Lothian

The Partridge

The Partridge

Pesticides, Predation and Conservation

G. R. Potts

COLLINS
8 Grafton Street, London W1

Collins Professional and Technical Books
William Collins Sons & Co. Ltd
8 Grafton Street, London W1X 3LA

First published in Great Britain by
Collins Professional and Technical Books 1986

Distributed in the United States of America
by Sheridan House, Inc.

Copyright © G. R. Potts 1986

British Library Cataloguing in Publication Data
Potts, G. R.
The partridge : pesticides, predation and
conservation.
1. Partridges   2. Birds, Protection of
I. Title
639.9′78617   QL696.G2

ISBN 0-00-383298-8

Typeset by V & M Graphics Ltd, Aylesbury, Bucks
Printed and bound in Great Britain by
Robert Hartnoll (1985) Ltd., Bodmin, Cornwall

All rights reserved. No part of this publication may
be reproduced, stored in a retrieval system or transmitted,
in any form, or by any means, electronic, mechanical, photocopying,
recording or otherwise, without the prior permission of the
publishers.

Contents

Preface		vii
Acknowledgements		xi
Statistical notes		xiv
1	Introduction	1
2	World-wide Decline of a Major Quarry Species	7
	Subspecies and varieties	8
	A quarry species	12
	Decline in numbers	21
3	Study Area and Methods	29
	Study areas	29
	Spring census	39
	Chick survival rate	45
	Insect monitoring	50
4	Predation at the Nest	54
	Predation as a density dependent factor	61
	Tests of the predation hypothesis	67
5	Chick survival	74
	Historical	75
	Theoretical considerations	80
	The Sussex study and situation in the field	84
6	Pesticides	94
	History of direct effects	95
	History of herbicide use	101
	Effect of herbicides and insecticides on insects	108
	Herbicides and herbicide-free cereal field margins	118
	Increase in chick mortality	123

7	Parasites and Disease	125
	Strongylosis	126
	Gapes	135
	Blackhead	139
8	Feeding Ecology through the Seasons	141
	Late summer to early winter	142
	Snow and ice	147
	Spring to summer	153
9	Nesting Cover and Spring Dispersal of Pairs	156
	Hedge removal	167
	Dispersal to avoid inbreeding?	173
10	The Causes of the Decline in Partridge Populations	175
	The Sussex model	176
	World-wide decline	187
11	Some Aspects of Traditional Partridge Conservation	193
	Estimating the shootable surplus	193
	Restocking	201
	Predator control	206
12	Avoiding the Adverse Effects of Pesticides	209
	Integrated pest control	209
	Unsprayed margins	219
	The future	223
13	Future Partridge Management: A Brief Survey of Recommendations	224

References 226
Index 263

Preface

I was very lucky to have been born into a farming family in North Yorkshire. It was a diverse farm (Plate XXIII) of 85 hectares, set in an exquisite landscape, with the layout much as it was in the mid-nineteenth century. Up until 1930 the farm had been part of the 2370-hectare (23.7 km^2) estate of Hornby Castle, seat of the Duke of Leeds. Before the outbreak of World War I, there were six gamekeepers on the estate and the game records show that partridges were abundant, probably averaging approximately fifty pairs per km^2 in spring. In 1968 I surveyed the area and found that partridge numbers were down by 80%, although on the family farm there were still good numbers. Today, these too have gone; in the spring of 1985 only three pairs were counted. The story must be similar for hundreds of thousands of farms, perhaps millions, world-wide.

I can claim some firsthand experience of pre-mechanised farming. Most of the farm work in the 1940s and early 1950s was done by horses, weeds were hoed or pulled by hand, grain was stooked, carried by horse and cart and threshed in stack-yards. Generally, there always seemed to be plenty of farm workers about the place and a great diversity of activities. I was a little over eleven years of age when herbicides were first used on the majority of cereals on the farm (1951) and I remember clearly the enormous impact of combine harvesters (1954) and electrification (1957).

My parents strongly encouraged me in the subject of natural history and my schoolboy diaries show my early interest in partridges – for example, measurements of snow-hole roosts (1952) and records of several partridge nests found. There were formative projects in ecology whilst at Scorton grammar school. My biology master, George Jefferson, recommended me to Professor Jim Cragg, Department of Zoology at the University of Durham. Then, as since, I was greatly helped and encouraged by Dr John Coulson.

Like many people in farming we knew of the work being carried out on partridges at Fordingbridge, though many ecologists were not fully aware of it until Terence Blank presented a paper on the work at a conference at the University of Durham in April 1961.

In May 1964, I learned for the first time that eggs of seabirds from the Farne Islands (collected by me as part of my post-graduate studies) contained relatively high levels of the insecticide dieldrin. It was at this point that I suddenly became aware of the fact that we knew dangerously little about the effects these compounds were having on the environment and also that little was understood about the ecological basis for their increased use year by year.

The following year I attended the NATO conference on pesticides at Monks Wood. John Ash was present and I approached him initially to ask a few questions concerning the Farne Islands (he had worked there too). It was then that I learned about the exciting findings on the side-effects of herbicides on partridges – the work carried out at Imperial College (chapters 5 and 6).

Due to the extraordinary efforts of Christopher Hunt, the 'Partridge Survival Project' was finally set up in February 1968 and John Ash encouraged me to switch from studying seabirds to studying partridges. This gave me the opportunity to continue to study the effects of pesticides and at the same time combine it with my interests in farming.

The great advantage of working on partridges has been that so much was already known about them, although comparatively little of the Fordingbridge work had entered the ornithological literature. There was great interest in the work – for example, James Fisher commissioned a *New Naturalist Monograph* on the partridge in 1954, but it was never possible to complete the necessary analysis of the Damerham data. About twenty monographs have been written on the partridge but all are now out of date, or primarily written for hunters, or not in English.

My first aim in writing this monograph was therefore to combine all the important ecological data on partridges and to publish it as a whole. My second aim was to examine the reasons for the enormous decline of the partridge, bearing in mind its value as an indicator of the way in which modern farming is affecting wildlife.

More important, I hope this monograph will show that in many areas it is still feasible and very desirable to restore partridge numbers. To do this the adverse effects of pesticides must be reduced, as explained in chapter 12.

Finally, I very much hope that this monograph will stimulate more research on the side-effects of modern farming, especially of pesticides, on wildlife. If the partridge is a 'barometer' of the welfare of farmland wildlife as a whole, then there is still a vast amount to be done and no time to be wasted.

Acknowledgements

It is an achievement in itself to have funded a research project for eighteen years, especially when it followed twenty-two years of continuous work along the same lines! Such is the regard that shooting sportsmen have for their quarry. A great many were involved in helping to secure funds – and the roles of Chris Hunt, Charles Coles, Richard Van Oss and Hugh Oliver-Bellasis have been crucial.

In Sussex, I was assisted principally by Stuart Pimm (1969), Andrew Williams (1970), Paul Vickerman (1972–1980) (funded by the Nature Conservancy Council and Agricultural Research Council), Keith Sunderland (1973–1979) (funded by the Agricultural Research Council and now, with a similar remit, continuing at the Glasshouse Crops Research Institute) and Stephen Tapper (1974–1977) (funded by Natural Environment Research Council). Many others have helped, including my wife Elsie on the secretarial side. The contribution of the gamekeepers, in particular Fred Allen, was immense; David Clark, Philip Adam-Smith, Robert Largen and many others gave a good deal of their time. Since 1980 Steve Moreby has carefully sorted and counted the D-vac samples, aided, as was much of this study, by grants from the Rank Foundation. The analysis of the insect data collected in Sussex is incomplete but a grant from the Ministry of Agriculture, Fisheries and Food to computerise the data has just been confirmed as the book goes to press.

A vital component in our work has been the extremely generous access given to farms and crops by the Sussex landowners and farmers, especially by the Goring family (Findon), Brian Morris and the staff at North Farm, the late Duke of Norfolk, Gordon Dickson (now Professor of Agriculture at Newcastle), Gordon Duke, David Lock, Toby Collyer, Basil Strudwick, Gerald Lee, Walter and Michael Langmead, the Passmore families at Coombe (Steyning) and Applesham (Shoreham) and John Metcalfe. In other parts of the country Roy Shepherd (Hampshire), Captain David Keith, Lady Margaret Barry,

Geoff Duke, John Wilson, Lord Melchett (all from the eastern counties), Robin Cowen and Mark Fearfield were particularly helpful, as on Salisbury Plain were the members of Bulford and Tidworth shoot. Most important were the experiments carried out at Manydown, thanks to the kindness of Hugh Oliver-Bellasis, his family and the farm staff.

Other research workers on partridges have given me a great deal of help. Professor Sir Richard Southwood gave much support from outset to completion and I would like especially to acknowledge the contributions of Doug Middleton, Terence Blank, Charles Coles and David Jenkins. Many helped enthusiastically with overseas data and in obtaining some obscure papers, especially Kevin Church (USA), Vladimir Litun (Soviet Union) with many most helpful translations from Russian by Mike Wilson, Marcel Birkan (France), Reino Hofmann and his team, especially Volker Döring at Giessen (FRG), Francesco Dessi-Fulgheri and Laura Beani (Italy), Zygmunt Pielowski and his staff at Czempiń (Poland), Erkki Pulliainen of Finland, Tso-Hsin Cheng (China and Tibet) and Kaj Westerskov. Betrand des Clers of the International Foundation for the Conservation of Game provided funds for me to attend conference/workshops on partridges in the USA, Idaho and Wisconsin and in Poland.

Professor Sir Richard Southwood, John Coulson, Raymond O'Connor, Eric Carter, Anthony Vandervell, Richard Van Oss, Colin McKelvie, Stephen Tapper (who also helped in many other ways), Mike Rands and David Hill read, and kindly commented on, and improved early drafts of the book. Doug Wise helped with several sections, especially Chapter 7, with the assistance of Roger Connan. Pete Hudson helped with the section on strongylosis and contributed Fig. 7.2. Keith Sunderland kindly updated sections of Chapter 12. Also Malcolm Brockless, Nick Sotherton, John Beer, Kevin Church, Nigel Boatman, Jonathan Reynolds and Pete Robertson checked relevant sections in a later draft. Gill Rands kindly drew the maps for Chapter 3 and assisted in preparing the book. Corinne Duggins helped with French, also the preparation of the index section. Past and present staff, research advisors and other officers at the Game Conservancy, and other colleagues, have all willingly helped as have many librarians and staff of the EGI, University of Oxford. I would particularly like to thank my wife and family who have given me the greatest possible support.

In producing this book I am most grateful to Mrs Patsy Hitchings. She tackled the secretarial work and typing of the manuscript with great expertise and with a dedication undaunted, whether by the awesome references or by what must have seemed a constant need to update and correct the text.

Illustrations at the beginning of chapters are gratefully acknowledged and appear by kind permission as follows. Tim Greenwood (2), Olga Patterson (3), Robert Gillmor (4), Winifrid Austin (5), Andrew Williams (6), David Jenkins (illustrations by C.F. Tunnicliffe) (7), Winifrid Austin (8), Dr Franz Müller (9), David Jenkins (illustration by C.F. Tunnicliffe) (10), Woodall (11).

I am particularly grateful to Rodger McPhail for his excellent front cover depicting a fine August covey (two males, one female plus fourteen young) in a weedy headland in the Sussex study area.

Lastly I would like to thank the publishers, William Collins, and especially Julian Grover, for their enthusiastic support.

Statistical Notes

1 km² (square kilometre) = 100 ha = 247 acres
    (this is the basic unit of area used throughout the study)

4 km² = approximately 1000 acres

1 section = 2.59 km²

1 township = 15.5 km²

Note The word 'per' is abbreviated throughout the book as follows: 10 partridges per square kilometre = 10 partridges km^{-2}; 10 partridges per km = 10 partridges km^{-1}

1 Kj = 1 kilojoule = 4.2 kilocalories

1 gram = 0.035 oz (28.35 g = 1 oz)

LD_{50} = dose lethal to 50% of population dosed

Confidence limits are usually given as ± (plus or minus) 1 standard error(s), though on graphs ± 2 standard errors are plotted. ± 2 standard errors indicate a 95% certainty that the true mean (i.e. if all data are available rather than a sample) lies *within* the confidence limits.

Probabilities are quoted as '*P*' less than (designated <) 0.05, which is the probability – here one in 20 (= 0.05) – that the difference between measurements could be the result of chance if there was statistically no significant difference between them.

Precision (p) is measured as the ratio of the standard error to the mean.

1 Introduction

In recent years there has been a growing concern for the loss of wildlife from farmland, due to the results of mechanisation, the use of pesticides, larger field sizes and so on. One of the prime examples has been the decline of the partridge, a species unique amongst the many affected by modern farming, for two reasons. Firstly, it was once a very common bird and it has been conserved for shooting one way or another for centuries; Louis XIV spoke of 'conserving' his partridges. Secondly, it has been studied by many ecologists for fifty years or more, so we have a fine opportunity to measure the extent to which a species of bird has been affected by the modernisation of agriculture, especially by the use of pesticides.

It is a dramatic story and in the next chapter I conclude that prior to World War II, the average world partridge population at the end of the breeding season was more than 110 million. This is now reduced to less than 25 million.

The grey partridge (*Perdix perdix*) is throughout this book referred to simply as 'the partridge' or as 'partridges'; *any other species of partridge is clearly indicated.* Alternative names for the partridge are: common partridge, grey or gray partridge (but not the Indian grey partridge *Francolinus pondicerianus*), the European partridge, the Hungarian partridge (or just the 'hun'), and English partridge (as opposed to French or red-legged partridge).

The partridge is a bird typical of open arable landscapes in what were originally the temperate grassland ecosystems of the steppes. For thousands of years the successive developments in agriculture, especially the clearance of woodland for grain production, must have created new habitats and helped increase numbers.

The partridge is potentially a prolific bird; it breeds in its first summer and lays the largest clutch of any species of bird, averaging fifteen or sixteen eggs. Despite cryptic colouring, furtive behaviour during nesting and a careful choice of a concealed nest site, predation of the hen and eggs is high.

The chicks hatch in mid to late June. They are looked after by both parents and spend most of their time in cereals or in other long grasses. The chicks feed mainly on insects and many of those selected by them for food live on weeds. The food supply to the chicks is thus indirectly reduced by the use of herbicides.

By late summer, surviving chicks, their parents and other adult birds form groups of about twelve birds known as 'coveys'. During this period both young and adults survive mostly by gleaning grain and by feeding on the seeds of stubble-weeds such as black bindweed. In winter and spring most partridges feed by grazing on growing cereals or alternatively on pastures, especially those with clover and grass leys.

Partridge pairs are usually formed in February, though the timing can vary with snow cover. Once formed, the pairs search for permanent grassy nesting cover, preferably on a dry bank, and the breeding cycle begins once more.

The spring dispersal of pairs takes place over short distances and many partridges spend their entire lives in the same three or four fields. Although a bird of the open fields, the partridge usually nests in hedgerows and so is inevitably affected by changes in field size and in field boundary management.

The research on which much of this book is based began at the University of Oxford – and with, surprisingly, a lecture on grey squirrels by Doug Middleton. The science of animal ecology was at that time still at an embryonic stage and Middleton was research assistant to Charles Elton, Director of the Bureau of Animal Populations. At the lecture in May 1931, Middleton argued that the 'new science' could help to eradicate the grey squirrel from Britain. Major Eley of the Eley Cartridge Company was among the audience and he questioned whether the same science could help the partridge, which was at that time suffering from an outbreak of strongylosis – the subject of an enquiry by the magazine *Country Life*.

At that time almost all cartridges used in Britain were made by ICI's subsidiary Eley, and overall sales in 1931 and 1932 were down by almost 12 million per annum – 17% of the total – mostly as a result of the strongylosis outbreak in partridges. Major Eley, a descendant of the family which began trading in the copper percussion cap business in the 1820s, described his thinking as follows:

'In the course of my work I began to realise that, while large sums were expended by the Company annually on research and experiments on the behaviour of cartridge cases, powders, caps, shots, etc. – in fact on all components that went into the breech end of a gun – nothing was being done, or ever had been done systematically, to improve things at the muzzle end, i.e. to ensure the continued existence of the game without which cartridge sales would vanish.'

The estate selected for the first field studies was Knebworth Park in Hertfordshire, where much of the work was carried out by Captain A. H. Moser. Two scientists were involved: Middleton, at the Bureau of Animal Populations, but moving to Jealotts Hill (ICI Plant Protection) in 1938, and Dr Phyllis Clapham, helminthologist at the Imperial Bureau of Agricultural Parasitology, St Albans.

With the outbreak of the Second World War all game research activities were interrupted, until 1946 when the ICI Game Research Station was established at Fordingbridge in Hampshire. The Research Station took a 14-year lease on West Park estate at Damerham, Fordingbridge – a 16 km^2 (4000 acre) mixed shoot. The estate was selected jointly by Eley, Middleton and Moser from many they visited together, and the studies there – particularly by Terence Blank and Dr John Ash – feature again and again throughout this book.

In October 1960, the lease of the shoot at Damerham expired, but the Eley Game Advisory Service (as the ICI Game Research Station was by then called) retained Terence Blank as the research biologist and a programme of less intensive partridge studies continued. In 1961 the Game Research Association was formed, supported by subscriber-members (initially numbering 461).

At the beginning of February 1968 the 'Partridge Survival Project' was set up by Chris Hunt (Plate I) and the Game Research Association with the help, in particular, of Lord Netherthorpe, former President of the National Farmer's Union, who was at that time Chairman of Fisons, the agrochemical manufacturers. The aims were 'to investigate the low breeding success in partridges with particular reference to the causes of chick mortality'. Hunt, a member of the Council of the Game Research Association and Managing Director of North Farm Ltd, Washington, made study areas available on the Sussex Downs, including the land farmed by him and owned by the Goring family. The Game Conservancy was formed by the merger of the Eley Game Advisory Service and the Game Research Association and Chris Hunt became the first Chairman, until his tragic and untimely death in September 1970. The Game Conservancy now has over 15 000 members.

The theme of this book is essentially the report of the work carried out by the Partridge Survival Project, here simply known as the 'Sussex

Plate I. Christopher Hunt, North Farm 1969, (N.Gray).

study', which began in a garden shed at North Farm in March 1968.

Chapter 2 reviews the status and distribution of the partridge worldwide, describing the contraction of its geographical range and quantifying the decline in bags and in breeding stock populations.

Chapter 3 details the methods used in the Sussex study to investigate the population dynamics, food and mortality rates through the life cycle. Mortality rates are not given as percentages or proportions but as log mortality rates or k values; k_1 = loss of eggs, k_2 = loss of hens in incubation, k_3 = loss of chicks, and so on. To simplify, the equivalent percentages are also given.

The subsequent chapters continue to examine the causes of these mortalities step by step, to build up a model of the whole life cycle system, and then to look at the causes of the decline in Chapter 10. Other available data, mostly from the extensive literature, are employed around the central theme of interpreting the Sussex partridge study.

Chapter 4 investigates nest losses, concluding that predation is the most important cause of loss and that the traditional methods of predation control employed by gamekeepers are (or were, prior to modern farming) highly effective in improving partridge nesting success.

Chapter 5 provides reasons for concluding that the supply of insect food determines the chick mortality rate, in a context which I hope explains why this has been such a controversial subject.

Chapter 6 outlines the history of the various effects of pesticides, direct and indirect, on partridges. The main adverse effect has been that of herbicides used on cereal crops, which reduce the supply of insects to the chicks. The status of various insect groups important as chick food is examined and the declines in insect food are quantified. It is concluded that these declines have mainly been caused by the indirect effects of pesticides, which explains the increase in chick mortality rates over the past thirty years.

High chick mortality rates were sometimes recorded before the use of pesticides and in Chapter 7 I argue that the disease strongylosis was often the cause. This disease no longer causes significant mortality, having greatly declined in incidence.

Chapter 8 outlines the feeding ecology of the adult. Long periods of deep snow cover are found to increase adult partridge mortality rates but this is normally due to the shortage of food which increases the incidence of predation rather than through direct effects of the weather. It is also argued that insect shortages have no adverse effect on adults.

Covey dispersal and the choice of nesting sites are described in Chapter 9, which concludes that pairs space themselves along hedges and other equivalent nesting cover to avoid an even higher predation rate than they already incur.

At this stage all the natural mortality factors (except shooting) have been dealt with one by one. Chapter 10 describes how a computer simulation model of the Sussex partridge population was constructed to determine the cause of the population declines. After considering data from other studies, it is concluded that for the most part the population declines have resulted from increased chick mortality.

Chapter 11 reviews the value of traditional management practices, outlining ways of obtaining the maximum sustainable yield by shooting. Little value is placed on restocking or, where pesticides increase chick mortality, on predator control.

Finally, Chapter 12 reviews the ways in which the adverse effects of pesticides on chicks can be minimised with little cost to agriculture and with considerable benefits to other farmland wildlife.

Pesticides affect many species, but none are specific to their particular target and the effects on the partridge provide a detailed example of how chemicals can indirectly affect wildlife and give some indication of what might have happened to many less studied species.

However, in order to keep the monograph of a manageable size, I have had to exclude information on the red-legged partridge and pheasant gained in the Sussex study and have also had to exclude the vast majority of the literature on these and other gamebirds, and on other species which might have been affected by the events which have influenced partridges. Unfortunately, due to a lack of resources, until 1986, I could also not complete analyses of the bulk of the data on insects collected in the Sussex study. Future work will therefore describe in more detail than is possible here the effects of weather on the insect populations, the effects of field boundary types and the differences between farms due to rotations, etc.

This monograph is intended to provide a detailed contribution to the wide international debate concerning how the countryside should be used and how adverse effects of pesticides can be monitored and understood. This debate will grow.

Given that the world's supply of possible arable land is finite, that the world's population at present needs more than two-thirds of the total to produce food, and that the population will probably double within the next thirty years, it is obvious that very large increases in production will be necessary in future. So there is no doubt that we are going to have to use more, not fewer, pesticides if the world's population is to be adequately fed. The optimistic view of Simon (1981) that the world's population can easily be fed at conceivable future levels rests on the assumption that pesticides will become increasingly used and what is more, increasingly effective.

Now, with vast grain surpluses it is widely recognised that there is more to be gained from farmland than food. It is therefore fortunate that our research shows that there are many practical measures which can be taken to offset the side-effects of pesticides on farmland wildlife, without significant hindrance to agriculture. Certainly ecologists concerned for wildlife on farms ought not to feel that they are up against inevitabilities of the kind demonstrated by King Canute.

2 World-wide Decline of a Major Quarry Species

'From all over the world come echoes of the peril that faces birds. The reports differ in detail, but always repeat the theme of death to wildlife in the wake of pesticides. Such are the stories of hundreds of small birds and partridges dying in France after vine stumps were treated with an arsenic-containing herbicide, or of partridge shoots in Belgium, once famous for the numbers of their birds, denuded of partridges after the spraying of nearby farmlands.' (R. Carson, 1962)

Subspecies and varieties

The partridge is one of three closely related species in the genus *Perdix*: the partridge originally classifed as a grouse and named *Tetrao perdix* by the famous Swedish taxonomist Carl von Linne in 1758; the similar but smaller, bearded or Daurian partridge *Perdix daurica* (Pallas); and the similar sized but differently coloured Tibetan or Ladakh partridge *Perdix hodgsoniae* (Hodgson).

In Europe the partridge occurs in many different varieties which can be divided into two groups, the one more rufous-brown, mainly in the west, and the other paler and with more grey, mainly in the east. Eight subspecies have been widely accepted but many others proposed. There have also been indications that the pigmentation of the plumage is a function of soil type and climate. The taxonomy clearly needs revising, using modern methods. Many hundreds of specimens are available in museums for such work and although there has been much trading of birds between countries, some of the original distributions might be more clearly established than hitherto.

Meanwhile some variations are clear and these are outlined below. I have to assume that there are no important geographical differences in population ecology between the various subspecies, though it is unlikely that regional genetic variations are restricted to plumage. An increase in clutch size in northern latitudes of Europe was reported by Lack (1947) and Pulliainen (1971). However, those partridges with the highest clutch size, in Ostrobothnia, Finland, had spread into the region relatively recently from areas with a lower clutch size (Westerskov, 1964b) and the variation may not be genetically determined.

hispaniensis   Reichenow (1892)   Pyrenees & Cantabrian Mountains in northern Spain and north-east Portugal, type locality La Coruña

– a dark subspecies with clear white streaks on upper parts (Bureau, 1905), bars across feathers of upper parts black-brown rather than red-brown, less chestnut on wing coverts and scapulars (as in summer plumage of nominate), horseshoe mark larger and darker. Breast and rump darker, especially in west, paler in Pyrenees (Castroviejo, 1967). A little known subspecies, originally *P.p. charrela*, with no population studies.

italica Hartert (1917)   Italy, type locality Chianti
– with a dark horseshoe, very like *hispaniensis* but not so clearly differentiated from nominate. Now listed in the Red Data Book as likely to become an 'endangered species'. Since 1920 when introductions to Italy became extensive, many specimens have lacked the very dark rump markings of the pure race (R. Massa, in litt). Birds in the Italian Alps probably nominate, those in Po Delta certainly so, being introduced from Yugoslavia and Czechoslovakia in the 1960s.

armoricana   Hartert (1917)   Armoricana (Brittany), Normandy, central France north to Morvan Mountains and Ardennes (but see *P.p. galliae* under nominate below), type locality Rialle, Loire-Atlantique
– upper parts more rusty-brown and less grey than nominate; throat and chest more washed brown Bureau (1911).

sphagnetorum   Altum (1894)   North-east Netherlands and neighbouring north - west Germany
– a clearly differentiated dark subspecies, known as the 'Moor partridge', it was at one time supposedly confined to lowland heaths in the Netherlands and north-west Germany, and considered not to interbreed with the nominate (Peus, 1929); it is now distributed widely through the countryside near Hamburg and in east Friesland (Knolle and Heckenroth, 1985). About 5500 pairs were found in Drente, Netherlands (Teixeira, 1979; see also Hens, 1938). Kelm (1979) extends the known range south and west into the flood plain areas of northern Belgium and north and east into Schleswig Holstein.

nominate *perdix*   Linnaeus (1758)   Scandinavia, Ireland and British Isles, south across central Europe to Alps and Balkans, North America
– almost all studies and illustrations in this book concern the nominate form. Hartert (1917) and Vaurie (1965) consider the area not inhabited by *armoricana* and *spagnetorum* to be occupied by the nominate subspecies but Kelm (1979) upholds the very pale *P.p. galliae* (Bacmeister and Kleinschmidt) which inhabits the plains from Normandy to

Cologne, and a much darker *P.p.hilgerti* (Kleinschmidt) from the Ardennes and Hessen. Yet further varieties are said to exist in isolated areas, such as the island of Borkum (Harrison, 1952). However, the short time available for subspeciation (<700 years in this case), plus the fact that mainland partridges do fly out to the islands, even Heligoland (40 km) (Gätke, 1895), casts doubt on the validity of the Friesland island varieties (see also Meinertzhagen, 1952).

lucida Altum (1894) — East of nominate from Finland, east Poland, east of Carpathians and northern Bulgaria across the Soviet Union to Urals and northern Caucasus (incorporates *P.p. caucasica*)

– paler grey on upper parts and breast than nominate, with narrower rufous bars. Kelm (1979) considers that the original Swedish description may have been of this form rather than the nominate! Occasional hard weather movements have been described, and, in the east, migrations.

canescens Buturlin (1906) — Turkey, Caucasus, Transcaucasia, Iran (incorporates *P.p. furvescens* (Buturlin))

– as *lucida* but with more dull grey upper parts and very little rufous, though the horseshoe is a rusty chestnut. The least known of all the subspecies, originally described from only two females shot in winter in a locality in Georgia.

robusta Homeyer and Tancré (1883) — East of lower Ural river basin and Urals to south west Siberia, Kazakhstan and Dzungaria (Sinkiang) (includes *P.p. arenicola* (Buturlin) and *P.p. rossica* (Johansen))

– a paler, greyer (see Colour Plate IV) and longer-winged subspecies (Stantschinsky, 1929), which migrates south in autumn (Formozov, 1946). The range overlaps that of the bearded partridge (*Fig 2.2*); hybrids have been reported, but not convincingly.

The chocolate-coloured variant once known as the mountain par-

Plate II. Incubating hen leaving nest, showing variety of summer plumage with scattered dark feathers for extra camouflage (Ogilvie-Grant, 1912), *Dennis Green.*

tridge (*Perdix perdix ab. montana* (Brisson)) deserves mention. Originally described in 1760, from the mountains of Lorraine, it occurred widely though very rarely throughout central north-west Europe and, despite its name, it was not restricted to mountainous regions (Stresemann, 1924). Stresemann recorded the bird in about a dozen localities in Europe over the period 1760 to 1912, mostly in eastern Europe and northern Germany. Several were reported in Belgium and France in the 1950s (map in Orts-Anspach and Dalimer, 1954; Lippens and Willie, 1972).

In Britain there were forty records from Northumberland in the period 1863–1891 but only three since then, despite enquiries to establish the position (Ash, 1966): one near Morpeth in 1911, one in 1919 and another in 1979 (also at Morpeth, now in the Game Conservancy Museum). In addition individuals were shot in Staffordshire (Ash, 1966), Cheshire and Kent (Harrison, 1968), and in North Cleveland (in 1984) (J. Hall *in litt.*).

The rate of incidence was never established but it was always uncommon (Naumann, 1833) and must now be exceedingly rare, perhaps with some pockets of relative abundance. It may well be a rare genetic recombination of rufous and melanistic forms, which at one time were much more common (Harrison, 1968). The first and so far only record from Poland, one in 1978, resulted from a detailed examination of over 18 000 shot in the period 1963 to 1985 (Olech, 1986). None have been encountered in Game Conservancy field studies.

A quarry species

The two most important distinguishing features of the partridge which set it apart from other birds are not the plumage, but the excitement it gives as a quarry species and its delectable flavour.

Even during medieval times the price of partridges was high and most were usually trapped in nets with setting dogs (setters) or hunted with the aid of falcons. Indeed in Britain and central Europe several principles of partridge conservation were well established before the sport of shooting at flying game began. For example in Czechoslovakia in 1630 a law existed whereby at least two hens and one cock should be released (for stock) from every covey netted or trapped (Koteš and Knobloch, 1947). Some of the released birds may have been marked and in Britain there is a report at the British Trust for Ornithology of partridges being ringed as early as 1667. Spring pair counts to assess stocks first began on estates near the border of Austria and Czechoslovakia in 1695 (Nováková and Hanzl, 1966).

Hunting with pointing dogs

The sports of falconry and game hawking with pointing dogs are generally thought to have originated in south-western Asia, perhaps being brought to Europe around the time of the Crusades. Such sports became popular wherever the country was sufficiently open so that a quarry such as the partridge would not easily reach the cover of a hedge. Large open areas such as the Yorkshire Wolds and Salisbury Plain were favoured for this reason in the nineteenth century.

In falconry, partridge coveys are located using setters or pointers (the choice of dog being a matter of personal preference). The falcon, usually a peregrine, is then unhooded, cast off and allowed to get to a pitch perhaps 200 or 300 feet above the covey. Then, on command, the dogs flush the covey which until then has been 'frozen' by the sight of the falcon, so enabling the dramatic vertical peregrine stoop to take place.

The percentage of partridges struck and killed outright is extremely high and non-fatal injuries to the quarry are virtually unknown.

Falconry can be very worthwhile when the density of partridges is too low for most shooting; the size of the bag is unimportant compared to the quality of the stoop. The quality of the bag is high too since the falcons do not pick, as is sometimes imagined, the sick or weak birds from coveys. Young (and more tender!) birds are however more likely to be selected, at least early in the season (M. Brockless *in litt.*).

It is not possible to bag large numbers with falcons. Indeed, 'nor is the sport of such a nature that the number of head killed can be always taken as a fair criterion of the amusement which has been afforded' (Lascelles, 1892). Three stoops a day per peregrine was considered sufficient (Salvin and Broderick, 1855). The open season was that prescribed for shooting, and usually two falcons would be kept; though at the top of the sport it could reach six. With four falcons the Duke of Leeds killed 260 partridges in eastern Scotland in the autumn of 1830, but the frequency with which the achievement is quoted in falconry literature indicates that this size of bag was exceptional.

Goshawks have also been flown at partridges, but there are far fewer accounts of this than is the case with the peregrine; goshawks usually take their prey on the ground after a somewhat unspectacular low-level chase.

There are many records of partridge shoots in the seventeenth century, particularly after the Restoration, but it was not until the various improvements in the design of the gun towards the end of the eighteenth century that shooting at flying game became popular. It was the invention of the percussion cap (1808), which replaced the old flint-locks, that spurred this on. Even then the awkward muzzle-loading shotguns in use were cumbersome and inefficient, especially in damp or windy weather. The sportsmen usually walked with a man-servant (to carry game) over stubbles behind pointing dogs (see Colour Plate I), often walking up to a mile for every bird shot. When a covey was found the shooter would then manoeuvre himself so that the covey was between him and the dog. In this way the covey could be dispersed and the birds to be shot selected.

One problem with this type of shooting later in the season, or when stubbles have been cut short (as they were after the introduction of reaping machines), is the ease with which partridges could then see the dogs approaching. If the wind is in the right direction, coveys can be prevented from moving too soon by flying a kite in the shape of a falcon high over the field, but this is a difficult technique to master.

Walking up

At higher densities partridges can be encountered without the use of pointing dogs, simply by walking, which has been the principal method of shooting in mainland Europe, as it was in Britain until the end of the nineteenth century (Alington, 1904). Now, due to the decline in numbers, the technique is again finding favour in Britain.

The most frequently used method consists of a team of shooting sportsmen walking in a line, with, between them, one or two beaters with retrieving dogs. Care has to be taken to keep the team in line whilst birds are being retrieved. When partridges were numerous some huge bags were obtained by walking up; for example in Czechoslovakia 30 000 were shot on one very large estate in eighteen days (Koteš and Knobloch, 1947).

Driving

In undulating country, and where partridge densities are high, the more formal method of shooting known as 'driving' became favoured. This was first tried out in Britain about 1845 in the eastern counties (Gladstone, 1922). The breech-loading gun, first patented in 1807 but not developed until after the Great Exhibition of 1851, was a key development. Driving became popular with the introduction of the pin-fire cartridge in 1847: cap, powder and shot in a convenient shower-proof case which could be quickly loaded at the breech end. It was some years before the much improved guns became widely available. In Britain there were approximately 200 in 1858, though 'thousands' by the early 1860s (Crudgington and Baker, 1979). The breech-loading gun and pin-fire cartridge were crucial to the development of driving since they speeded up the whole shooting process.

The methods of driving partridges are clearly explained by Payne-Gallwey (1892) and also by Alington (1904). Beaters walk in a line carrying white flags, with the outer members, known as flankers, carrying distinct flags. The beaters, like the birds, are out of sight of the guns so the centre member, usually the headkeeper, and also with a special flag, carries a whistle or horn in order to signal that coveys are flying towards the guns. There is generally a line of about eight guns, plus their retrieving dogs, and the aim is to drive birds high to give testing shots – usually by using shelterbelts, tall hedges or by placing the guns along the bottom of a valley (Colour Plate II). In the Sussex study area, the area from which the birds were driven would average half to a full km² per drive. Driving partridges is made easier if root crops are available, in which case the flanked coveys are first encouraged into the holding cover afforded by the roots and then driven out of this cover so as to put them over the guns.

In 1963 and 1964 the Eley Game Advisory Service attended 167 drives; 1475 partridges were killed. It was, they found, possible to take aim effectively at only a small proportion of the birds driven and there were 3.3 shots per bird bagged. This is why it is desirable that high numbers are available for driving.

The highest documented density of wild partridges prior to the open season is about 450 km^{-2} and the record partridge bag in Britain (2069 shot in one day) was made on 3 October 1952 on the North Lincolnshire Wolds near Rothwell, at a density of about 400 partridges km^{-2}. Even higher daily bags, with a record of 4000 obtained in Czechoslovakia in the nineteenth century (Maxwell, 1911) and 2333 in France (Chantilly, in 1785), indicate that some higher densities occurred in these countries than in Britain.

Sources (Fig 2.1): Norway, S. Myrberget *in litt.*, Hafthorn (1971); Sweden, Dahlgren (1986) extended *in litt*; Finland, P. Vikberg *in litt.* (Hunters' Central Organisation); Denmark, Strandgaard and Asferg (1980); Britain and Ireland, British Trust for Ornithology Atlases, Sharrock (1976), Thom (1986), Lack (1986); France, Birkan (1983), Lebreton (1977); Belgium, Lippens and Willie (1972); Netherlands, W. Doude van Troostwijk *in litt.*, F. Leeuwenberg *in litt.*, Teixeira (1979); German Federal Republic, V. Döring *in litt.*, R. Helfrich *in litt.*, H. Brüll *in litt.* (Schleswig-Holstein), A. Roese *in litt.*, Nyenhuis (1985), Thieme (1985); Austria, F. Tataruch *in litt.*, H. Gossow *in litt.*; Switzerland, Schifferli *et al* (1982); Italy, Matteucci and Toso (1985), Moltoni (1964); Spain, Seoane (1891), Castroviejo (1967), J. de la Peña Payá (ICONA) *in litt.*; Yugoslavia, Makatsch (1950), Romić (1975a), Vućković (1967); Greece, E. Papaevangelos *in litt.*; Turkey, Ornithological Society of Turkey Annual Bird Reports (to 1985), R. Porter *in litt.*; Albania, C. Prigioni *in litt.*; Hungary, A. Havasi *in litt.*, Mátrai and Vallus (1981), Statistical Office of Ministry of Agriculture, E. Nikodémusz *in litt.*; Bulgaria, Georgiev (1955), Petrov (1966); Romania, Manolache (1970); Czechoslovakia, Sekera (1966); Poland, Pielowski (1986), B. Olech *in litt.*; Soviet Union, Osmolovskaya (1966), Logminas and Petraitis (1970), V. Litun (1982, plus unpublished surveys and correspondence); Iran, Cergh (1943), E. Kahrom; Portugal, Joao Bugalho *in litt.*

Sources (Fig. 2.2): Dementiev and Gladkov (1952); Cheng *et al.* (1983); Cheng (1976); Inskipp and Inskipp (1985).

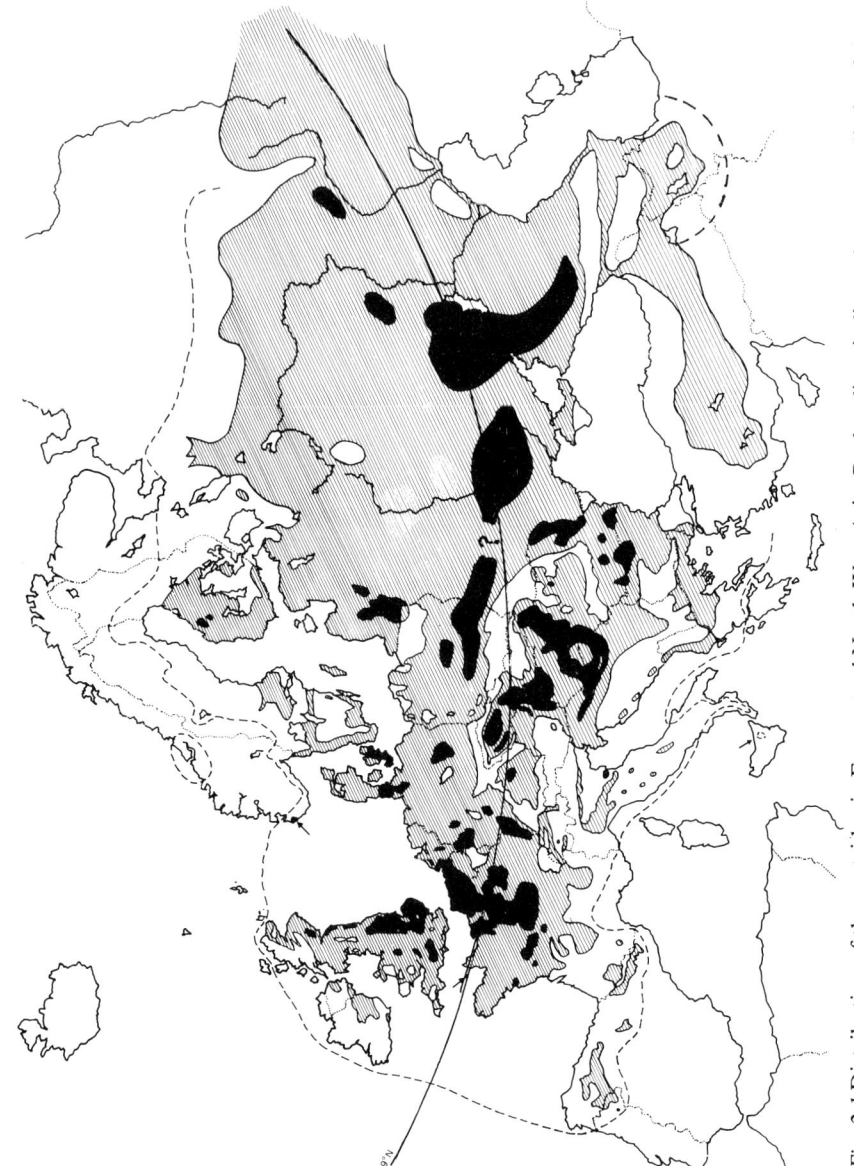

Fig. 2.1 Distribution of the partridge in Europe and North West Asia. Broken lines indicate the extreme limits of the distribution of the species, with hatched areas where the species is currently present. Dark areas indicate that densities of >5 pairs km^{-2} would be expected with no use of herbicides in cereals.

WORLD-WIDE DECLINE OF A MAJOR QUARRY SPECIES 17

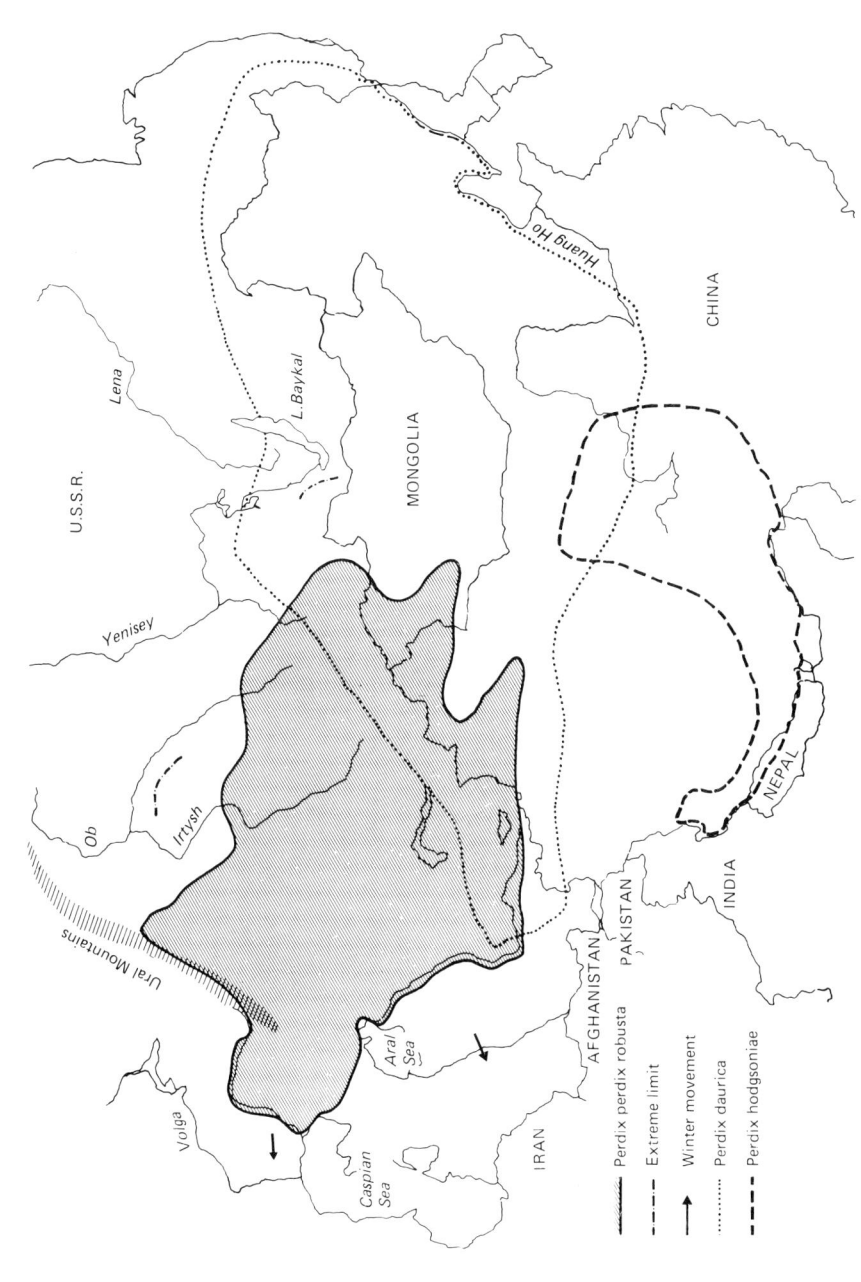

Fig. 2.2 The distribution of partridge, bearded partridge and Tibetan partridge, to show the overlap of ranges.

World distribution

Europe and Asia

The geographical ranges of *Perdix perdix, P. daurica* and *P. hodgsoniae* in Europe and Asia are mapped in Figs 2.1 and 2.2 indicating in the former case the regions of high density, the best of which were in the areas east of Prague in Czechoslovakia, in parts of Hungary and in the south Paris Basin, especially in the Plains of Beauce between Orléans and Chartres.

Marked contractions of range have taken place this century. At the northern periphery there has been a distinct retreat south, in Scandinavia and the Soviet Union, often of 200 miles or more.

Until about 1910 the species occurred, after introductions, as far north as Trondelag, around Trondheim in Norway (63°N). After that time and especially in 1925–1930 the species declined and retreated towards the south east (Haftorn, 1971). A few birds still breed at Jaeren near Stavanger (S. Myrberget *in litt.*) but probably not in the south east around Oslo and Ostfold (V. Holthe *in litt.*). At the end of the last century it spread almost to the Arctic Circle (66.5°N) in Sweden (Dahlgren, 1986) (Colour Plate XVII), and to Archangel in the Soviet Union (65°N) (Osmolovskaya, 1966). The contraction of range southwards in Sweden has been particularly well documented (Dahlgren, 1986).

In Portugal and in north-west Spain, the range was contracting 'alarmingly' in the 1960s (Castroviejo, 1967), as it is currently in many valleys of the Pyrenees (F. Roucher *in litt.*), in the Massif Centrale and the foothills of the Maritime Alps (Birkan, 1983). Some declines in France have been, at least locally, spectacular. For example at Sandricourt, north of Paris, the partridge bag on the same area of land in similar seasons was 5000 in 1938, 1500 in 1976, and 12 in 1984 (H. Goelet *in litt.*). The Office National de la Chasse conducted surveys in 1974–75 and 1983–84 which indicate a 60% decline of partridge bags over the period (Landry, 1985).

The reduction of numbers in Italy is also alarming (Matteucci and Toso, 1985) and as already mentioned the subspecies *italica* is listed as an 'endangered species'. The range seems to have been most extensive in the 1890s (Moltoni, 1964) and at this time a small 'colony' was found at Francavilla, Sicily (Lovari, 1975). Most of the reductions in range have occurred since the 1950s (Matteucci and Toso, 1985); in the Italian Alps since the mid-1950s and especially after 1975 (Paolo and Piodi, 1986).

Many of the farms on the hills of Tuscany (Colour Plate XVIII) were once famous for their partridge shooting. Most bags were obtained by walking up, and twenty to thirty brace shot per day was not unusual in the Chianti Classico region. Some detailed information was made available to me by the Brandini family on their 5 km² estate at Castello di Rencine. There the annual bags of the partridge declined, but only slightly, from 1948 to 1967 from about 20 km^{-2} to 10 km^{-2}. Then there was a rapid decline until shooting of this species was stopped in 1973. Breeding stocks now average approximately 1.5 pairs km^{-2} (A. Cecchi *in litt.*), which is only about a fifth of the minimum necessary to provide the bags of the early 1950s.

In Greece, partridges occurred south to the Gulf of Corinth prior to modern farming (E. Papaevangelos *in litt.*) but they have now retreated far to the north. The birds' current status in Iran is not known but a decline is suspected in their limited range (E. Kahrom *in litt.*).

Some of the earliest and most dramatic population declines were in Ireland where the species was regarded by the Duke of Ormonde as 'plentiful' in the seventeenth century. Large bags were achieved in Kildare up to the end of the nineteenth century but since then numbers have declined all over the country and the partridge may soon be extinct in Ireland. In Wales a general decline in bags through the first half of this century has been particularly well documented (Matheson, 1956a, b, 1957, 1960).

North America

Partridge trapping had long been a tradition in much of the old Austro-Hungarian Empire, with many birds being exported for restocking programmes in western Europe. It was therefore not surprising that attempts were also made to introduce the species to other countries. In the USA and Canada there were several such attempts in the nineteenth century, but with little success. The introductions were documented by Phillips (1928). During the period 1905 to 1914 almost 175 000 were imported, continuing, but on a reduced scale, in the 1920s; astonishingly successful results were achieved. Most of these partridges were trapped in autumn in Europe and released in the following spring in America. The progeny of pairs which were penned for egg production did not usually do well, although some did breed (Leopold, 1931, 1933).

The distribution and stocks of partridges in the USA and Canada were given considerable attention at the Perdix Workshops in 1980 (Peterson and Nelson, 1980) and in 1983 (Dumke *et al.*, 1984). The main area, known as 'primary range', extends from north-west Iowa through the Prairie pot-hole region of the Dakotas, across Saskatchewan to the parklands of Alberta (Fig. 2.3). Densities are also quite high in southern

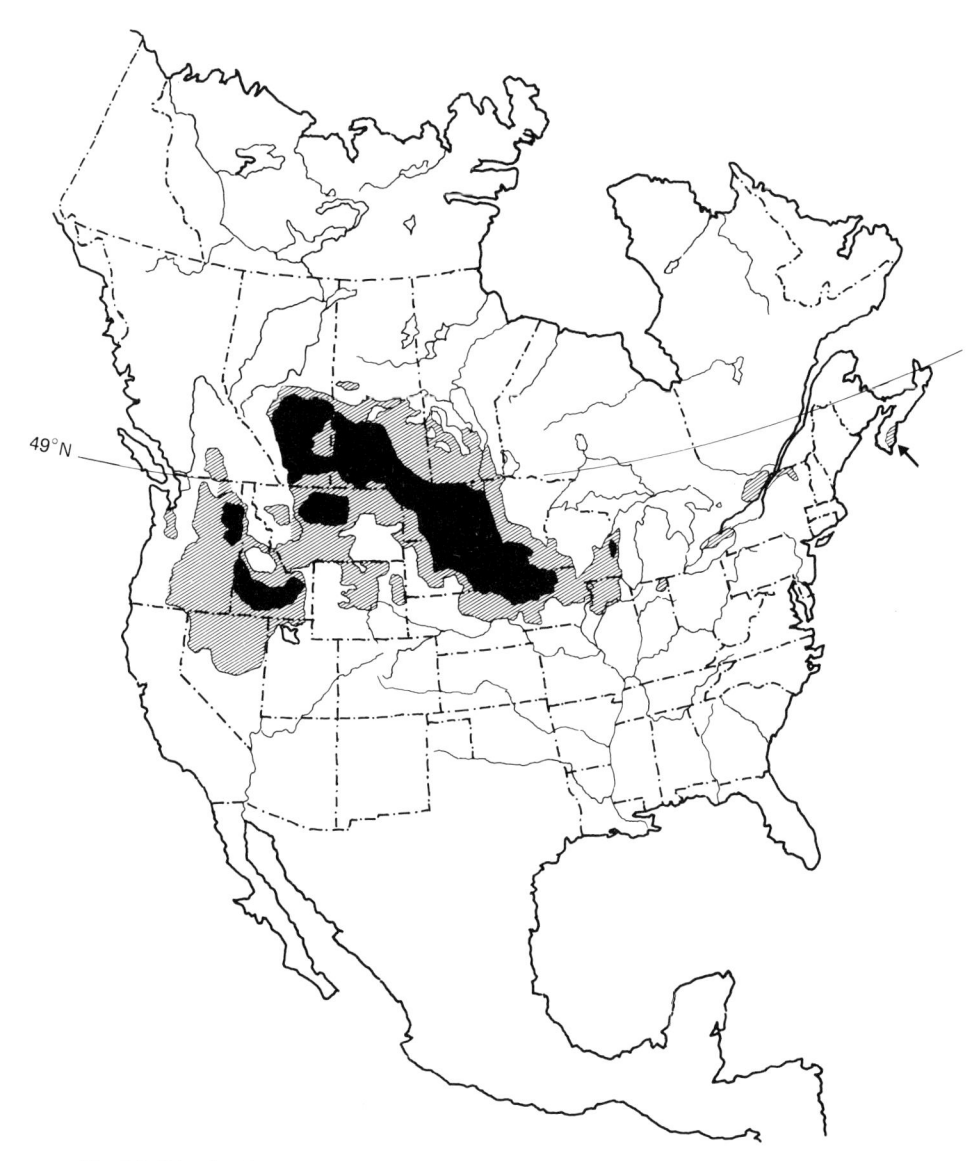

Fig. 2.3 Distribution of partridge in North America. Results of a survey conducted for Perdix III: Partridge/Ring-necked Pheasant Workshop, 28–30 March 1983, Campbellsport, WI. (Plus K. Church and J. B. Dawson, *in litt.*) Dark areas indicate densities probably >5 pairs km^{-2} with no use of herbicides in cereals.

Idaho, and another prime area was the Palouse prairie of Washington State, habitat which has however deteriorated greatly through removal of nesting cover (Colour Plate XIX).

Releases, often successful at first though always in the end failures, have for a number of years been made in most of the states of the USA, from California across to Florida. The reasons for failure have never been clearly documented, but competition, one way or another, with bobwhite quail has been considered. However, the partridge does not thrive in areas which are too hot, too dry (see Twomey, 1936), or thickly wooded and this could be part of the explanation. Temperature during laying should ideally range from 9–11°C (Moilanen, 1968).

Since the 1950s a marked contraction of range has occurred east of the Great Lakes, especially in Ontario and the maritime states (Dawson, 1961; Johnston, 1972; Thomas, 1973), partly due to reversion to woodland as in Michigan and New York State (e.g. Murtha, 1967). Further contraction is accompanying the agricultural depression of the mid-1980s (J. Enck *in litt.*). However, in North America there has apparently been no general retreat southwards as has occurred in Europe and the species still occurs to 56°N in Alberta (R. Melinchuck *in litt.*).

All other documented attempts to extend the range, in Hawaii, Chile, Australia (including Tasmania) and New Zealand, were failures (Long, 1981).

From 1864 many shipments of partridge were sent from England to New Zealand, but often resulting in a high mortality; in one case only nineteen birds out of 240 survived the long journey. No releases succeeded (Westerskov, 1960) and in 1870 the native quail (*Coturnix novaezealandiae*) also became extinct (King, 1984).

Early in 1959, 300 eggs were flown from Denmark to New Zealand under the guidance of Kaj Westerskov, who had earlier been Director of the Game Research Station at Kalø, Denmark. Although this did not establish a population some birds did breed in the wild for some years.

Decline in numbers

Bags

An overwhelming decline in numbers has been documented in most countries in which the partridge is found. Indeed, it is possible that the species has declined in all of the thirty-one countries in which it is found!

The relevant data are of two kinds: a vast documentation of numbers shot (bags) which has been collected and analysed in many different ways, and the more localised census of pairs in spring.

There are obvious sampling problems with the bag record and there is no universal relationship of bag size to actual partridge numbers, although it is very clear in many cases (see later). Many of the estimates of national bags and populations are also difficult to substantiate in detail but in most cases it seems that the right order of magnitude is achieved; the major exception may be the Soviet Union.

The estimated population size or bag in the Soviet Union is by far the largest contribution to the whole, but more uncertain than most, partly due to the lack of early data and also because of the temporary effects of occasional devastating winters. The cultivated area (arable land) in the Soviet Union totals about 2.27 million km^2, of which 1.2 million km^2 are given over to grain, including the Virgin Lands (41 million ha), first ploughed in the 1950s.

Osmolovskaya (1966) estimated that prior to the shooting season there were about seven partridges km^{-2} of 'cultivated landscape' west of the Urals (i.e. in the European Soviet Union) in the early 1960s. There are also two estimates of the rate of decline of post-breeding numbers from the early 1950s to the period covered by Osmolovskaya's survey. Near Stavropol in the North Caucasus numbers declined from 20 km^{-2} at a rate of about 8% per annum (Loshkarev, 1976) and at Zuevka, near Kirov, numbers declined at about 7% per annum (Litun, 1980).

Taken together, these two estimates suggest that the density of 7 km^{-2} in 1965 would be equivalent to about twenty birds km^{-2} in 1952, indicating that the North Caucasian region studied by Loshkarev was typical, at least in the period 1946–1955. The estimate of 9 km^{-2} for Gatchina (Dits, 1917) concerns an area outside the main range of the partridge whereas most of the Soviet Union is climatologically similar to the main range in North America, e.g. Kazakhstan similar to Saskatchewan and the Ukraine similar to North Dakota (Brady, 1974). The latter state had post-breeding densities of 20–30 km^{-2} in the 1940s (Hammond, 1941; Schulz, 1977). A density of 75 km^{-2} in 1941 south of the Urals was quoted as being exceptionally high (Dal, in Dementiev and Gladkov 1952). Densities in Poland in the early 1960s, prior to the decline there, averaged 35 km^{-2} (Olech, 1971) and often up to this level in the 1950s in Lithuania (Logminas and Petraitis, 1970) and Azerbaydjan (Khanmamedov, 1962).

An early 1950s estimate for the Soviet Union of twenty partridges km^{-2} on 1 September therefore seems reasonable, but on arable land alone

Table 2.1 Decline in national bags of the partridge

	Mean pre-1940 bag or pre-decline era	1984 bag (or most recent year)	Authorities
Sweden	25000	2000	Ulfstrand and Hogstedt (1976), Dahlgren (1986)
Finland	18000	3250	Merikallio (1958), P. Vikberg in litt., Hunters' Central Organisation
Denmark	350000	49000	Dansk Vildtforskning
Britain	2000000	100000	Game Conservancy
Ireland	7000?	<100	C. McKelvie in litt.
France	4000000	2150000 (many released)	Westerskov (1958b), ONC (1976), Landry (1985)
Belgium	100000	<40000	Westerskov (1958b)
Luxemburg	20000	<2000	Lippens and Willie (1972)
Netherlands	>50000	10000	Koninklijke Ned. Jagers Vereniging
Germany (FR & DR)	1500000	28000	Deutscher Jagdschutz-Verband Handbuch (1986), Horstman and Zörner (1986)
Austria	300000	29000	Glutz von Blotzheim et al. (1973), Reichholf (1973), F. Tataruch in litt.
Italy	500000	<100000 (mostly released)	Toso et al., Calabria Conference
Yugoslavia	152000	153000 (inc. releases)	Isaković (1970), V. Varićak in litt., statistical review.
Hungary	1290000	0	Nagy (1977), Matrai and Vallus (1981), MEM STAGEK (1984)
Bulgaria	200000	<20000	Petrov (1966)
Romania	377000	<36500	Manolache (1970)
Czechoslovakia	2400000	0	Sekera (1966), IUGB Conf. (1984)
Poland (present boundaries)	750000	100000	Pielowski (1986)
Soviet Union	4500000	4000	See text
USA	1084000	<777000	Dumke et al. (1984), Westerskov (1985b)
Canada	200000?	<189800	Dumke et al. (1984), J. Brindle in litt.
TOTALS	20 million	3.8 million	

this would amount to over 40 million partridges. If only 10% were shot the bag would be larger than in any other country and there have always been plenty of hunters – a million in the Ukraine alone. No complete data are available but at least 300 000 dead birds were exported annually from Leningrad in the early 1930s (Dementiev and Gladkov, 1952) compared to 30 400 shot in the whole country except Kazakhstan in 1971 (Priklonsky and Sapetina, 1978) and 4000 shot in the whole country, mainly in Kazakhstan, in 1981 (V. Litun *in litt.*), which indicates a huge decline.

To a lesser extent difficulties such as these occur in all countries, but the overall picture is clear (Table 2.1). The changes are so dramatic and the demand for partridge shooting is still so strong that it is obvious that the cause of the fall in bag sizes is a decline in the partridge population itself.

The partridge was also formerly shot in Norway, Switzerland, Spain, Portugal, Albania, Greece, Turkey and Iran; there are no reliable statistics available for these countries, but the total was probably about 150 000.

The decline in the Eastern Bloc countries has been of great concern; the partridge was of considerable economic importance until the late 1970s, though now shooting has virtually ceased. The only exception seems to be some areas of south-east Poland which are in the hands of private farmers and which still have many partridges. The situation in Hungary and Czechoslovakia is well documented and we shall return to the decline in these two countries later in this chapter.

Establishing starting points for these declines is difficult from the bag records since the upheavals of World War II were still reducing bags, especially in Germany, until well into the 1950s. However, *in the main range of the species*, there is no evidence of a widespread decline in partridge populations, as opposed to the bag, until after 1952 (Potts, 1970a).

I cannot resist an estimate of the size of the pre-decline population which can be based on the assumption that the bag represents 12% of the population at the end of the breeding season in Poland and the Soviet Union, 30% in Britain, Hungary, Czechoslovakia, France and Italy and 15% elsewhere (Chapters 10 and 11). Assuming the above to be correct the world population would have been about 110 million at the end of the close season, prior to about 1953.

Decline in breeding stocks

In Britain, breeding stock densities have been carefully monitored, at least on keepered areas, 1933. The decline since 1952 has been from around twenty-five pairs km^{-2} to around five pairs km^{-2}, or 80% (Fig. 2.4). The graph indicates higher numbers in the early 1950s but only ten selected estates were involved, compared to fifty or more from 1956, and these were situated in prime areas of Hampshire and north west Norfolk. Judging from counts on these originally selected estates from 1956 onwards (when the sample was much larger), it appears that there were generally about twenty-five pairs km^{-2} in the early 1950s. The trend is given on a log scale in Fig. 2.5, and the mean slope calculated at –0.021 of logs pairs km^{-2} per annum.

The trend through available estimates of breeding pair densities from all the detailed studies in Europe and North America (see Table 10.4, later) is plotted in Fig. 2.5. This suggests that breeding stocks may have averaged about eleven pairs km^{-2} prior to 1953; three pairs km^{-2} in 1985. The overall trend from the detailed studies is –0.016 log pairs km^{-2} per annum.

The overall rates of decline in Hungary (–0.020 log pairs km^{-2} per annum), Czechoslovakia (–0.027 log pairs km^{-2} per annum) and the Soviet Union (–0.028 log pairs km^{-2} per annum) have been very similar. Schulz (1977) reported a rate of –0.025 log pairs km^{-2} per annum for North Dakota for the period 1947–1975.

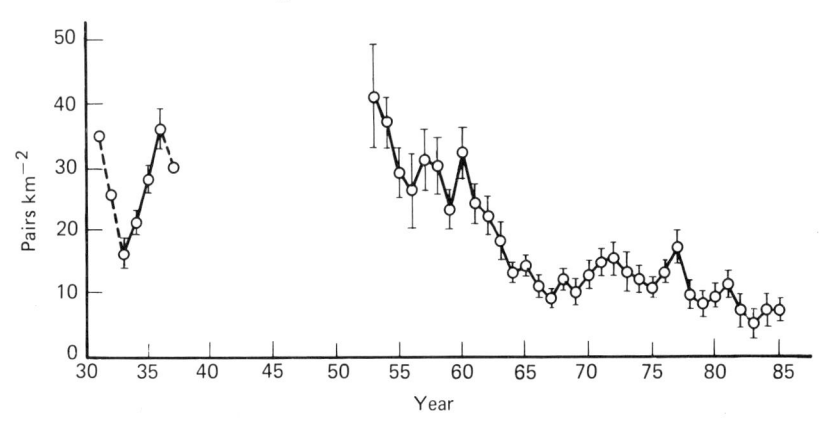

Fig. 2.4 The Game Conservancy's National Game Census March pair counts for the partridge from 1933 to 1985, with estimated minimum densities for the early 1930s ±2 standard errors.

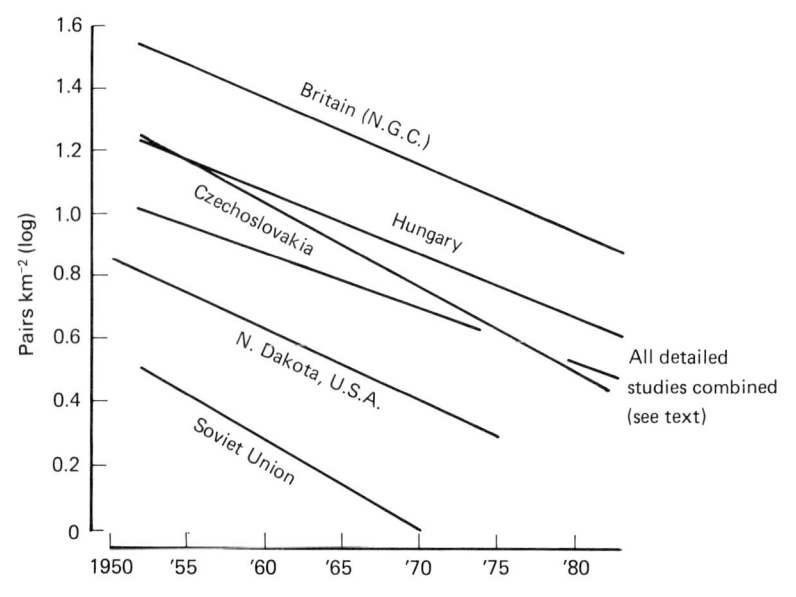

Fig. 2.5 The trend in density of breeding pairs km^{-2} over the period 1952 to 1985 for various regions of the world range.

Sources: Britain, National Game Census; Hungary as Table 2.1 plus A. Zajak *in litt.*, Fasankert Field Research Station; Czechoslovakia as Table 2.1, detailed studies see Table 10.4; North Dakota, Schulz (1977); Soviet Union in text.

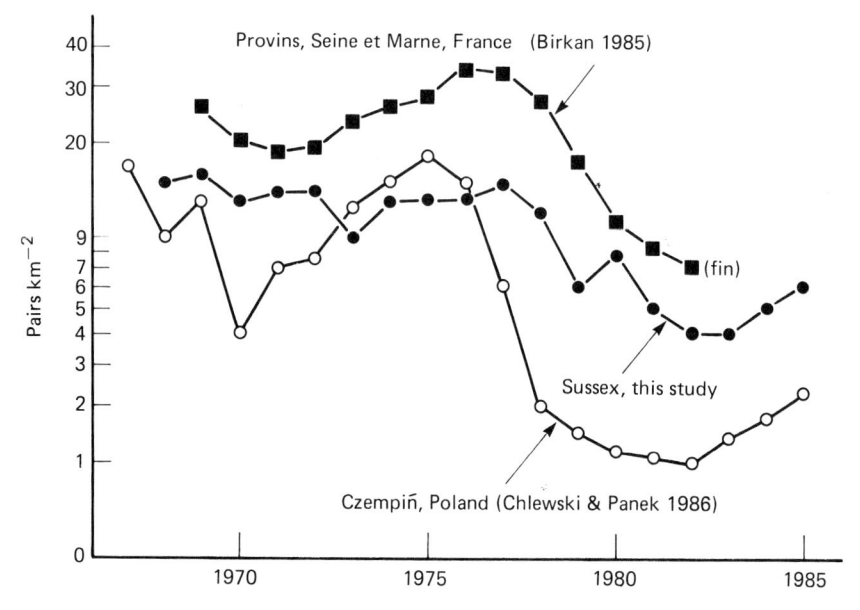

Fig. 2.6 Comparison of the three recent long-term studies on partridge populations: trends in spring stocks.

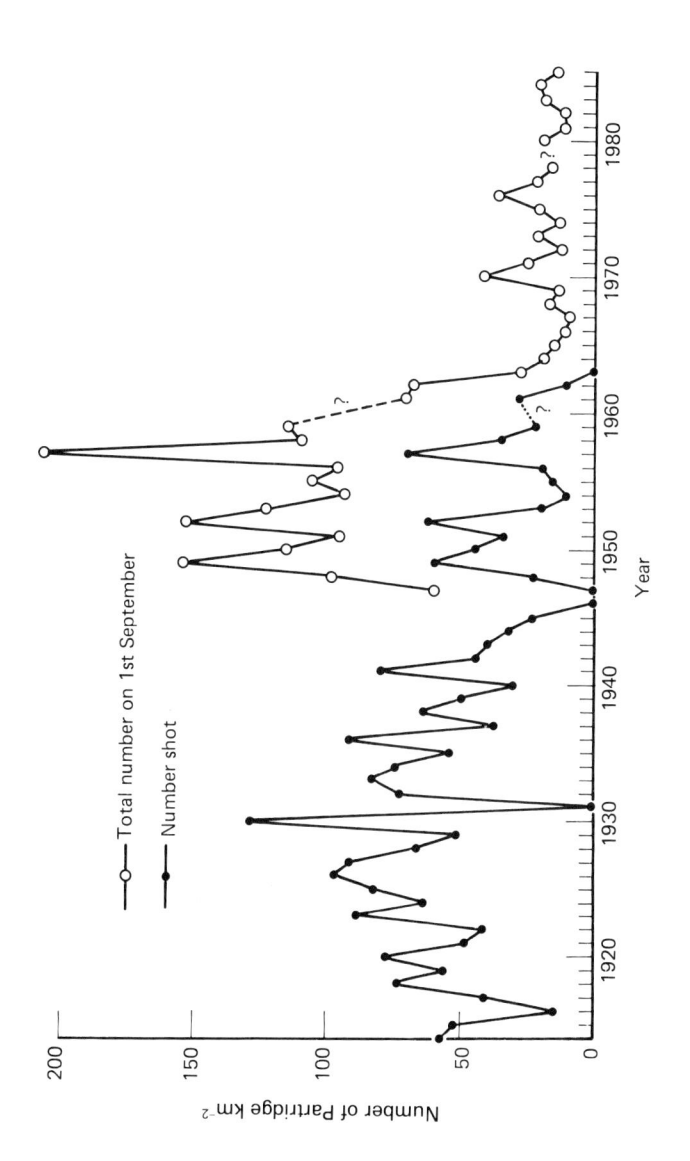

Fig. 2.7 The bag km^{-2} for the partridge at Damerham, Fordingbridge from 1914 to 1985 and the numbers km^{-2} on 1 September (from 1946 to 1985).

We thus arrive at a picture with six independent estimates of statistically significant declines (all $p<0.05$), each with slopes ranging only from -0.016 to -0.028 log pairs km^{-2} per annum, equivalent over the thirty-two years of decline to a loss of from 70% (detailed studies) to 86% (Czechoslovakia) of the breeding stock.

The decline of spring stocks in the Sussex study area is compared to that resulting from two other more or less contemporary studies in France (Birkan, 1985) and Poland (Chlewski and Panek, 1986); the overall similarity is striking (Fig. 2.6).

To summarise, we are searching for factors which could have caused a world-wide decline in the wild partridge population, before shooting, of about 80%.

The changes in spring stocks in the Sussex study area during the period 1968-1985 varied from nil to 70-80% depending on the farm concerned and at Damerham the decrease has been approximately 85% (Fig. 2.7). So we believe our experience of these two uniquely well-documented studies should provide insight into what has occurred elsewhere in the world.

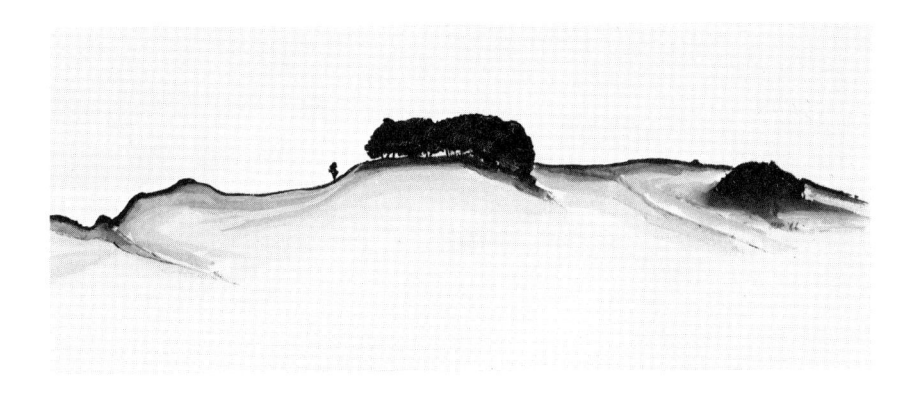

3 Study Area and Methods

In this chapter, the methods employed in the Sussex studies of the Partridge Survival Project are explained. The central feature is the stubble count or post-breeding survey used to estimate nesting losses, the mortality rate of hens during incubation and the mortality rate of chicks during the first six weeks. The ways in which these statistics are calculated and the precision obtained are described in detail. Other methods include the radio-tracking of broods and identification of diet by analysis of faeces collected from roosting sites of tracked broods.

Study area

Sussex

This, by far the main study area, was based at North Farm, Washington, West Sussex, and covered an area of 62 km², with partridge numbers monitored on 29.2 km² in the same way each year from 1968 to 1985 inclusive. All land was privately owned and we did not seek any influence over crop or game management practices. Bag data were available from 1946, partridge counts from 1956 and cereal insects monitored from 1969; we covered fields on fourteen farms with twelve different owners.

The boundary to the west of the study area (see maps, Fig. 3.1) is the flood plain water-meadow area of the Arun valley. The Adur valley, much of which has now been drained and used for cereal growing, lies to the east. Thick woods, predominantly of beech or ash, or hawthorn scrub, cover most of the 200 m scarp slope of the South Downs and form the northern edge of the study area. The southern border consists of wooded areas, villages or coastal conurbations. Thus, for much of the length of the boundary, the habitat is less suitable for partridges than the study area itself. The whole area is freely drained open downland with dry valleys running across the dip slope towards the sea (Plate III and Colour Plates VII and XVI. Fields are relatively large for Britain, averaging 16 ha, with 50% over 20 ha (Colour Plate VIII); there are very few houses in the area and only two short stretches of road.

Much of the area, particularly North Farm, was used for military training during the period 1939–1945, and it was not until the early 1950s that extensive areas of hawthorn scrub (with some oaks) were cleared from the higher parts of the downs which had not hitherto been cultivated.

The soil is mostly a chalk rendzina including flints, with some isolated areas of clay. Until about 1966 the predominant system of arable farming was a rotation of spring-sown barley with clover leys established by undersowing. For a time, especially from 1967 to 1973, several farms abandoned the traditional ley in favour of oilseed rape and beans but more recently some form of rotation with grass has become popular and the percentage of the total land area in cereals has remained constant at about 60%. The types of cereal grown are given in Table 3.1.

Other details are given in the text where appropriate, for example those for the cereal crop flora and invertebrate fauna are in Chapter 6, nesting cover in Chapter 9. There are two areas of downland grassland designated as 'Sites of Special Scientific Interest', one at North Farm and the other on the area known as North Stoke (see Fig. 3.1). The latter was carefully selected in 1968 as a 'control' area. This was planned to enable us to discount the possible effects of trials with released partridges which had taken place at North Farm but not at North Stoke, prior to 1968. The number of gamekeepers on the farms where partridge numbers were monitored varied through the study from two to six.

Table 3.1 The main types of cereal crops in the West Sussex study area in 1971 and 1985 (16% of the crop which was spring-sown in 1971 is now sown in autumn)

	1971	1985
Fields sampled	174	110
Winter wheat	30%	40%
Spring wheat	4%	5%
Winter barley	9%	21%
Spring barley	51%	34%
Winter oats	5%	0%
Spring oats	1%	0%

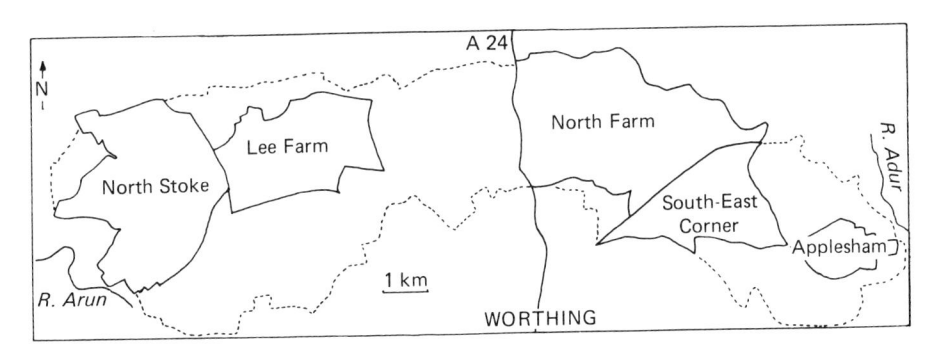

Fig. 3.1 Key to distribution of the five areas monitored, Lee Farm on page 32, others on succeeding pages except South East Corner not shown and Applesham as Fig. 3.4.

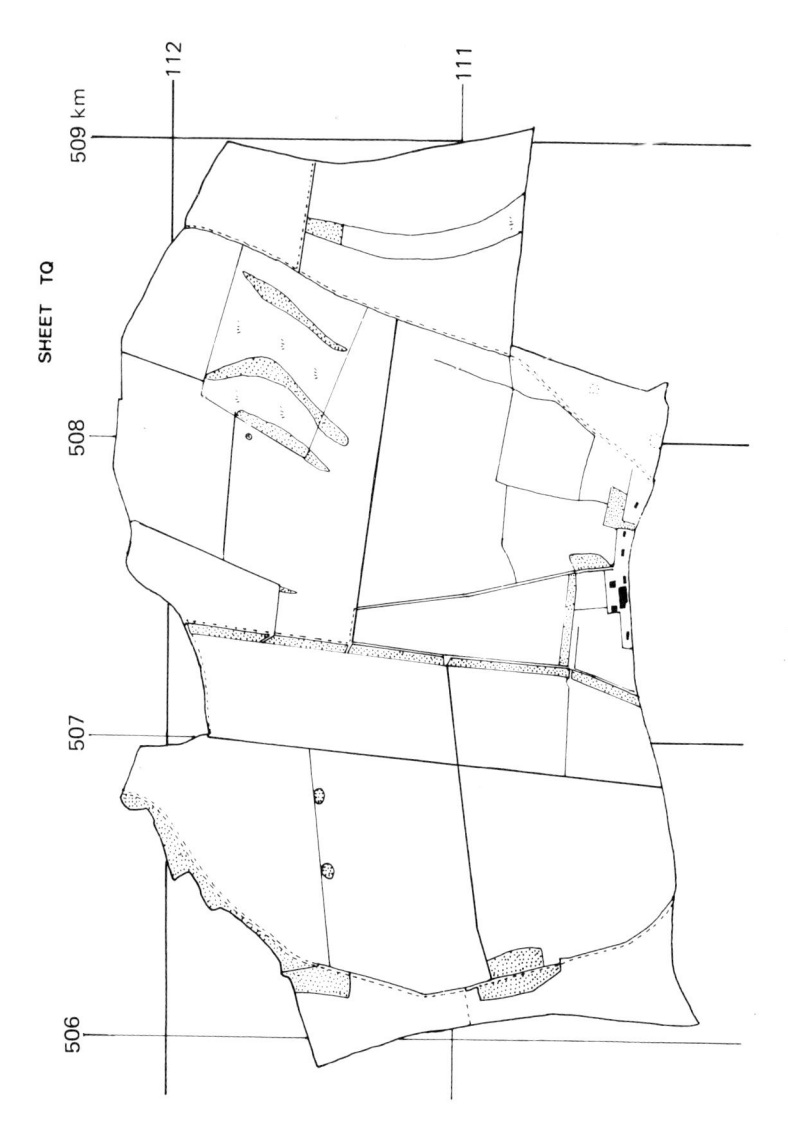

Fig. 3.1(a) Lee Farm; note woodland or scrub is stippled and all permanent field boundaries, fencerows, shown. No significant changes 1968–85.

STUDY AREA AND METHODS 33

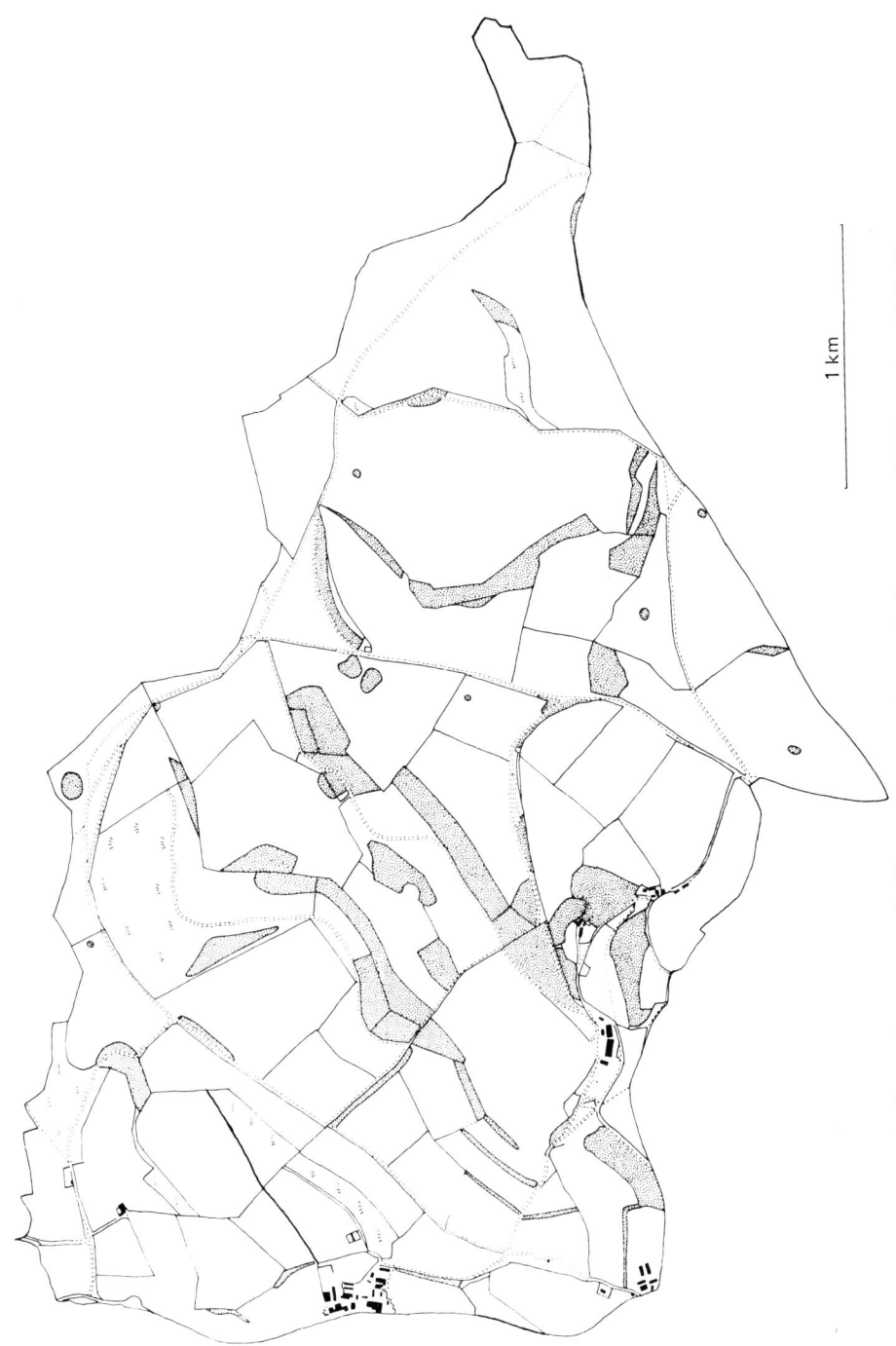

Fig. 3.1(b) North Farm; no significant net change in length of permanent field boundary 1968–85.

34   THE PARTRIDGE

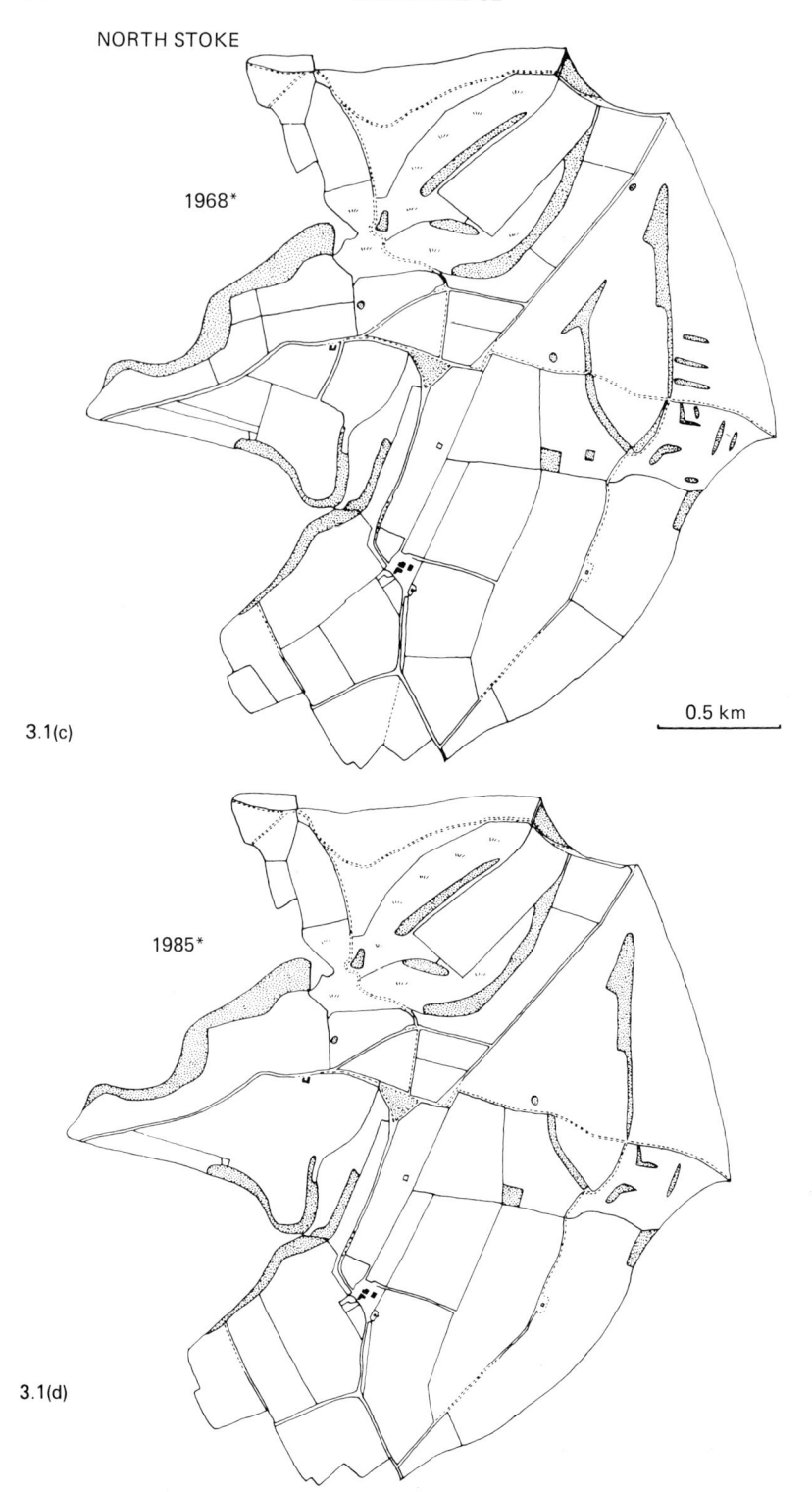

NORTH STOKE

1968*

0.5 km

3.1(c)

1985*

3.1(d)

*Note the changes are quantified in table 9.1

I. Shooting over pointing dogs (*Henry Alken c.1820*).

II. Driven partridges in September (*Derick Bown, 1983*).

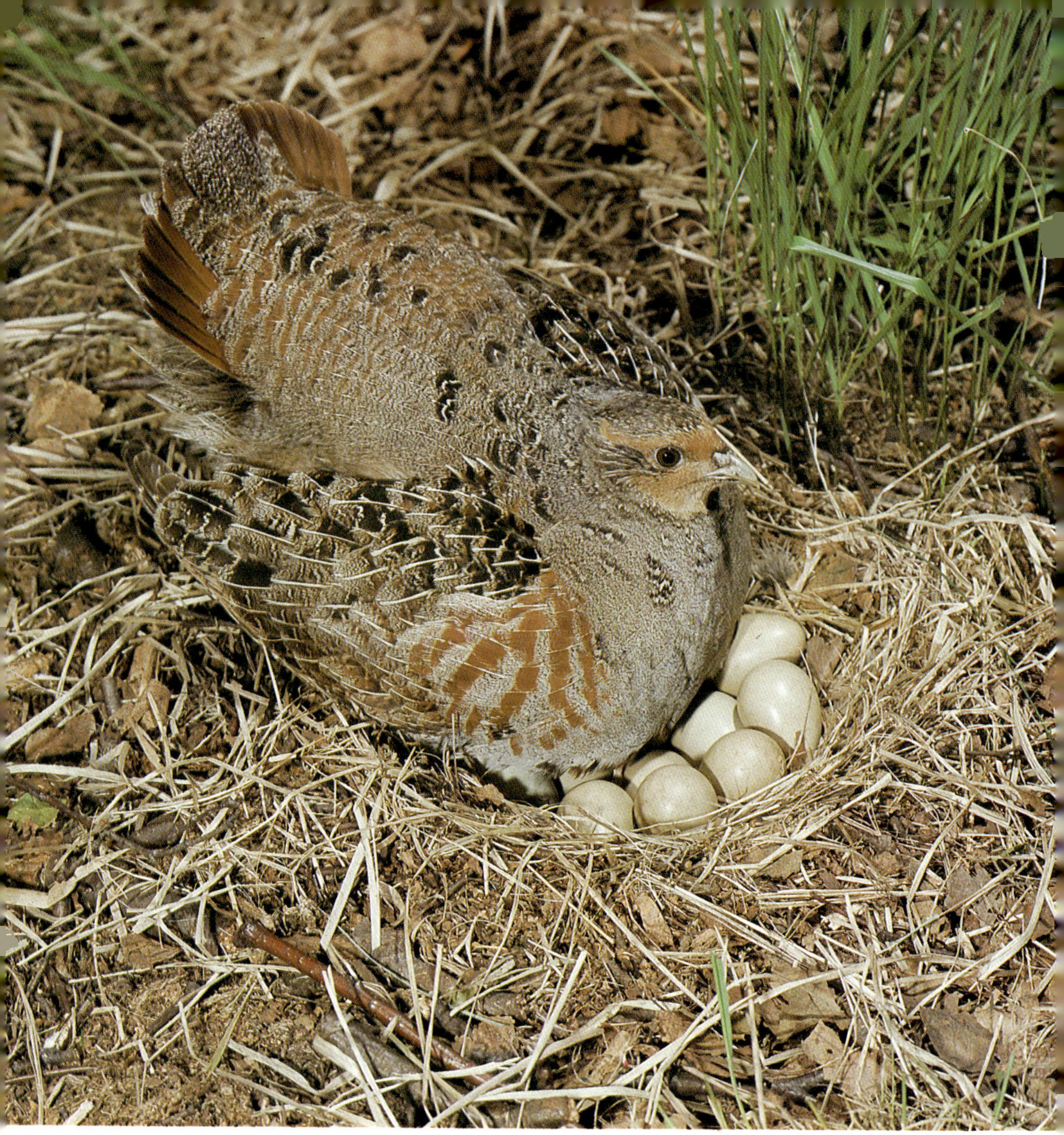

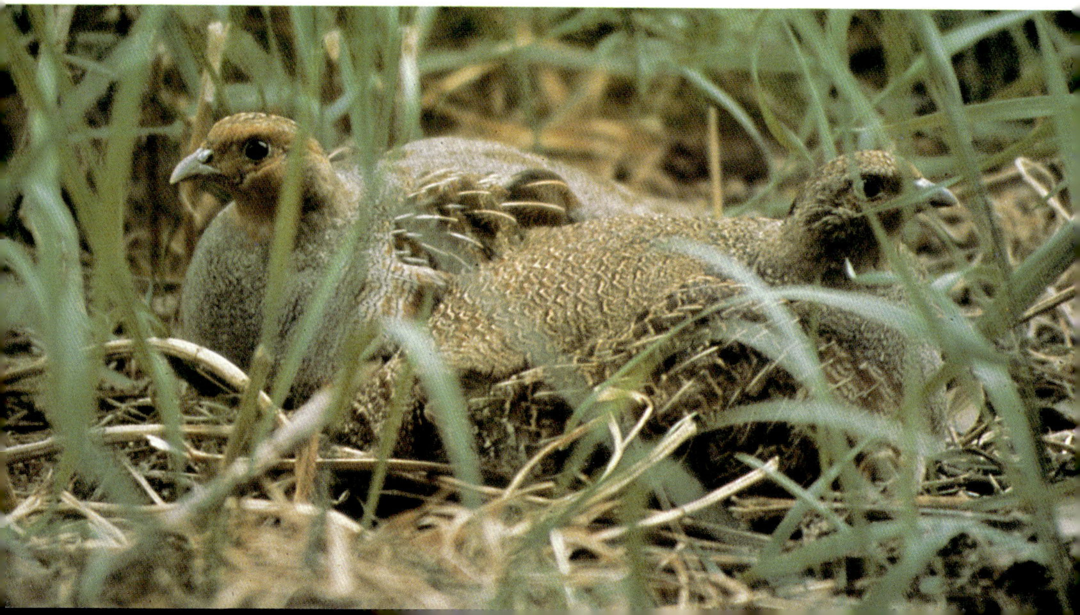

IV. (Above) Partridge plumage variation, three on right *P.p. robusta* from Altai of Mongolia (*G. Mützel, 1885*).

III. (Left) Variety of hen partridge at nest. Note the odd dark feathers on neck and back. These are grown prior to incubation (*Dennis Green, 1977*).

V. (Above) Fred Allen, North Farm, stoat caught in Fenn trap (*Stephen Tapper*).
VI. (Left) Pair in May, Yorkshire, female in front (*Dick Wilkinson*).

VII. Sussex study area, Valliers, North Farm (1979) (*Richard Prior*).

VIII. Sussex study area, Applesham (1979) (*Christopher Passmore*).

Plate III. Sussex study area, looking north to Chanctonbury Ring, North Farm

Damerham, nr. Fordingbridge, Hampshire

In this case the boundary was that of the 14 km² West Park Estate, Damerham. Although under one owner throughout the study, the area was farmed mostly by tenants (eleven in 1946, four in 1986). The shooting was rented from the owner by the ICI Game Research Station (now Game Conservancy) from 1946 to 1961, during which time there were five gamekeepers. Bag data are available for the period 1914 to the present, partridge counts from 1946 and insect data from 1978. Although woodland is scarce (5% of the area), the southern boundary is thickly wooded. There are two broad valleys running west to east, one dry, the other with a stream and water-meadows, Fig. 3.3. On the higher ground (although the highest point is only 120 m) the soils are derived from gravel beds, the rest rendzinas derived from chalk. A little under 50% of the area was in cereals through the period 1948–1965, since then 60%, the remainder being grass, mostly leys.

Manydown, Hampshire

Although partridge counts on this area began in 1933, experimental studies did not begin until 1982; the trials with unsprayed headlands are described at the end of Chapter 6. The area consists of 11 km², 65% in cereals with a wide variety of other crops and grass. There is more woodland (9%) than in either the Sussex area or Damerham. Details of the experimental procedures (controls and replications) are given by Rands (1985).

Courtyard Farm, Norfolk

Courtyard Farm, 3 km², was part of the Hunstanton Estate which joined the National Game Census in 1933. Fields are relatively small (10 ha) and the hedgerow layout is much as it was in 1858; woods amount to 3% of the area. Pair densities have reached 81 km^{-2} (1962) (the highest on record in the National Game Census) with over 300 km^{-2} in August for several years until the mid-1960s. Numbers shot exceeded 247 km^{-2} (one per acre) on two occasions, a figure which has been achieved on only about ten estates in Britain. Predator control was methodically carried out until 1975 but not since. Our main interest in Courtyard Farm is the change in predator control during a period in which the distribution and quality of nesting cover has remained excellent.

National Game Census

Through its membership, the Game Conservancy has organised a National Game Census of partridges and other game, beginning in 1956. This collates spring counts, August counts for 50 to 100 estates per year and bag records from these and approximately a further 400 estates. These records are used here as we have seen in the previous chapter. In addition, the estate currently with the highest density of partridges in Britain, West Barsham, near Courtyard Farm, is treated as an individual case (e.g. in Table 10.4).

Differentiation of the sexes

Differences in the plumage between the two sexes were well described around the turn of the century (e.g. Ogilvie-Grant, 1891; Saunders, 1899), yet in most popular bird books today, if the sexes are separated at all, they are usually depicted with an incorrect plumage. In particular the horseshoe mark on the breast is not a reliable indicator of sex. The horseshoe mark is wider in the male than in the female and it is always present in males, but is also found in 54% of females (Nagy, 1975; Fábián, 1979).

The post-juvenile moult is usually completed at the age of sixteen weeks (McCabe and Hawkins, 1946; Westerskov, 1958a), and from that time the sex can be determined from the plumage with good 10×50 binoculars at a range of up to approximately fifty yards. The main differences are well illustrated in the colour plate of Portal and Collinge (1932) and by the diagrams of Birkan (1977a) and in Colour Plates IV and VI. The principal diagnostic feature is the transverse bars, the so-called 'cross of Lorraine effect' on the feathers of the tertiary coverts or scapulars of the female and this feature has been checked by inspection of the gonads of shot birds (this study and Weigand, 1977b).

There have been reports of a statistically significant excess of females among late hatched young which have been shot before October in Denmark (Westerskov, 1957), in Czechoslovakia (Hell, 1965) and in France (Birkan, 1977b). However, Olech (1969, 1971) showed that males have often been mistaken for females prior to the completion of the post-juvenile moult of the wing coverts, which in some birds is not until the end of September. When the birds shot in September are omitted, the remainder of partridges shot in their first autumn show a 50:50 sex ratio ($49.5 \pm 0.05\%$ were females in a sample of almost 10 000

Fig. 3.2 Ageing guide for juvenile grey partridge.

examined; (Potts, 1980a)).

A unique feature of the Sussex study was the separation of male from female adults in the stubble counts. I estimated the sex ratio in counts made by other observers by assuming that 'single adults' were males and that other odd numbers in groups of adults were due to an excess of males (i.e. 3 adults = 2 males and 1 female). The Sussex counts suggested that 90% of males not attached to females will be detected in this way.

Age

Until the age of about eight weeks young partridges can easily be separated from the adults by size (Fig. 3.2). In addition the buff feathers on the ear coverts and neck are clearly diagnostic until the post-juvenile moult is complete; excellent colour paintings of these features are given by Habermehl and Hofmann (1963). It has been known since at least 1792 that the outer two primaries have pointed tips in young partridges, and rounded tips in the case of adults. The pointed juvenile primaries are retained for approximately fifteen months (Westerskov, 1958a; Olech, 1969).

Spring census

Fortunately the partridge is one of the easiest non-colonial birds to count. Moreover the techniques have been established and proved to be worthwhile in a practical sense on many estates for many years, such as those contributing to the spring counts of the National Game Census. The guidelines for this count issued for this census are given below.

'The aim of the spring census is a complete record of all partridges in the area, pairs and single birds. In most regions it should be carried out in the middle of March, when birds have paired and before the crop cover is too high. Counts should be made in the two hours after dawn and the two hours before sunset, when the birds should be feeding in the open: the best weather conditions are calm and dry.

A Landrover makes a good mobile 'hide' and the largest fields can be surveyed through binoculars from the headlands. Up to 200 hectares (500 acres) can be covered in about two and a half hours, the birds showing up readily on recently sown fields, but the vehicle may have to criss-cross well grown leys. As seen, the birds should be plotted on a map, scale about 1:10 000

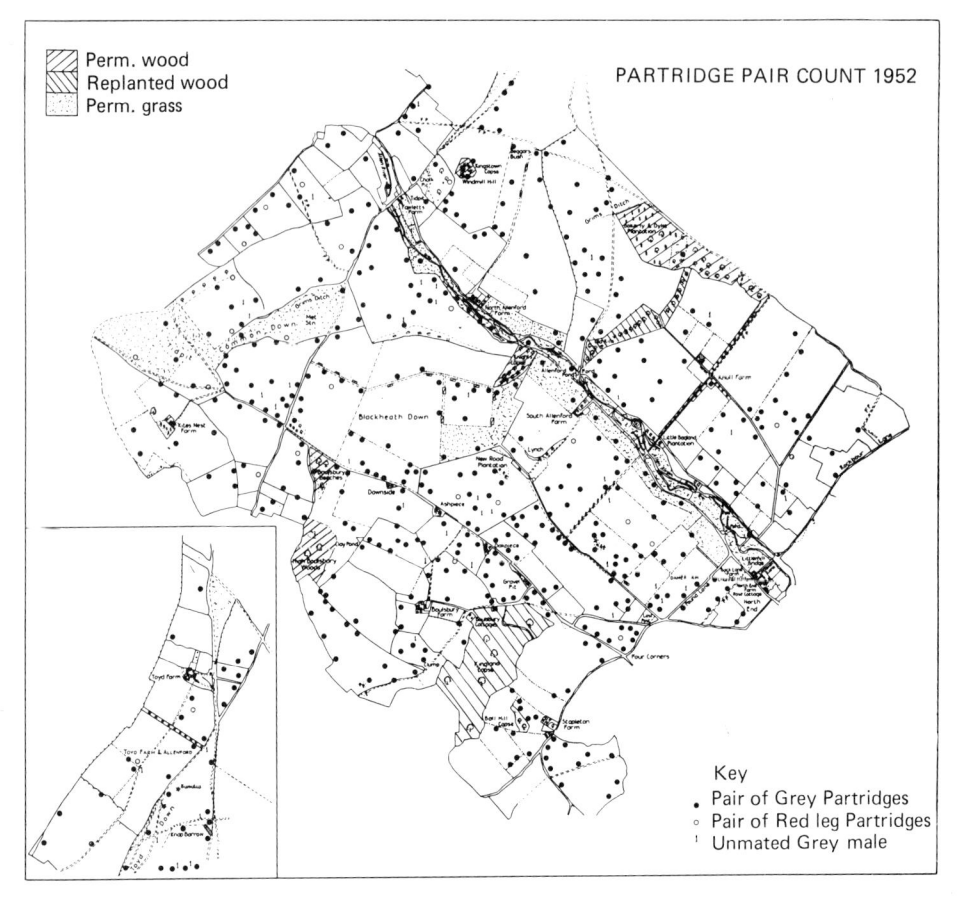

Fig. 3.3 Damerham. Result of the spring pair count 1952; 468 pairs of partridge and red-legged partridge on 14 km².

(6″ to 1 mile); grey partridge pairs are conventionally marked as '●' and single birds as '1' (see Fig. 3.3).'

An analysis of the Damerham spring census maps which included observations of marked birds showed that 85% of pairs nested within 200 m of where they were seen during the spring count. This, combined with the high visibility of feeding pairs before the spring crops start to grow, makes the spring count a relatively easy, accurate and useful census.

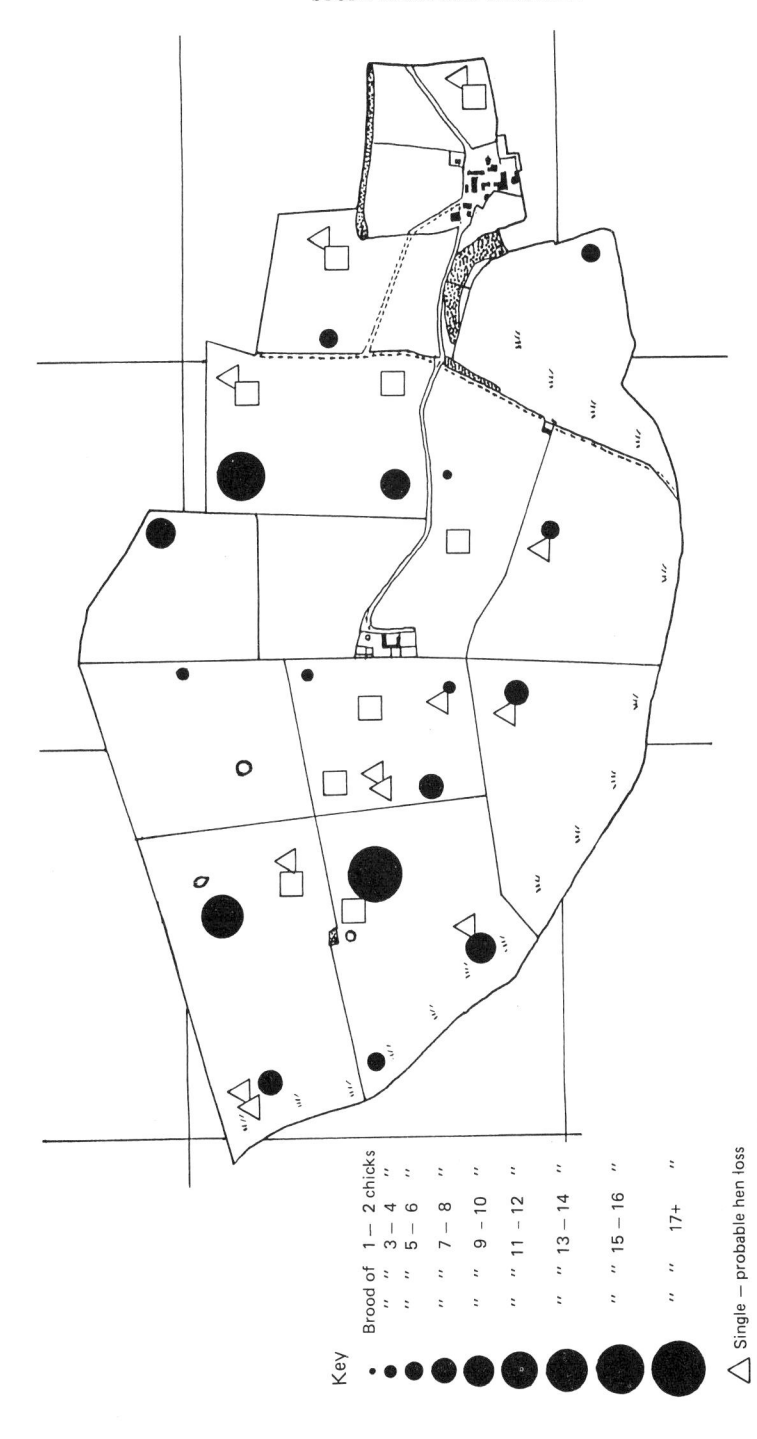

Fig. 3.4 Applesham. Diagrammatic representation of count in September 1984.

Post-breeding: The august stubble count

This count was originally used to sample the breeding success:

'Counts should be made in the early morning, in the two hours after sunrise while the crops are still wet with dew. A slow drive around the headlands will give a good idea of brood successes or failures after the partridges have hatched. Pairs without young, as well as successful pairs, will be seen feeding on stubbles or other patches of open ground. With the aid of binoculars it is easy to distinguish young birds from old, even when they are nine or ten weeks old.'

In Sussex the annual stubble counts began at the end of July and were completed in mid-September – they provide the core data of the Sussex study; some 23 000 individual partridges of known age and sex were plotted on maps in the years 1968 to 1985 inclusive, providing information of the kind shown in Fig. 3.4. In most other studies on partridges the stubble counts have been of a sample of birds; *in our case the aim was a complete census*, derived as follows.

The survival of individually marked paired and surplus males from April to August was determined in the Damerham study and found to be $85 \pm 2\%$ and $54 \pm 5\%$ respectively. In the Sussex study, $84 \pm 1\%$ of the total males in April had formed pairs, with no unpaired females.

Using these percentages we can take an example of 100 males in spring which would include eighty-four pairs. The total number of males surviving to August would be eighty. Therefore to assume that the density of males seen in August was the same as the density of the breeding stock would be to underestimate the breeding stock by a little less than 5%. In fact this is cancelled out by the higher proportion of partridges found compared to spring.

After harvest we found it easy to cover all fields several times to check and double-check estimates. By contrast in a mild spring, even in March, it is difficult to see all pairs, birds being hidden in crops of oilseed rape or winter cereals (the latter having greatly increased in area through the study, itself creating a possible bias).

Arguments that stubble counts are preferable in estimating spring stocks would not be strong in areas where potatoes, sugar-beet or maize are grown – crops in which coveys would be able to hide during the post-breeding period.

In Sussex the August census was also preferred because some dispersal continued after the spring pair count. Thus where we predicted five pairs km^{-2} in August from the spring counts, we found more: 6.3; and where we predicted twenty pairs km^{-2} we found less: 18.9. In years when counts were carried out earlier in the season than normal, these effects were statistically significant. Moreover, in the hilly parts of the study area we could not see all parts of fields from the edge and a thorough spring count necessitated driving over the cereals. In very wet years it was difficult to drive vehicles over all crops without causing damage.

Throughout the analysis of the Sussex data I have assumed that the male density in August is the same as the pair density in spring. As we have seen, mortality of paired males since spring is offset by unpaired males surviving to August and by the increased efficiency of counting in August.

Individual marking

In the early 1950s the research team working at Damerham developed the 'back-tab' as a means of marking partridges individually (Blank and Ash, 1956a). The next development, in 1970, was the numbered 'poncho' (Pyrah, 1970). It was used mainly in France but never became popular because it blew forward when the birds were feeding, and it was superseded by the 'back fin-tab' (Green, 1984b), originally developed for blackbirds in Switzerland (Furrer, 1979). As the number was in a vertical position it could be read far more easily.

Meanwhile in North America the development of radio-tracking proceeded, beginning in 1970 with the work of T. Upgren in North Dakota. There was no evidence that radio-marked partridges behaved differently (Schulz, 1977), even though the radios were somewhat heavier (16 g, 4% of body weight) than those used today.

Major advances in the radio-telemetry of partridges include the cage trapping of incubating hens, allowing subsequent tracking of broods (McCrow, 1982); solar rechargeable batteries (Church, 1979) and the location of faeces at roost sites in cereals (Green, 1984a). Smith *et al.* (1980, 1981) used a temporary anaesthetic to calm hens caught on the nest to help prevent desertion. In the later stages of incubation this is not necessary and desertion is not a problem with this technique.

Judging from the literature, over 250 partridges have now been radio-tracked in ten studies, not including the projects currently under way in the USA and in France.

Finding nests

Partridge nests are difficult to find even though they are mostly confined to the long (old or residual) grass areas alongside hedges and tracks. In our Sussex study area, as in Britain generally, most nests are situated alongside hedges (Chapter 9). Our method of nest searching is to walk along the hedges looking for a 'hole' or sign that the birds are using a particular entrance to a possible nest site.

In typical open countryside, with reasonable nesting cover, the time taken to find nests varies according to their density. With very careful searching our experience at the Game Conservancy suggests that it is possible to find approximately 20% of nests with one pair per 600 m of hedgerow, rising to 70% of nests with one pair every 200 m. An example of a nest map with a very high density is given as Fig. 3.5.

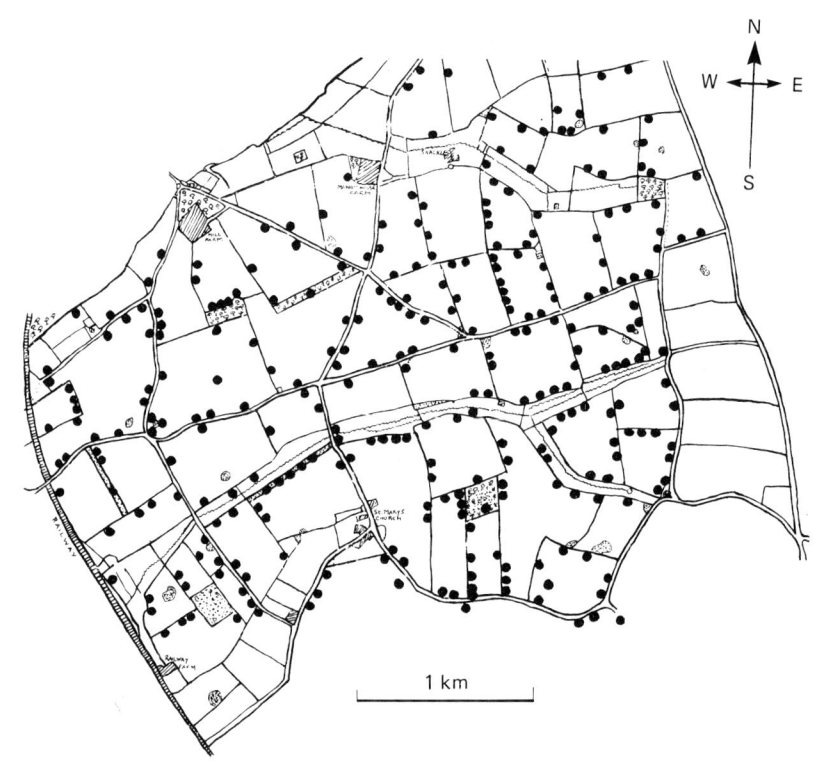

Fig. 3.5 Great Witchingham in Norfolk, original distribution map of partridge nests in 1906; each one had a number and detailed nest records made (see Table 10.4).

Young hatched per successful nest

With or without shooting (it makes little difference; see Chapter 11) the average expectation of life of an adult partridge is normally about 11 months, so unlike longer-living species they must try to breed in the first year.

There was no significant relationship between age and clutch size (Table 3.2) and there has never been any indication that even a small proportion of hens do not lay in their first year.

Table 3.2 Clutch size in relation to age of the hen: Damerham study 1952 to 1959

Age	Clutches	Mean	± standard error
First year	78	15.6	±0.21
Older	57	14.7	±0.32
All ages	135	15.2	±0.20

The number of young hatched per successful nest was remarkably constant over the years and between studies (Table 3.3).

Chick survival rate

An indirect method was needed to measure the survival rate of wild partridge chicks, to overcome the difficulty of finding large numbers of nests of individually marked hens.

On most farms the brood size can only be accurately determined after harvest, normally in August, since most chicks spend nearly all of their time in cereal crops. However it is not possible to equate pairs without young as brood sizes of zero, because the mortality could have occurred during the egg stage and the proportion of pairs which lose all their chicks is often high. Nor does brood size give a direct indication of chick survival because entire broods are lost when chick mortality is high.

Using geometric rather than arithmetic mean brood sizes (because brood sizes tend to have a log normal frequency distribution), I found (Potts, 1980a) that the chick survival rate (CSR) up to the age of approximately six weeks can be estimated by the power-curve equation, where the geometric mean brood size = x:

$$CSR = 3.665 x^{1.293}$$

though where $x>10$, CSR $= x/13.84 \times 100$

(*Note:* when a brood has more than sixteen chicks and there are more than two adult females in the covey, it is assumed that two broods were present i.e. a correction for the merging of broods. An approximation of the geometric mean is $-0.95 + 0.95 \times$ the arithmetic mean.)

Since the above technique was developed the results from some radio-tracked broods have verified the method. From eight broods in Norfolk, Green (1984a) obtained:

$$\text{CSR} = -7.81 + 7.81x \quad (P<0.05)$$

Table 3.3 Annual variation in the number of partridge chicks hatching per successful nest in the UK from 1907–1984, studies in areas with predator control

Period or year	Study areas	Mean chicks hatched per successful nest ± se	Nests found per annum in special studies
1907–1914	Charterhall (Berwicks)	13.27±0.43	353
1911–1916	Hursley Park (Hampshire)	13.93±0.18	243
1915	Clemor Hall (Norfolk)	14.30 –	358
1916	Clemor Hall (Norfolk)	13.40 –	367
1919–1922	Hursley Park (Hampshire)	13.70±0.09	293
1919–1932	Charterhall (Berwicks)	14.60±0.33	235
1933	16 UK estates	13.62±0.26	–
1934	21 UK estates	14.16±0.17	–
1935	30 UK estates	13.98±0.24	–
1936	30 UK estates	14.03±0.21	–
1937	14 UK estates	12.64±0.51	–
1948	3 UK estates	13.93	–
1949	5 UK estates	14.07±0.20	–
1950	5 UK estates	14.23±0.24	–
1951	4 UK estates	14.27±0.49	–
1952	6 UK estates	13.28±0.20	–
1953	8 UK estates	13.87±0.58	–
1954	4 UK estates	14.17 –	–
1955	4 UK estates	12.83 –	–
1956	3 UK estates	14.73 –	–
1949–1959	Damerham (Hampshire)	13.48±0.20	214
1949–1961	Sandringham (Norfolk)	13.60±0.59	854
1960–1966	Sandringham (Norfolk)	14.20±0.21	81
1969	this study (Sussex)	13.40 –	67
1970	this study (Sussex)	13.86±0.40	45
1971–1976	this study (Sussex)	13.71±0.36	9
1978	4 UK estates	14.34±0.35	–
	27 studies mean	13.84±0.10	–
1984	Manydown (Hampshire)	14.71±0.97	54

From nine broods at Manydown, M. Rands (*in litt.*) obtained:

$$CSR = 3.07 + 5.89x \ (P<0.05)$$

These relationships fit the power-curve equation well (Fig. 3.6) and I have retained it throughout.

The statistical precision (p) with which we can estimate chick survival is important, and here it is measured as the ratio of the standard error (s.e.) of brood size to the mean. A plot of the standard errors of brood size against the numbers of broods counted is given in Fig. 3.7. Where the number of broods is less than 10, $p>0.10$ of the mean; perhaps unacceptably large. An example with a geometric mean brood size of 5 and where $p = 0.10$ is set out below:

Upper 95% confidence limit = 37% chick survival
Mean = 29% chick survival
Lower 95% confidence limit = 22% chick survival

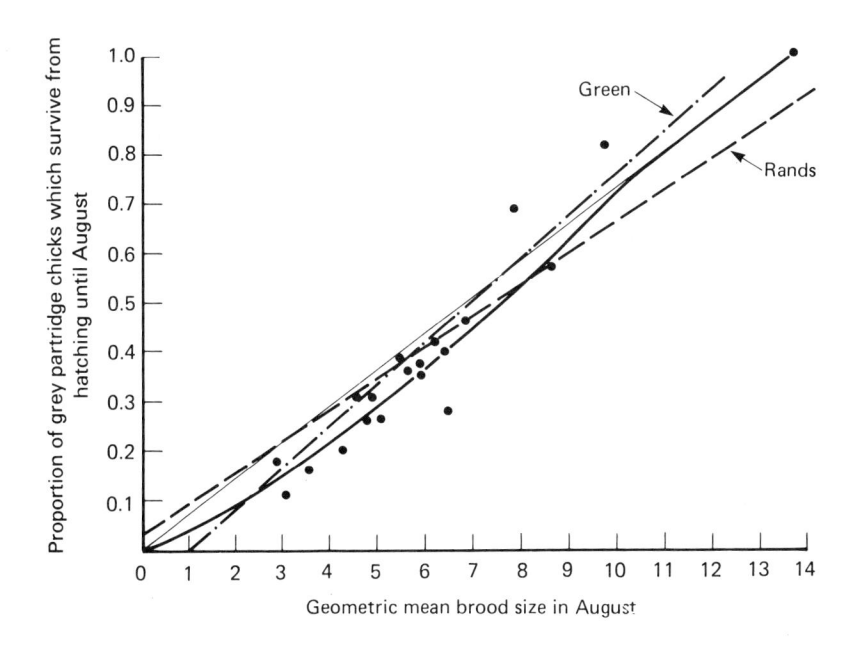

Fig. 3.6 The power-curve equation used to estimate chick survival rate (to six weeks) in the partridge. Individual points are annual means for the Damerham study and those of Jenkins (1956). The regressions obtained by Green (1984a) and M. Rands (*in litt.*) are indicated. See text for full explanation.

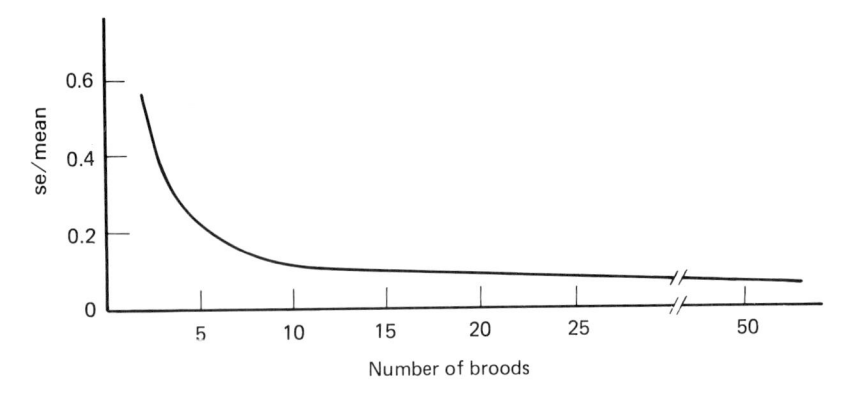

Fig. 3.7 Precision (se/mean) in measuring brood size, in relation to number of broods counted; the overall relationship in the Sussex study.

Brood production rate and nesting success

The brood size on hatching averaged 13.8 (from Table 3.3) so it is a short step to calculate the number of chicks hatching from the chick survival rate:

(1) Chicks hatching $= \dfrac{\text{chicks surviving (observed)}}{\text{proportion of chicks surviving (calculated)}}$

(2) Broods hatching $= \dfrac{\text{chicks hatching}}{13.8}$

(3) Broods hatching per pair (BPR) $= \dfrac{\text{broods hatching}}{\text{males seen in August}}$

From these equations it is obvious that errors in chick survival rate will carry over to brood production rate (BPR). Moreover, the number of broods is itself a function of the brood production rate. Errors will therefore inevitably be higher with increased nest losses, because there will be fewer broods. The number of broods from which brood production rates were calculated averaged thirty-one in areas with predation control but only nine in the areas with no predation control.

The implications of this can be further explored by taking the earlier example and assuming sixty chicks seen at age six weeks.

Chicks hatched		
− 2se	273 (CSR = 22%)	or 20 broods
Mean	205 (CSR = 29%)	or 15 broods
+ 2se	162 (CSR = 37%)	or 12 broods

So, with thirty males (for example) the respective brood production rates would be: 0.67, 0.50 and 0.40; a range of ± 0.27 of the mean.

Although the variance in BPR was relatively high this did not invalidate any analysis undertaken here.

Shooting

We attended all shoots on the study area and each bird shot was examined to determine sex, age, weight and the presence of numbered wing- (patagial-) tags (used on all released birds in the main studies reported here). The crop was extracted for identification of food eaten and the trachea (windpipe) examined for the presence of the gapeworm (*Syngamus trachea*). Great care was taken to retrieve all shot birds and we estimated that the proportion of birds shot but not retrieved was negligible. Therefore no correction was made for this.

Mortality rates using logarithms

It is now usual for the number of animals dying between successive stages in their life history to be expressed as k values (k for 'killing power'), which are the differences between log population densities at the start and at the end of life history stages. k values are more useful than simple proportions or percentages dying because they give a better representation of the changes which tend to occur at the same daily rate at the same stage (stages being; eggs before incubation, during incubation etc.). The use of k values also avoids some statistical distortions involved in the use percentages: those that require the angular (arc sine) correction. A simple example of their value when dealing with rates as opposed to absolute changes is given below:

Method 1 (invalid)
(1) 10 chicks at start day 1; 5 chicks at end day 3
(2) Mortality $= \frac{5}{10} = 0.50$
(3) But mortality per day does not equal 0.50/3, i.e. 0.1667 per day, since this gives 4.214 chicks dying, not 5

Method 2 (valid)
(1) Log 10 chicks day 1 = 1; log 5 chicks = at end day 3 = 0.699
(2) Mortality = (1 −0.699) = 0.301
(3) Mortality per day = 0.301/3 = 0.1003 per day − this gives 4.999 chicks dying

Logs are to the base 10 throughout; some authors use log to the base e, but since this is equivalent to $\log_{10}/2.3$ it is of no advantage here.

Losses were divided into five main stages:

(1) Egg mortality $\quad k_1 = \log\left(\dfrac{\text{males}}{\text{broods}}\right) - k_2$

(2) Hen mortality $\quad k_2 = \log(\text{males}/\text{females})$

(3) Chick mortality $\quad k_3 = \log\dfrac{\text{chicks hatched}}{\text{chicks at six weeks}}$

(4) Shooting mortality $k_4 = \log\left(\dfrac{\text{Partridges before shooting}}{\text{Partridges after shooting}}\right)$

(5) Winter mortality and losses of full grown birds prior to nesting
$\quad k_5 = \log\left(\dfrac{\text{All female partridges Sept Year 1 - shot Year 1}}{\text{Old male partridges Sept Year 2}}\right)$

Unlike percentages, k values can be added or subtracted. The logarithmic scale is also very useful when comparing trends of rare and abundant populations over the same time period; as we saw in Chapter 2, the slopes of graphs plotted on a log scale directly indicate rates of change, important in attributing changes to causes.

(Although analyses were in k values the equivalent percentages are given in the text, where it might be helpful.)

Insect monitoring

Our insect monitoring studies began in 1969 and are based on the use of the Dietrick vacuum insect sampler ('D-vac') (see Dietrick, 1961). Each year the 100–150 cereal fields have been sampled in the first two or three days of fine weather following 17 June. Vacuum samples (Colour Plate XII) consisted of five randomly placed sub-samples, each of 0.092 m², taken along a diagonal transect 25 m into each field, the sampler head being placed over the crop, dropped vertically and pressed to the soil surface for ten seconds. Five is the number of sub-samples used because it is the maximum number which can be taken without reducing the sampling efficiency and necessitating the use of another net. Taking samples in this way, relatively near the edge of the field, reduces crop damage and yet gives densities which are representative of the fields as a whole (Carter *et al.*, *in press*), though densities in many arthropod groups (especially plant bugs) are higher at the edge of fields than in the centre. Most partridges feed near the field edge.

The arthropods were first killed with ethyl acetate and then stored deep-frozen, awaiting transfer to alcohol and identification under a microscope. The samples were then placed in permanent storage.

As soon as each sample had been taken the areas sampled in the field were revisited to record crop type, growth stage, weeds (on a simple ranking system we devised at the outset), presence or absence of undersowing, and crop diseases.

Crop growth varied annually but shifting the insect sampling dates was not necessary because the dates of chick hatch were not subject to notable annual variation. At Damerham the median date of hatching varied only between 17 and 25 June over an eleven-year period.

A study of British Trust for Ornithology nest record cards from all parts of Britain, over several decades, showed that two-thirds of chicks hatched between 15 and 25 June (Potts, 1980a).

The types of pesticide used and the date and method of use were obtained from field records kept by farmers throughout the study.

Precision

The accuracy of the method of monitoring cereal insects with the D-vac has been assessed by Carter (1984) for a number of key species using the method of Finch *et al.* (1978) which is based on Taylor's power law (Taylor, 1961). In this the variance (S^2) of a sample varies with the mean (m):

$$S^2 = am^b$$

where *a* is largely a sampling factor and b a constant for a given species in particular environmental conditions.

The relationship can be expressed as:

$$\log_e S^2 = \log_e a + b \log_e m$$

This equation can be used to test whether the regression acounts for a significant proportion of the variance and whether it is linear.

This analysis was carried out for several groups of insects and other invertebrates, and Taylor's power law fitted the data well; in a sample of twenty-eight taxa (species and groups of similar species) the coefficient of determination, r^2, averaged 0.93. The degree of aggregation measured by b, varied from 1.01 for *Agonum dorsale* (when b = 1 the population is randomly distributed) to over 2.0 for aphids and thrips (highly aggregated), but averaged 1.5.

The sample size (N) needed for a given precision level (p = standard error/mean) is calculated from:

$$\log_e N = (\log_e a - 2\log_e p) - (2-b)\log_e m$$

Thus if $a = 1$ and $b = 2$ then sample size (N) is independent of the sample mean and only varies with the required precision level (Fig. 3.8).

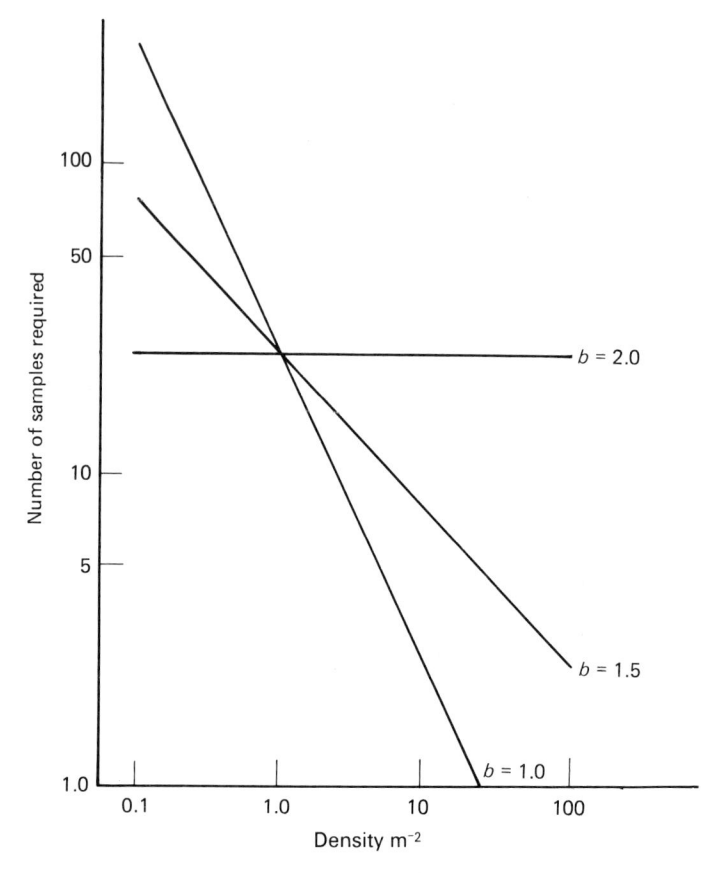

Fig. 3.8 The effect of mean density (m) and index of aggregation (b) on the number of samples (N) required to maintain a precision level (p) of 20% (with $a=1.0$).

For cereal aphids, thrips and for relatively abundant predators, the number of samples taken gave p<0.20, as did most species with mean densities more than 1.3 m^{-2} (Fig. 3.8). For the sum density of insects preferred by chicks, p ≏ 0.10.

Chick diet and faecal analysis

Partridge chicks stay close to their parents, so brood movements could be tracked from the radio-marked hen, using an aerial with attached prismatic compass. Hens were located during the night, within a radius of 5 m, using two bearings at right angles to each other. The exact roost site was located the following day so that the piles of chick droppings could be collected (Green, 1984a). When chicks in a brood died, this was often indicated by reductions in the number of small faeces at the roost; most chick losses occurred during the first ten days.

The methods of dissection of faeces, identification and calibration to diet are described by Green (1984a).

Each sample of faeces collected from a roost site was broken down in water with a mounted needle and washed over a 0.2 mm sieve. Remnants of prey arthropods and plant foods were identified by microscopic examination. Arthropod structures such as labra, mandibles, wings, tibiae, tarsi and elytra (wing cases) were counted in each faecal sample and the minimum number of individuals required to account for the numbers of remnants was calculated; e.g. the number of aphid tibiae divided by six. Feeding trials were carried out in order to determine the relationship between the composition of faecal remnants and that of the diet. For some species more research is needed to identify the appropriate remnants to count. For example, Green (1984a) estimated sawfly consumption from mandibles but in faeces there are normally three eye rings per mandible, not one as might be expected.

Interpretation of other population studies

Data from other published population studies were recalculated in the units and terms used for the Sussex study. The mortality rates were then calculated in the same way and with the same assumptions as described in this chapter. It was not possible to estimate confidence limits (e.g. Table 10.4) but it is obvious that some of the data, especially those covering a short period of years, will have little precision. In addition, methods used were often not explicit, especially in the older investigations.

However, the purpose was to investigate general and simple patterns in the data set as a whole. For this purpose representation and coverage are at least as important as precision, especially when, as here, the same set of rules was used throughout.

4 Predation at the Nest

'The amount of food for each species of course gives the extreme limit to which each can increase, but very frequently it is not the obtaining food, but the serving as prey to other animals, which determines the average numbers of a species. Thus, there seems to be little doubt that the stock of partridges, grouse and hares on any large estate depends chiefly on the destruction of vermin. If not one head of game were shot during the next twenty years in England, and, at the same time, if no vermin were destroyed, there would, in all probability, be less game than at present, although hundreds of thousands of game animals are now annually shot.' (C. Darwin, 1859)

In the first two full seasons of the Partridge Survival Project (1969 and 1970) we found 111 nests which progressed beyond the four egg stage. These nests were visited regularly and when the clutch was complete we removed five eggs from each, replacing them with wooden dummies of the kind used in the Euston System (see box 4.1). We were very interested in the subject of egg quality and each batch of five eggs was labelled and placed separately in an incubator so that the viability of the

---

Box 4.1   THE EUSTON SYSTEM

Once a hen partridge nears the end of incubation she can be lifted from her eggs or gently moved off the nest without fear of desertion. Nowadays we take advantage of this tameness by trapping females on the nest in order to radio-track their broods.

At the end of the nineteenth century a system originally developed for pheasants at Euston was used for partridges in the Belvoir fox-hunting country of Leicestershire. Whenever possible, partridge eggs were collected for incubation by bantams, being replaced by an equal number of specially made and widely available wooden 'dummy eggs'. The original eggs were returned to the nest – if the hen survived – at the chipping stage. Some hens even continued to sit during the exchange.

The advantage of this system is that eggs are protected from fox predation and that in turn foxes could be preserved for hunting. However, because the hens were still killed by foxes, the number of eggs shared among the surviving hens was often well above the normal clutch size. Also, because the control of foxes was not thought to be so vital, it increased hen losses generally, and egg losses from nests not 'Eustoned'. Perhaps because of these factors the system became unpopular even before the cost of the labour involved became a serious drawback. Whatever the cause of the system's demise it has always been clear that: 'The presence of foxes on an estate vastly complicates the question of partridge preservation'. (Maxwell, 1911)

chicks could, under controlled conditions, be related back to the site where the eggs were laid.

The aim of this approach was to check the biological significance of some variation in hatching success found on Lord Rank's Sutton Scotney estate (Southwood, 1967). We had in mind the approach of Jenkins and the team at Banchory, which stressed that most of the variation in the survival of grouse chicks was determined before the chicks hatched – by the 'quality' of their eggs. Different views had resulted from some studies on pheasants and partridges but the subject was controversial and many points needed verifying (Jenkins, 1965).

At North Farm (Sussex study area) the hatching success of eggs was very high, both in the incubator and in the nest: 90 and 95% respectively. In captivity the chicks survived well in both years (85%), though in the wild they survived poorly (25%) in 1969 but well (60%) in 1970.

Table 4.1 summarises the causes of loss among the nests we found. Less than half the clutches hatched and almost 80% of the losses could be attributed to predation. Moreover it was clear from the estimates of nest loss derived from the stubble surveys that our own presence at the nest had not increased the predation rate on eggs.

The difference between the average estimate of 40% lost in 1969 and 1970 derived from the stubble count, and of 53% lost from the sample

Table 4.1 Estimates of overall percentage nest loss and hen loss in the Sussex study area: a comparison of results from nests found and of estimates calculated from stubble counts, including the percentage lost to foxes

	1969	1970
Nests found (excluding early desertion)*	59	40
Nest loss		
(i) observed †	56%	50%
(ii) calculated ‡	43%	37%
Hens lost		
(i) observed	23%	32%
(ii) calculated	23%	28%
Hen loss attributed to fox§	20%	26%

* <4 egg stage

† *Gross*, includes clutches found and later lost, some of which might be replaced

‡ *Net*, the losses per pair per year allowing for successful replacement layings

§ Signs or smell at nest, hen found at earth (den) etc.

of nests found, is attributable to the success of repeat clutches. Comparison of the percentages suggests a repeat laying success rate of 26% in 1969 and 1970, similar to the calculated rate of 27% for the years 1964 to 1967 inclusive (see Table 4.2).

Table 4.2 The effect of collecting completed first clutches on final brood production rate in the Sussex study 1957 to 1984

Years* (inclusive)	Predator reduction	First clutches	First clutches collected	Broods produced
(1) 1957–1961	intensive	944	0	585 (62%)
(2) 1964–1968	intensive	398	143 (36%)	175 (44%)
(3) 1969–1980	less intensive	1447	0	666 (46%)
(4) 1981–1984	little	263	0	71 (27%)

* Data for 1962 and 1963 have been lost

The rate of replacement laying can be calculated from the data in Table 4.2, as follows:

Step 1   Taking the average of rows (1) and (3) gives an expected brood production of 215 (54%) for row 2, in the absence of clutch collection.

Step 2   In row (2), if there had been no repeat laying the 255 'not collected' would have had a brood production of 137 (54%), thirty-eight broods less than observed.

Step 3   These thirty-eight broods, attributed to replacement layings for the 143 collected clutches, gives a brood production rate for hens from which clutches had been taken of 27%.

Ornithologists studying the nests of song-birds often consider that their tracks to the nest and the disturbance of revisits could increase the risk of predation. It is therefore important to stress that in our case the main method of determining nest losses was independent of nest finding and possible nest disturbance.

Generations of gamekeepers were taught to visit partridge nests at least every other day with the aim of reducing losses. As soon as any nest was predated, gin traps (a few of which were always carried) would be set near neighbouring nests or under remaining eggs. (Of course gin traps have been illegal for many years; since 1958 in England and Wales, and 1969 in Scotland.)

Our study of nest losses revealed high predation on what was at the time one of the best partridge shoots in south-east England. At North Farm there was an organised campaign against foxes in the spring, yet foxes took almost a quarter of the sitting hens. (Incidentally, our dummy eggs were often ruined by fox tooth marks; they must have given the foxes something of a surprise!) More seriously, one wondered what was happening away from our study area, or where nest predators were not controlled.

The western block of the Sussex study area, the North Stoke Shoot, was well known for its partridge shooting. There was no releasing of partridges, yet the bag averaged over 20 km^{-2}, with in addition a useful population of wild red-legs. On 3 October 1961, 273 partridges were shot in seven drives and, according to Fred Scott, the gamekeeper, this was 'less than a quarter of the number present'.

The partridge population at North Stoke fluctuated in parallel with that of North Farm from 1957 to 1967 inclusive but not thereafter. In 1968 North Stoke was, for the first time for many years, not keepered at all and in the August count it became clear that nest losses had been unusually high. In 1970, after a return for one year to intensive predator

Plate IV. Predation by fox, the hen has been killed and removed late in incubation (*T.H. Blank*).

Plate V. Predation by feral cat (*T.H. Blank*).

reduction and low nest losses, the gamekeeper left and was not replaced for three years, each of them with high nest losses.

In the early 1980s systematic predator reduction ceased on two of the three beats at North Farm (and in the adjoining area, South-East Corner, see Fig. 3.1). On these areas partridge nest losses increased to the high level typical of the unkeepered years at North Stoke. We return to a detailed analysis of these effects later in the chapter.

Many nest predators leave clear signs of their presence and most traditional gamekeepers can correctly diagnose the cause of predation in about seven cases in ten (Middleton, 1967). For example, corvids pierce eggs and leave the insides of the shells clean, badgers crush shells and leave surrounding vegetation flattened. Rats often roll eggs away, stoats leave distinctive punctures on shells from their canine teeth, hedgehogs leave tiny indentations and leave many small pieces of shell. Foxes ignore eggs or leave some dented and often only partly eaten. They deftly remove the hen, leaving only a few saliva-dampened feathers, whereas cats maul hens, scattering feathers (Plates IV and V), and dogs often make a grab for the hen at the back or tail, leaving a large bunch of feathers. Many mammal predators leave a few hairs in nearby brambles, barbed wire, etc.

All the previous studies in Britain were carried out on well keepered estates with rigorous predator reduction, yet predation was the main cause of nest loss, most of it by only a few species (Table 4.3), though partridge bags were higher where predator reduction was most intensive (Middleton, 1967).

Table 4.3 Percentage of partridge nest losses attributed to major predators on estates with predator reduction, from Middleton (1967)

Nests lost, cause determined	3214
Mainly egg predators:	
Corvid	10%
Rat	7%
Hedgehog	3%
Badger	2%
Total	22%
Mainly hen predators:	
Fox	22%
Stoat	5%
Cat	5%
Dog	4%
Total	36%

Approximately half the area studied in Sussex was patrolled regularly by gamekeepers who were very 'enlightened' in their attitude to predators, especially kestrels, owls and rarer species even before they received full protection. Even some numerous predators were largely unmolested from July through to the end of February, except around the vicinity of release pens. However, in the 1960s trapping continued virtually all year round to protect released partridges.

In all years a vigorous campaign was organised against the resident carrion crows and magpies, beginning in February, resulting in a 70% reduction in the number of adults present and in addition preventing breeding amongst the survivors (Potts and Vickerman, 1974). From

March until early June, spring traps were set in tunnels (see Colour Plate V) at a density of about one per 250 m of hedgerow or similar nesting cover; almost 300 were set on the North Farm Shoot at any one time. The aim was to eliminate stoats, which was to all intents and purposes achieved (Tapper *et al.*, 1982), and also to reduce the rat population as much as possible. At the onset of incubation and through May and June foxes were the main target for predator reduction; some snares were set and any active earths gassed, but most foxes were shot at night. As a result foxes became few and far between, and cubs were not normally resident. Monthly bags of key predators during the entire study are given in Table 4.4, to show seasonal peaks.

Table 4.4 Monthly totals of key predators removed to show the spring campaigns, Sussex study area

Month	Carrion crow	Stoat	Fox
January	26	35	51
February	48	27	22
March	172	75	41
April	113	75	52
May	57	70	79
June	18	25	26
July	11	45	39
August	4	32	27
September	19	23	20
October	23	34	35
November	23	55	37
December	24	69	48
Totals	538	565	477

Predation as a density-dependent factor

Throughout the studies there were no areas where predators were totally eliminated, nor areas where predators were entirely protected, and there was a continuum of predator control activity between these extremes involving shepherds and poultry keepers as well as gamekeepers. However, the tunnel trapping policy gave a clear means of distinguishing between areas with traditional keepering and those without. Any keeper with the time to maintain a line of tunnel traps properly was able to do the other work that predator reduction demanded. Most non-trapped areas had only a very thin presence of gamekeepers (1 per 14

62   THE PARTRIDGE

Table 4.5 Summary of long-term data available of the effect of predator control on nesting success, indicating paired comparisons

Locality	Period	Trapped		Area-years
(1) North Farm, North Stoke, Lee Farm	1957–1967	yes		25
(2) North Farm, North Stoke, Lee Farm, South-East Corner	1968–1984	no	} Fig. 4.2	39
(3) North Farm, North Stoke, Lee Farm, South-East Corner	1968–1984	yes		36
(4) Applesham	1970–1985	no	Fig. 4.1	16
(5) Damerham, Hampshire	1947–1960	yes	} Fig. 4.3	14
Damerham, Hampshire	1962–1984	no		23
(6) Courtyard Farm, Norfolk	prior to 1975	yes	} Fig. 4.4	15
Courtyard Farm, Norfolk	since 1975	no		10

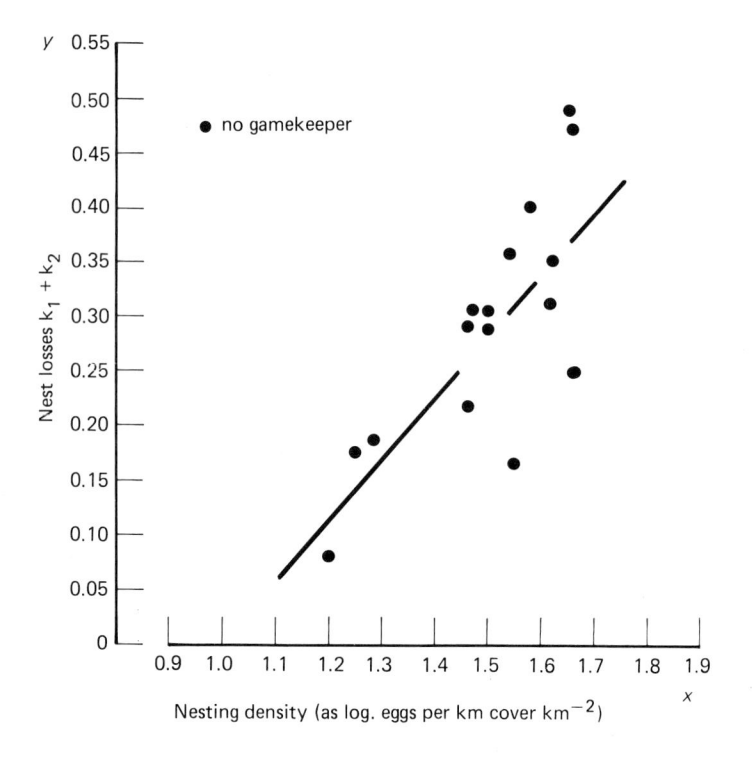

Fig. 4.1 The Sussex study: Applesham Farm 1970–1985 inclusive. Increased nest losses (k_1+k_2) at higher densities of nests. Most losses were attributable to predation ($y = -0.55 + 0.56x$, $P < 0.001$).

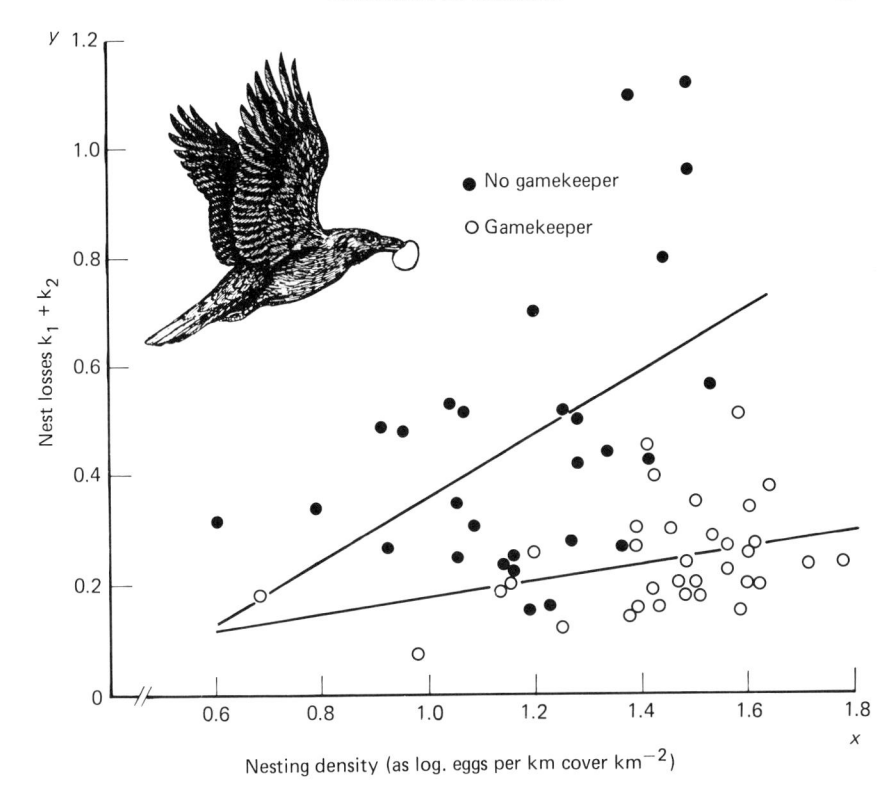

Fig. 4.2 The Sussex study: increased nest losses (k_1+k_2) at higher nest density; each point represents one area-year.
y (no predator control) $= -0.22 + 0.58x$ $P<0.01$ s.e. slope ± 0.19
y (predator control) $= -0.03 + 0.15x$ $P<0.05$ s.e. slope ± 0.07

km^2), with most attention directed to the rearing of pheasants and red-legged partridges. On thirteen area-years no attempt was made at predator reduction (in row 2, Table 4.5).

On this basis we could classify the area-years of the Sussex study and make paired comparisons (Table 4.5) with the same approach for the other study areas at Damerham and Courtyard Farm.

An analysis of the data in Table 4.5 shows clearly that losses of potential broods before hatching (i.e. $k_1 + k_2$) increased with nesting density; the Applesham data are given in Fig. 4.1.

It is not possible to judge from this data whether hen predators were responding to sitting hen density, or to nest density. One reason is that clutch losses continue through the incubation period and so the density

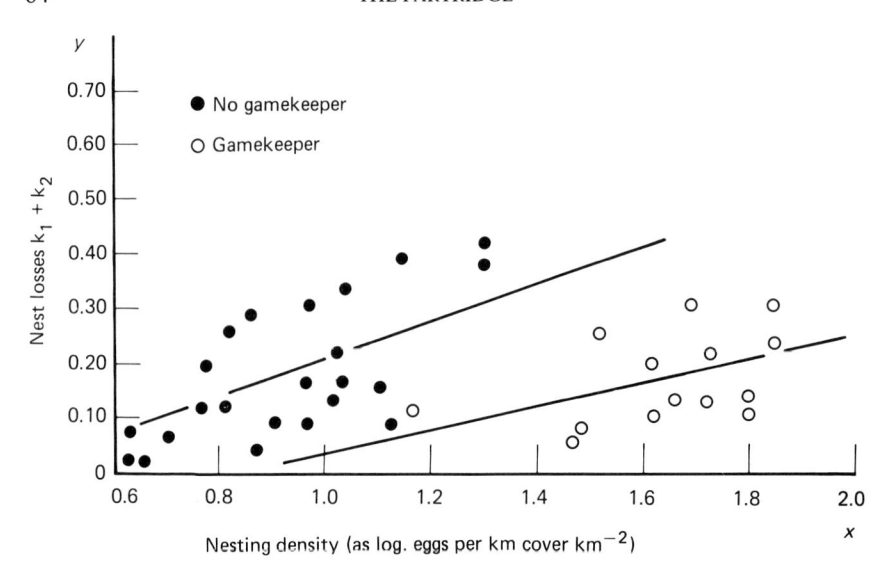

Fig. 4.3 The Damerham study: increased nest losses (k_1+k_2) at higher nest densities; each point represents one year.

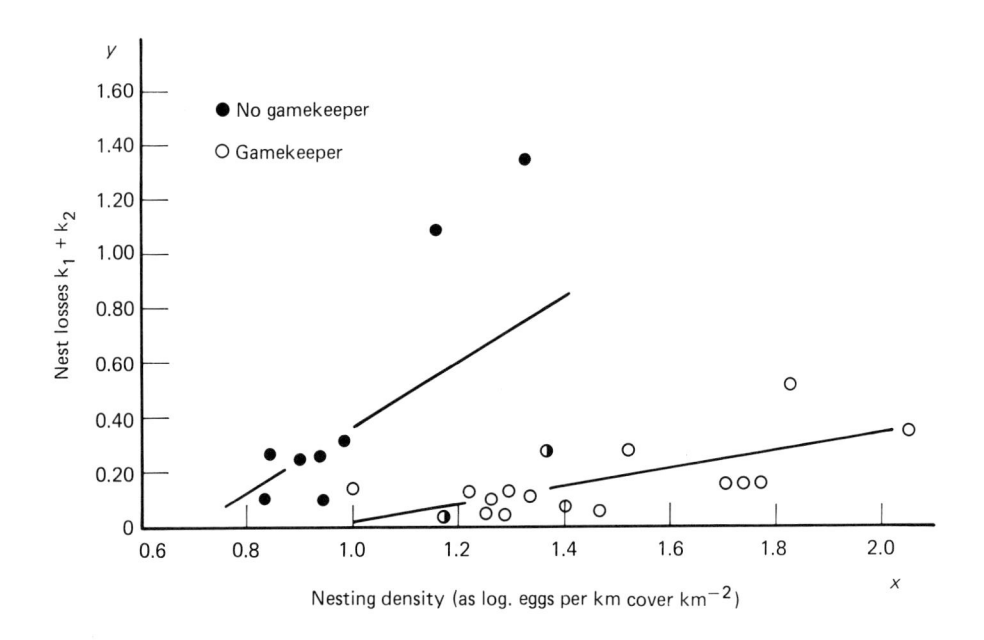

Fig. 4.4 Courtyard Farm: increased nest losses (k_1+k_2) at higher nest densities; each point represents one year.

of incubating hens is not known. It is therefore necessary to deal with both types of nest loss together in relation to nest density. The paired comparisons showing the effects of predator reduction on overall nest losses are given in Figs 4.2, 4.3 and 4.4.

In all cases, the slope of nesting losses on density is significantly different from zero in areas without predator reduction (each $p<0.05$), and not significantly different in areas with predator reduction. Predator reduction therefore clearly had a marked beneficial effect on nesting success.

Before investigating the nature of the density dependent relationships further, we should examine some other variation in nest losses.

Weather during the nesting period

Where possible, partridges select well-drained areas for their nests, which is why they prefer to nest alongside hedges planted on banks rather than in hedges planted on the flat (Chapter 9). Sometimes however they are forced, due to a lack of good nesting cover, to nest on sites where heavy rainfall may flood nests. Even good sites are affected in poor conditions, thus 'hundreds' of hens were 'drowned off' their nests at The Grange, Hampshire, in 1888, and in a well-documented case in Suffolk 61% of nests were flooded (Alington, 1904), see also Plate VI.

Early on the morning of 2 June 1981, most partridges in the Sussex study area were about one-third of the way through incubation and were therefore mostly unable to relay (Jenkins, 1956; Janda, 1966). Within a few hours, 75 mm (3") of rain fell, causing considerable flooding, especially in the area South East Corner (A. S. Potts, 1982). Based on estimates of nest density and keepering, nest losses ($k_1 + k_2$) might have been expected to average 0.24, a 42% loss (in 1981), but in fact they averaged 0.50, a 70% loss. By swamping nests the rain thus appears to have caused an unreplaced loss of 28% of clutches. However, the event was by the far the most severe in the seventeen-year study and has at this locality a return time frequency of only about once every 100 years (Table 4.6).

Mowing

Analyses of the causes of nest loss from fifteen studies in Europe and North America showed clearly that there are only two important causes of regular nest loss: predation and mowing (Potts, 1980a). Some clutch desertion has been recorded (e.g. in the British Trust for Ornithology

Plate VI. Incubating hen partridge after heavy rain, note sheep tick (*Ixodes ricinus*) bottom right of eye (*T.H. Blank*).

Table 4.6 Calculated annual maximum daily rainfall for various return periods (frequency) (A. S. Potts, 1982)

	Return period	
	10 years	100 years
Worthing (south of study area)	49.5 mm	67.6 mm
Parham House (north of study area)	50.2 mm	66.7 mm

Nest Recording Scheme) but in reality desertion might be an undetected loss of the hen.

In the Sussex study area mowing caused the loss of a considerable number of pheasant nests, but by contrast very few partridge nests, perhaps 2% per annum. Large blocks of fields were given over entirely to grass and these showed a similar rate of nest loss to areas where mowing for silage or even hay was frequent. In other studies where mowing was considered an important cause of nest loss, the areas were characterised by poor nesting cover outside the crops (e.g. few hedges), and also by the presence of relatively good nesting cover in the fields. Yocum (1942) and McCabe and Hawkins (1946) described areas where birds were nesting in meadows of lucerne (alfalfa) which had been undersown the previous year and which had strong admixtures of brome grass. By comparison the dense swards of Italian ryegrass in the Sussex study area were unsuitable for nesting, especially when heavily rolled in spring, as most were.

The speed of modern mowing machines was once considered a hazard to partridges, and so it is interesting that deaths were also frequent in days when scythes were used (Naumann, 1833) – in fact the hen sits so tightly that speed does not seem to matter.

Trials with a flushing bar mounted on the mower were carried out in North America in the 1930s and later at Damerham, Hampshire, in Hungary and in Czechoslovakia – but all with no success (e.g. see Skultéty, 1965). Neither did ultra-sonic and high-frequency sounds, or even a whistle (driven by the tractor exhaust!) frighten hens away from their nests. Only a small proportion of sitting hens were ever saved, but many eggs (below the cutter bar) were successfully transferred to incubators. Now it is known that the best solution to the problem is to attract nesting birds to better and safer sites in the field boundary (see Chapter 9).

Tests of the predation hypothesis

So it appears that predation is by far the most important cause of nest loss; a conclusion which if sustained would have far-reaching implications.

A mass of anecdotal evidence and the evolution of the gamekeeper's work suggests that predator reduction was always effective for partridges. However, technical weaknesses in the lines of reasoning used so far were:

(1) the changes in predator control did not occur at random,
(2) the pairings were not replicates, and
(3) the areas studied in Sussex, Hampshire and Norfolk were not chosen at random, so they may not be typical.

In 1984 we therefore chose two areas typical of the arable areas around the edge of Salisbury Plain for an experiment. Each area was of

Table 4.7 Salisbury Plain experiment to assess the effects of predator reduction

	1984 A	1984 B	1985 A	1985 B
	pre-treatment		predator reduction	predator protection
Area km^2	5.67	5.26	5.67	5.26
Stock of pairs	39	52	69	67
Broods seen at six weeks	21	16	34	17
Nest losses ($k_1 + k_2$)	0.15	0.35	0.08	0.37
Chick mortality (k_3)	0.39	0.34	0.57	0.68
Total 1 September	223	230	338	196

similar size, well separated geographically, in the same landscape and with the same management techniques for farming and shooting. By a series of counts from spring to mid-winter and by recording numbers shot, we established that the population dynamics are as expected from the Sussex model for an area with this kind of habitat, 5 km of nesting cover km^{-2} and a level of predation midway between keepered and unkeepered; the area as a whole has been 'lightly keepered' for many years. On the toss of a coin, we began predator reduction on area A (Colour Plate IX) and predator protection on the other area, B. These regimes will be reversed after three years. The 1985 results are given in Table 4.7 with differences in the nest losses which are almost exactly as predicted; low nest losses in A in 1984 being attributable to low nest density, and even lower nest losses in A in 1985, at higher nest density, being attributable to predator reduction. But at the time of writing we are still at an early stage in the project and the definitive conclusion of this work will not appear until 1991 – about 100 years after the zenith of predator reduction in the British countryside!

A similar though less comprehensive experiment was carried out from 1959 to 1969 on a flat, rich, arable area west of the Rhine near Bonn (Frank, 1970). The predator reduction area was 35 km^2 with two full-time hunters employed for the purpose. Unfortunately a problem developed over a strip of land which projected into the predator reduction area where the owners were not sympathetic to the experiment. Despite this, the results are clear.

The bags on the predator protection area were typical of much of the surrounding area and were less than those attained in the predator

Table 4.8 Effect on partridge bags of predator reduction (Frank, 1970) compared to computer simulation of results, which assumed the effect was entirely attributable to a reduction in nest predation

	Mean bag per annum km^{-2} (observed) 1959–1969	Mean bag per annum km^{-2} (model)
Predator reduction	10.9 ± 1.9	10.7 ± 1.5
Predator protection	5.7 ± 0.8	3.6 ± 0.4

reduction area. The results are given in Table 4.8 and compared with a computer prediction of the results based on an adaptation of the Sussex computer simulation model (described in Chapter 10).

In this particular version of the model we used the Sussex chick mortality rates and assumed that there was a constant shooting rate in both predator reduction and predator protection areas of 20% of the 1 September population per annum. Only the nest losses ($k_1 + k_2$), a function of predator control, were changed.

The results of the experiment showed a statistically significant response of partridge numbers to predator reduction and similar responses were observed in hares and pheasants. There were no stubble counts to show what was happening to the population, but the results are consistent with the view that nest predation was reduced and *as a consequence* bag sizes increased.

Trautman *et al.* (1973) described a large-scale predator removal project in eastern South Dakota from 1964–1971 involving eight 2.6 km^2 plots. Pheasants responded with a 75% increase compared to a 19% decrease in the normal plot. Unfortunately no details for partridges were given but scientists carrying out studies on waterfowl nesting success (also improved by predator removal) found that 'partridge broods were unusually abundant on the areas where predators were controlled but were quite rare in the remainder of the nearby countryside, including the plots where predators were not reduced' (J. Lokemoen, *in litt.*).

Change in behaviour of predators with higher partridge density

Density-dependent predation on eggs inevitably means that the predators are eating a higher proportion of partridge eggs at higher nest densities. If we can explain the mechanisms which are involved it would strengthen the validity of the general claim put forward.

It is certainly clear that the partridges' nesting strategy attracts a high probability of predation on two counts. First, the clutch, or at least the first egg, is on the ground for twenty-one days during which time the clutch is completed, and for a further twenty-five days during incubation. Pliny observed with admiration that the eggs of the partridge are covered during the laying period which gives them effective concealment: in contrast to those laid by the red-legged partridge (Green, 1984b). The only exceptions are that the first egg is not covered until the second is laid and that eggs are not covered between spells of incubation.

Second, where only a small proportion of a habitat is usable by prey, which is inevitably the case with farmland species nesting in permanent cover, the impact of predation can be intense especially where the predators can exploit most of the habitat, or move in from adjoining habitats such as woodland. A predator such as a fox need only follow the hedgerows to pick up the scent of partridges; about 2% of the habitat with nests arranged on the ground (i.e. at fifty times their overall density) and in a row (an example is given in Fig. 4.5). A parallel with the partridge restricted to hedgerows could be some of the ground-nesting arctic waders restricted to a few snow-free areas on the tundra, where predation is often high (Byrkjedal, 1980).

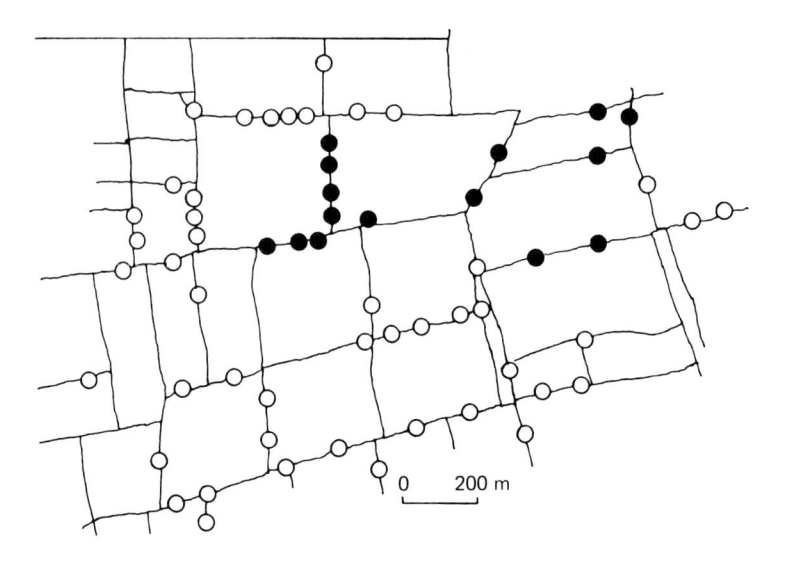

Fig. 4.5 Partridge nest records showing predated (●) and successful (○) nests. Map shows field boundaries with locations of nests along hedges and fencerows: part of the Hunstanton Estate in 1944; in this case all predated nests were attributed to a single stoat.

Table 4.9 Percentage losses of clutches per day during incubation: comparison of Sussex and Norfolk (latter from Green, 1984b)

	Losses (%)	
	Predator reduction	Predator protection
Sussex	1.8	4.5
Norfolk	>1.3	3.9

In studies of nest losses in the field sparrow, Fretwell (1972) showed that density-dependent relationships of the kind we observe in partridges can arise from a linear relationship between daily predation rates (given for the partridge in Table 4.9) and daily nest density. But is this a response by a few predators switching to a diet of partridges, or a gradual increase in preference for partridges by all predators? We need to account for the mechanisms if density dependent predation on partridge nests is to be plausible.

An increase in the density of the predators (known as a numerical response) is unlikely since partridge eggs account for such a small fraction of the overall diet of the predators as a whole (for carrion crow and other corvids see Holyoak, 1968). Nor can the predators be aggregating in areas with high partridge nest density, because most predators are territorial or have fairly exclusive home ranges. Moreover it appears that the territorial predators, which know their localities especially well, are those which account for most of this type of nest predation (Myrberget, 1972), probably finding nests by watching the movements of birds.

Initial contacts between predators and nests will be a function of the density of the predators and the density of the nests. However, once a nest has been found and the eggs eaten there is the potential for the formation of a searching image specifically for partridge clutches, which could explain at least some of the density-dependence. Unfortunately the theoretical basis for such an image is unclear. It was originally formulated by von Uexküll in 1934 (Curio, 1976), revived by Tinbergen in 1960, and then much criticised through the next two decades (Taylor, 1984). The problem was not the lack of evidence for searching images, nor was the concept implausible (Taylor, 1976), after all it *is* more difficult to look for two or three things at the same time, as has been demonstrated by experiments with carrion crows (Croze, 1970). What was not clear was the way in which the searching image spreads through a population of predators in relation to the density of prey sought.

In Sussex we had little data on predator densities, though in the years 1971–1976 inclusive, carrion crows and magpies were systematically recorded through the summer. During this period the percentage egg loss increased with the density of adult, resident, carrion crows and magpies km^{-2} in June (x) as follows:

$$\% \text{ egg loss} = 16.4 + 12.4x \qquad (P<0.01)$$

At one Sussex carrion crow nest in 1972 and 1973, we found the shells of at least 260 game bird eggs (195 pheasant, 56 partridge and 9 red-legged partridge) and in 1985 the shells of 172 pheasant and partridge eggs were found in similar circumstances (R. Helmsley, *pers. comm.*).

In the case of carrion crows, at least, it therefore seems that encounters with nests could result in a proportion of them becoming specialists searching for partridge nests. If so it is likely that only a small proportion of the predators in any one locality eat partridge eggs, but that this small proportion eats a large number of eggs. This occurs in the great skua (*Catharacta skua*) where individuals have been shown to specialise in their predation on eggs (see Table 4.10), and similar results might be expected for carrion crows. If this was the case the functional response (proportionately more eggs eaten as nest density rises) then results from a change in the proportion of specialists rather than from the average predator changing its preference (for further discussion see Murdoch and Oaten, 1975).

Specialist predators have long been considered by gamekeepers as 'rogues' – but there are unexpected conclusions if the above arguments are broadly correct and if specialists have an important role. For example it seems that the partridge specialists might just as easily occur (in proportion to their numbers) in rare generalist predators. Or as Naumann (1833) wrote, 'All birds which eat meat will eat partridges given the chance', and there are documented cases of individual

Table 4.10 Specialist egg predators in a colony of the great skua, Faroe Islands 1961 (Bayes, *et al.*, 1964)

Food brought to broods	Broods	Eggs eaten
Mainly eggs	1	200
Some eggs	12	145
No eggs	52	0
Totals	65	345

predators such as the snowy owl, merlin, sparrow hawk and badger specialising in partridges.

Despite this the number of predators will be most important, and a great deal of predation is clearly random and not attributable to the density-dependent specialists or rogues. Much of the reduction in nest predation brought about by gamekeepers may result from lowered numbers of predators rather than lower numbers of specialists. This would explain the difference in nest losses between predator reduction and predator protection areas which is not attributable to density-dependent predation (see particularly the difference at low densities in Fig. 4.2).

One feature of ecological research in recent years has been the large number of experiments increasing or decreasing the number of predators. Thus Sih *et al.* (1985) were able to review 139 studies over the period 1965 to 1984 which yielded 1412 estimates of prey densities in experimental areas and in controls. An astonishing 86% of these comparisons showed significant effects on at least one prey species; 36% of all prey species were affected, like the partridge, by predation.

The effects of nest predation on partridge populations are examined in Chapter 10, and effects on the shootable surplus in Chapter 11.

5 Chick Survival

'... Also if you take the partridge eggs and set them under a hen that sitteth she will hatch them and bring them forth, and nourish them like house chickens. They must be fed with ants' eggs till they be of more strength and of a good bigness.' (Maskall, 1581)

In many ways the most surprising fact about partridge ecology is that it has taken so long to establish that insects are important to chick survival

Historical

Small partridge chicks face rather obvious problems arising from the fact that they can only produce (by themselves) about a third of the heat necessary to keep warm (Koskimies, 1962); they must obtain the rest from brooding parents. Chicks can only feed for short periods before they again need the warmth from brooding. It seems obvious therefore that cold weather will limit feeding time and perhaps reduce chick survival rates.

However, none of the many attempts which have been made since the 1870's to correlate chick production with summer weather have proved satisfactory. There are several reasons for this, for example the measures of chick survival were indirect, usually young to old ratios in the bag. If heavy rain flooded nests, the reduction in young to old ratio would be misinterpreted as a reduction in brood size.

Middleton (1936a) illustrated an apparent dependence of young to old ratios in the August counts at Great Witchingham on weather in a graph, using June and July sunshine hours. He recognised the problems involved in interpreting such a correlation and judged that it 'may of course be due to variety of indirect environmental factors brought on by dry warm weather, rather than by direct effects'.

Some very interesting studies were made of geographical variation in breeding success in relation to weather but the most detailed investigations each only covered two years (Nolte, 1934; Cartwright, 1944). Nolte thought breeding success to be a function of temperature multiplied by food supply divided by rainfall, but he had no data on food supply.

The Royal Races at Ascot are traditionally (since 1711) held in the third week of June and many people concerned with partridges have thought that the weather during this event (the peak week for hatching) determines whether the forthcoming partridge shooting season will be good or bad. This reasonable view is, however, difficult to prove, if only because weather, as it affects partridge chicks, could not be measured and in many ways it still cannot, as we shall see later. In his *Diary of a Partridge Rearing Field* (for Knebworth Estate in 1937), published by Eley, Moser attributed much of the chick mortality to the often cold and wet conditions at daybreak, adding, with some justification since he was referring to the weather in June, 'people in their beds have no realisation of these conditions'.

We do not know when it was first realised that insects might be an important factor in chick survival, but 'ant eggs', i.e. pupae (cocoons) of *Lasius flavus*, the yellow or mound ant, were probably used to hand-rear chicks centuries before people began to write of such things, and Montagu (1813) considered ant pupae and grasshoppers to be a specially favoured and important food of chicks. Naumann (1833) noted that the young fed mainly on insects but that adults would also do so if they had the opportunity; insects he mentioned included grasshoppers, various beetles, larval insects of many kinds, ants and their pupae and craneflies. Jäckel (1891) reported ground beetles, weevils, ants (especially *Lasius* pupae), crane flies and sawflies.

On the Sussex Downs, the cold dry spring of 1901 was considered to be the cause of 'a great loss' of young partridges – 'except where ants were common'. 'Instead of the usual stock of creepy-crawly beasts there was no life (grasshoppers, beetles) among the grass and weeds at all, except a few butterflies' ('Partridges and insect food', *Country Life*, 7 September 1901). Poor chick survival was also attributed to a 'shortage of insects' by gamekeeper Dix at Great Witchingham in 1913, 1929 and 1931, and to an 'unseasonal lack of insect life' by the owner of the Manydown Estate in 1937. No doubt such views were widespread, even before the use of pesticides.

Analyses of the crop contents of chicks began to appear early this century and have continued, providing evidence that insects are at least numerically dominant in the chick diet, e.g. Poland (Rörig, 1900; Oko, 1963b); Hungary (Csiki, 1912); Britain (Ford *et al.*, 1938; Southwood and Cross, 1969; Potts, 1970a); Soviet Union (Poyarkov, 1955); Denmark (Hammer *et al.*, 1958); Czechoslovakia (Janda, 1959) and France (Thonon, 1974; Launay, 1975; Serre and Birkan, 1985).

The possibility that natural shortages of insects were contributing to poor chick survival was not considered, although in 1927, a year of very poor chick survival generally, broods did well on one estate where 'ant-heaps were carted daily to the vicinity of hatching nests and young coveys' (Portal and Collinge, 1932).

On Lord Rank's estate (at Micheldever), David Jenkins kept meticulous records throughout his three-year study, and these show clearly how his thinking on the causes of variation in chick survival progressed. He began by contrasting two areas. Chick survival was 24% higher in 'a' than in 'b' during the disastrous summer of 1953. He attributed this to the fact that 60% of the chicks on 'a' hatched after 22 June when the worst of the rain was over. Yet in 1954 when the weather was also very poor but with no heavy downpours, only 4% of chicks survived in 'a' compared to 50% in 'b', with no difference in hatching dates between 'a' and 'b'. At the end of his third and final season, he wrote 'the fact that chick losses consistently occur, even in periods of perfect weather and when no disease is traceable, suggests that some other, far less obvious lifeline is at the root of the trouble'. Unfortunately, at the time, he did not consider that some of the chicks could be starving.

Through his company manufacturing poultry feed, Lord Rank became greatly interested in chick nutrition and believed insects could be important to partridges in the wild. With this in mind, in the late 1950s he organised the distribution of lorry loads of ant hills around parts of his estate – but unfortunately the supply of ant hills was limited and transplanted hills did not succeed.

The Game Conservancy (then known as the ICI Game Research Station) reviewed for Lord Rank the possible importance of insects but concluded (in August 1960) that, 'for partridge chicks it would be more profitable to persevere with the idea of providing a readily available artificial food than with an idea of encouraging insects'. Fortunately this did not discourage Lord Rank and in March 1961 he contacted Dr Southwood (later, Professor Southwood) at Imperial College Field Station, and attention soon switched to the role of insects.

Work started in May 1961 on Lord Rank's estate and David Cross began his PhD studies under Southwood's supervision. In Bournemouth, at the 1963 International Union of Game Biologists Congress, Southwood reported:

'Shortage of insects could easily be a vital factor and chicks may need from 2000 to 3000 insects per day. The difference between partridge numbers pre- and post-war, commented on by Mr. Middleton, might be due to the effect of herbicides – our *preliminary* data suggest that chicks need to walk just over 1 mile per day in unsprayed fields but nearly 4 miles per day in barley fields sprayed with herbicides.'

Questions were asked as to what one could do for the partridges that would be compatible with farming, but these were unanswered. On Lord Rank's estate the partridge management shifted to restocking on a large scale and progress on the ecological front began to focus on North Farm, Sussex.

Sussex studies

At North Farm, partridge chick survival had been very low during 1963 and 1964. In 1965 survival was lower still and at first the June weather was thought to be the cause. However, during extensive August counting, Chris Hunt and Fred Allen found several large broods grouped on one farm. This stirred a good deal of interest since the fields had been spread with mushroom compost the previous winter – which started a host of questions! The following year (1966) was a poor one both for summer weather and chick survival, but chicks survived little better in 1967 during very good weather. It was this last failure of chicks to survive, more than any other factor, that directly led to Chris Hunt's desire to promote research on the subject, culminating in the formation of the Partridge Survival Project in 1968.

All those involved in the setting up of this project were encouraged by the results obtained by Southwood and his co-workers at Imperial College Field Station. In particular there were significant correlations between annual (June) insect abundance (measured in an aerial suction trap) and partridge young to old ratios obtained in the NGC (Southwood and Cross, 1969). Southwood greatly encouraged the Game Conservancy initiative at North Farm and it seems ironic that the insect trap that he and his students used was within sight of Ascot!

In the first systematic stubble counts (1968), I was almost immediately impressed by the patchy occurrence of areas in which the brood size was, relative to elsewhere, very high. In 1969 we found that good patches such as these were associated with the distribution of chick food, especially sawfly larvae, and at my family farm in Yorkshire, sawfly larvae were abundant and partridge brood size high. So I concluded that 'these and the other food insects might be at least as important to chick survival as the weather' (Potts, 1972a). In the remainder of this chapter I review the factors which eventually confirmed that correlations between insect abundance in cereal fields and chick mortality rate are ones of cause and effect and that the direct effects of weather are less important than was once thought.

From the analysis of crop contents of chicks collected mostly as a result of mowing accidents in their first week of life in the years 1934 to 1937, Ford *et al.* (1938) concluded that 95% of items eaten were insects. In our own studies during the 1970s we also found that 95% of items eaten in the first week were insects, though with fewer insects per chick compared to the findings of Ford *et al.* (1938) (Vickerman and O'Bryan, 1979). Even taking the first two weeks together, about 80% of all items eaten were insects (Table 5.1), the remaining food being weed seeds.

Pupae of ants, especially *Lasius flavus*, feature little in the diet for the first week in Sussex and in five other studies, but were the dominant food in two (Janda, 1959; Birkan and Serre, 1986), and after the first week they usually predominate. Thus in the Sussex sample they were not present in the crops and gizzards of a sample of eight chicks from the first week, but 68% of all the insects eaten in a sample of twenty-one chicks aged from two to six weeks were ant pupae.

Taking all the published studies together the most substantial items in the early diet were species of Coleoptera, especially weevils, particularly *Phytonomous variabilis* (now *Hypera postica*) and leaf beetles such as the knotgrass beetle. Most of the chicks in the Ford *et al.* (1938) and Janda (1959) samples were from hay fields so that the insect fauna of forage legumes, such as the lucerne springtail (*Sminthurus viridis*), also feature strongly.

In France a brood predated by a stoat was found to have eaten a large number of crane flies and adults of the ground beetle *Amara fulva* (Launay, 1975). In another case, in Beauce, eleven of sixteen chicks (aged up to ten days) had eaten 266 of the smaller, ground beetle *Trechus quadristriatus* (Serre and Birkan, 1985), which other considerations (later) suggest is a most important food.

Other important groups were grass and cereal aphids, plant bugs and the caterpillars of sawflies and lepidoptera. A particular feature of the diet of partridge chicks is their preference for relatively large, immature leaf-dwelling insects. Further comments on selectivity will be given later in the chapter, but first we must consider whether insects are likely to be important to chick survival.

Table 5.1 Grey partridge chicks: insects per chick and insects as a percentage of items in the diet in the first two weeks

	Chicks	Insects per chick crop	% items	Authority
Czechoslovakia, England and Scotland 1934–1968*	105	98 ± 5.0	82	Janda (1959), Ford *et al.* (1938) and T. Blank *in litt.*
Sussex 1969–1977	14	38 ± 10.5	77	this study

* includes two from the Sussex study area

Theoretical considerations

It is inconceivable to me that partridge chicks would go to so much trouble finding and eating such large quantities of insects unless such behaviour had evolved, because in most situations it confers some advantage. I tried to make this point and argue the general importance of insects as game chick food at the International Ornithological Congress in the Netherlands in September 1970, but without success.

Grouse workers at the conference accepted the fact that the chicks of many species of galliformes, including the red grouse, feed on insects but considered that they were not a factor important in limiting chick survival. Maternal nutrition affecting egg quality was, by contrast, thought to be vital – which had the illogical effect of weakening the case for the role of chick nutrition. Recently, from the North of England Grouse Research Project, we now have direct evidence from radio-tracking of broods that growth and survival rates of red grouse chicks are much improved if chicks are able to find and eat more insects (Hudson, 1986b).

The chicks of a few species of bird do not apparently need to feed on insects, so why should partridges need to? Examples given at the conference included the crossbill, linnet and woodpigeon, though here the role of pre-digestion, e.g. producing the so-called 'pigeon's milk', was unclear. Goslings too were said to grow on a diet of 'grass' alone, though now there is increasing evidence that crustaceans, such as *Daphnia* can be important (Wright and Street, 1985).

Research on partridges at Imperial College showed insects to be important to growth, especially to feather development (Cross, 1966; see Plate VII) and in trials at Fordingbridge in 1977, we confirmed that chicks of both species of partridge do not grow properly on a diet of cereal weeds or weed seeds alone, even when higher protein leaves such

Table 5.2 Effect of diet on the daily growth rates of partridge chicks

	Average weight increase per day	
	Grey (45 chicks)	Red (60 chicks)
Starter crumbs ad lib	+ 11%	+ 17%
Insects not ad lib, seeds etc. as below *ad lib* (NB they would have eaten more insects)	+ 6%	+ 12%
Ad-lib *Polygonum* seeds, weeds (*Stellaria media*), legumes and *Poa annua* spikelets	+ 0.5%	+ 1%

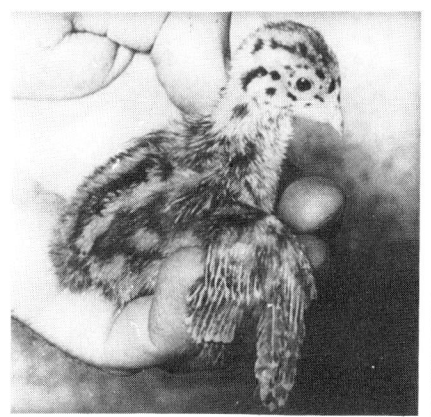

Plate VII. Two chicks from the same brood used in feeding trials at Imperial College. The chick fed with insects is shown right.

as those of clover are available. We cannot be certain that we fed the chicks on the best possible vegetarian diet but we did try to choose the best mixtures of *Polygonum* seeds and *Poa annua* spikelets and buds of forage legumes, especially clover, in order to raise the protein level. We also provided pelleted lucerne and ensured plenty of grit and water and of course the chicks had no difficulty keeping warm.

In these trials the rate of growth of chicks (grey and red-leg) was found to respond very much to their diet (Table 5.2); those feeding on plant food grew so slowly that it was barely measurable.

More recent work shows that partridge chick gizzards are unable to grind grass seeds open, indicating that many vegetable proteins may not be available to young grey chicks even when they are eaten. By contrast red-legged chicks have gizzards which are able to grind grass seeds open two or three days after hatching; in grey partridge chicks the same efficiency takes about ten days to develop (Green *et al.*, in press). Presumably this is why we find the grey partridge to be more dependent on insects at least after the first 3 days than the red-legged partridge.

Chick mortality is certainly at its peak during the ten-day period of maximum dependence on insects; 2.1% per day for the first ten days compared to 0.5% per day from ten to seventy-four days (Church, 1980). A comparable study found 1.6% per day and 0.3% per day for the same age intervals (J. Enck *in litt.*).

Cross (1966) considered certain amino acids to be of particular importance, for example the sulphur amino-acids essential to feather growth, and this line of reasoning has been developed using the example of red grouse by Wise (1982). His calculations (modified for the partridge) (Table 5.3) are based on the following assumptions:

1. The amino acids methionine and cystine are the most likely amino acids to be limiting to the growth of young galliforme birds, especially in feather growth (Almquist, 1952; see also Bagliacca *et al.*, 1985). Also, it is more likely that these amino acids will limit growth than dietary energy levels.

2. A chick growth rate gain per day of 2.2 g (11% per day for a ten-day old, 20 g chick) would probably require 38 mg per day of the amino acids methionine (M) and cystine (C). D'Mello (1978) demonstrated that M+C requirements for growth were probably the same for a wide range of vertebrate species.

3. The concentration of M+C in protein from insects is usually higher than that in plant protein, quite apart from the fact that the concentration of protein in insects is higher than that in plants.

On these assumptions Wise calculated the daily needs to satisfy the chicks' requirement of methionine and cystine (Table 5.3).

Table 5.3(a) Example of calculations of the available methionine and cystine in various foods

Foodstuff	A % crude protein in dry matter	B % M+C in protein	C % availability of M+C for poultry	% available M+C in dry matter $= \dfrac{A \times B \times C}{10\,000}$
Grassmeal	21.5	2.8	80	0.48
Field bean	28.0	1.5	82.5	0.35
Wheat	12.8	3.1	95	0.38
Fishmeal	67.0	3.9	95	2.48
Meatmeal	59.0	2.6	90	1.38
Insects	53.0	3.3	93	1.63

Table 5.3(b) Effect of methionine and cystine concentration on amount of food required to maintain normal rate of growth of partridge chicks

Foodstuff	A % available M+C in dry matter	B Available M+C needed (mg)	C Dry wt food needed	C as % body wt
Insects	1.63	38	2.33	11.7
Fishmeal	2.48	38	1.53	7.7
Wheat	0.38	38	10.00	50.0
Grassmeal	0.48	38	7.92	39.6

Without animal protein in the diet the daily weight intakes of chicks are likely to exceed the chicks' own weight per day, which is absurd.

One outcome from our feeding trials was that partridge chicks, even those from game farm stocks, were very obviously selecting certain types of insects such as plant bugs, types that also feature strongly in partridge diet in the field. Vickerman and O'Bryan (1979) investigated this further and produced a preference list derived from trials where young partridge chicks were given a choice of different insects in paired tests. This produced the following preference order: plant bugs = sawfly larvae > grasshopper nymphs > knotgrass beetles > ant pupae. In tests with coloured ant pupae it was found that the chicks preferred green to yellow, and green and yellow to blue, red or black. Green insects occur in chick diet more often than expected from their abundance in the habitat e.g. aphids, plant bugs, *Hypera postica* larvae, *Sminthurus* and some sawfly larvae (see also Birkan and Serre, 1986).

Insects were considered to be 'preferred' when they occurred more than twice as frequently ($P<0.05$) in the faeces samples as in the vacuum insect net samples from the field where the faeces were collected (Green, 1984a; Rands, unpublished).

So to summarise, chicks are eating insects; this behaviour is likely to improve the chances of survival, and certain types of insect seem particularly important. The question is now: what evidence exists that chicks are actually dying from a *shortage* of the preferred insects?

Before we can answer this question we must consider the possible density dependence of the chick survival rate, because it was at one time considered that chick survival rates were density-dependent (at Damerham – Blank *et al.*, 1967). In a later analysis I showed (Potts, 1980a) that this occurred for only a limited period of years there and was not the case on six other estates with similar contemporary records. In Sussex there was no indication of a dependence of chick mortality rate on either the density of the breeding population or the density of broods hatching.

In Sussex the maximum number of chicks per day m^{-2} of cereal crop would (at a population of seventy insect-feeding chicks km^{-2}) amount to only 0.00007 chicks m^{-2}. Even if there were only five preferred insects m^{-2} this would give 70 000 preferred insects per chick. Feeding tends to be restricted to the field edges (McCrow, 1982; Reitz, 1983; Green, 1984a; Rands, 1986a), because it is there that insect densities are higher. However, broods move considerable distances, as radio-tracking studies have shown. So given the considerable daily change in insect populations, for example in newly emerging ground beetles, it is difficult to see how chicks could depress their own insect food supply.

Russian, Polish and Czech biologists have claimed that partridges reduce insect pest damage, particularly by eating larvae of the Colorado beetle (*Leptinotarsa decemlineata*). For example in a three-year study (1979-1981) in the Stavropol district of the Soviet Union an average of twenty-five larvae was found per partridge crop – a large proportion of the contents (Khokhlov *et al.*, 1983). Similar results were obtained in Poland in 1960 (Oko, 1963b). The partridge also preys on various species of plant bugs known as tortoise-bugs, sunn pests, or wheat bugs (*Eurygaster* spp.). In the region of the Lower Volga, perhaps the best area for partridges in the Soviet Union, Nefedov (1943) found that 35% of the food of adult partridges in summer was insects, 90% of which were classified as crop pests with a maximum number of fifty-three *Eurygaster* eaten per bird. A level of only two to five of these bugs m^{-2} is the economic threshold for spraying with insecticide, so perhaps in this particular case the theory that partridges could reduce numbers is not so improbable as it at first appears to be (Barbulescu, 1973; Popov *et al.*, 1981).

The Sussex study and situation in the field

Background: cause of chick mortality

Radio-tracking studies have shown that broods with the highest chick mortality are those which had to move furthest in order to obtain food. Where y is the distance in metres between successive night roost sites for the first twenty days and x the percentage chick survival, we have, for Norfolk (Green, 1984a) and Manydown combined (Rands, 1986a): $y = 93.7 - 0.46x$ ($P<0.05$). Pheasant broods in cereals at Damerham gave the same equation: $y = 86.6 - 0.45x$ ($P<0.02$), although in this case home range size gave a better indication of survival of broods (Hill, 1985). Actual distances moved daily will of course be greater; Wood-Gush *et al.* (1978) calculated that some feral bantam broods moved up to 3 km per day.

How do chicks die of insect shortages? This is a difficult question to answer since very few young chicks have actually been found dead, even in the detailed radio-tracking studies. For example five chicks were found dead in the Sussex study, two during Green's work and two more by Rands in 1984 and 1985. On post-mortem examination the cause of all deaths was found to be hypothermia and hypoglycaemia (cold and starvation), disease was absent and very little insect food was found in the crops or gizzards.

Cold weather will naturally increase energy needs, for example in turkeys appetite increases 1.2% for every 1°C fall in temperature below 20°C (Jones and Barnett, 1974; see also Chapter 8). Small chicks are particularly at risk from hypothermia (Koskimies, 1962), thus the growth rate of chicks must be important to survival. Cross (1966) related growth, survival and chick diet by comparing time to torpor (on chilling in relation to weight). A group of chicks were fed insects and another

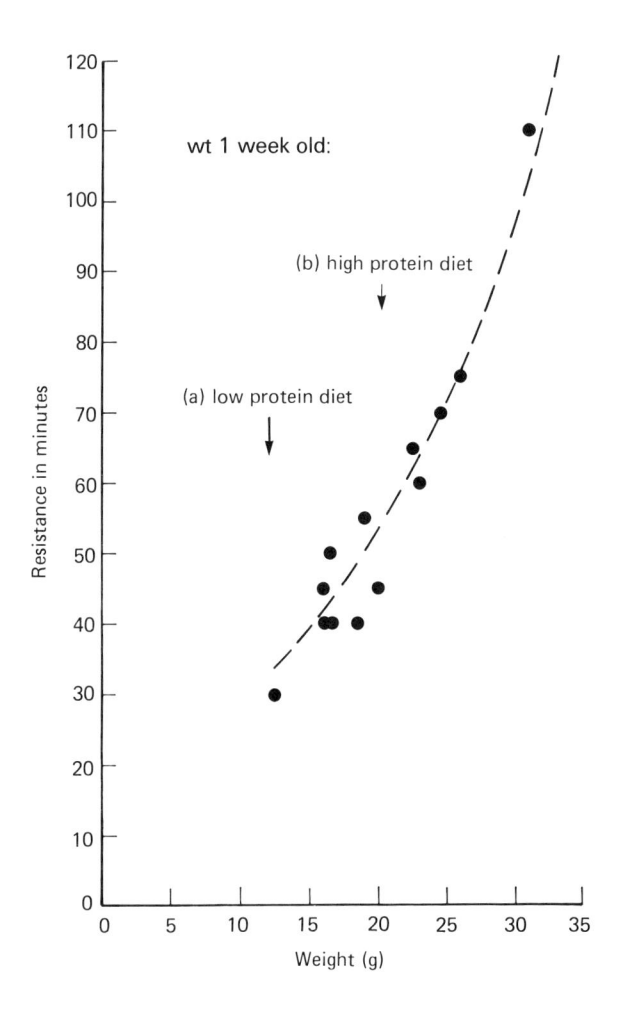

Fig. 5.1 Relationship between time to torpor for partridge chicks kept at 10°C, and weight.

Plate VIII. Team of the Partridge Survival Project, North Farm 1976. Left to right, the author, Stephen Tapper, Paul Vickerman, Keith Sunderland and Fred Allen.

Table 5.4 Feeding behaviour of broods of domestic fowl (feral) in relation to weather

	percentage of time hens and chicks were feeding	
	mornings	afternoons
Wet	44	50
Dry	67	85

group fed chick starter crumbs (24% protein). The results plotted in Fig. 5.1 show that one-week old chicks on the high protein diet did not succumb to the effects of torpor for almost an hour, whereas those on the low protein diet did so after only thirty-five minutes.

Chicks growing at a faster rate will also be able to fly earlier (at about ten days) and therefore be able to escape ground predators. Some chicks will inevitably be predated, mostly by weasels or stoats, but on farmland, predation is unlikely to be an important factor if broods are able to feed in the cover of cereal fields. Without such protection chicks may be vulnerable to predators, as has recently been shown for four species of grouse in northern Sweden (Marcstrom and Engren, 1985).

In Sussex approximately 4% of partridge chicks were taken by weasels and stoats (see Tapper, 1976) and in years of reduced vole numbers, weasels did feed on more birds (Tapper, 1979) but chick survival rates during these years were not lower than expected after taking account of insect food abundance (see later). Chicks from more widely-ranging broods may be more susceptible to predation so that predation becomes, as it were, the final executioner and not the ultimate cause of death.

Multiple regression study

An evaluation of the separate effects of insect abundance and weather on chick survival was needed. The multivariate technique selected for this was the multiple regression model with chick mortality, k_3, as the dependent variable, and weather and insects as the independent variables, using the data from the Sussex study area.

Annual chick mortality rates k_3 were used for the 29 km² monitored (Plate VIII) for the seventeen-year period 1969–1985 inclusive. There were comparable data on insect abundance and weather from 10 June to 10 July.

It has been shown (Green, 1984a) that the wetness of the vegetation is an important factor restricting chick activity and Reitz (1983) found that activity ceased altogether in all but the lightest of rain. Wood-Gush *et al.* (1978) also found that the activity of chicks of feral bantams was lower in wet weather (Table 5.4). Green (1984a) also showed that chick activity decreased in wet conditions and increased with a rise in temperature and Reitz (1983) found that brooding periods were 25% longer in cooler weather.

The wetness of the vegetation was not measured in the Sussex study but an attempt was made to calculate this from the number of days where rainfall was >5 mm at both Worthing and Applesham. However when this was incorporated in Green's regression equations with daily temperature to produce a chick activity index, the index was less well correlated to chick mortality than temperature alone. In fact chick mortality rates tended to decrease (but not at $P<0.05$) as the number of wet days increased between 10 June and 10 July. Many of the wet days were warm, with the rain in the form of thundershowers. By contrast, very dry weather reduces the activity of many insects. A refinement to allow for the length of wet weather periods used in an earlier analysis of historical records (Potts, 1972b) did not improve the correlations, so wetness as a variable was abandoned.

The measure of temperature used was the mean of the daily Stevenson screen temperatures from 10 June to 10 July at the Worthing Meteorological Station, five miles south of the centre of the study area (see Fig. 3.1). Records kept at Findon (part of the study area) for the years 1972 to 1978 gave temperatures indistinguishable, over this period, from those in Worthing.

With so many groups of preferred insects, problems arose because they were often varying through the study in parallel with each other (Fig. 5.2). So (1) the small diurnal ground beetles e.g. *Trechus quadristriatus*, (2) the knotgrass beetle *Gastrophysa polygoni* (Colour Plate XXVI), other leaf beetles and weevils, (3) plant bugs (Colour Plate XV) and (4) sawfly (especially *Dolerus* spp.; Colour Plate XXXI) and lepidoptera larvae were combined. Of these groups the plant bugs were most important, in fact they gave the single highest negative correlation coefficient with chick mortality obtained in this study. The remaining insects and arthropods (but not including thrips and Collembola) were combined. Cereal aphids were consumed in large numbers on occasion and in some studies have been considered preferred (Potts, 1970a; Thonon 1974; Birkan and Serre, 1986). However they were not correlated with chick mortality. When most abundant (1975) these aphids occurred mostly on the ears of winter wheat, well out of the reach of chicks.

The chick mortality rates used in the multiple regression analysis for the seventeen years 1969–1985 are plotted in relation to the densities of preferred insects in Fig. 5.3.

The data on insect densities and weather were then incorporated in a step-wise multiple regression analysis, which was first run to quantify any trend in the unexplained variability in chick mortality through the study. There was no such trend despite the fact that the partridge population density had decreased considerably over the period 1969–1984; providing further evidence that chick survival is not related to the density.

A total of 58% of the variation in chick mortality was explained as follows:

$$k_3 = 1.532 - 0.016x_i - 0.048x_{ii} \quad P<0.005$$

where x_i = sum density of preferred insects m^{-2} cereals, third week in June

CHICK SURVIVAL 89

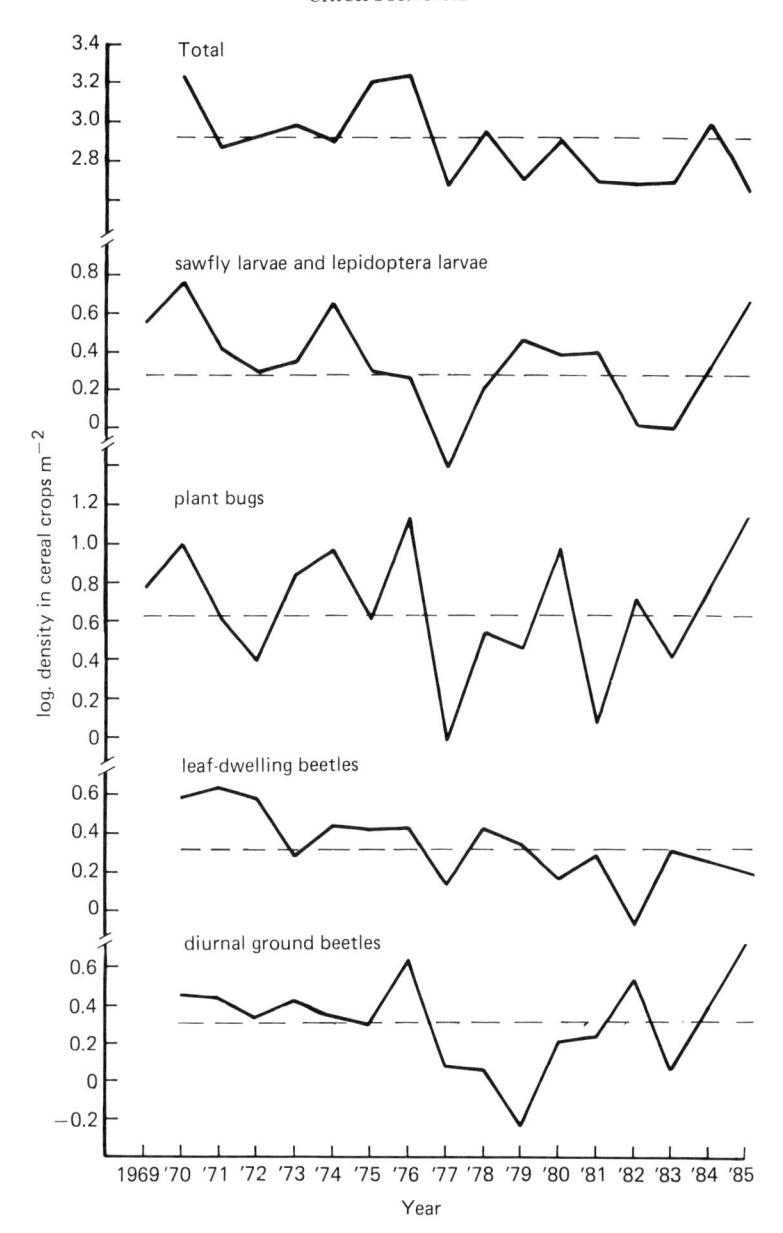

Fig. 5.2 Trends in densities of preferred insects in cereal crops 1969–1985, in the Sussex study area, third week of June, total non-preferred insects for comparison.

x_{ii} = mean daily temperature 10 June–10 July

The densities of cereal aphids and of all other non-preferred insects together were found not to relate to chick mortality rates, though

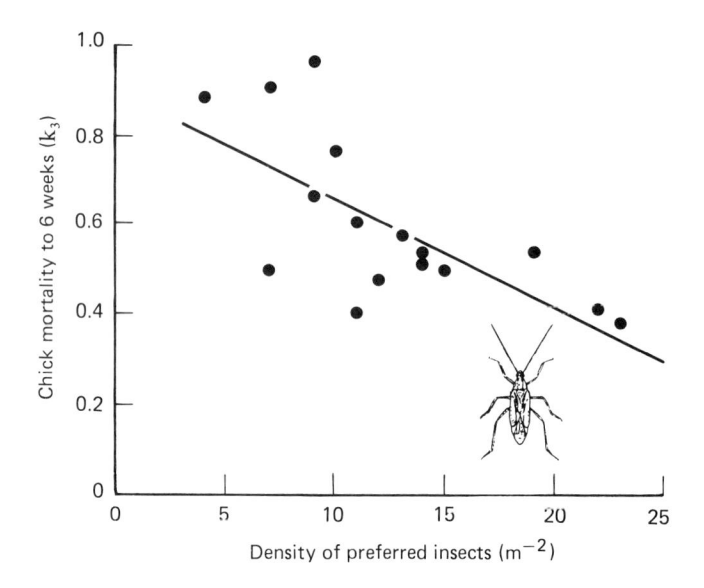

Fig. 5.3 Annual chick mortality in relation to the density of preferred insects, third week of June, Sussex study 1969–1985.

undoubtedly some non-preferred insect species were contributing to the variation in chick mortality. Preferred insects in general account for over a third of the biomass of insects eaten, but only an average of 5% of the individual insects sampled.

The annual variation in densities of preferred insects alone explained 48% of the variation in chick mortality ($P<0.001$) and an additional 10% of the chick mortality was explained by the variations of temperature ($P<0.001$). In simple correlations, the sum of preferred insects, the densities of plant bugs and the densities of the small diurnal ground beetles were each more highly correlated to chick mortality than temperature.

A further comparison of the relative importance of preferred insects and temperature can now be gained by changing the values for the variables independently, using the multiple regression equation. For each variable two standard deviations (sd) were added to the observed means, as in Table 5.5.

This suggests that the effect on chick survival of variation in the weather is almost as great as that of the preferred insects, but this may be a recent phenomenon. Evidence of reduced levels of preferred insects in recent years is given in the next chapter. With less food available, the amount of time needed for feeding determined partly by the weather would become *more* critical.

Table 5.5 Comparison of the role of temperature and insect food supply on the mortality rate of partridge chicks, Sussex study 1969–1985, from the multiple regression model

	k_3	% chick survival	Adding
Insects and temperatures as observed	0.61	25	
Mean insects + 2 sd	0.43	37	12%
Mean temp. + 2 sd	0.46	35	10%

The next step was to examine the role of insects in reducing partridge chick mortality, by experiment. This was carried out by increasing the supply of insect food – herbicide exclusion trials – and by decreasing the supply – the effects of insecticides. These aspects are fully dealt with in the next chapter.

The fact that weather and insects interact to determine chick mortality rates partly explains why it has taken so long to establish the importance of insects. The other reason is that weather is so important in determining annual variation in insect levels. For example plant bugs are more abundant in June if the weather in May has been warm. Cold wet weather has an adverse effect on most of the preferred insects.

Field studies in cereal areas on chalk rendzina soils (in south-east England) have shown that shortages of insects are increasing chick mortality. So what about the insect food supply in cereal crops elsewhere?

Wider relevance of the Sussex insect data

To find whether the Sussex cereal fauna were representative, at least so far as preferred insects are concerned, I took sweep net samples from the family farm in Yorkshire (1969 and 1970), from Hampshire (Sutton Scotney, 1969; Damerham, 1971), north Norfolk (West Barsham, 1970), and areas in eastern Scotland (Strathmore and Angus, 1970). D-vac samples were taken on my family farm in Yorkshire (1972), Northants (Thorpe Malsor, 1972), and in 1975 and 1976 from seven farms in the eastern counties (including Great Witchingham and Courtyard Farm) as part of the Game Conservancy's Eastern Counties Partridge Study.

The overall conclusion from extensive sampling was that the densities of preferred insects were fairly similar to those in Sussex. Sawfly larvae were more abundant in the north and west, plant bugs more numerous in the eastern counties.

Chick mortality rates were in line with expectations from the Sussex model and the relationship between expected and observed chick mortality rates was 1:1 and statistically significant ($P<0.02$) through a wide range of variation.

In 1981 Green (1984a) took samples by D-vac and sweep net from fourteen farms in Norfolk and Suffolk, including those sampled in 1975 and 1976. Though it was a poor year for preferred insects and chick mortality was high, there was a statistically significant inverse relationship between chick mortality rate and the densities of larval sawflies and lepidoptera, larval leaf beetles, plant bugs, aphids and also some flies (Empids and Dolichopods). Other beetles were not sub-divided into preferred and non-preferred and, as in Sussex, there was no relationship with the two groups combined.

Overseas, for practical reasons, I could only use the sweep net and surface searching techniques. Samples were taken in Germany in 1978–1982 (forty-three fields in Hessen, Rhineland-Pfalz and Bayern) and in 1983 in Italy (Po Delta, Tuscany and Montalto de Pavese). Some of the results are summarised in Table 5.6; *Trechus quadristriatus* is particularly important in mainland Europe, as has already been reported for cereal crops in Germany (Brasse, 1975). Grasshoppers also were more numerous outside Britain. A large outbreak of grasshoppers in cereals in North Dakota in 1938-39 was accompanied by very low chick mortality (Hammond, 1941) and it seems likely they have wider

Table 5.6 Densities of some insect groups in cereals at peak partridge hatch in the years 1978–1985. A comparison of data from Hampshire, where experiments (Chapter 6) have demonstrated that there is insufficient food for many partridge chicks, with preliminary data from Germany, Italy and New York State

	Hampshire, Britain*	Germany	Italy	New York State†
Plant bugs per 20 sweeps	16	11	9	present
Sawfly larvae per 20 sweeps	3	2	0	present
Grasshoppers per 20 sweeps	0	1	1	?
Trechus m^{-2}	7	30	12	?
Other insects m^{-2}	c. 500	460	?	250
" per 20 sweeps	355	420	140	234

* N. Sotherton *in litt.*
† J. Enck (1986) extended *in litt.*

importance. The sampling of cereals in North Dakota in 1985 revealed no sawfly larvae in the crops (J. Schulz *in litt.*) though some were found in samples in New York State (Table 5.6).

Very little information is available on the densities of preferred insects in maize (corn) but weed densities are particularly low in this crop due to the very effective use of atrazine herbicides, sowing dates relatively late, and insecticide use much greater than in other cereals. Data on ground beetles show that these are scarcer in maize than in small grain cereals (e.g. Dritschilo and Erwin, 1982).

Some pioneering studies in the Soviet Union should also be mentioned. In the 1930s surface searches were made in the wheat fields of the Orenburg Steppes, south of the Urals, once famous for their large population of partridges (e.g. S.T. Aksakov's late nineteenth century classic, *Notes of a Gun Hunter in the Orenburg Province*). Bey-Biyenko (1939, 1961) and colleagues found only about thirty insects m^{-2} but the sample plots (covering only 40 m^2) yielded nineteen species of plant bug and 6.4 ants m^{-2} including *Cataglyphus cursor*, a major food of young partridges (Poyarkov, 1955). Densities of insects on the feather-grass (*Stipa lessingiana*) steppes were given as 112 m^{-2}, but including plant bug 9 m^{-2}, ants 50 m^{-2}, as well as grasshoppers and other preferred species.

At least 33% of species of spiders are the same in wheat in the Soviet Union as in Britain (Sunderland, 1986); the situation with preferred insects is likely to be similar. The biomass of insects in wheat fields along the Volga, as measured by sweep net, is only about a fifth of that found on the feather-grass steppe (Kubantsev and Vasil'ev, 1982).

It therefore seems that partridge chicks evolved in a habitat far richer in preferred insects than modern cereals.

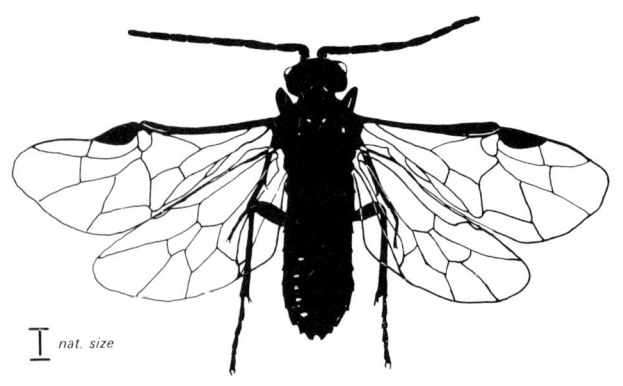

Adult sawfly (*Dolerus*)

6 Pesticides

'... The farmers cutting up the grass-banks for fuel, and thereby driving partridges to breed in open fields, at the mercy of hawks, wet weather, and scythes – putting among their seed-wheat vitriol (to prevent smut), which poisons partridges that would otherwise be left to breed ...' (P. Hawker, 1844)

This is a subject which must be considered in detail, for it is a controversial one and even fairly recently fears concerning the effects of pesticides on game have been considered 'hysterical and unjustified' (Broadbent, 1980).

Pesticides can affect partridges in three fundamentally different ways. Firstly, there may be direct poisoning by ingestion or contact. Secondly, a sub-lethal level of pesticides in the body can upset the physiology and reduce reproductive potential. The classic example in this case is DDE, a breakdown product of DDT, which was thought to be quite harmless for over twenty years. DDE can accumulate in birds such as the peregrine falcon and sparrow hawk which then, as a result, lay thin-shelled eggs. Thirdly, there are the indirect effects arising from the ecological changes caused by the use of pesticides.

It is not possible to estimate the number of partridges lost to these three different effects of pesticides in our Sussex study. Nevertheless from 1968 to 1984 I consider that only a small number could have died directly from the effects of poisoning. Only two cases have ever been confirmed as death by pesticide poisoning in the Sussex study area (one dieldrin, in 1958, the other DNBP, in 1971). Nor is there any reason to suspect significant physiological effects attributable to sub-lethal doses of pesticide, a subject dealt with in this chapter. By contrast I consider, from the increase in chick mortality, that at least 10,000 chicks died from the ecological effects of herbicides during the 18 years (1968–1985) of the Sussex study alone.

History of direct effects

There has been a long history of pesticide use in cereals, with amounts used and types of ingredients steadily increasing year by year. At the time of writing eighty-two active ingredients are currently approved for cereal growing in Britain, but few are directly toxic. They include seed dressings, herbicides, fungicides, insecticides and slug pellets.

Lead arsenate was used to dress wheat in the late nineteenth century and there are two reports of partridges dying as a result of arsenic poisoning prior to World War I (Maxwell, 1911). Although no reliable data are available, this compound does not seem to have had a serious impact on game.

A potential problem, but again with no discernible effects on partridge population size, was the use of the mercury seed dressings; tolyl mercury acetate (TMA) was introduced in Britain in 1938 and a mixture of ethyl-mercury acetate and TMA in 1945.

The main environmental concern over mercury-based pesticides has been with methyl-mercury dicyandiamide (MMD) (Table 6.1). When used in Sweden the resultant mortality (Plate IX) to birds was extensive, though when similar methyl-mercury compounds were used in Britain and Germany (e.g. 'Panogen') no significant adverse effects were recorded. Nor have adverse effects been observed with phenyl-mercury acetate, widely used on cereal farms in Europe. In Sweden MMD seed dressings were used at higher rates per grain than in Britain yet the effects on partridges were not clear and other pesticides such as aldrin or dieldrin were often involved in the mercury incidents. Only one partridge (with 56 ppm mercury in the liver/kidneys) was included amongst hundreds of other species reported dead. Partridges shot or trapped had higher levels of mercury than normal at autumn sowing time but significant mortalities were not noted at that time of year (Borg et al., 1969).

In the USA Weigand (1971) examined the possible impact of mercury seed dressings on partridges, but could find no evidence that the birds suffered any significant adverse effects. In his study in Montana and in a separate study in the Canadian Prairies (Fimreite et al., 1970), levels of these compounds were found to be low, in the tissue analyses, 1–2 ppm. The more toxic phenyl- and methyl-mercury seed dressings were withdrawn from use in the USA and Sweden over the period 1965–1975 and in most of Europe in the mid-1980's.

In Sussex mercury seed dressings were mostly of the less toxic methoxy-ethyl type and no adverse effects were suspected. In general, mercurial seed dressings do not appear to have caused significant

Table 6.1 Examples of toxicity to partridges of some pesticides known to cause direct mortality to gamebirds, and of toxicity of some other pesticides mentioned in the text

	LD_{50} in ppm	Direct mortality to gamebirds? + yes − no
(1) Herbicides		
dinoseb	26	+
DNOC	32	+
2,4-D	472	−
2,4,5,T	750	−
difenzoquat	>5000	−
dicamba	>10000	−
(2) Seed dressings		
dieldrin	9	+
methyl-mercury-dicyandiamide	15	+ Sweden
gamma BHC	118	−
carbophenothion	123	−
methoxy-ethyl-mercury	550	−
thiram	673	−
(3) Insecticide sprays and granules		
monocrotophos	9	+ not used
parathion-methyl	10	? in Britain
demeton-s-methyl	15	−
dimethoate	20	−
fenitrothion	30	?
heptachlor	34	+
DDT	600	+ (see text)

Borg et al., 1969; Giban, 1953, 1965; Grolleau and Giban, 1966; Hudson, R. et. al., 1984; Lavaur, 1967; Moore, 1967; Worthing and Walker, 1983.

Plate IX. Partridge poisoned by seed dressing containing mixture of alkyl-mercury and aldrin, Sweden March 1960 (*K. Borg*).

mortality to partridge populations.

The di-nitro-ortho-cresol known as DNOC was discovered in 1892 and used as a winter spray against red-spider mite in orchards for many decades. In 1932 French scientists discovered that it could be used to control broad-leaved weeds in cereals; it was introduced to Britain in 1939 and partridge mortalities due to this chemical peaked in 1950 (see Table 6.2).

One of the very earliest warnings that DDT might have harmful side-effects on farm wildlife came from a game biologist, Leopold (1945). By 1946 this insecticide was being widely used (for example on my family's farm, to control turnip flea beetle). No adverse effects were noted and elsewhere very few deaths of partridges have been attributed to DDT, except in orchards.

The real impact of the direct effects of pesticides came in the mid-1950s with the use of dieldrin, when about half of the total reported incidents of mortality involved partridges (Ash, 1965). Spring use of dieldrin seed dressings was subject to a voluntary ban in 1962 and incidents soon became much less frequent (Table 6.2). The development of the research in Britain which led to this ban is described by Sheail (1985); the contribution made by the staff of the Game Conservancy was considerable.

Twenty-six post-mortem examinations of wild partridges over the

Table 6.2 Number of incidents of mortality in partridges (both species) and pheasants in Britain according to year and type of pesticide involved. Game Conservancy archives, plus BTO, RSPB and Game Conservancy Joint Committee Reports 1–6, 1961–1964, and MAFF Tolworth Laboratory, 1964–1984

	DNOC (herbicide)	cyclodienes (mainly dieldrin)	other insecticides	aldicarb (nematicide)
1947	1	–	–	–
1948	–	–	–	–
1949	1	–	–	–
1950	10	–	–	–
1951	2	–	2	–
1952	6	–	10	–
1953	4	–	2	–
1954	2	–	–	–
1955	2	–	1	–
1956	–	2	–	–
1957	2	37	7	–
1958	3	44	12	–
1959	?	'many'	?	–
1960	–	39	7	–
1961	–	125	6	–
1962	–	23	4	–
1963	–	19	–	–
1964	–	13	2	–
1965	–	2	2	–
1966	–	1	–	–
1967	–	1	–	–
1968	–	5	3	–
1969	–	–	–	–
1970	–	3	2	–
1971	1	4	1	1
1972	–	1	3	–
1973	–	3	2	1
1974	–	1	1	–
1975	–	4	–	–
1976	–	2	1	2
1977	–	–	2	–
1978	–	–	1	3
1979	–	–	–	1
1980	–	–	1	–
1981	–	–	2	–
1982	–	2	3	–
1983	–	–	–	–
1984	–	–	2	–
Total incidents	34	331	79	8

Note: Excludes six cases arising from the illegal use of mevinphos (to control predators)

IX. Salisbury Plain study area 'A' 1985 large fields cover between (*Malcolm Brockless*).

X. Partridge habitat, near Weissenheim, Bavaria 1982 smaller fields little cover between (*G.R. Potts*).

XI. Cereal flora, chalk soil, yellow charlock, pheasant eye (*David Hill*).

XII. Sample from the vacuum insect net, Sussex study (*G.R. Potts*).

XIII. Cereal flora, acid soil, corn marigold (*G.R. Potts*).

XIV. (*Below Centre*) Aerial spraying of aphicides, North Farm, June 1975 (*Stephen Tapper*).

XV. (*Above Right*) Larval plant bug, favourite chick food (*Charles Coles*).

XVI. Sussex study area, North Stoke, August 1977 (*G.R. Potts*).

period 1977–1985, carried out at the Game Conservancy, showed that only three had died from pesticides – all from aldicarb, a carbamate used as a nematicide on sugar-beet to control 'docking disorder'.

Whether a poison will actually kill or not is indicated only in part by its toxicity. Assuming the chemical is used correctly and is not repellent (as the most widely used seed dressings with gamma BHC appear to be: Ash and Taylor, 1964), then the rates of use and biodegradation are also important. Thus the insecticide most used in partridge habitat today, demeton-s-methyl, is forty times as toxic to birds as DDT (Table 6.1), yet it appears to cause no direct poisoning because it has a half-life of a few days, does not accumulate in the body and is used at low field application rates.

There has been a welcome decline in the toxicity of pesticides to vertebrates, and an increase in their biodegradability, for example amongst insecticides with the advent of the synthetic pyrethroids. Widespread deaths appear not to occur much above an LD_{50} of about 50 ppm (Table 6.1) and fortunately the average LD_{50}s of pesticides currently used in Britain (to gamebirds) are approximately: insecticides 700 ppm, herbicides 2900 ppm and foliar fungicides 4300 ppm (calculated from Worthing and Walker, 1983). This is one of the reasons why the direct effects of pesticides are not at present the cause for much concern.

The direct adverse effects of pesticides on partridge populations have not been anything like as great as those found in the predatory birds such as the sparrow hawk or even in the granivorous species such as the stock dove, which were especially at risk (O'Connor and Mead, 1984; O'Connor and Shrubb, 1986). Nor is it likely that they approached the level of mortality in the woodpigeon, which was estimated at 16% of the population in south Cambridgeshire, in the spring of 1962 (Murton *et al.*, 1963b).

Mortality in partridges might even have been offset by mortality to predators; one case in particular was the high mortalities which occurred amongst foxes in eastern England in 1959–1960, as a result of eating birds which had ingested dieldrin (Taylor and Blackmore, 1961).

Hopefully direct poisoning of birds and mammals is a thing of the past, but it is still necessary to be vigilant because, as in the case of carbophenothion and geese (Stanley and Bunyan, 1979), it is often not possible to predict how wildlife will be affected when a pesticide graduates from the scale of a few field trials to one of counties or regions.

Sub-lethal effects

Sub-lethal effects have been recorded in partridges with thiram (Grolleau and Biadi, 1966), a seed dressing usually used on maize, but only in the laboratory.

One of the most common seed dressings used within the partridge's range in Britain is chlorfenvinphos (used to control wheat bulb fly after dieldrin was phased out), which has been shown not to cause lethal or sub-lethal effects on partridges when used at normal field rates (Janda, 1974).

Parathion-methyl poisoning may have occurred in parts of the partridge's range overseas and sub-lethal effects have been recorded in captive pheasants at normal field dose rates (Messick *et al.*, 1974). This pesticide is still used frequently, for example in Italy and the USA; and at much higher rates of application it is used to eradicate weaver birds in Africa. However, parathion has a very short half-life and sub-lethal effects did not occur in the laboratory trials with partridges, which revealed that dieldrin caused a significant reduction in egg output (Neill *et al.*, 1971). In one long-term experiment it was found that chick weights on hatching were actually increased if laying adults were kept on a diet of 8 ppm parathion (Muller, 1971).

So far as partridges are concerned the greatest controversy has centred on the use of the herbicide 2,4-D. At the University of Strathclyde it was found that when this chemical was injected into domestic fowl eggs it reduced hatching success (Dunachie and Fletcher, 1967). Later, in trials in France, it was found that when 2,4-D was sprayed on partridge eggs a high mortality of embryos resulted, with malformations amongst chicks (Lutz and Lutz-Ostertag, 1971). The latter results were at variance with general experience (e.g. Dobson, 1954), hence the controversy surrounding these results.

It was later confirmed that some 2,4-D is absorbed through the shell but that mortality was not increased (Somers *et al.*, 1974) and that adverse effects did not occur until rates of application were equivalent to at least five times the field dose rate (Grolleau *et al.*, 1974). Similar results have been obtained with 2,4,5-T (Hoffman and Eastin, 1982). In view of the above findings, the results of the 1971 trials on 2,4-D, though worrying at the time, now seem best discounted.

Some reports (Blank, 1968; Lutz-Ostertag and Henou, 1975) that paraquat sprayed on eggs can harm or even kill pheasant embryos, may have been justified and the LD_{50} to mallard through the shell is equivalent to a rate of between 2 and 4 kg ion/ha, i.e. in the range at which it is used (Hoffman and Eastin, 1982). However even in these cases the defoliating effects on the vegetation, thereby exposing the incubating bird and eggs, are likely to be more important than direct toxicity to the eggs. Partridge eggs are normally covered and therefore not exposed to direct effect of sprays such as paraquat.

In the Sussex study we were particularly interested to find out whether any of the herbicides used on cereals reach the developing embryos *via* the food of the hen; so we sampled chickweed sprayed with CMPP and collected eggs laid by hens eating this weed. However we could not find anyone who would complete the necessary analyses (and solve the problem of the co-extracts of the chloro-phenoxyacetic acids). Fortunately it turned out that most currently used herbicides do not appear to have any adverse effects on the hatchability of eggs or viability of chicks (e.g. Somers *et al.*, 1974; Gyrd-Hansen and Dalgaard-Mikkelsen, 1974) but excluding, of course, the ecological effects. Although we were unable to study the direct and sub-lethal effects of pesticides to any great depth, it soon became abundantly clear that the direct effects of pesticides attributable to their toxicity were dwarfed by the indirect effects on the ecosystem, especially from the use of herbicides.

History of herbicide use

The systematic hand hoeing of cereals fell into decline during and after World War I with the shortage of labour, but some annual weeds were kept in check by light chain-harrowing and perennial weeds by rotation with summer fallows and cleaning crops such as potatoes or grass, and by a form of hoeing known as 'looking'. Gangs of farm workers were sent out into the fields to pull tall weeds such as thistles and docks, a practice which survives to some extent as the hand roguing of seed crops for wild oats and other undesirable cereals. Cereal crops were much taller than today, another factor which tended to suppress weeds, and most weeds and weed seeds were of course removed from the field in sheaves for threshing, whereas after combining most are left on the stubbles.

Despite these measures to keep weeds to a minimum they would always be present in crops, and the change in diet of the partridge (Potts, 1970b; Pulliainen, 1984) and the results of the Official Seed Testing Station at Cambridge (see Fig 6.1; Potts, 1970a) both show that weeds were far more numerous prior to the use of herbicides.

Similar changes in the cereal weed flora of West Germany over the

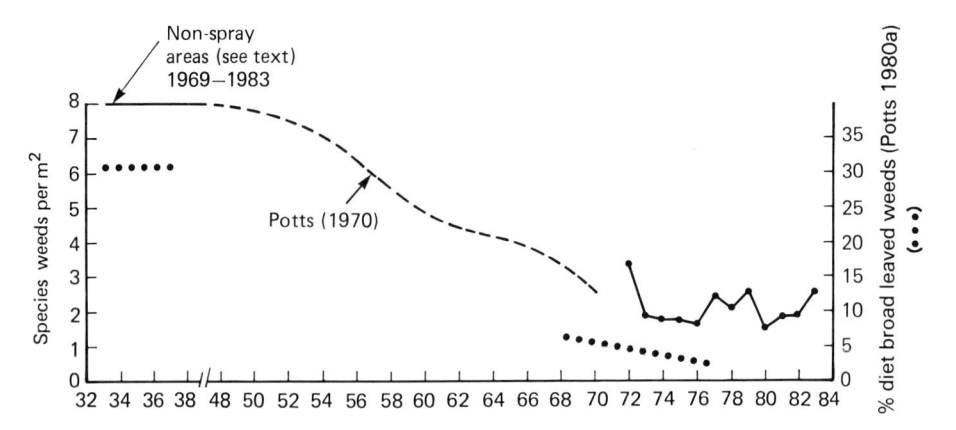

Fig. 6.1 Estimation of the number of weed species per m² from cereal crops based on monitoring from 1969 to 1980 in Sussex, 1930s estimate from the number of weeds per m² in unsprayed sites. The trend between the two is obtained from analysis of cereal seed samples (Potts, 1970a, and see text). The percentage of autumn partridge diet consisting of broad-leaved weeds is shown below and right; see also Chapter 8.

period 1955–1969 were quantified in a series of surveys (Bachthaler, 1967) and field trials (Rademacher *et al.*, 1970), likewise for 1953-1965 in Hungary (Ubrizy, 1968). Long-term (twenty-year) trials in Canada showed a reduction of susceptible weeds amounting to 70% of emerging plants with MCPA, 85% with 2,4-D (McCurdy and Molberg, 1974).

Weeds such as poppies were a most distinctive feature of the European countryside:

'The landscape was characterised by fields of cereals full of colourful and often rampant patches of yellow charlock, red poppies, blue cornflowers and white chamomile, which brought little joy to the farmer; this picture of the countryside remained basically the same until after 1950.' (Hanf, 1983)

It was a rare occurrence to find more than twenty species in any particular field, but over 700 species of broad-leaved weed occurred in arable crops in Europe (Hanf, 1983).

The hesitant beginnings of the use of herbicides in cereals is well illustrated by records from my family's farm in Yorkshire. In 1934 and 1935 efforts were made to control infestations of wild radish in barley using sulphuric acid. Usually only the worst parts of the field were treated and such attempts were abandoned in 1936. In the 1940s Norfolk was said to be 'red and yellow with poppies and charlock'; but the most harmful weed was wild radish which also 'defied all attempts to eradicate it with copper sulphate and sulphuric acid' (Kirby, 1980).

According to my father's diary it was not until 2 May 1944 that he managed to obtain a quantity of DNOC (and then only sufficient to spray two acres of barley). The chemical (a yellow dye) was not popular and in North Yorkshire two farm workers died as a result of using this herbicide; but they were, however, stripped to the waist. There were other reports of death due to the use of this chemical (Sheail, 1985).

By 1944 there were still only about 2000 crop sprayers in Britain; often horse-drawn, they were not strongly made and easily became corroded. However by 1962 most cereal growers had a tractor-mounted (or drawn) sprayer – amounting to a total of over 51 000 machines.

MCPA was fortunately much simpler to use and far safer than DNOC; it was introduced on my family farm in 1946. One problem with the early techniques of using this chemical was that it had to be dusted onto cereals, not sprayed. At North Farm the weed control achieved with this technique was described, at the time, as 'pathetic'.

By 1950 13% of cereals were being sprayed with herbicides nationally, 30% by 1955 and 63% by 1960 (Woodford, 1964). Obviously some areas were more advanced in their usage than others and in Yorkshire a survey conducted in 1956 showed 72% of wheat was being treated in the Vale of York but only 25% on the Wolds (Long, 1969). Farm records of pesticides used in the Sussex study area show 70% of all cereals were sprayed by 1958 (Table 6.3). One factor encouraging this spread was the increasing number of combine harvesters which needed clean crops in which to work efficiently.

Similar upward trends in herbicide use, with the main increases occurring from 1955 to 1975, have been reported in North America and from nine countries in mainland Europe. Data from the United States Department of Agriculture giving the production figures for 2,4-D in the USA suggest that only a very small percentage of cereals was treated prior to 1952. Only 40% of cereals (28% of wheat) received herbicide treatment in 1970 (Pimentel, 1976). On the Northern Plains a decline of charlock occurred in the mid-1960s as a result of herbicide use (Hay, 1968) but herbicides were used on only 26% of cereals in 1971, increasing to 40% in 1976 (United States Department of Agriculture). In North America herbicide use on small grained cereals is still much lower than in Europe. However in Idaho by 1980, it seemed to me that most farmers were not only using basic herbicides such as 2,4-D and MCPA, but also 2,4-DP and dicamba which are particularly effective against *Polygonum* spp. (knotgrass, black bindweed, etc.).

In France herbicides are now used on practically all cereal crops in the major cereal growing regions (Lescar, 1984) yet as late as 1970 studies in the south east Gatinais showed almost no herbicide use. Crops in this region developed a rich flora dominated by *Polygonum* spp., *Chenopodium* spp., chickweed and seven other species, some now quite rare, such as *Stachys annua* (Gindre and Allion, 1971).

Table 6.3 Pesticides applied to cereal crops in the Sussex study area contrasting 1958, the first year of the data set, with 1969, the first year of insect monitoring, and 1984. Excludes seed dressings and pre-emergence, and post-harvest treatments

Fields sampled	1958 50	1969 100	1984 87
No spray	15	10	1
Herbicides			
MCPA	24	71	46
MCPB	2	–	–
dicamba	–	51	36
CMPP	9	43	79
2,3,6-TBA	–	23	–
2,4-D	–	12	–
benazolin	–	7	1
2,4-DP	–	5	2
2,4-DB	–	2	3
ioxynil	–	–	6
bromoxynil	–	–	7
bifenox	–	–	1
iso-proturon	–	–	21
chlortoluron	–	–	9
tri-allate	–	–	2
difenzoquat	–	–	5
Insecticides			
cypermethrin	–	–	9
permethrin	–	–	4
demeton-s-methyl	–	–	15
chlorpyrifos	–	–	1
gamma BHC	–	–	3
Foliar fungicides			
propiconazole	–	–	48
carbendazim	–	–	40
triadimefon	–	–	37
captafol	–	–	28
thiophanate-methyl	–	–	5
fenpropimorph	–	–	7
Molluscicides methiocarb	–	–	5
Total active ingredients per field	0.70	2.14	4.83

Note: two split or successive treatments with the same foliar fungicide are counted as one

In Schleswig-Holstein, herbicide use on cereals grew rapidly in the period 1955 to 1970 and by 1973 almost all cereal fields in Germany (FRG) were being sprayed (Schönnamsgrüber, 1970; Madel, 1970; Frode, 1977). The situation was much the same in Finland and Sweden (Markkula, 1969; Fagelfors, 1985). A rich flora existed in cereals in Finland until about 1964, with fat hen as the second most numerous species (Mukula *et al.*, 1969). In Denmark the main increase in the use of herbicides on cereals was between 1961 and 1972 (Nøddegaard, 1984) and in Poland during the mid-1970s (Chlewski, 1976).

In eastern Europe few herbicides were used in the early 1960s (Sokolov *et al.*, 1964) though with dramatic increases later, especially in Czechoslovakia and Hungary in the mid and late 1970s and early 1980s (Food and Agriculture Organisation statistics and Nagy, 1977) and, if the five-year plans were near fulfilled, in the Soviet Union (see Chesalin in Sokolov *et al.*, 1964). This last point is difficult to confirm since the relevant data seem to have been restricted from 1975 (Komarov, 1980). This aside, the position is much the same throughout the partridge range, though with Britain leading the way in herbicide use (Fig. 6.2).

The herbicide 2,4-D, discovered in the USA in 1942 (about the same time as MCPA in Britain), seems not to have been used to any great extent in Britain in the 1950s although, known as 'Dikonert' or as a component of 'U46 combi', it was widely used in Europe. Thus MCPA,

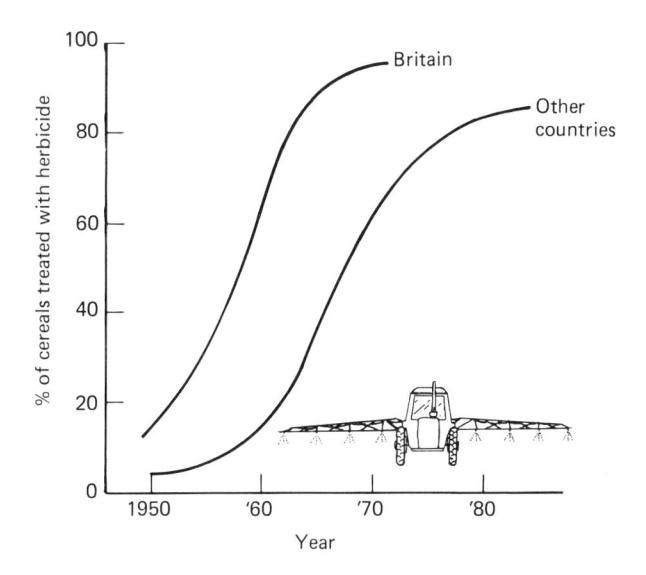

Fig. 6.2 Trend in herbicide use on cereals.

sold by the company Nickersons as 'Gamesafe' (to distinguish it from DNOC), and CMPP, introduced to control chickweed and cleavers in 1956 by ICI Plant Protection, dominated the scene until 1961 (e.g. in the Sussex study area, Table 6.3). Neither MCPA nor CMPP were efficient in controlling knotgrass, an important food for partridges.

Some years ago I made an attempt (Potts, 1970a) to estimate the overall impact of herbicides on weed populations since the 1940s (see Fig. 6.1). From the results it was clear that major reductions in broadleaved weeds did not become marked until the early 1960s and would be virtually complete by the early 1970s.

Some declines of weeds in the Sussex study area occurred before herbicide use could have been the cause. The corncockle disappeared in the 1920s and also the cornflower and corn cleavers in the early 1950s (Hall, 1980). Better seed cleaning might have played a part in the declines prior to the use of herbicides. The eradication of the parasitic dodder (*Cuscuta*) from clover seed in the 1920s was attributed to better methods of cleaning (Wellington, 1971). But these are exceptions and there is no doubt that the use of herbicides has enormously reduced the flora of cereals and, as Moore (1962) wrote, 'the total ecological change must be immense'.

In the Sussex study area approximately a dozen species of weeds once formerly common are now very rare, examples being yellow charlock, wild radish, pheasant eye, hemp nettle, corn gromwell, corn buttercup, corn spurrey, narrow fruited corn-salad, various thistles, white campion and the two species of fluellen (Colour Plate XI).

Annual frequencies are plotted in Fig. 6.3 to indicate relative trends in grass weeds and in broad-leaved weeds. The dominant species are listed in Table 6.4, indicating their importance to partridges and to cereal growers.

On areas with acid soils a calcifuge flora develops in cereals which is quite different from that in the Sussex study area, with such species as corn marigold and corn spurrey dominating (Colour Plate XIII). Shepherd's cress (*Teesdalia nudicaulis*), an indicator of the cereal weed community of acid soils, still dominated the flora of cereal fields in Poland in the early 1970s (Borowiec *et al.*, 1975) but has been very rare in Britain for some time (Hall, 1980). In Hungary the cereal weed community was dominated by wild radish and larkspur, both of which were eliminated by the use of the first herbicides (Ubrizy, 1968).

For Europe as a whole, at least fifty-five species of cereal weed are listed in the Red Data Book as 'endangered'. Herbicides are the major cause of their decline, but fourteen of the species were already declining

PESTICIDES 107

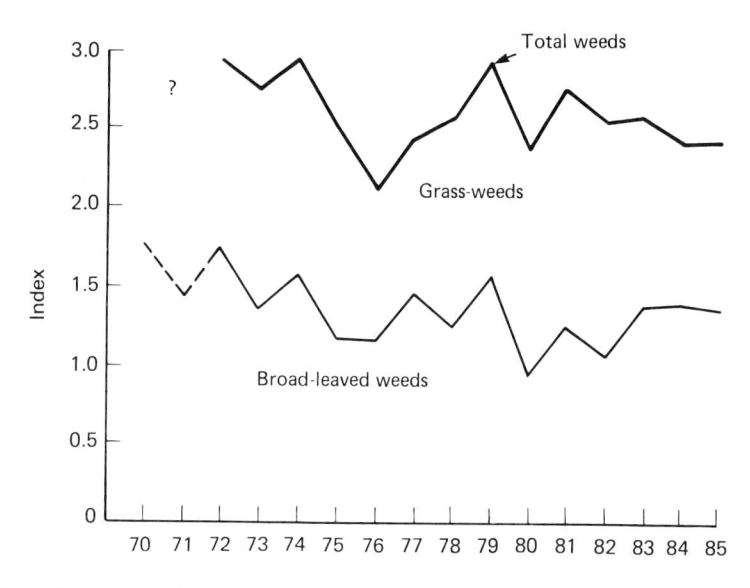

Fig. 6.3 Sussex study: annual indices of abundance of cereal weeds in mid to late June.

Table 6.4 Sussex study: mean annual percentage frequency per D-vac site of dominant broad-leaved weeds in the years 1972 to 1985 inclusive, combined

Species	Frequency per site	Importance to partridge (– = none)
Speedwells *Veronica* spp.	50 ± 2%	–
Chickweed *Stellaria media*	27 ± 3%	adult food
Mayweed *Matricaria perforata*	27 ± 2%	insects*
Knotgrass *Polygonum aviculare*	22 ± 2%	adult food + insects†
Black bindweed *Polygonum convolvulus*	14 ± 2%	adult food + insects†
Field pansy *Viola arvensis*	12 ± 2%	–
Forget-me-not *Myosotis arvensis*	10 ± 1%	–
Red poppy *Papaver rhoeas*	9 ± 1%	–
Cleavers *Galium aparine*	7 ± 1%	none and most harmful to cereal grower
Henbit dead nettle *Lamium amplexicaule*	6 ± 1%	–
Yellow charlock *Sinapis arvensis*	4 ± 1%	–
Hemp nettle *Galeopsis tetrahit*	3 ± 1%	adult food

* Plant bugs
† *Gastrophysa polygoni*, the sawfly *Ametastegia glabrata*, plant bugs and a leaf weevil *Phytobius* spp.

Note: a further thirty-eight species were recorded less frequently at the June D-vac sample sites

before herbicides were used, e.g. corncockle, shepherd's needle and field nigella; the use of fertilisers and improved drainage have also been very important factors (Eggers, 1984).

Effects of herbicides and insecticides on insects

Ever since the early 1950s it has been widely accepted that herbicides would deprive adult partridges of weeds and that insecticides could deprive chicks of insects (Lynn-Allen and Robertson, 1956; Wentworth Day, 1957). What was not realised at the time was that by removing weed-eating insects the herbicides could have the same effect on chick mortality rates as the use of insecticides, i.e. the effect first described by Southwood (see Chapter 5).

In the early 1950s landowners began to show a great deal of concern over the possible effects of DNOC on partridge chick food since it was known to have insecticidal qualities. As a result, in 1954 work was carried out at Rothamsted Experimental Station which confirmed that considerable insect mortality occurred when this herbicide was used (Johnson *et al.*, 1955). However, DNOC was largely replaced by the new chlorophenoxyacetic acid herbicides (see Table 6.2) and the work did not extend to them.

Some early work in Germany by Heydemann (1956) had shown how important weeds were to many insects in cereal crops, and work in Hungary by Jermy and Saringar (in Ubrizy, 1968) and later in England by Southwood and Cross (1969), and the present studies, have shown that herbicides have a dramatic impact on the insect and other arthropod fauna (Table 6.5), reducing overall densities by 50%. Long-term effects were not measured in these within-season trials and because the insect fauna of cereals was not properly described prior to the use of herbicides, it is difficult to estimate the overall impact on the cereal field insect fauna.

In Britain very little was known about the natural history of the pest insects in cereal crops in the nineteenth century, although grain aphids, the major insect pests of recent years, were recorded. Indeed, they were known to be a problem in Norfolk as early as July 1797. However, Curtis (1883) considered the plant bug *Notostira elongata* to be 'abundant' in cereals, and grain thrips 'very common'.

At that time the turnip sawfly dominated the arable insect pest scene and now it illustrates our lack of quantitative data on the farmland arthropod faunas before the use of pesticides. This pest was sometimes

Table 6.5 Reduction in densities of insects preferred by partridge chicks caused by herbicides

	Log 'reduction' insects	Direct effect (+ yes − no)	Year	Authority
(1) DNOC	0.61	+	1954	Johnson et al. (1955)
(2) 2,4-D	0.44	(+)*	1960	Ubrizy (1968)
(3) MCPA (some MCPB)	0.33 ± 0.06	−	1963–66	Southwood and Cross (1969) (extended in litt.)
(4) Various	0.31	−	1972–76	Vickerman and O'Bryan (1979)
(5) CMPP + simazine + metoxuron	0.24	−	1973–74	Vickerman (1974)
(6) Various	0.27	−	1983	Sotherton et al. (1985)
(7) Various	0.25	−	1984	Sotherton et al. (1985)
(8) Not undersowing (but appropriate herbicides)	0.20	−	1970–85	Potts (unpublished)

* Sotherton (1982c)

Note: the situation with the grass weed herbicides is not clear but in the above case number (5), the effect of grass weed removal alone in a severe infestation of *Poa trivialis* was 0.24, about half the effect of the broad-leaved weed herbicides

very common indeed throughout the nineteenth century and turnip fields were often 'laid waste' after its devasting effects; this occurred in the Sussex study area in 1837. In one of the earliest references to biological control in Britain, Curtis wrote 'ducks and poultry will devour these sawfly caterpillars with avidity: the birds may either be carried or driven into the field according to the distance'; an observation somewhat reminiscent of the duck brigades still used in China to clear rice paddies of particular insect pests.

Later the turnip sawfly became extinct in Britain and we do not even know when it disappeared or why (Benson, 1935); certainly the ducks could hardly be held responsible! So, if we know so little about such a notable pest, we know little indeed. The situation was much the same in other countries. A Russian entomologist wrote:

'It is quite amazing that even wheat which provides the staple diet of hundreds of millions of people throughout the world, has not been studied in any country as a specific plant and animal association, as a specific ecosystem ...' (Bey-Biyenko, 1939).

In the 1950s some ecological work was carried out on farmland near the University of Kiel and by Tischler and other workers throughout Germany. But the amount of research conducted in cereals was not in proportion to the acreage of the crop. One problem may have been that in the West nothing dramatic was yet perceived in cereal growing:

'What plant community is more stable than the wheat fields of the Canadian prairies? Here identical crops pass through identical cycles year after year for generations, crop rotation practices never move a crop further than a few hundred yards ...' (Turnbull and Chant, 1961)

In fact, dramatic events had occurred, but in western Siberia and Kazakhstan. In 1954 Kruschev began to organise the rapid ploughing up of the feathergrass steppes and the planting of a vast spring wheat 'monoculture' on an area larger than the total arable land in Canada. The majority of insect species became less abundant in the cereals than in the original steppe grasslands, but over the period 1957 to 1967 the remainder showed improved population stability as the monoculture settled into a routine. Grigor'yeva (1970) thus concluded:

'Monoculture as a farming practice does not make conditions in an agroecosystem more unstable and does not increase the threat of invasion by insect pests; consequently there is no need for more intensive chemical control to protect the harvest against pests.'

Unfortunately the conclusion is in fact invalid because the crops were not, in the ecological sense, a monoculture; they were full of weeds! (McCauley, 1976).

Several studies were carried out on cereal dwelling insects in the 1960s, but were each highly focussed on a particular pest species; for example, the studies on the wheat-bulb fly at Rothamsted Experimental Station. Often the emphasis in this kind of study was on the potential for control by pesticides and most trials were not in cereals but in more intensively grown crops; in Britain, at that time, there were few pest insects considered to be of economic importance in cereals (Gair, 1975).

At the time of writing we have monitored cereal insects and other arthropods for seventeen years on the Sussex study area, giving most of our attention to the second half of June and early July and using the methods described in Chapter 3. Our overall conclusions from these studies are that the short-term annual variations in the abundance of the arthropod fauna are dominated by cereal aphids and that in the long-term the insect densities of most species are much lower than formerly and still declining (Fig. 6.4); but many effects of pesticides are complex and difficult to differentiate from more natural causes of fluctuations.

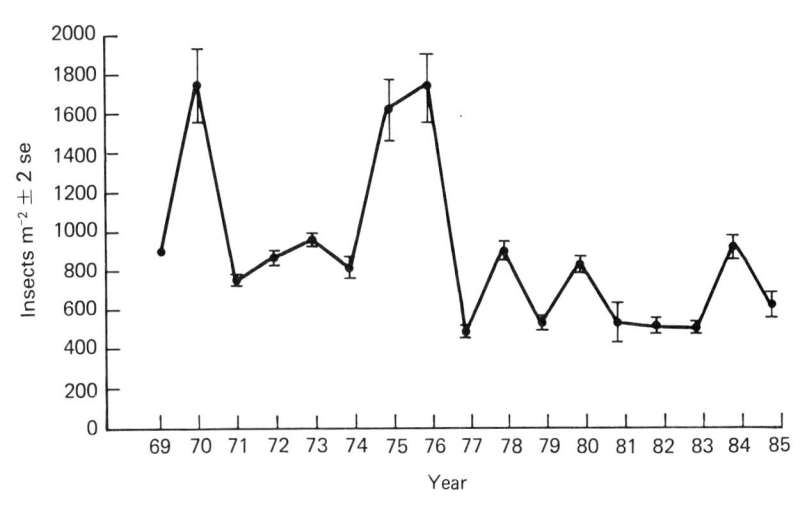

Fig. 6.4 Mean density of insects per m² from cereal fields in the Sussex study area, monitored in the third week of June 1970–1985, with an estimate for 1969. ±2 standard errors. Collembola are excluded.

Leaf-dwelling beetles (weevils and leaf beetles)

In part, the long-term effects of herbicides on arthropods are not easy to quantify because of the parallel decline of undersowing which quickly followed their introduction. Many insects formerly included in the diet of partridge chicks fed on clovers, sainfoin, trefoil and the other forage legumes used in undersown leys. One example, the weevil *Hypera postica* which feeds on forage legumes especially sainfoin (Tischler, 1965), has greatly declined. In the samples of partridge chick food obtained in the 1930s, it was the most frequently occurring species (Ford *et al.*, 1938) and it was also very numerous in partridge chick diet in Czechoslovakia in the 1950s (Janda, 1959). The larvae of this species exhibit behaviour unusual for weevils, in that they feed fully exposed on leaves, hence their attractiveness to chicks. They were sufficiently numerous in crops of sainfoin and lucerne to be a significant pest and were included in the MAFF (ADAS) reports which showed that 'severe damage' to crops occurred in seven of the twelve years between 1945 and 1956. Since that time the weevil has only been recorded once, having caused 'slight damage' in 1959. In most areas it is now very rare; we never observed it in the Sussex study area though it is still common on Salisbury Plain, where patches of wild sainfoin grow.

Sotherton used the example of knotgrass, food plant for the knotgrass beetle *Gastrophysa polygoni* (Sotherton, 1982a), to explore the insect/

weed relationship in detail (Colour Plates XXVII and XXVIII). Both weed and beetle feature largely in the diet of partridges throughout its world range.

A female knotgrass beetle lays approximately 750 eggs per generation and there are usually two generations per season. Losses of eggs and young larvae are very high, accounting for most of the mortality occurring throughout the life cycle and the key factor accounting for fluctuations in numbers. The main cause of these losses appeared to be predation by other beetles (Sotherton *et al.*, 1984b).

Experiments using predator exclusion techniques showed that the main egg mortality was caused by predation by ground and rove beetles. Among these groups the ground beetle *Agonum dorsale* and the rove beetle *Philonthus cognatus* appeared to be particularly important (Sotherton, 1982b). *Philonthus* is a widespread and opportunistic predator, for example it was the major cause of density-dependent mortality in winter moth pupae on oak trees studied at Oxford.

Whether predation was density-dependent on knotgrass beetle eggs and larvae could not be determined in a three-year study, but on the data available it seemed likely that this was the case.

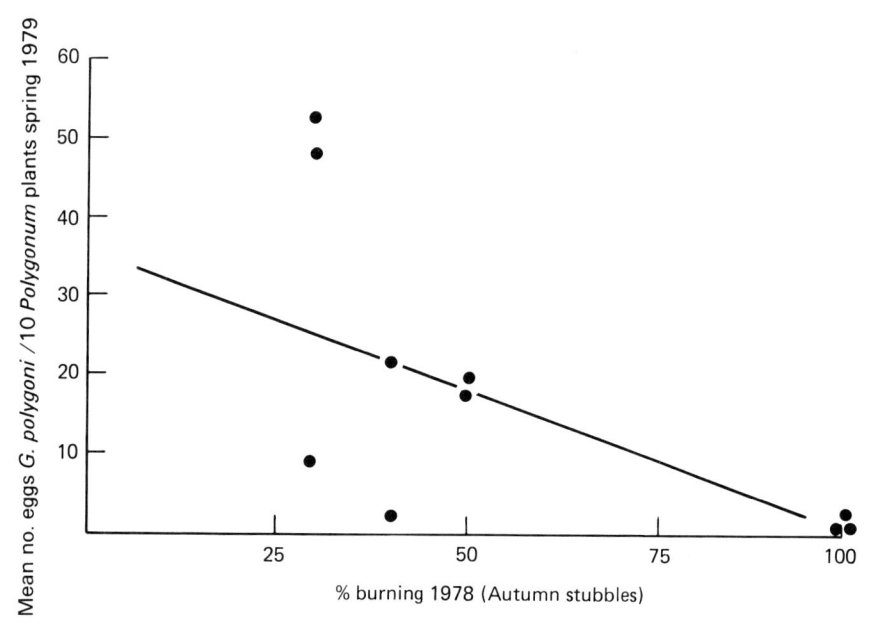

Fig. 6.5 Relationship between percentage field area covered in autumn straw burning and egg density of knotgrass beetle (*G. polygoni*) the following spring ($P<0.05$).

If predation pressure accounts for the low numbers of knotgrass beetles in cereal fields, what are the reasons for the very patchy distribution?

Firstly, the knotgrass beetle is only able to feed and lay its eggs on two or possibly three species of *Polygonum*. These weeds are under increasing pressure from the use of herbicides, more so in the 1980s than ever before (see Chapter 8). On many cereal farms in Britain there are now only remnant populations of this weed, found on farm tracks, in gateways and field corners.

Secondly, the knotgrass beetle does not fly and has such poor powers of dispersal that even when ideal conditions prevail it is very slow to recolonise cereal fields. So an interruption in the density of host plants, for example when a field is sprayed with a *Polygonum* specific herbicide, may mean that the knotgrass beetle is absent for years even if the knotgrass is not sprayed in subsequent years. At the outset of the Sussex study knotgrass was abundant in the cereal fields on one farm (Potts and Vickerman, 1974, map fig. 10) – the only farm where anti-*Polygonum* herbicides had not been used.

Thirdly, several agricultural practices have been shown to increase mortality, such as the direct effects of herbicides where the host plant survives (2,4-D) (Sotherton, 1982c) and also fungicides (benomyl and thiophanate-methyl) (Vickerman and Sotherton, 1983) and straw burning (Sotherton, 1982a) (Fig. 6.5).

Plant bugs (Heteroptera)

The effects of herbicides on the plant bugs (Colour Plate XV) are also neither simple nor straightforward to assess. A number of species of plant bug feed on broad-leaved weeds but those which are especially favoured such as fat hen and various thistles (Southwood and Leston, 1959) are now very rare in cereal fields. There are no records of plant bugs preferring such common cereal weeds as yellow charlock or red poppy.

Many species of plant bug also feed on clover or other forage legumes and on wild and cultivated grasses, and there exists an association between the abundance of plant bugs and the ranked density of grasses in the cereal crop (Table 6.6) which is not found with the broad-leaved weeds. The situation is similar with other hemiptera such as the Jassids (Cicadellidae) and Delphacids. Grass weeds increased as the broad-leaved weeds were reduced by herbicides, so it is possible that some plant bugs were not greatly affected by the use of herbicides. However

Table 6.6 Relationship of rank abundance of grass weeds and plant bugs in D-vac samples mid-late June 1971–1978, Sussex study

Grass weed index (fields)	Mean ratio of Hereroptera to overall mean for year, and 95% confidence limits	
0 (213)	0.89	(0.78–1.02)
1 (259)	0.87	(0.79–0.95)
2 (136)	1.25	(0.95–1.65)
3 to 5 (75)	1.32	(1.10–1.58)

evidence from Sussex suggests that there has, if anything, been a decline since 1969 (Fig. 5.2). Plant bugs were clearly adversely affected and reduced in numbers by cold wet weather, i.e. in 1968, 1977, 1979, 1981 and 1985. McNeill (1973) showed that rainfall was a significant cause of mortality in the plant bug *Leptoterna dolobrata* and that the seasonal onset of flowering of the host grass (Yorkshire fog) was important. *Leptoterna* is, like several other plant bugs, a pest of cereals in Scandinavia and Poland but not Britain (Zadoks and Rijsdijk, 1984).

Sawfly larvae

The sawfly fauna of cereal crops in the Sussex study area is dominated by leaf-eating species of the genus *Dolerus* (Colour Plate XXXI). This dominance seems to be typical, being the case in all sweep-net samples I have taken in cereals in north east Scotland, North Yorkshire, Norfolk, Hampshire, in the Wetterau (near Frankfurt) and in Bavaria.

The seasonal abundance of *Dolerus* larvae has been monitored in winter wheat fields in Halle (East Germany) from 1971 to 1981 with evidence of cyclic fluctuations but no long-term trend was apparent (Freier and Wetzel, 1984). These sawflies were common in the cereals of eastern Europe (Oko, 1963a; Mühle and Wetzel, 1965; Dabrowska-Prot et al., 1974; Ermolenko, 1983). In Kazakhstan cereal leaf-eating sawflies form an important food of some species of birds such as the reed bunting (Badulin, 1983). However the genus *Dolerus* appears to be rare in the South Paris Basin; only one of over 6000 adult sawflies collected in cereal fields there belonged to the genus *Dolerus* (Chevin and Chambon, 1984). Also, I did not obtain any by sweeping cereals in several parts of Italy at the end of May 1982.

Eleven species of *Dolerus* occurred in cereal crops in Sussex but 93% of 1568 adults collected over an eight-year period consisted of *D.*

puncticollis, D. gonager and *D. haematodes* (Potts, 1977a). A comparable figure is as yet not available for larvae since the key of Lorenz and Kraus (1957) did not include *D. puncticollis*.

Some detailed but largely unpublished work by Dr F.L. Waterhouse of the University of Dundee showed in the 1930s and 1940s that adult *Dolerus* feed on nectar and that the females can reproduce successfully with a complete absence of males (i.e. parthenogenesis), so they are clearly an interesting group to study.

In Sussex we obtained data on the fecundity of sawflies by placing captured individuals in breeding cages and by dissection of females trapped in cereal crops. Density estimates were from D-vac samples, but we used cast skins to correct for the absence in samples of larvae of more than 3 mg dry weight, which are not (as Thonon, 1974, also showed) efficiently sampled by this suction method.

A preliminary analysis of these data suggests that 88% of the total annual mortality of the three main species of *Dolerus* occurs in the pre-pupae and pupae stages. Annual fluctuations of larval density appear to be cyclic (technically, phase-remembering quasi-cycles) and the over-winter mortality is of the delayed density-dependent type (see Fig. 6.6), typically found in species which are affected by parasites. If this is the

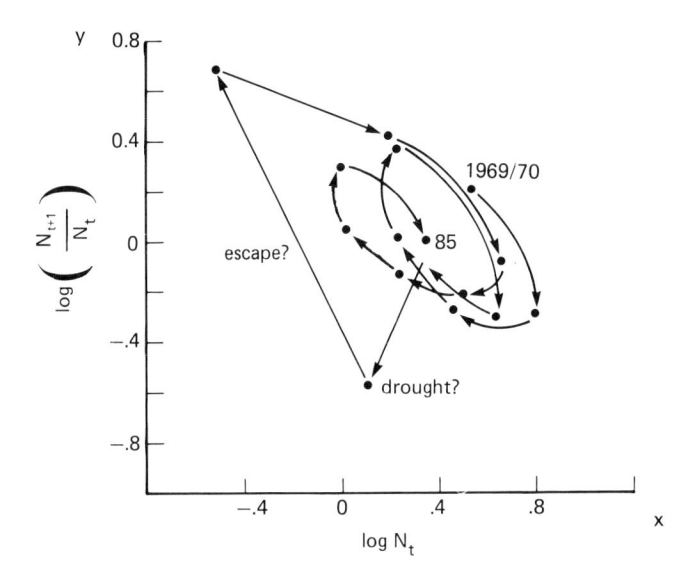

Fig. 6.6 Sequential plot of densities of larvae of cereal-leaf-eating sawflies m^{-2} (x) from 1969 to 1985. Pupal 'survival' (y) is reduced by parasites, it is of the delayed density-dependent type and results in quasi-cycles.

case in Sussex it could explain the cycles in adult and larval numbers, as its relatives do in some cyclic forest lepidoptera, e.g. grey larch bud moth (Van den Bos and Rabbinge, 1976).

The eggs of a parasitic wasp, *Tryphon* spp. (Ichneumonidae, Tryphorinae), are frequently found attached to the 'neck' behind the head capsule (Colour Plate XXXII) and it seems likely that parasitism is the cause of the delayed density-dependent mortality amongst *Dolerus* sawflies. *Tryphon* has been described as an important parasite of *Dolerus* sawflies in the Soviet Union (Kasparyan, 1973).

Several cereal pests were inadvertently transported from Europe to North America. These included the European wheat stem sawfly *Cephus pygmaeus* (L.), found rarely but regularly in the Sussex study area. The importation of its natural enemies from Europe was suggested as early as 1864 (twenty years before the first publicised success of biological control in the Californian orange groves). Eventually this approach proved successful when the European sawfly was reduced permanently to very low densities by *Collyria calcitrator*, a parasitic wasp related to *Tryphon* (Turnbull and Chant, 1961).

Having no cocoon, merely a cell in the soil, the pre-pupal sawfly is also susceptible to dessication by cultivation of the soil, and the exceptional drought of 1976 was associated with the highest observed between-season mortality amongst sawflies during the Sussex study. It seems that a significant proportion of total mortality is caused by ploughing and cultivation, even though the main source of (delayed) density – dependent loss is probably parasitism by *Tryphon* spp.

In the Sussex study in 1970 and 1971 the emergence of insects in spring was measured in fields where the cereals had been undersown the previous year and in fields where the stubbles had been burnt, cultivated and ploughed in the usual manner. In both years the necessary traps were placed in rows in adjacent fields. Like other hymenoptera, the number of adult sawflies emerging increased in the undersown fields to a level three times that in the cultivated fields even after allowing for the fact that undersown fields start with higher densities (Vickerman, 1978).

It seems likely that this difference can be attributed to the physical damage caused to overwintering pupae by ploughing and cultivation but one other contributing factor could also be that some species of sawfly, those which have cocoons on the soil surface, will be destroyed by straw burning, e.g. *Pachynematus* spp.

In traditional ley farming the proportion of cereal fields undersown is about one third, thus increasing the emergence of adult sawflies on a farm scale by two thirds. Applesham Farm is the only farm in the Sussex study which still maintains traditional undersowing (25% of cereals) and there the mean density of sawfly larvae is, in line with the above reasoning, 50% higher than on the other farms ($P<0.001$).

Other preferred insects

The small diurnal ground beetles typically include *Demetrias atricapillus*, a generalised predator with a preference for cereal aphids (Sunderland and Vickerman, 1980), and *Trechus quadristriatus*, another generalised predator but this time with a preference for small earthworms (Mitchell, 1963). *Demetrias* overwinters in dry, grassy-bottomed hedges and breeds in summer (Sotherton 1984), whereas *Trechus* overwinters in open fields and breeds mostly in autumn (Mitchell, loc. cit.). Both species were found in particularly low numbers in the three years 1977 to 1979, the years of highest chick mortality.

Finally we should consider the status of the ants, especially *Lasius flavus*. The mounds of this species are destroyed by cultivation and also by shading (Pontin, 1960). Thus the combination of the ploughing of downland and the growth of shrub species and other vegetation (kept down by rabbits until 1955 – myxomatosis reached the Sussex study area in August 1954) must have resulted in a drastic reduction in numbers in the Sussex study area.

Despite indications to the contrary in 1969 (Potts, 1970a), no increase in chick mortality could be readily attributed to the absence of ants from parts of the Sussex study area. The best area for *Lasius flavus*, Amberley Mount, is certainly not an area of unusually low chick mortality. Probable reasons could be that partridge chicks tend to feed on ants when they have fledged and can move out of cover, often to dust in old ant hills rather than to feed. Almost by definition chicks will not encounter many *Lasius flavus* in their first ten days or so because during this period they prefer to feed in the cover afforded by cereals, which presumably protects them from aerial predators.

Lasius flavus tends to be most abundant in southern England (see map in Brian, 1977) and many well-known partridge shoots of the past in Norfolk, Yorkshire and further north have never noted significant populations of these ants. Although there is no clear evidence, my own view is that the limitation of ant distribution described above will have made chicks more dependent than they would otherwise be on preferred insects in cereals, but that it has not affected the overall situation greatly.

Herbicides, and herbicide-free cereal field margins

In March 1970 I prepared a map of North Farm indicating headlands of spring barley where herbicides might not be used, i.e. those above grassy banks ideal for nesting partridges, to provide weedy strips. The farm manager did not like the idea one bit! The harvest of 1968 had been made very difficult by the presence of weeds and he did not want a repetition. Eventually only two strips, 6 m wide and 500 m long were not sprayed, the others being replaced by 4 m wide strips of buckwheat, vetches or fodder-radish, since it was thought easier to take strips out of cereals altogether than to compromise standards of cereal husbandry. In any case the buckwheat did not attract preferred insects, the vetches were soon reduced to stalks by woodpigeons and unfortunately the experiments had to stop.

On one Sussex study area farm in 1974 and on another in 1979, no herbicides were used at all on cereals. These were not experiments but chance events (e.g. illness of the staff involved). In both cases chick survival was excellent. The 1979 case was particularly interesting because chick survival at 40% was much higher than in the rest of the study area (15%); 1979 was generally a poor year for partridge chick

Table 6.7 Effects of spraying of herbicides and insecticides on the log mortality rates of partridge chicks (k_3)

Study	Year	Method	No h (6 m margins)	h all field	h + some insecticide (part field)	h + insecticide (all field)
(1)	1976	Enquiry (NGC) (Potts, 1978)	–	0.24	0.29	0.60
(2)	1980	Enquiry (NGC) (Potts, 1981)	–	0.36	0.54	–
(3)	1982	Manydown trial	0.22	0.32	–	–
(4)	1983	Manydown replicated experiment (Rands, 1985)	0.31	0.72	–	–
(5)	1984	as 1983, but reversed	0.20	–	0.42	–
(6)	1984	as 1982, 8 farms (NGC)	0.40	–	0.70	–
(7)	1984	Sussex trial	–	0.37	–	0.59
(8)	1985	Manydown experiment	0.54	0.92	–	–
(9)	1985	5 farms (NGC)	0.56	0.88	–	–

h = herbicide

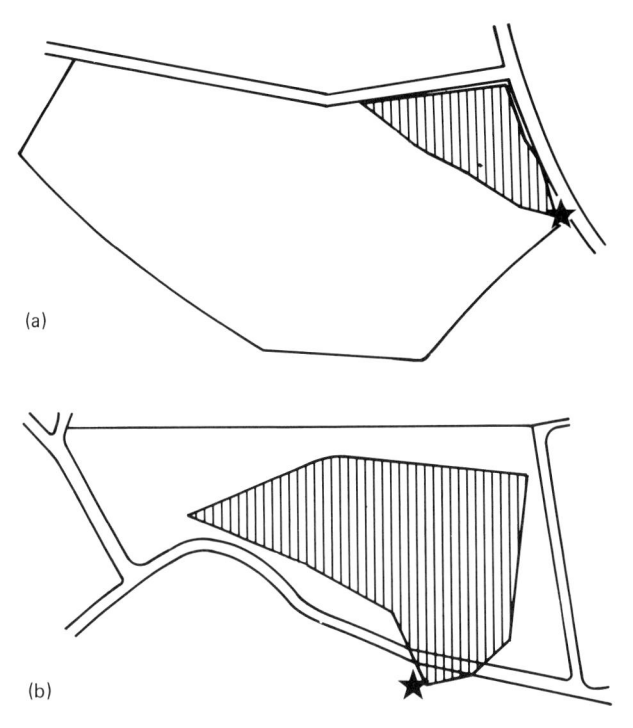

Fig. 6.7 Home range size (hatched) for two grey partridge broods during the first 21 days after hatching. (a) a brood in an 11.8-ha field of spring barley with unsprayed margin. (★ marks the nest sites.) (b) a brood in an 8.8-ha sprayed field of spring barley (from Rands 1986a).

survival, 1974 (a good sawfly year) was generally good even where crops were treated with herbicides.

At the Game Conservancy we instigated some trials in the mid-1970s in which strips of cereals were undersown with lucerne to encourage insect food for chicks. However, these trials were on a small scale and not properly replicated.

In 1982, the first farm scale trials were initiated when headlands of spring barley were left unsprayed at Manydown in Hampshire (Colour Plate XXIX), with controls. The result was a very encouraging lowering of chick mortality rates (Table 6.7) and in the following year, 1983, a farm-scale trial was organised using a layout of control and experimental blocks of fields (Rands, 1985) which was reversed in 1984 (Rands, 1986a) when the radio-tracking of broods was also undertaken (Fig. 6.7). Eight farms scattered throughout eastern Britain carried out trials of this kind in 1984 and five in 1985. Chick mortality rates in 'sprayed' and 'unsprayed' areas are compared in Table 6.7. At first sight it is astonishing that restoring the weeds to only a 6 m width at the crop margin is equivalent to not using herbicides at all. However it should be noted that broods fed mostly in unsprayed margins (Rands, 1986a) even though these amounted to only 6% of the area of the field. Also the density of plant bugs on sprayed headlands is five times higher than in the rest of the field (Carter, 1984), so that the effects of not spraying are correspondingly greater.

Insecticides

In recent years insecticides have been increasingly used to control cereal aphids (Colour Plate XIV; Fig. 6.8) and during the summers of 1976 and 1980, records of spray use were collected from those farmers involved in the August count scheme covered by the National Game Census. Results showed that increasing levels of spraying (allowing for the insecticide used, the area covered and the timing of the spray) were having significant adverse effects on chick survival (Potts, 1978, 1981).

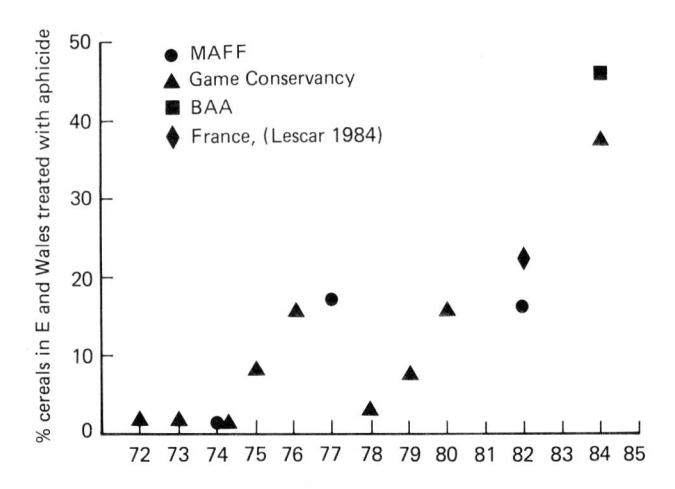

Fig. 6.8 Increase in use of insecticides for the control of cereal aphids. Percentage of sown area treated 1972–1984.

Sources: MAFF (Pesticide usage survey report 8, Sly (1977), preliminary survey, Steed and Sly 1979, preliminary report 35, Sly 1984). Game Conservancy surveys by members 1984, excludes autumn use. British Agrochemicals Association 1984 included autumn 1983 when aphicides were recommended by ADAS and widely used.

Poor chick survival has also followed use of aphicides on wheat in France and in this case it was shown, by using caged chicks placed in fields, that the chemicals (pirimicarb, phosalone, bromophos, dimetho-

Table 6.8 Effects of insecticides on mortality rates of preferred insects

Chemical	Log mortality attributable to chemical	Authority
(1) demeton-s-methyl	0.38	Moreby and Potts (1985)
(2) dimethoate	0.70	Vickerman and Sunderland (1977)
(3) pirimicarb	0.83	Potts unpublished (sawfly larvae only, lab. study)
	0.30	Powell *et al.* (1981)
(4) pyrazophos	0.42	Sotherton and Moreby (1985) (extended *in litt.* 1986)

Table 6.9 Densities of insects in winter wheat seven to ten days after spraying with insecticides, early June 1984 (Potts and Moreby, 1985)

	No insecticide	Insecticide demeton-s-methyl
Fields	25	13
Aphids	208.0 ± 28.0 $^{-2}$	79.5 ± 16.2 m^{-2}
Plant bugs	6.1 ± 1.2 m^{-2}	3.54 ± 0.9 m^{-2}
Sawfly larvae	1.9 ± 0.5 m^{-2}	0.36 ± 0.1 m^{-2}
Beetles	5.1 ± 1.0 m^{-2}	1.23 ± 0.6 m^{-2}
Total insects, including above	1562 ± 120 m^{-2}	650 ± 70 m^{-2}

Table 6.10 Game chick mortality rates and the use of insecticides to control cereal aphids in winter wheat, early June 1984 (Potts and Moreby, 1985)

	No insecticide	Insecticide
Fields	25	13
Broods seen	22	15
Log chick mortality rate to August	0.37 ± 0.09	0.59 ± 0.08
Log chick mortality rate expected from insects	0.40	0.74

ate, fenthion and parathion) did not directly cause mortality (Saint-André de la Roche and Douville de Granssu, 1982).

The effects of aphicides on preferred insects are, not surprisingly, drastic (Table 6.8). It is unfortunate that pirimicarb, the most specific aphicide now available, is so toxic to sawfly larvae. Some comparative data are given in Table 6.8, including that for pyrazophos, an insecticidal organo-phosphate fungicide now used on cereals.

These effects are very severe since they are measured in faunas already depleted by herbicides and by the other trends towards monoculture.

In 1984, for the first time, aphicides were used in the Sussex study on a large scale (Table 6.3) before most chicks would have switched to vegetarian diets. Data show (Table 6.9) that preferred insects were reduced and that the chick mortality rate was increased (Table 6.10) by a level consistent with the multiple regression model of Chapter 5.

Thus the multiple regression model is supported by experimental evidence; it predicted the effects of increasing or decreasing the insect food supply.

It is interesting to draw parallels between the effects of insecticides used in cereals in reducing partridge chick survival rate, and similar effects arising from the use of DDT to control spruce budworm, where juvenile ruffed grouse (Neave and Wright, 1969), woodcock (Wright, 1960) and probably black duck (Hunter *et al.*, 1984) all showed increased mortality attributable mostly to reduction in their insect food supplies rather than to direct toxic effects. Even with canopy species the

Table 6.11 Summary of estimates of partridge chick mortality rates grouped according to herbicide and insecticide use

	Up to 1952 (no herbicide)	Mean $k_3 \pm$ se 1953–1961 (some herbicide)	1962–1985 (herbicide + some insecticide)
National Game Census	0.33 ± 0.02	0.45 ± 0.05	0.51 ± 0.02
Damerham	0.32 ± 0.05	0.50 ± 0.06	0.59 ± 0.05
Lee Farm	–	0.44 ± 0.06	0.67 ± 0.07
North Farm	–	0.45 ± 0.05	0.63 ± 0.04
Sussex study	–	0.40 ± 0.05	0.61 ± 0.04
Mainland Europe	0.29 ± 0.03	0.37	0.45 ± 0.03
North America	0.25 ± 0.07	0.28	0.36 ± 0.04

Sources: Table 10.4; also for North America, (Hart 1945, Porter 1955).

PESTICIDES 123

direct effects of insecticides were small compared to the indirect effects (see also Brown, 1978; DeWeese et al., 1979; Herman and Bulger, 1979).

Increase in chick mortality

Four sources of data can be used to estimate chick survival rates prior to herbicide use (Table 6.11). In addition, thirty years of continuous monitoring at Great Witchingham gave a figure of $42 \pm 3\%$ ($k_3 = 0.38$), including some years in which strongylosis depressed chick survival

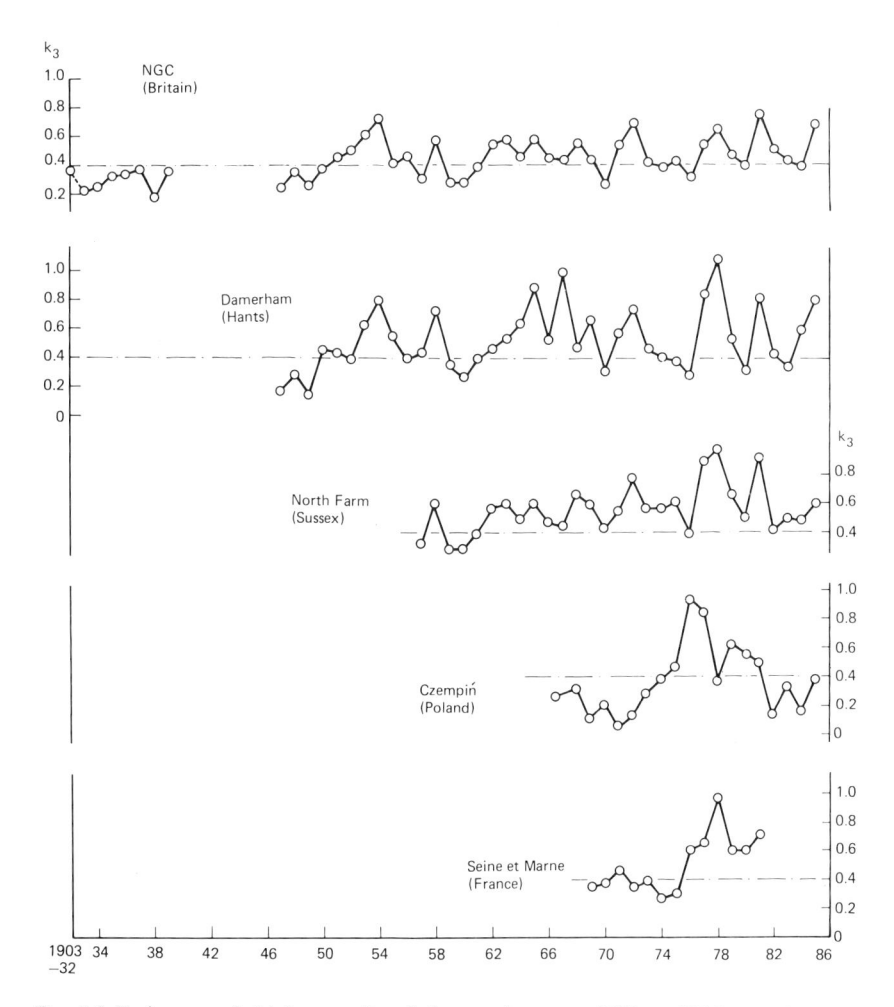

Fig. 6.9 Estimates of chick mortality (k_3) over the years 1932 to 1985, showing the increases prior to population declines (cf Fig. 2.6).

rates significantly (see Chapter 7). The data suggest a mean k_3 of 0.32 for Britain prior to 1952; 0.27 for the rest of the world range. In the continental areas of Europe and North America, warmer summer climates are more suitable for chick survival.

There was no indication of any trends through any of these data prior to 1952 but significant increases in chick mortality rates have occurred since then (see Table 6.11).

The most systematically recorded long-term data are those from the Sussex study area, and the upward trends in chick mortality are not significantly different from those in the National Game Census. The rate of increase in chick mortality in North America is, on these analyses, less than that recorded in Britain, as would be expected from the lower herbicide use there. In France, Birkan's 1969–1981 study shows low mortality compared to Sussex followed by a clear increase in chick mortality up to the rates currently recorded in Sussex (Fig. 6.9) (Birkan, 1985 extended *in litt.*). The data from Czempiń, western Poland, shows a dramatic rise in chick mortality in the mid-1970s following the introduction of herbicides (Chlewski, 1976), with a short-term recovery in 1982 when herbicides were not available (Chlewski and Panek, 1986).

There is therefore very clear evidence of an increase in chick mortality in each of the long-term studies showing population declines.

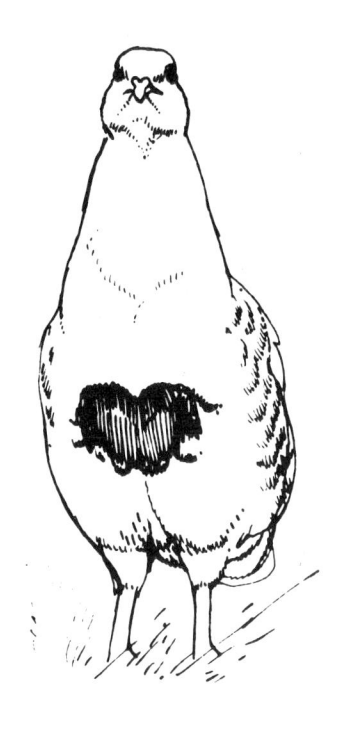

7 Parasites and disease

'Although many species of worm appear to have little or no effect on their host, this is, in all probability, because we cannot ask the hosts about their symptoms.' (Rothschild and Clay, 1952)

Most ecologists who have studied populations of wild birds have not ranked disease high in importance, whereas by contrast, most breeders of poultry and waterfowl devote a good deal of their time to controlling disease. Partridges, once managed at far higher densities than most wild birds, lie somewhere between these extremes.

In Britain, twenty-one species of parasitic worm have been found in the partridge (Clapham, 1935) and in Czechoslovakia fifteen species have been found (Páv *et al.*, 1961). The proportion of partridges carrying parasitic worms (mostly nematodes) was, in Poland from 32% to 50% (Kozakiewicz *et al.*, 1983, and Bezubik, 1959, respectively), in Yugoslavia 53% (Vrazic, 1957), in Romania 25% (Chiriac *et al.*, 1972) and in south-east Kazakhstan 83% (Gvozdev, 1957). So, just how significant is their presence?

From 1933 to 1958 over 1280 post-mortem examinations were carried out on wild partridges by Dr Phyllis Clapham and her successors at Fordingbridge. A total of 690 had died of non-violent natural causes and parasitic worms were implicated in the death of 442 (64%). As with many herbivores the most important of these worms were nematodes. Three species were particularly important: the caecal threadworm *Trichostrongylus tenuis* (Mehlis), cause of 'strongylosis'; the gape worm *Syngamus trachea* (Von Sieb), cause of 'gapes'; and the caecal worm *Heterakis gallinarum*, (Schrank). The latter transmits an amoeba-like flagellate protozoan *Histomonas meleagridis* (Smith), which causes the disease 'blackhead'.

Strongylosis

Strongylosis (as it is known; strictly Trichostrongyliasis), the disease caused by *Trichostrongylus tenuis*, was first described in 1846 and discovered in red grouse in 1854 (Macdonald, 1883). Whether it then occurred in partridges is not known but some deaths of full grown birds in coveys occasionally observed during harvest in the nineteenth century might have been caused by strongylosis. The disease was first confirmed in the partridge when the pathologist to the magazine *The Field* found that twenty-six (31%) of eighty-three adult partridges had died from the effects of *T. tenuis* in 1913 (Smith, 1913). In 1926 the same pathologist found that twenty-five (31%) out of a total of eighty birds had died from strongylosis (Parker, 1927).

The most notable outbreak of strongylosis in partridges occurred in 1931. As previously mentioned, this event stimulated the research on which much of this book is based. This particular outbreak was investigated by *Country Life*, which engaged W. E. Collinge (a specialist on the food of birds), employed by the Natural History Museum in York. Unfortunately the data published as a result of this investigation (Portal and Collinge, 1932) were inadequate and the original files have since been lost. Total counts of worms in both caeca were used, rather than counts based on sub-sampling. This was so laborious and time-consuming that there was time for only a few counts, and we do not know how typical they were. Despite these difficulties I have carried out an analysis and attempted a reconstruction of the data which suggest that the main effect of strongylosis was to increase chick mortality and not, as Portal and Collinge supposed, to result in clinical effects on the adults.

Numbers of parent birds and hatched young were derived from censuses of partridges in spring and August from twelve estates in Hampshire and the eastern counties (i.e. see Portal and Collinge, 1932: Table iv). Based on the assumption that the brood production rate was 0.75 and the number of young hatched per brood was fourteen, we can estimate the mortality of adult birds for each estate by further assuming that chick mortality rates never exceeded 90% on any estate. (Chick mortality was estimated on only two estates; one gave 89% and the other 83%.)

On this basis comparisons of the pre-breeding and post-breeding censuses suggest an adult mortality between spring and August of probably less than 45% and a chick mortality probably greater than 85%.

There is also evidence to suggest that high chick mortality occurred again in 1932 (e.g. Great Witchingham, Table 7.1), though in 1933–34 the numbers of *T. tenuis* dropped to low levels and chick mortality returned to normal (Clapham, 1935).

Table 7.1 Chick mortality rates (k_3) before, during and after an outbreak of strongylosis at Great Witchingham 1931/32 and Six Mile Bottom in 1952/54

Year	Great Witchingham (12 km^2) Pairs km^{-2}	Chick mortality k_3	Year	Six Mile Bottom (23 km^2) Pairs km^{-2}	Chick mortality k_3
1929	57	0.21	1950	?	0.35
1930	80	0.24	1951	>25	0.57
1931	46	0.92*	1952	22	0.64*
1932	35	0.66*	1953	21	0.64*
1933	29	0.28	1954	16	0.72*
1934	27	0.42	1955	13	0.35

* Years in which post-mortem examinations confirmed deaths of adults due to *T. tenuis*. Most adults died in June or July

This persistence of high mortality occurring in the second or even the third season of an outbreak was also a feature of the latest significant outbreak of strongylosis in partridges in Britain, that which began at Six Mile Bottom, Cambridgeshire, in 1952 (Table 7.1). Much interest was initially drawn to this incident because the weather had remained reasonable throughout and because only a few miles away (e.g. Stetchworth and Chippenham) the mortality of chicks was low. Predation as a cause could be ruled out; at that time there were no foxes, carrion crows or magpies in the area and the estate was very well keepered. Judging from August counts and nest records from 1936 to 1948 the log female mortality rate (k_2) on this estate could be expected to be 0.09 (18%); in 1952 the estimate was 0.11 (23%). Adult mortality was not therefore notably increased in this particular case.

At the beginning of the 1952 breeding season the stock appeared to be in good condition but by July the birds' plumage began to darken noticeably and as a result it was decided to shoot a sample of nineteen birds and send them to Dr Clapham, the pathologist at Fordingbridge. These partridges were found to be significantly below normal weight

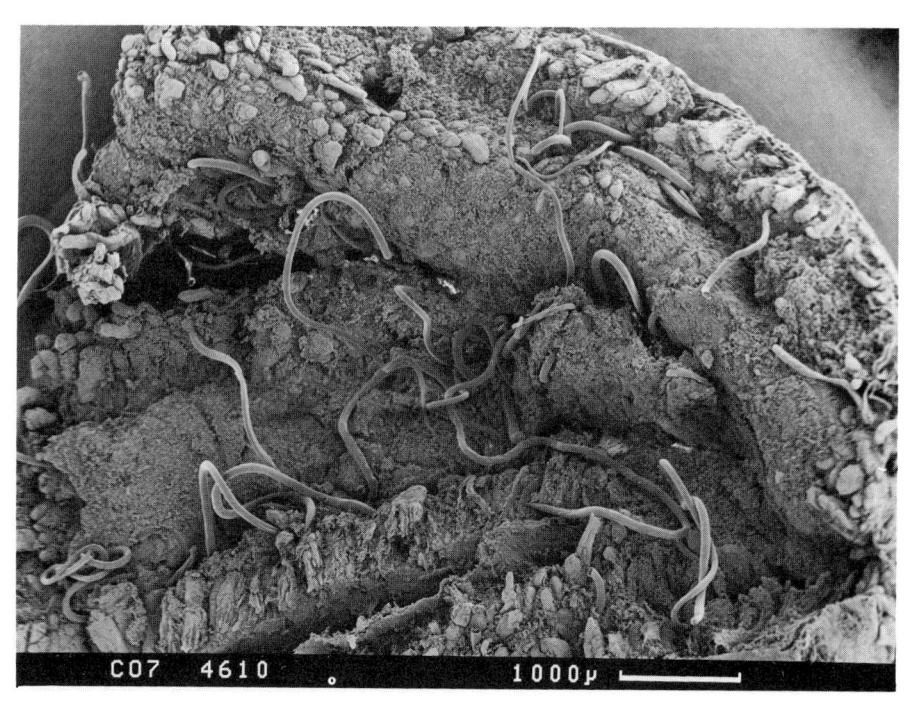

Plate X. Scanning electron micrograph of caecal threadworms burrowing into the caecal wall of a red grouse (*by kind permission of H. Watson and Professor D.L. Lee, University of Leeds*).

and seven showed severe inflammation of the caecal walls caused by the burrowing activity of parasitic worms (Plate X). During the following year an incubating female died from *T. tenuis*; two more in 1954.

The weather during the breeding seasons of 1953 and 1954 was very poor (unlike 1952) and breeding success was generally well below average, so it is not clear that *T. tenuis* contributed significantly to the high levels of chick mortality during these years.

After 1954 further study was not possible simply because there were no notable outbreaks of the disease and only a few recorded cases of confirmed death from strongylosis (see Fig. 7.1); one of them was an adult female, found on 24 April 1958, in the Sussex study area. The last reported case of death due to strongylosis in the wild was in July 1958, but the disease continued to cause problems on game farms for some

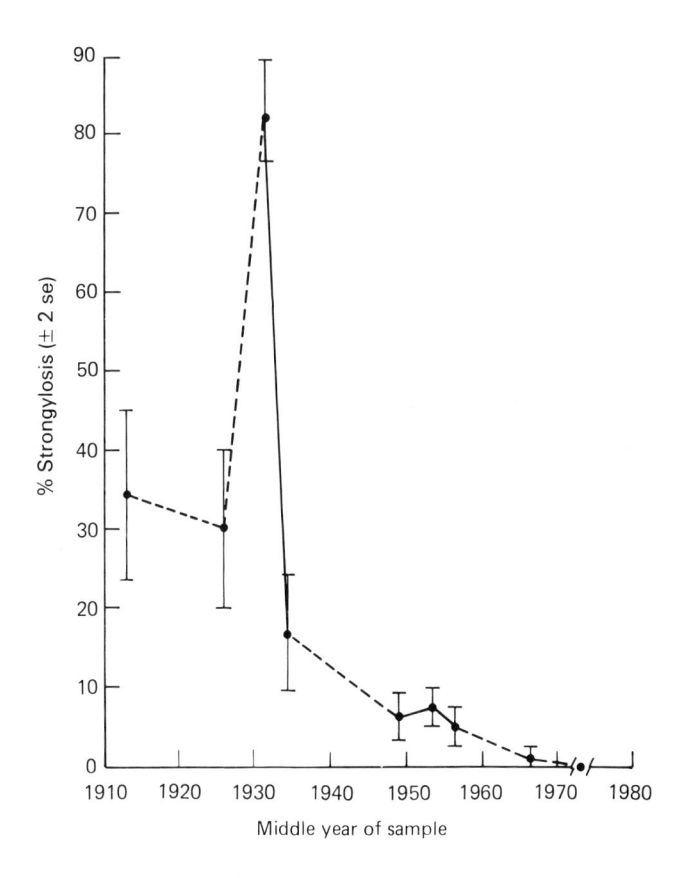

Fig. 7.1 Incidence of death caused by strongylosis in samples of partridges submitted for post-mortem examination over the past 80 years. The decline, like that of the partridge itself is clearly evident.

years. *Trichostrongylus tenuis* is now practically absent in partridge populations but an underweight bird killed on 8 December 1985 by a sparrow hawk on our predator reduction area on Salisbury Plain contained forty-three worms (H. Watson *in litt.*).

Portal and Collinge (1932) stressed the importance of 'persistent damp but not too cold weather' as a precursor of strongylosis, as occurred from September 1930 to May 1931. However, since most outbreaks were in areas of high density such as Norfolk and Hampshire and not in the wetter, milder areas of western Britain, it appears that high density was also a prerequisite.

In Britain it seems likely that partridge densities were below the threshold necessary for maintaining *T. tenuis* before the wet seasons of 1964, 1965 and 1966, which might otherwise have favoured the disease. Only a small change in density might have been necessary if it occurred in combination with another factor. One possible variable is the very marked decline of undersowing of clover, especially in the eastern counties in the early 1960s (see Potts, 1970a). Ogilvie (1902) and Portal and Collinge (1932) describe how partridges tended to concentrate on undersown leys in the spring and the latter showed that larvae of the strongyle worm could be present in considerable numbers on the growing tips of clover. These leys would certainly seem to be a better environment for *T. tenuis* than cultivated fields and the survival rate of the free-living stages is an important factor in determining *T. tenuis* burdens in red grouse (Hudson *et al.*, 1985).

Densities of the partridge overseas have usually been lower than on estates such as Great Witchingham and Six Mile Bottom and it is clear that *T. tenuis* has rarely been a problem world-wide – for example it has only once been recorded in partridges in North America (North Dakota; Bach, 1943), although in bobwhite quail it occurs quite frequently. On the European mainland strongylosis has proved to be a problem on game farms (Madsen, 1952; Páv *et al.*, 1961) – perhaps providing further evidence that high densities are a precursor of the disease.

The succession of two, or occasionally even three seasons of high chick mortality which apparently occur with outbreaks of *T. tenuis* in partridges is typical of red grouse (Potts *et al.*, 1984). However, we have not detected true quasi-cycles in any partridge bag series, so severe outbreaks were probably infrequent.

It should also be noted that no cyclic behaviour has been confirmed in any partridge population, though in Alberta partridges are affected by cyclic predation related to the ten-year cycle in species such as snowshoe hares (Rowan, 1954; Wishart, 1977). Middleton (1934b) claimed that a cycle of eight years was apparent for a number of estates in England, and Wing (1953) described a twenty-three year cycle in Czechoslovakia. In these cases the methodology was incorrect and these cycles have not been confirmed by modern time-series analysis.

The question of how important strongylosis has been in determining partridge chick mortality requires investigation. Some cases of high chick mortality in the past (before the use of herbicides) might be attributable to this disease and not to severe shortages of insect food which (before the use of herbicides) seem implausible. With partridge host densities at such low levels it was too late to monitor strongylosis in partridges, but the responses of the red grouse and the partridge to this disease are probably similar. On further analysis of the twenty-one post-mortem examinations cited by Portal and Collinge (1932) it would appear that the burden which causes death in partridges is about 4100 worms (geometric mean), the comparable figure for red grouse being 5800 (see Potts *et al.*, 1984). These numbers represent virtually the same burden when an adjustment is made for the different body weights of the partridge and grouse.

However, workers on red grouse minimised the role of strongylosis in that species and the matter rested until:

'The current ideas of the grouse research team suggest that infections of threadworms (i.e. *T. tenuis*) are secondary to social stress. I am speculating that a combination of the two may occur. Thus in certain circumstances of grouse population density and climatic conditions, threadworms might kill grouse even though in most circumstances they are adapted to live together.' (Wilson, 1977)

Further work (Wilson and Wilson, 1978) resulted in an early emphasis on *T. tenuis* in the initial investigations of the Game Conservancy's North of England Grouse Research Project. Over the next five years Hudson (1986a) demonstrated (experimentally) the effects of *T. tenuis* by dosing red grouse with levamisol hydrochloride (see Box 7.1), in order to reduce worm burdens.

In this way he demonstrated that increasing loads of *T. tenuis* caused increased mortality among chicks, mortality attributable to diseased hens laying poor quality eggs and to their poor incubation and brooding behaviour. Where percentage grouse chick mortality $= y$, and number of worms per hen $= x$:

$$y = -33.2 + 0.005\,x \qquad (P<0.05)$$

– a relationship which underlines much of the reduction of breeding

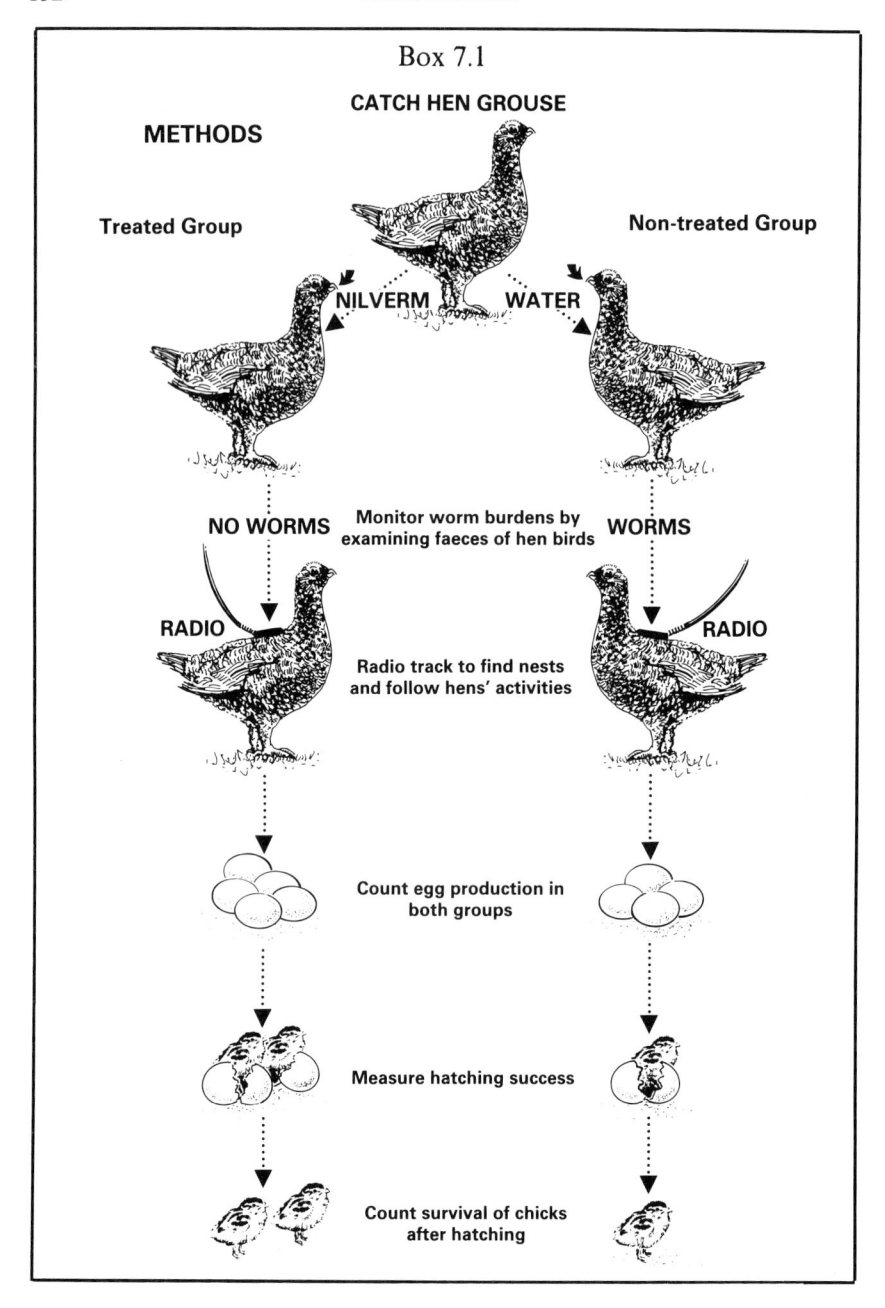

> **Box 7.1**
>
> **METHODS**
>
> **CATCH HEN GROUSE**
>
> **Treated Group** — NILVERM
> **Non-treated Group** — WATER
>
> NO WORMS / WORMS — Monitor worm burdens by examining faeces of hen birds
>
> RADIO — Radio track to find nests and follow hens' activities
>
> Count egg production in both groups
>
> Measure hatching success
>
> Count survival of chicks after hatching

Experimental methods for dosed and not dosed grouse in 1982 and 1983. Nilverm = levamisol hydrochloride (from Hudson, 1986b).

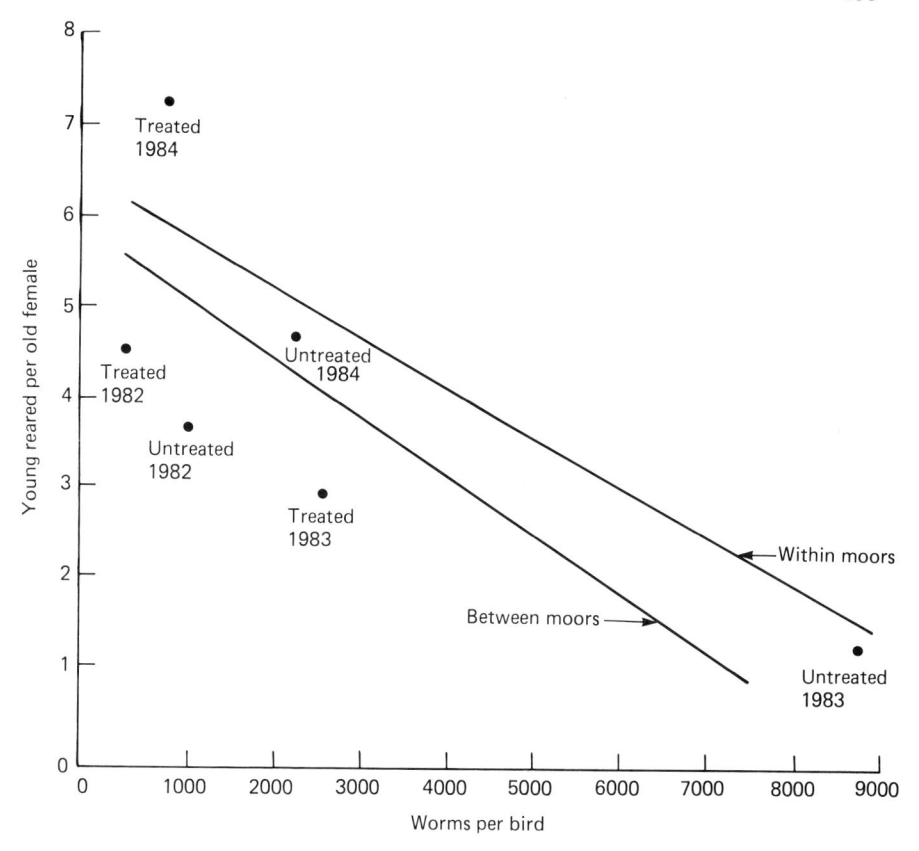

Fig. 7.2 Brood size of red grouse in relation to numbers of caecal threadworms; comparisons between moors and within moors. The experimental results from treated and untreated hens confirm these relationships (from Hudson, 1986a).

success in red grouse which occurred with high numbers of *T. tenuis* (Fig. 7.2).

So, to summarise, it is clear that some of the low partridge chick survival rates reported in the pre-herbicide era can be attributed to strongylosis. Any effects would have been, as with red grouse, *via* the hen, and the prevalence of *T. tenuis* would have been negligible in the young chicks. This in part explains why it has taken so long to elucidate the effects of the disease – the main reason being that scientists were looking for clinical effects and adult mortality. It is now established in red grouse that the main effects are sub-clinical and that these result in increased chick mortality.

Box 7.2 TREATMENT OF GAPES

The symptoms of the disease gapes are distressing and many attempts have been made to find a cure, but until recently with little success. Products were sold but were not effective, e.g. the gamebird wormer tetramisole was only effective against larvae (Connan and Wise, 1977). Thiabendazole, however, was effective (Sharpe, 1964) but the treatment was expensive and needed to be carried out over two to three weeks.

Wise and Connan (unpublished) therefore carried out a controlled trial to immunise pheasants by injecting irradiated *Syngamus* and were successful in preventing the disease at North Farm in 1974. This approach demonstrated the importance of immunity but was not a practical method of prevention in reared birds because of the cost involved. Meanwhile attention was directed to a successor of thiabendazole: mebendazole. This compound was sold from 1978 as Mebenvet, and has been effective even though it has to be mixed with food and administered over fourteen days. Also at virtually the same time as the introduction of mebendazole, the water soluble nitroxynil was introduced as Gapex. These two compounds have been widely used and by 1984 there was no doubt that gapes was much less prevalent than in the past, at least in reared birds (Beer, 1985). Fenbendazole (Wormex) was introduced as a twenty-four hour feed treatment in 1984.

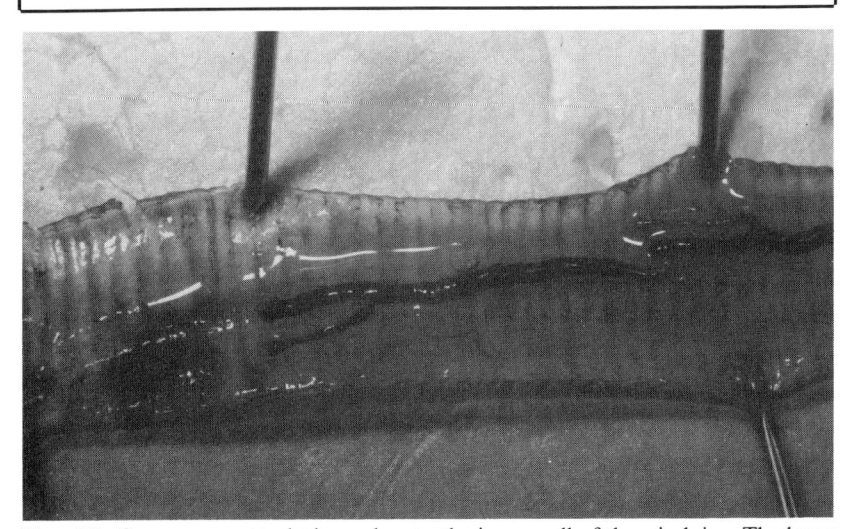

Plate XI. Gapeworms attach themselves to the inner wall of the windpipe. The large female and small male are in permanent copulation, forming the characteristic Y-shape (*T.H. Blank*).

Gapes

This disease, caused by the gapeworm, has probably been known for centuries (Montagu, 1813). At the beginning of our Sussex study we considered that gapes might be the cause of death of many chicks, especially in 1968 and 1971 (Potts and Vickerman, 1974).

The worm lives as an adult in the trachea or windpipe causing, if sufficient are present, death by asphyxiation. The worms live in pairs with the tiny male permanently in copulation with the female (Plate XI).

The life cycle of the gapeworm can be summarised in Fig. 7.3:

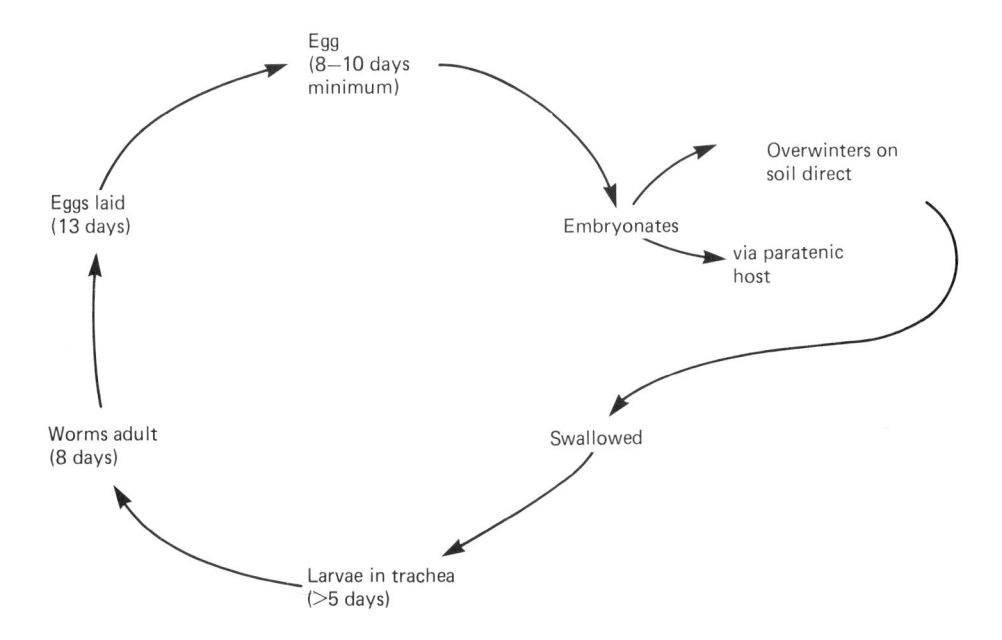

Fig. 7.3 Life cycle of the gapeworm.

Wise (*in litt.*) considers direct cycles to be the most important (i.e. no involvement of paratenic host). However, it is difficult to eradicate the disease, partly because earthworms may live and carry infective *Syngamus* larvae for several years.

Clapham (1934) showed that earthworms, especially *Eisenia foetida* (and to a lesser extent *Lumbricus terrestris*), often contained large numbers of encysted *Syngamus* larvae and that by eating these worms gamebirds could contract the disease. This was later confirmed by Wright *et al.* (1980). Gapes occur in at least thirty-eight species of birds

(Anderson and Shapiro, 1955); young rooks are perhaps most prone to infection and as long ago as 1903 it was thought they were the cause of gapes among pheasants (Clapham, 1940). This has not been established; indeed, such transmission probably cannot occur directly and happens only if the worm loses its species specificity by passing through a paratenic host. Ways of dealing with gapes in captive birds are described in the Box 7.2.

From 1949 to 1959 the prevalence of *S. trachea* was measured each year in partridges shot at Damerham. Prevalence was low (7 ± 1%) in old birds but higher (23 ± 1%) in young birds, with a peak in them of 50 ± 3% in 1958, which led to a widely publicised enquiry into the distribution of gapes in Britain. However, out of 3000 questionnaire forms distributed, only 732 were completed and of the 43% who reported gapes as present only 10% considered the disease as 'increasing'. Surprisingly it emerged that the incidence of the disease was not higher in the high game density areas, and also that areas with light soils (such as south Wiltshire) had a higher incidence rate than Essex with its heavy clays. This was surprising because most people had, until then, the contrary impression (Ash, unpublished manuscript, 1963).

In the Sussex study there was a high prevalence of gapes in birds shot in the first season (1968) and like Whitlock (1937), I found that females were most affected even amongst the young; of young females shot 65% had at least one pair in the trachea or at the top of the bronchi c.f. 35% for young males (for all years amongst young $\chi^2 = 21$, p<0.001).

The next stage of the investigation was to establish the number of worms which would be sufficient to kill chicks or adults. In 1973 Connan and Wise (unpublished) therefore carried out a trial with thirty-two red-legged partridge chicks dosed with large numbers (≈ 600) of infective larvae at age six days. The first chick death took place after eight days (i.e. when aged fourteen days), and twenty-nine had died by the nineteenth day (aged twenty-five days). It was concluded that five pairs of worms were sufficient to cause death in chicks aged three weeks (c.f. Plate XI).

Only 8% of one-day old pheasant chicks given an average of 470 active larvae each died by the fifth day (when all worms were in the lungs) (Connan, *in litt.*), and even in the unlikely event that a massive dose of infective larvae was ingested by partridge chicks within their first day, the chicks would probably not die until aged at least ten days. Yet another trial, this time with two groups of six-day old pheasant chicks, gave the following results:

Died or would die	4 birds averaging 13 pairs of worms
Gaping but might survive	2 birds averaging 6 pairs of worms
No clinical signs	6 birds averaging 2 pairs of worms

In this case the average age at death was in excess of twenty-four days.

At Micheldever the first deaths attributable to gapes were encountered when chicks were over three weeks old (Jenkins, 1955). In the Sussex study area three ailing partridge chicks were found on 13 July 1969, all females from the same brood of nine, aged a little over three weeks. They contained five to sixteen pairs of worms and we concluded that they were indeed dying of gapes.

In the Sussex study area the disease gapes was very unevenly distributed, with an area of high incidence in a valley which had a ten-year history of gapes in a large pheasant release pen (see Potts and Vickerman, 1974: map 18 (vii)). In July 1973, before any pheasants were released, we made a collection of faeces from the area around (but not inside) the pen. This revealed about 300 eggs per gram of faeces for the pheasant compared to 50 eggs per gram for the partridge (both species). We also collected eight representative groups of invertebrates from the same vicinity which again confirmed the importance of earthworms as the carriers of infection, though larvae were also found in one batch of snails. However, young partridges rarely eat earthworms, in fact Wright *et al.* (1980) had to colour worms green and mix them with other food before partridge chicks would eat them; but they do, however, eat snails, perhaps for their shell calcium content. The *Syngamus* larvae found present in them could be a possible source of the infections. Eggs from the previous year, on the soil, are the other source.

Of the twenty-one chicks on which post-mortem examinations were carried out during our studies, only four had died of gapes and as we have seen, three of the four were in one brood. Of fifty-eight post-mortem examinations of chicks (to age six weeks) carried out at Fordingbridge, 19% were considered to have died of gapes.

In Sussex partridge chick survival rates were lower in the valley with a high frequency of gapes than elsewhere in years which were generally poor. Because most chicks died during the period of their main dependence on insects and before gapes could be a problem, we interpret the correlation as due to food shortage and not gapes *per se*. Our studies in the laboratory and experience in the field lead us to believe that the early disappearance of chicks, to which we have drawn attention in Chapter 5, could not be caused by gapes. In fact the prevalence of gapes seems likely to have been over-emphasised because it becomes relatively obvious when the chicks, being old enough to fly, come out of crops.

One further piece of evidence confirms this view. In the high gapes area (in Sussex) and in both 1968 and 1971 when incidence of gapes was highest, we found a slight surplus of females among young in the bag, yet as our surveys of shot birds showed, the prevalence of *Syngamus* is higher in females than males. This was especially so in young aged ten to twelve weeks shot during our studies ($P<0.001$). Had gapes been a significant source of mortality we would have expected a *shortage* of young females. This, together with the low number of pairs of worms per bird in the shot sample, suggests to us that gapes was not very important, at least in the Sussex study area (Table 7.2). Thus, although it was not possible to estimate the proportion of chicks dying from gapes, all the signs were that it was low.

Table 7.2 Prevalence of *Syngamus trachea* in partridges in the Sussex study area and in post-mortem examinations where it was the cause of death

Pairs of *Syngamus* in trachea	Number of partridges	
	Shot, North Farm	Died of 'gapes' (Clapham, 1952–1958 data)
0	476	0
1	52	6
2 + 3	26	9
4 to 10 inclusive	14	36
>10 (maximum 90)	0	37
Totals	568	88

Blackhead

Poultry feeding on stubbles, which they did regularly until the 1950s, were often infested with the caecal round-worm *Heterakis* which transmits the disease blackhead. For example, a survey in France gave a 57% incidence in domestic fowl (Clapham, 1933). Now the disease is rare in turkeys and other poultry, even where anti-blackhead drugs are not used, due to better housing and concrete floors.

In the Sussex study as a whole we found thirty-eight adult or full grown wild partridges dead which were sent for post-mortem examination and the most frequent disease amongst these birds was blackhead. It was a contributory factor in the death of five adults and was considered to be the sole cause of death in four.

The prevalence of blackhead in adult partridge dying of non-violent causes appears to be about 16% and may not have changed since the 1930s (Table 7.3) (the comparable figures being 25% for red-legged partridge and only 3% for the pheasant).

Table 7.3 Incidence of blackhead and *Heterakis* in post-mortem examinations of partridge

	1933–1936	1947–1951	1952–1955	1955–1958	1964–1969
Number examined	101	276	458	320	125
Blackhead (*Histomonas*)	8%	18%	16%	18%	18%
Heterakis	2%	2%	1%	<1%	0%

Heterakis itself only occurs in <2% of partridges (Table 7.3), compared to about 1% of red-legged partridge and 3% of pheasants. In North America levels of parasitism may be similar; Brugger (1941) reported a 4% incidence of *Heterakis* in the partridge.

Much remains to be discovered concerning the life-cycle of *Histomonas*, the amoeba-like flagellate which causes the disease blackhead, but we do know it is found inside *Heterakis* eggs. How *Histomonas* is able to penetrate the *Heterakis* eggs is not known. Nor is it known how partridges ingest the *Heterakis* eggs, although it is likely to be by direct contamination. Several species of insect eaten by chicks contain *Histomonas*, for example grasshoppers (Lund, 1972a, 1972b). The main seasonal occurrence of the disease is during the months July to September, the time when most invertebrates are eaten.

Other diseases

A range of other internal parasites are found in partridges but are of even less significance than gapes or blackhead (e.g. coccidiosis).

Feather lice, fleas and other external and feather parasites are frequently found on partridges. Ticks are very occasionally found (Plate

VI) and the sheep tick *Ixodes ricinus* has been reported from the partridge (Milne, 1949). Most partridges even in hill areas are found on improved land where sheep ticks are scarce or absent, but some will encounter these ticks along the moorland edge.

Judging from work on red grouse (Hudson, 1986b), ticks do not have much adverse effect unless they are transmitting disease. In north-west Britain there is a relatively high probability that nymph ticks carry the virus louping-ill (Potts, 1980b). Louping-ill, a disease of the central nervous system found only in the British Isles, is, where it occurs, the cause of very high mortality in red grouse chicks (Duncan *et al.*, 1978) and might have the same effect on partridges. Most nymph ticks on red grouse chicks pick up the virus when as larvae (a year earlier) they feed on sheep (Duncan, 1981).

However, in Scotland and northern England we have found no difference in the partridge bag between estates according to whether or not their sheep (and therefore presumably grouse) were affected by louping-ill. By contrast red grouse bags were 55% lower ($P<0.001$; Barnes unpublished data, 1985).

In conclusion it seems clear that disease is not currently a significant factor. In the past strongylosis is likely to have increased chick mortality rates. The disease is now infrequent, but presumably will increase again if partridge densities are restored.

8 Feeding Ecology through the Seasons

'As is known, most birds resist cold very well if there is an abundance of food.'
(Formozov, 1946)

Late summer to early winter

Much of the countryside is relatively peaceful in July. In the cereal crops partridges are safe from disturbance, the weed populations there are recovering, to some extent, from herbicides used earlier in the season and, relative to other months, insects abound. Later, however, when the main bulk of the winter wheat straw is burned, any weeds and other favourite foods suddenly disappear from the partridge environment (Colour Plate XVI). In the areas of cereal monoculture there seems to be an obvious scarcity of food, particularly where large areas are left as ploughed or when there is snow (Colour Plate XXIV). Today there are fewer stubbles than formerly (Colour Plate XIX) and no stackyards where the birds can seek grain, nor is there as much food as was formerly obtained around folded sheep or other outwintered stock.

In Sussex, none of these factors seemed to matter. We recorded no mortality of partridges due to straw burning and found that they survived far better in autumn and winter than in summer.

After the cereal harvest, partridges are essentially gleaners, feeding on waste grain left on stubbles and seeds of weeds, especially those of knotgrass (knotweed), black bindweed (smartweed or wild buckwheat) and hemp nettle. Partridges normally awake at daybreak and begin feeding soon after sunrise, although feeding may be delayed for as long as two hours if the weather is wet or very cold (Haugen, 1941). In autumn feeding continues, but leisurely, throughout the day, though there is an intensive session to fill the crop before sunset and a short flight to the ground roost site. Filling the crop thus effectively lengthens the available feeding time, which is particularly important at high latitudes in winter. Where grain and seeds are not available, partridges must resort to grazing pasture foods such as grass, clover, such weeds as dandelions (see Vetiska, 1979) or the green shoots of autumn-sown cereals such as wheat and rye, and at these times feeding is less leisurely.

The effects of farm modernisation have resulted in a large decrease in the availability of grain and weed seeds. When the first combine harvesters were used in North America, cereal grains were left on stubble at a rate of 600 m^{-2} (Yocum, 1943). Over the next thirty-five years the amount of grain left on stubbles decreased by 67% for wheat; 62% for barley (Kobriger, 1977). In the eastern counties of England in the late 1950s and early 1960s, cereal grains were present on stubbles immediately after harvest at 100–150 m^{-2} (Murton *et al.*, 1963a). Even larger quantities of grain were probably left on the uneven fields of the Sussex study area though a big reduction followed the use of self-levelling combines from 1964. Nevertheless, despite these changes, there was probably more grain on stubbles in the early 1980s than in the days of reapers and reaper-binders. However, this extra food will not have had much effect on partridge food supplies because most stubbles are now burned or cultivated – with spilt grain being encouraged to germinate. The major exception is where cereals are undersown.

The effects of herbicides and in particular the burning and subsequent cultivation of stubbles have also greatly reduced weed seed abundance in autumn. Thus the amount of *Polygonum* spp. seed in partridge crops declined from 31% of total food in 1933 to 1937, to 8% in 1968 and 2% in 1977 (Potts, 1984a). In Finland, Pulliainen (1984) records similar declines of hemp nettle (Colour Plate XXV) seeds in partridge diet, especially between 1970 and 1979. Prior to the use of herbicides the dry weight of broad-leaved weed seeds was usually about half the dry weight of grain in the autumn diet of partridges (Potts, 1970b), but recent estimates have ranged between 4% (Sussex 1977, this study) and 17% (Austria 1975–77, Vetiska, 1979).

Comparisons of the incidence of weeds on stubbles and in the diet of partridges show that the seed of the black bindweed is the most preferred food (Kiessling, 1923; Potts, 1970b; Kobriger, 1977). This species is potentially an important contaminant of seed grain and its history is more quantifiable than most.

There have been twenty-six major investigations on autumn food of partridges, including the examination of the crop contents of a total of well over 6500 partridges in eleven countries. In twenty-four of these studies the black bindweed (Colour Plate XXVI) and its close relatives ranked in the top three weed seeds eaten (Table 8.1). From 1898 to 1968 an average of twenty seeds of black bindweed were found in the crops of partridges shot in autumn; from 1968 to the present, the comparable figure is five.

Weed seeds are recorded in the returns of the Official Seed Testing Station (Cambridge) and from 1928 to 1968 there was no sign in the data of any long-term change in the status of black bindweed in cereals. On average about 14% of grain samples through this period were contaminated with black bindweed seeds (Broad, 1952; Gooch, 1963; Tonkin, 1968). In the Sussex study area there was a determined campaign to control black bindweed, beginning on two farms in 1968 with specific herbicides for the purpose. Returns from the Seed Testing Station confirmed that the control was very effective. By 1971 30% of the Sussex study area cereal fields still contained the weed, but a notable decline was already evident both in fields and in samples of grain. In the early

Table 8.1 Summary of twenty-six studies of partridge diet in autumn, showing the relative importance of seeds of the main broad-leaved weeds

Weed in order of preference	1st	Studies in which ranked 2nd	3rd	Total
Black bindweed (smartweed) and knotgrass (knotweed)	19	3	2	24
Hemp nettle	4	–	3	7
Fat hen (lambs quarters) Orache	–	8	3	11
Chickweeds	–	4	3	7
Corn spurrey	–	2	1	3
Corn gromwell	1	–	3	4
Cornflower	1	–	2	3

Sources: Brüll and Lindeman, 1954; Brüll, 1969; Campbell, 1936; Hammer *et al.*, 1958; Hick, 1950; Hunt, 1974; Huss, 1983; Janda, 1956; Kelso, 1932; Khanmamedov, 1962; Kobriger, 1980; Lebeurier, 1958; Litun, 1983a; Middleton and Chitty, 1937; Nefedov, 1943; Oko, 1963a; Penev, 1983; Potts, 1970b (updated); Poyarkov, 1955; Pulliainen, 1965, 1984; Rey, 1907; Rörig, 1900; Thaisz and Csiki, 1912; Vertse *et al.*, 1952; Westerskov, 1966; Yeatter, 1934; Yocum, 1943.

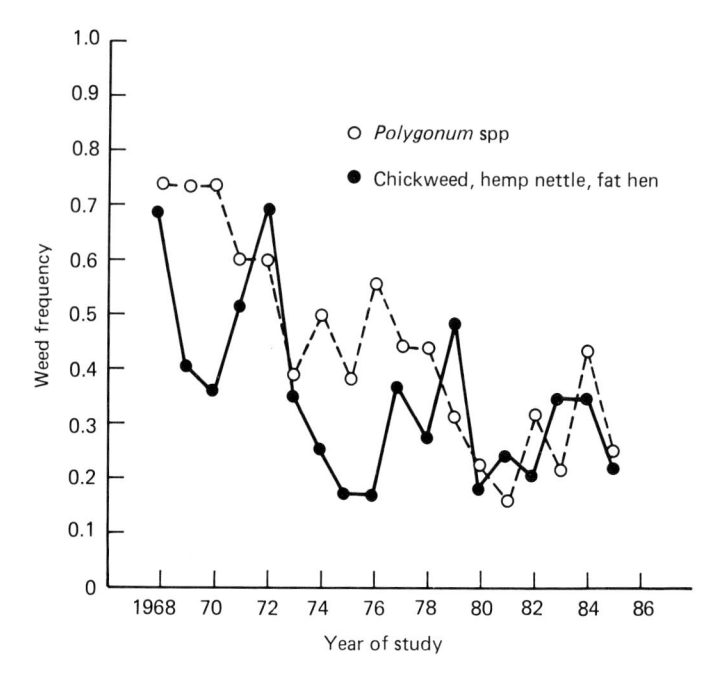

Fig. 8.1 The frequency of weeds in Sussex cereal crops, 1968–1985; June samples for species favoured as food by adult partridges.

1980s the species was recorded in less than 10% of fields and judging from herbicide use, these changes and those amongst the other preferred weeds (see Fig. 8.1) are likely to be typical of cereal growing areas. For example, in a south central England survey of cereal crops, black bindweed was present in only 4% of cereal fields in 1982 and hemp nettle was not recorded (Chancellor and Froude-Williams, 1984).

In North America the situation is probably more favourable for partridges feeding on weeds. As late as 1979 80% of cereal fields in Saskatchewan and Manitoba still contained black bindweed plants in significant numbers (Hume *et al.*, 1983).

In Finland, Pulliainen (1965, 1984) considers that the disappearance of weeds such as hemp nettle (Colour Plate XXV), which have a high fat content and which are a favourite food in the autumn, could mean that the birds are more often in a negative energy balance in winter than they were formerly. This is an interesting possibility but in Britain, at least, the decline of weeds has not had a statistically significant effect on the weights of birds in autumn (Potts, 1980b) nor, as we shall see, on mortality rates.

Winter

Temperature

There are eleven independent estimates of either the food consumption or the existence energy needed by partridges in relation to temperature. These are plotted in Fig. 8.2 (corrected where necessary to Kjoules per bird per day and to total energy needed) and give a picture of the food requirements in winter in relation to temperature; an approximate halving from −15°C to +15°C.

The energy assimilation efficiency of an adult partridge is considered high for a vegetarian bird; Reitz (1983) found 72% assimilation of mixed diets in his trials and this is assumed in calculating the energy value of food intake per bird from data on respiratory metabolism. The results are plotted in Fig. 8.2. On this basis the total food intake ranges from approximately 650 Kj per day at −15°C, to 300 Kj at +15°C.

In Finland, Pulliainen (1966) found that feeding occupied 80% of total daylight activity at −15°C and about 60% at 0°C, a decrease of 25%, in line with the data in Fig. 8.2; for example the line of Delane and Hayward (D+H in figure) predicts a decrease of 27%.

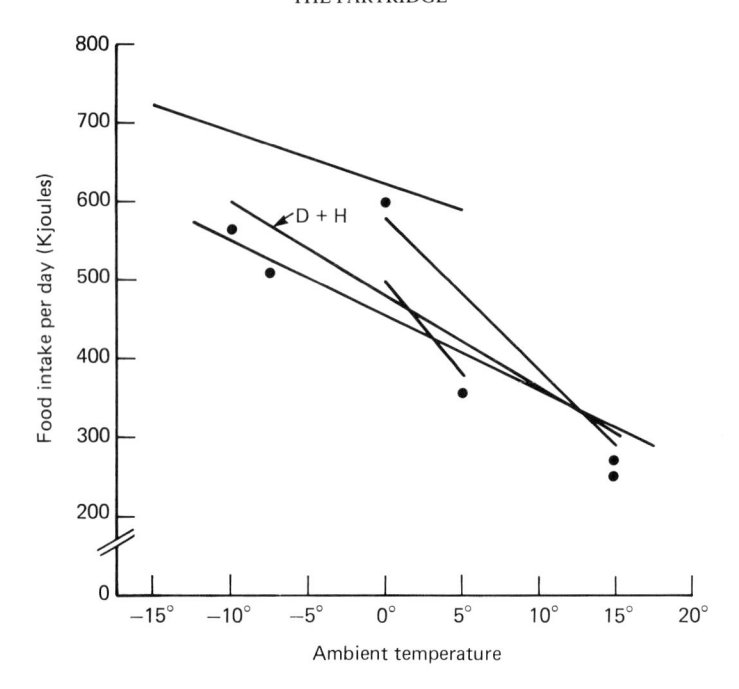

Fig. 8.2 Relationship between temperature and daily food requirement in the partridge, in eleven investigations, various diets.

Sources: Aschoff and Pohl, 1970; Beljanksi, 1960; Delane and Hayward, 1975; Gavrilov, 1980; Hawkins, 1937; Janda and Fišer, 1960; Kendeigh, 1970; Lasiewski and Dawson, 1967; Middleton and Chitty, 1937; Reitz, 1983; Westerskov, 1965, 1966.

Note: In Westerskov's study partridges were feeding in the wild, the others were in captivity. Wild partridges fly very little and the difference between wild and captive birds may not be great. However, wild birds would often be able to avoid low temperatures at night by hole roosting in snow, in turn reducing the amount of food required. At higher temperatures in spring and summer the energy costs of breeding, especially incubation and the moult, need to be considered, and, above 25°C, the cost of cooling.

Some of the main foods from which this energy can be obtained are compared in Table 8.2, which shows that food gathering will be far more efficient when partridges have access to grain. It is therefore not surprising that grain is such an important winter food in some regions. For example in North Dakota it accounts for 76% of the diet by volume (Kobriger, 1980), in Canada 69% (Westerskov, 1966) and in Washing-

Table 8.2 The value of major types of partridge foods in winter and amount needed assuming similar assimilation efficiencies (see text)

	Kj/gram dry weight	% water (field)	Grams needed daily (wet) −15°C	15°C
Wheat grains	13	17	49 (60)	22 (27)
Black bindweed seeds	19	12	34 (39)	15 (17)
Wheat/rye leaves	13	80	49 (246)	23 (116)

ton State 63% (Yocum, 1943).

Each wheat grain weighs approximately 0.05 g dry weight, each peck of wheat shoot 0.002 g dry weight (Dean, 1978). So a partridge existing at a mean temperature of −15°C, as many do in northern Alberta and in Siberia, has the alternative, so to speak, of 1000 pecks per day feeding on wheat grains or 24 500 pecks per day feeding on wheat leaves. Woodpigeons often achieve 35 000 pecks of food per day (Murton *et al.*, 1963a) so such feats are not impossible – unless snow or ice intervenes.

Snow and ice

During the winter of 1964–65 a detailed study of partridge feeding behaviour was made in Finland by Pulliainen (1966). He found that about half the potential feeding time was spent on fields of autumn-sown wheat and rye, leaves of the former being preferred. He also confirmed the findings of Suomus (1958), that about 80% of food was obtained from beneath snow.

Partridges scratch through snow looking for food to a depth of about 35 cm (10 inches) (e.g. Hawkins, 1937; Hammond, 1941), but no deeper even if the snow is soft. Naumann (1833) commented on this and, like most others since, concluded that neither cold nor snow was much of a problem for partridges but that ice-encrusted snow (known as 'nast') caused considerable mortality.

In Bulgaria it has been shown that partridges can maintain body temperature (41°C) for at least three days at −30°C even when they have not fed (Branković *et al.*, 1967). Moreover, partridges often roost in burrows in the snow, a method which enables gamebirds to produce a local ambient temperature above freezing (Marjakangas *et al.*, 1983).

Nevertheless partridges which are entirely deprived of food die in as little as five days at −18°C (Gerstell, 1942), or seven days at 10°C (Pulliainen, 1965). Incidentally, in both these studies and that of Kobriger (1980), weight loss involved metabolism of proteins and weight at death amounted to 40% of normal, the same as encountered at death in diseases such as strongylosis. It therefore seems very clear that if snow or ice prevents partridges from getting sufficient food, then mortality will be difficult to avoid.

When food is difficult to find in the fields partridges have to resort to farm buildings, especially to spillages around grain silos, corn cribs and in areas where cattle are being fed (Colour Plate XXIII) or where manure, which often contains undigested grains, is available. At one time, in the Soviet Union, the undigested grains in horse manure were an important source of food for partridges (Litun, 1980) and currently in Wisconsin, New York and eastern Canada, the slurry from cow kennels provides a food source in mid-winter (Church, 1985).

In severe winter conditions partridges in North Dakota obtained most grain from around farmsteads. A systematic aerial search in January 1979 located fifty-nine coveys in an area of 93 km^2; fifty-four were closely associated with farmsteads (Schulz, 1980); seven out of eight radio-tracked coveys concentrated their activities around farmsteads. Likewise in Finland, hay seeds are an important mid-winter food of partridges and these seeds are mostly obtained around barns. In Ostrobothnia, the area of highest partridge density, hay is kept in small wooden barns scattered across the farmland at about 50 km^{-2} (Sulkava, 1965).

For 24 February 1947, my father's diary comments 'many rabbits and birds are dying around the farm buildings, we found both the resident barn owls dead and partridges were wandering around the stackyard in poor shape'. Conditions worsened over the next three weeks, in fact it was rather reminiscent of R. D. Blackmore's *Lorna Doone*, and on 13 March several cattle were killed when a fold-yard collapsed under the weight of snow.

However, detailed meteorological records kept by my father show that these were by far the worst conditions in a forty-three year period, although at the end of January 1941 and in mid-February 1963, conditions were somewhat comparable. It is therefore interesting that in all three winters partridges did not appear to be so much affected as red grouse, which were forced down from the nearby moors to feed on hawthorn buds and even cabbages. Nevertheless, in the winter of 1947, many partridges must have died of starvation. When one estate (West Barsham) employed a snow plough to clear clover leys for the partridges, large numbers benefitted.

Migration

Formozov (1946) commented on the fact that the bearded partridge manages to survive very well in the extremely cold but relatively snowless areas of the eastern Siberian Steppes, by making extensive and regular migrations to avoid the worst conditions. Ringing has shown movements of up to 470 km (Litun, 1982). Formozov also describes annual migrations of the *robusta* sub-species from areas which regularly experience snow depth greater than 50 cm, with snow lying over a period of five months. Large numbers of partridges migrated south along the Volga with some flocks reaching as far west as Odessa (Dementiev and Gladkov, 1952). In exceptional winters some migrations were reported from the *lucida* race as far west as the Baltic coast of Poland. Naumann (1833) and later Hartert (1894) recalled seeing flocks of 200 or more, in one case 500, of these 'migratory partridges'.

In the severe winter of 1981/82, in northern New York State, Church (1985) recorded daily movements of coveys of up to 1.6 km but no migrations have been recorded in North America, with one possible exception, along the Wisconsin shore of Lake Michigan in 1951 (R. McCabe *in litt.*). Most partridges in North America originated from Hungary and Czechoslovakia, where annual migrations do not occur.

Siivonen (1956) gives some data on winter severity and subsequent population levels in south-west Finland, which explain the adaptiveness of these movements. The data have been summarised in the multiple regression equation:

$$\text{Population change} = 0.48 - 0.14x_i - 0.02x_{ii}$$

where x_i is the population level (an index) before the winter concerned, and x_{ii} is the mean depth of snow in mm from 1 November to 30 April (see Potts, 1980a, for this reworking of Siivonen's data). This equation suggests that partridges in Finland could be expected to decrease when mean snow levels, over a period of years, were greater than an average of 16 cm from November to March.

Perhaps the partridges' affinity for feeding around farm buildings led to the idea of overwintering them in barns. We do not know how many were netted for this purpose but it may not have been great; Kotes and Knobloch (1947) cite one instance of 20% of the partridge population being brought into temporary captivity during the winter of 1940–41, in Czechoslovakia. Conditions in the barns were not recorded, nor mortalities, but from what we know of the poor success rate of spring releases in Britain, the practice could only be of benefit where partridges not in barns suffered exceptionally high mortality.

Mortality

Mortality is not easily attributed to hard weather, even where sudden losses are documented. For example Knapton (1980) followed four coveys through the winter of 1974–75 on a 5.3 km² area. The rate of loss was three times higher than normal during a severe storm but the cause of death was not determined and no bodies found. Pulliainen (1965) gave data which enabled calculation of the rates of loss at an average of 0.7% per day from December to March, but in his case losses to the sparrow hawk seem to have been important, as has recently been reported for losses of the bearded partridge in winter (V. Litun *in litt.*).

In studies in northern New York State, Church (1986) has shown that more than half the winter losses were known to be attributable to predation (Table 8.3). The condition of the birds killed was not poor and in Winconsin in 1979 the winter weather was more severe but, with fewer raptors, there was very little partridge mortality (Church, 1980).

Judging from the relative abundance of raptors in the two states, particularly in late winter, and from his wide experience of partridges in North America, Church put forward the hypothesis that three conditions were necessary for a major crash in partridge numbers to occur as

Table 8.3 The importance of raptor predation on partridges in winter, in New York State (Church, 1986)

	Winter and spring Mortality rate	k_5	Percentage mortality attributable to raptors*, minimum based on known deaths, maximum assuming all unknowns due to raptors (died)
Jefferson County (range)	0.89	0.96	71 – 82% (14) (17)
Springport (potential range)	0.66	0.47	47 – 80% (20) (34)

* Primarily red-tailed hawk and great horned owl

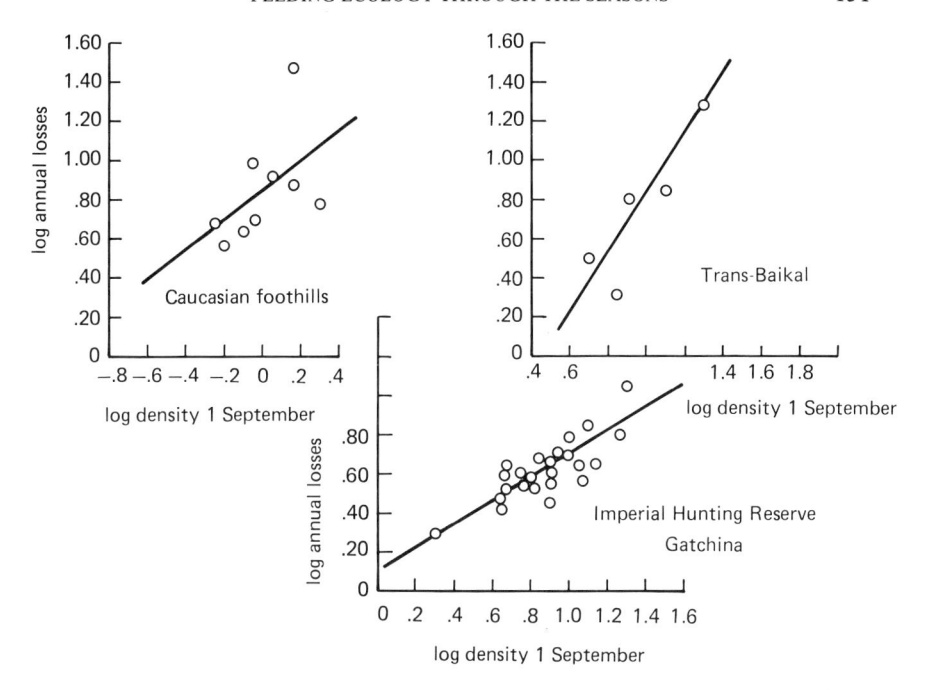

Fig. 8.3 Relationship between density of partridges on 1 September (i.e. before shooting) and adult losses in subsequent year, mostly in winter, at three sites in the Soviet Union.
Sources: Loshkarev (1976); Litun (1983b); Dits (1917).

a result of winter weather. These were (1) severe winter weather and dramatic reduction in food availability, (2) high density of raptors, and (3) a high partridge density. Certainly in other crash declines recorded elsewhere, densities were relatively high (Fig. 8.3) and this seems also to be the case in the sudden crash which occurred in parts of Sweden in the winter of 1978/79 where goshawks were the main immediate cause of death (J. Dahlgren *in litt.*).

The time available for feeding, or indeed any activity, is related to covey size. In particular, Jenkins (1961a) observed that one bird in a partridge group, the 'sentinel', was always on guard. One sentinel represents 50% of a pair, only 8% of a covey of twelve. Lone partridges will therefore be vulnerable to predation which might explain why, in summer, bereaved males quickly join coveys. More research is needed on the subject, but it also appears from Church's work that partridges become vulnerable to predation when pairing for the first time. Pairing is delayed a month or two in colder climates, but not indefinitely, and it has been established that it was snow in April rather than through winter which was the main adverse factor for partridges in Finland (Siivonen,

1956). Maybe partridges, which are always highly visible on snow (Colour Plate XXIV), are also relatively vulnerable if in pairs rather than coveys.

Estimates of annual losses of full grown birds are available for thirty-five studies (Table 10.4, later). From these data mortality (k_5) was found to increase with winter snow cover (months with snow lying = x) (Fig. 8.4).

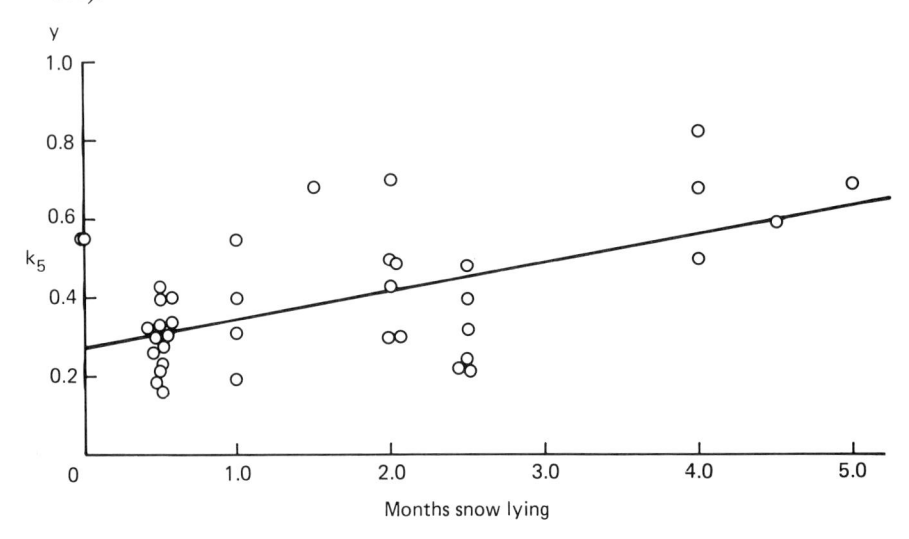

Fig. 8.4 Overwinter mortality (k_5) increases with the number of months of snow cover. The northern limit of the species coincides with five months of snow cover. (Sources as Table 10.4) $y = 0.27 + 0.07x$ ($P < 0.001$).

A high estimate for Cornwall (where snow cover = approximately 0, see Fig. 8.4) has recently been confirmed by a release of partridges which had an estimated first winter mortality of at least 90% (to unknown cause, but possibly predation by buzzards; for similar examples see Sladek, 1966). A similar group released in Northants, where there were no buzzards, had a mortality rate of 55% ($P < 0.005$). More research would be needed to establish whether buzzards were an important cause of mortality, but I have watched two healthy wild partridges killed by them, in an area where buzzards are very infrequently seen.

It is interesting to note that the northern limit of the partridge range coincides with five months of snow cover on low ground. At this point there is a winter loss rate of 0.62 (76%) (Fig. 8.4), which I calculate to be equivalent to the shooting of 38% of partridges per annum in Sussex, and a level sufficient to extinguish most partridge populations (Chapter 11).

Spring to summer

Egg quality

Lack (1947) noted that the average size of first clutches of the partridge varied (but only a little) from year to year and he suggested that variations in food supply were responsible. Siivonen (1956) thought that clutch size was reduced after a late winter but gave no evidence. The average clutch size of the partridge in Finland is, at nineteen (Pulliainen, 1971), the highest of any bird species in the world.

In Yugoslavia, Romić (1975a) further developed Siivonen's hypothesis by suggesting that laying is later and clutch size smaller as a result of poorer habitat and deteriorating food supply caused by modern agriculture. His data do show an apparent 6% reduction in hatching success (Table 8.4). But there was no significant difference in the size of eggs or the weight of the shell, albumen or yolk. Most clutches were found as a result of mowing, and it is possible that the effects Romić noted were attributable to a higher proportion of repeat layings.

Table 8.4 Hatchability of partridge eggs taken from nests in hay fields in Croatia, Yugoslavia, before and after modernisation of farming (from Romić, 1975)

	Eggs hatched	Did not hatch	Total
1933–1939	3105 (73%)	1166	4271
1955–1966	2033 (67%)	990	3023

Note: the difference is statistically significant ($P<0.001$)

In Austria, Huss (1983) has focussed on the partridge's need for proteins in order to lay good quality eggs. Most weeds and clovers contain more of these than grass and cereals (e.g. see Dutt *et al.*, 1982), but I find no reason to suspect that there is a general shortage of protein sufficient to reduce egg hatchability. Even in red grouse, which have a far inferior diet to partridges, the adverse effects of poor quality food are not easy to quantify, being dwarfed by the tax that internal parasites exert on food quality (Hudson, 1986a).

Incubation and brooding

In April, growing cereal leaves average 23% protein (this study) and probably represent a better diet than would be available on uncultivated steppes, where the partridge originated. It is notable that at this time of year partridges make no attempt to seek the high densities of insects overwintering in the hedgerows. For example the diet of two radio-marked hens was determined daily from 5 May to 5 July in southern Sweden (J. Dahlgren *in litt.*). Grass and cereal leaves dominated the diet, together with *Poa* spikelets until early June, when chickweed seed heads were also present in the diet. Insects (mainly ants) were eaten but much later in the season, whilst the chicks were being led by the parents.

Data collected at Damerham show that during the twenty-five days of incubation the hen leaves the nest only three times per day, less if the weather is wet, with each absence lasting about forty-five minutes (Fant, 1953). Assuming that partridges can feed at the same maximum rate as woodpigeons, this would be equivalent to 12000 pecks per day. Setting aside the question of the considerable extra energy cost for incubation (and possible difference in assimilation efficiency) this compares to 13500 pecks needed if the birds are existing on cereal leaves, and only 520 pecks if feeding on cereal grains. Obviously grain is not available but there will be a high premium on equivalent alternatives and on relatively high value foods such as clover leaves and weed seeds, especially chickweed. Insects are probably scarce enough in cereal crops during incubation to incur a considerable time penalty through searching. Pleshkov and Fowden (1959) reported cereal leaves as being an excellent supply of high quality proteins, including methionine, which may be one reason why we have found no evidence of poor nutrition despite finding very few insects in the diet of incubating birds.

After hatching, the time for feeding is less restricted and parents have to show insects to the chicks and to encourage chicks to eat them. Protein may have been lost during incubation (weight certainly is) and there may be a premium on insect food for hens if they are feeding partly to restore a protein balance.

It is difficult to estimate weight loss during incubation from the literature available since this has never been measured directly and the large weights of 440 grams or so, often recorded in May, could include a considerable amount of material to be used in egg production. However, a loss of at least 10% of normal weight is indicated by the data from Poland, given by Olech (1971).

Some indication of the possible reasons for adults eating insects might be obtained from a comparison of the diet of the sexes (Table 8.5).

In Kazakhstan 95% of the insects eaten by partridges were ants, with a preference for insects amongst the females. However, in North Dakota the males were eating more insects (grasshoppers), so any differences

Table 8.5a A comparison of the diet of male and female partridges in summer, Kazakhstan 1952 (Poyarkov, 1955)

	Green leaves (% volume)	Seeds/bird	Insects/bird
20 males	25	112	19
17 females	15	61	147

Table 8.5b A comparison of the diet of male and female partridges in summer, North Dakota (Kobriger, 1980)

	% with ants	% with grasshoppers	Total insects (% volume)
43 males	33	28	13
24 females	33	13	6

between the food of the sexes at this time of year are not likely to be important. Other data show clearly that insects are eaten by adults (e.g. Middleton and Chitty 1937), especially in July, but the data are insufficient to show differences between the sexes.

Partridges undergo a complete body moult (apart from the two outer primaries), normally beginning soon after the chicks hatch, and a ready supply of the feather-promoting sulphur amino acids which are found in large and readily available quantities in insects, may then be a vital component of the diet – for both sexes.

Middleton and Chitty (1937) reported that 12% (by volume) of the diet of adult partridges in summer was composed of insects. In Czechoslovakia, in the early 1950s, the percentage of insects in the diet (again by volume) increased from 1.3% in March to May, to 16% in July, the insects being mainly grasshoppers (Janda, 1959). In England insects increased from 0% to 12% in the diet (mainly ants) over the same period. If adult partridges require insects in July (for the moult) there will usually be plenty; even on modern farms there is a peak in the abundance of insects at that time.

Whatever the need for insects by the adults, it is considered to be minor; not nearly so vital for survival or production as it is for the chicks.

9 Nesting Cover and Spring Dispersal of Pairs

'... Our tests have shown that predation pressure can cast a powerful vote for scattering (of the prey) in the evolutionary compromise which determines the ultimate density of a prey species' (H. Croze, 1970)

In order to complete the investigation of mortality through the annual cycle it now remains only to deal with the annual losses of full-grown females between the end of the shooting season and the onset of nesting, i.e. for practical purposes, k_5.

The Sussex study area was divided into the five groups of farms (as before, Fig. 3.1) giving a total of seventy-seven area years in which these losses, mostly occurring in spring, were known. It should be noted that emigration, where it exceeds immigration, cannot be differentiated from mortality, which is why the term 'mortality' is not used here.

The most important result (Table 9.1) was that overall annual losses were very low, only a quarter above the mortality rate of females during the three weeks of incubation! Or to put it another way, whereas the hen mortality (k_2) over the twenty-five days of incubation amounts to 0.15 (or 1.4% per day), over the remaining 340 days, losses (k_5) amount to only 0.20 (or 0.14% per day). On a daily basis incubation is therefore ten times as hazardous as routine behaviour.

Losses over winter and spring increased with the density of females and decreased with the availability of suitable nesting cover. Thus the clearest picture emerged when density was expressed as females per linear km of permanent nesting cover km^{-2}. (Some isolated patches of good nesting cover, such as the grassy sides of marl pits or derelict dewponds, were counted as 200 m each.)

On four of the five study areas losses were significantly greater at higher female densities ($P<0.05$; and the overall relationship was significant at $P<0.01$, see Table 9.1). At a constant density of four females per km of cover km^{-2}, losses would be similar in four of the groups of farms but a little higher in the fifth, North Stoke, where the quality of some of the nesting cover was relatively poor. The analyses summarised in Table 9.1 suggest that at least a quarter of the variation in losses was related to nesting cover, using the linear value, and that overall losses were similar throughout the Sussex study area, despite differences in farm type.

Table 9.1 Sussex study 1968–1984. Loss of full-grown female partridges between shooting season and nesting, in relation to farm type and availability of nesting cover

Area	Mean annual losses (k_5)	Nesting cover per km km^{-2}	Maximum nests km km^{-2}	Losses dependent on availability of nesting cover
North Farm (excluding releases)	0.19 ± 0.03	6.2	4.9	$P<0.05$
North Farm (including releases)	0.28 ± 0.03	6.2	4.9	not sig.
South-East Corner	0.12 ± 0.05	6.9 → 6.7	4.2	$P<0.05$
Applesham	0.27 ± 0.04	4.3	3.5	$P<0.05$
North Stoke	0.14 ± 0.05	5.6 → 4.6	3.0	$P<0.05$
Lee Farm	0.18 ± 0.04	5.8	4.6	not sig.
All combined (excluding releases)	0.20 –	5.8 → 5.6	–	$P<0.01$

158   THE PARTRIDGE

The increase in losses with female density per km of nesting cover is plotted in Fig. 9.1, a relationship which indicates that the females are clearly spacing themselves out, given that in Sussex there was no known density-dependent *mortality* (i.e. as opposed to losses) of females outside the nesting season. The movement of pairs across the boundaries of our

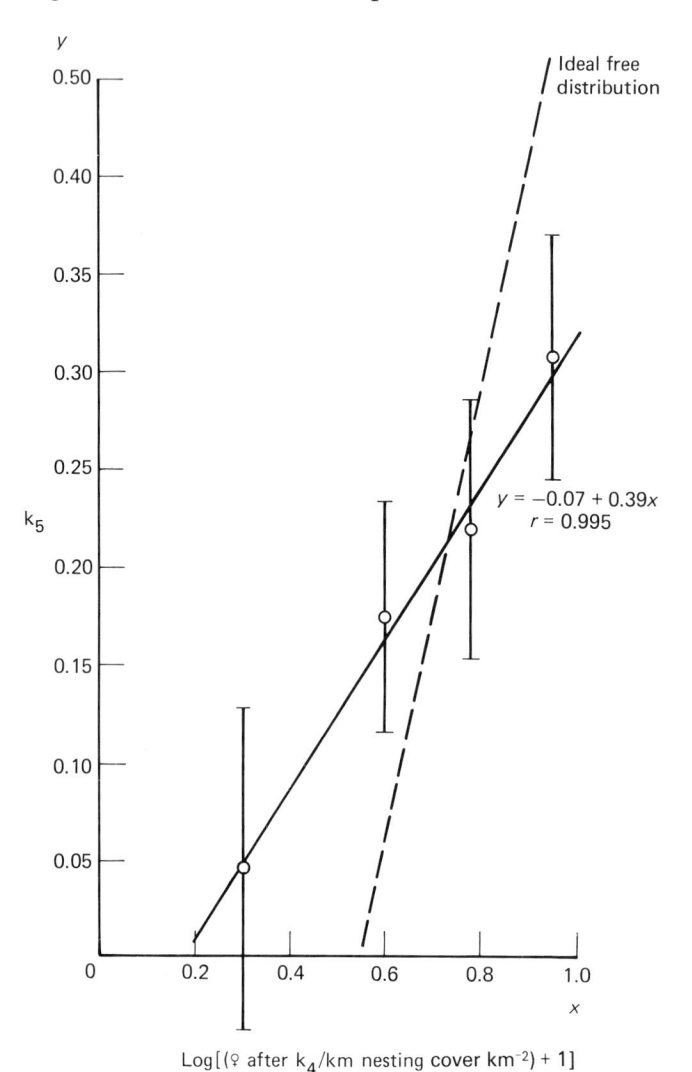

$y = -0.07 + 0.39x$
$r = 0.995$

Log[(♀ after k_4/km nesting cover km^{-2}) + 1]

Fig. 9.1 Sussex study: overwinter loss (k_5) as a function of the log density of females after shooting, per unit of hedgerows and other permanent nesting cover. The dashed line is a theoretical one, known as the *ideal free* distribution in which the birds are spacing themselves perfectly through the habitat (see text). Note log 1=0, so 1 is added to density index; ±two standard errors plotted.

five blocks of farms was obvious in spring and where densities were low at the end of the previous season, we often found an increase in the number of females.

My interpretation of these movements is that the pairs were spacing themselves out to avoid an even higher penalty than they already incur from density-dependent predation. This conclusion was reached through studies of prey but, ironically perhaps, it was experiments with carrion crows which provided an experimental basis for it (Croze, 1970). To illustrate how efficient partridges are at spacing themselves out in an area, we can employ a theoretical consideration based on the reasoning of Fretwell (1972), i.e. that individuals:

(1) select the nest sites best suited to their breeding requirements. Natural selection favours individuals with the ability to do this and if the selection pressures (i.e. nest predation) have been great enough, such favoured individuals will predominate – these Fretwell termed *ideal*.
(2) Are *free* to select nest sites on an equal basis with other partridges. Obviously many individuals are not free in this sense because nest sites may be too far away.

If both assumptions were met the distribution of females (i.e. pairs) would follow Fretwell's *ideal free* distribution represented in Fig. 9.1. If all females were able to follow this *ideal free* distribution, they would have equal opportunities for breeding and it follows that density-dependent effects could not be observed. In fact the actual distribution of females is about half-way to the *ideal free* distribution (Fig. 9.1). How do partridges do it?

The answer came from studies in Wisconsin where small, rechargeable solar-powered radio-transmitters were fitted to nine seven-month old female partridges which had not paired or nested before. Three radio fixes were taken each day and each location was plotted successively on maps. The results (Church *et al.*, 1980) showed that there are three quite distinct behaviour patterns associated with pair dispersal:

(1) Isolation

For about two weeks after the initial pairing, the females confined their movements to the general area hitherto occupied by the covey. Social interaction with other pairs was minimised and pair bonds reinforced. When severe weather occurred during this period the pairs tended to join up and the coveys reformed, though often loosely. The females in such coveys would mostly be sisters, but the young males not their brothers, since sibling pairs (pairs of sister and brother) are unknown in partridges. (The fact that it is the young males which disperse was discovered in the Damerham study, whereas in the red-legged partridge by contrast, the young males stay, leaving the young females to disperse (Green, 1983).)

(2) Exploration

Church *et al.* (1980) defined this as a non-goal orientated movement in any direction, way beyond the isolation area. In 1979 movements like this began on 1 April and lasted three to four weeks, during which time the maximum distance travelled from the winter covey range averaged 2.2 km (range 0.9–9.6 km) – much further than in Britain. At Damerham twenty-seven females nesting for the first time did so at a distance of only 0.42 ± 0.076 km from the site of capture the previous September. Although movements were greater in Wisconsin, five of nine females still nested within the outer limits of their winter range.

(3) Habitation

Exploration ceased as nest sites were selected (Colour Plate XXII) and the home range established. Selection for ranges with residual grass nesting cover was evident. This cover accounted for only 2.5% of the study area but 52% of all radio fixes of partridges were plotted in these areas before nesting, with preference for such cover increasing as nesting approached. Throughout the entire study, pairs occurred twenty-one times as frequently in residual grass nesting cover as would have been expected at random – steadily increasing from about sixteen times during *isolation* to thirty-two times during habitation.

Nest site quality

In Britain partridges begin to choose their sites quite early in the season; a number of scrapes can usually be found before the end of March. The first egg is laid a few weeks later and at North Farm the median onset of laying was 30 April for first clutches in the years 1964–1970. The eggs are laid in an unlined bowl scratched from friable soil up to 10 cm deep (Krüger, 1961). Thus nests are liable to flooding in heavy rain and it has been known for many years that partridges prefer well-drained areas, a fact recognised by Yeatter (1932) and demonstrated in Hungary by Szederjei and Szederjei (1960). We saw the extent to which flooding can reduce nesting success in the Sussex study in 1981.

Much interest has been shown in the value of differing qualities of nest site and the availability of nesting cover to partridges.

'Hedges are by far the commonest choice, and it is very hard to tell why some particular hedges are so very popular. Thus, I know a hedge, perhaps 200 yards long, which year after year holds eight or nine nests; and another close by, in much the same condition, which rarely holds more than one. Speaking generally, I think they like hedges that are not too high, as these latter often get thin at the bottom; on the other hand, they dislike too thick a bottom; possibly it holds the wet too much, or, possibly, they cannot see enough of their surroundings when on the nest' (Ogilvie, 1902).

A modern study of nest site selection has been made by Rands (1982) who selected the most complete sets of data arising from the 1961 to 1978 National Game Census and August Count Scheme records of seventeen estates scattered from Tayside to Hampshire, but mostly in the eastern counties. The Sussex study area was included and in each area the nesting cover was quantified as follows:

(1) Length of nesting habitat (permanent field boundary) per km^2.
(2) Width of permanent field boundary (metres).
(3) Height of permanent field boundary (metres).
(4) Height of bank at base of permanent field boundary (metres).
(5) Amount of dead grass in the field boundary ground vegetation (%).
(6) Amount of nettle in the field boundary ground vegetation (%).
(7) Amount of bramble in the field boundary ground vegetation (%).
(8) Visibility through the field boundary ground vegetation (%).
(9) Amount of cover provided by the field boundary ground vegetation (%).
(10) Number of trees per km of permanent field boundary.
(11) Number of gaps per km of permanent field boundary.
(12) Proportion of total boundary length with a ditch (%).
(13) Proportion of total boundary length with a fence (%).

The next step was, by multiple regression and principal component analysis, to select those features of the quantity and quality of nesting cover which were most important in determining the recruitment efficiency of each partridge population, defined as: 'The density of yearlings entering the breeding population, for a given existing density of adults and yearlings' (Rands, 1982). It was an attempt to measure how many of the previous year's offspring an estate could retain – a measure of the attractiveness of the area to potential breeding birds, independent of the existing density of partridges.

In this case linear cover included fences and other permanent field boundaries with no grass cover at the base, which were excluded from the measure of cover used in the Sussex analyses. Nevertheless, the variable availability of linear cover explained most of the differences in recruitment between estates (see Fig. 9.2).

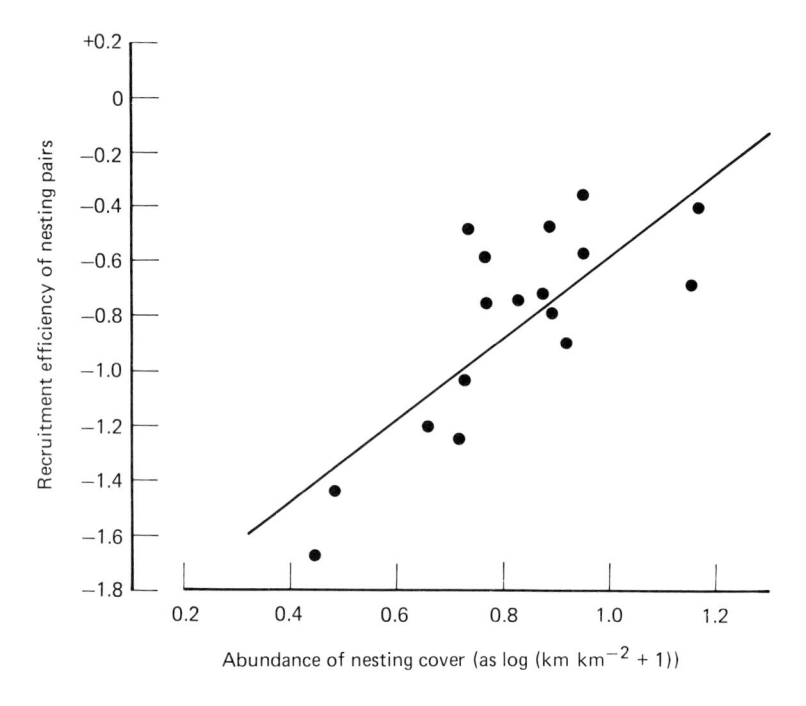

Fig. 9.2 The relationship between partridge recruitment efficiency (see text) and the abundance of nesting cover on seventeen estates studied by Rands (1982). (National Game Census data, adapted from Rands, 1982.)

After allowing for the quantity of nesting cover (log length of hedgerow (or equivalent) km^{-2}) which explains 51% of the variation in recruitment efficiency in the seventeen estates, only two quality variables were statistically significant:

XVII. Former partridge habitat near Uppsala, Sweden (*G.R. Potts*).

XVIII. Former partridge habitat near Florence, Tuscany, Italy (*G.R. Potts*).

XIX. Poor partridge range in autumn, Palouse Prairie, Washington State, USA (*Steve Peterson*).

XX. Czempiń, Poland, October 1975. Zygmunt Pielowski describes removal of nesting cover (*G.R. Potts*).

XXI. Grassy nesting cover becoming shaded out by untrimmed hedge, Damerham, Fordingbridge (*G.R. Potts*).

XXII. Hessen, F.R.G., pair prospecting for nest site (*Rolf Helfrich*).

XXIII. Mixed farm, good partridge range in winter, Craggs Lane Farm, North Yorkshire (*G.R. Potts*).

XXIV. Good feeding conditions, Norfolk, deep snow can prevent feeding altogether (*Chris Knights*).

$$\text{Recruitment efficiency} = -1.187 + 0.476x_i + 0.283x_{ii}$$

where x_i and x_{ii} are the standardised regression coefficients for percentage of dead grass and bank height. On their own these two variables explained 35% of variation in recruitment efficiency. These analyses were essentially between estates and between years, so checks were made to ensure that the conclusions held within estates and within years, which they do (Rands, 1986b). Similarly in Norfolk the spring dispersal of young red-legged partridges was greater where hedgerows were less frequent (Green, 1983).

In a separate approach Rands (1982) analysed site characteristics of partridge nests found in north Norfolk and in Wiltshire. He compared

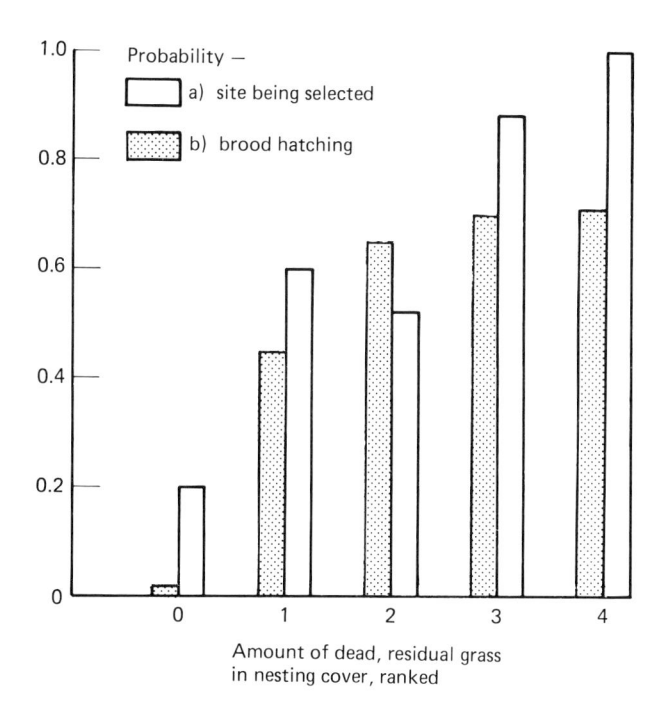

Fig. 9.3 The effect of dead (residual) grass on the probability of a random site being selected for nesting by the partridge, and on the probability of a clutch avoiding predation. *Note:* Most potential broods are lost due to predation. Source 42 nests, Rands 1982.

the characteristics of the nest site to those of sites chosen at random and in this way confirmed the importance of residual grass (Colour Plate XXI; see Fig. 9.3) and bank height. Finally he looked at nest predation and confirmed that it was lower where there was more residual grass available (Fig. 9.3). This was the first demonstration of the value of long grass as nesting cover, although it was given top priority in a list of recommendations for partridge management almost a century earlier:

'The first thing is to give the birds suitable ground for nesting. To this end do not allow the tenant farmers to plough within two yards of a hedge on either side. You will then have strips of high coarse grass along the hedges for the birds to nest in – a cover they are very fond of for the purpose and which also conceals their nests from winged marauders as well as from ground vermin.' (Payne-Gallwey, 1892).

The value of residual grass as nesting cover has always been much emphasised in North America; Yeatter (1932) pleaded with farmers not to burn it during the springtime 'clean up'. Since then other studies emphasising the importance of this grass have included McCabe and Hawkins, 1946; Blank *et al.*, 1967; Gates, 1973; Hunt, 1974; Weigand, 1977a; Church, 1980; Hupp *et al.*, 1980; McCrow, 1982; and Döring and Helfrich, 1986.

Most nests (perhaps nearly all first nesting attempts) are to be found in the non-crop habitat. Few studies included searches for nests in both the crop and non-crop cover alike but where this has been done the selection for permanent cover is clearly evident (e.g. see Table 9.2).

Despite the necessity of permanent nesting cover the partridge is a bird of open landscapes, with little cover overall:

'Fond of rambling into waste or pasture grounds, which are covered with long grass, gorse or broom; but it does not often enter woods, and never perches on trees.' (Macgillivray, 1837).

Even earlier, Gilbert White (1756) pointed out an aversion to trees and hedges; the way in which partridges roost in the larger fields or in the middle of small ones 'to avoid polecats and other vermin'.

Rands detected an intolerance to trees in the form of lower recruitment than might be expected where there were more than ten trees per km of linear cover. Though there were not enough data available to establish this aversion as a significant factor, it certainly corresponds with the preference shown by the partridge for open country. Presumably this is an adaptation to avoid goshawks and other predatory birds; certainly most partridges killed by goshawks are within

Table 9.2 Distribution of partridge nests on farmland according to availability of habitat, Hungary 1950–1954 (Szederjei et al., 1959)

	% of total nests	% of total farmland
Hedges, grass strips	68	1
Forage legumes	12	17
Cereals	15	57
Other crops	5	25

Note: selection for sites in hedges etc. and aversion to nesting in cereals and 'other crops' is clear ($P<0.001$), using Neu et al. (1974)

about 70 m of trees (Döring and Helfrich, 1986). Some partridge biologists refer to trees as raptor perches!

On rare occasions nests are built near trees and a photograph of a pair emerging with chicks from a nest inside the fork at the base of a large tree is given by Lynn-Allen and Robertson (1956).

In Germany, a farmer once took me around an old derelict house. The wooden floors were bare but in each room, up and down, there was a partridge hen incubating on a magnificent nest, carefully made from hay that the farmer had provided. There were nine pairs in all, each hen quietly incubating, with a view of nothing but old wallpaper.

Although hedgerows and similar nesting cover are important in mediating the dispersal of pairs prior to nesting, the amount of nesting cover does not often limit the density of nesting populations. The availability of nesting cover did not explain a significant amount of the variation in breeding density between estates with predation control (Rands, 1986b). Game conservation was taken seriously on all study areas and not one of the estates had drastically reduced the available nesting cover.

Breeding densities in Britain are now highest in the arable areas of the eastern counties, on the southern chalk downlands and on Salisbury Plain, all areas with large fields and few hedgerows (Colour Plate VIII). In these areas, grassy nesting cover with odd bushes along fences seems sufficient for the resident birds, so is the shrubby cover of a planted hedge (Plate XII) necessary? Are hedges important?

In most of central and eastern Europe and in the Northern Plains, hedgerows are scarce (Colour Plate X). In such areas fencerows and the strips of residual grass on baulks (Colour Plate XX), which are used to separate the cultivated areas of different farmers, often assumed great importance in attracting and holding pairs in spring (Colour Plate

Plate XII. Hedge in Eastern Counties of England showing grass bank at base, providing vital nesting cover for partridges but with some trees, which tend to be avoided. Courtyard Farm. (*C. L. Coles.*)

XXII). This is true even where pairs prefer to nest in the crop edge rather than in the residual grass (Döring and Helfrich, 1986). In areas of Poland where rye is grown (the first crop to grow in spring), or in central France where winter barley growth is very early, pairs may nest in the crop even though they were originally attracted to the nesting vicinity by residual grass in the field boundary. This explains the apparent paradox that the removal of permanent nesting cover reduces pair numbers although many pairs eventually succeed by nesting in crops (Birkan, 1977c; Döring and Helfrich, 1986).

In the crop the nest is at risk from mowing and, being on the flat, from flooding. However, nests in the cereal crop are safer from predators, as has been shown by studies of the pheasant; most pairs eventually succeed in hatching their young by making repeat nests in the crop rather than in the hedge (Hill and Ridley, in prep.). In the partridge, renesting attempts often take place in the crop (Porter, 1955; Jenkins, 1956; Blank and Ash, 1962; Hunt, 1974) but annual nesting success is highly dependent on the success of the first nesting attempts. Moreover, if first nests are not in the crop boundaries then they are mostly within

5 m of the edge of the crop (McCabe and Hawkins, 1946; Sekera, 1959; Szederjei *et al.*, 1959; Petrov, 1963). Any increase in field size will therefore, at least initially, increase the density of pairs in the possible nesting area, and (because it is density-dependent) increase nest predation.

Hedge removal

We do not know when the enclosures and hedge planting schemes actually began – in fact rather too much is made of this as a distinct movement; in the west of Britain many areas have been enclosed for centuries. One attempt at enclosure was made as early as 1236, but the bulk of hedge planting took place as the Industrial Revolution developed in the eighteenth and nineteenth centuries (Pollard *et al.*, 1974). We can begin to see why some earlier attempts failed in an intriguing passage from the famous chronicler Holinshed, in 1521:

'The King (Henry VIII), having regard to the commonwealth of this realm, considered how, for the space of fifty years past and more, the gentlemen of England, being given to grazing of cattle and sheep, had invented a mean how to increase their yearly revenues, and studying how to increase their pastures more than to maintain tillage, began to decay husband tacks and tenements, and to convert arable ground into pasture, furnishing the same with beasts and sheep, so inclosing the field with hedges, ditches and pales, ingrossing wools and selling the same, and also sheep and beasts at their own prices. Hereof a threefold evil chanced to the commonwealth: one, that thereby the number of husbandmen were sore diminished; another, that many towns and villages were left desolate and became ruinous; the third, that both wool, and cloth made thereof, and the flesh of all manner of beasts was sold at far higher prices than was accustomed. So commandment was given that the decayed houses should be built up again, that enclosed grounds should be laid open, and sore punishment against them that disobeyed.' (Baker, 1911)

Before the Napoleonic Wars most of the arable areas of Europe were therefore farmed on the open field system. The vast majority of the farmers lived in villages surrounded by many small, hedged plots and pastures which led out to three or four very large open cultivated fields. At Laxton, in Nottinghamshire, there were four large fields which averaged 132 ha (Orwin and Orwin, 1967). Meadows and woods were situated in the areas between the large fields of adjoining villages. The landscape was varied and it is quite misleading to equate, as some have, the large fields of the open field system with those created recently by hedge removal. To begin with, drainage on the non-free-draining soils was achieved by the ridge and furrow system, whilst on the free-draining soils, land was divided into hundreds of strips separated by paths and narrow grass ridges or baulks.

Although each open field was of the same crop type, successively fallow, winter cereals, and spring cereals, there would be a high diversity of crops if only because the adjoining strips would be farmed by different villagers. The arable strips at Laxton averaged only 10 m in width and 300 m in length; or a third of a hectare in size. The total permanent boundary length would have exceeded 100 km km^{-2}, though only about 4% of this could be classified as a proper hedge. It is true that many of the strip boundaries and grass headlands would be grazed after harvest and otherwise made unsuitable for nesting partridges, but the overall impression gained is one of a habitat well suited to the bird. It seems inconceivable that the partridge would have been short of nesting cover. The highest densities of partridges in mainland Europe today are found in those parts of central and south-east Poland where the strip system still survives, with average field sizes as low as 1 ha (Dudzinski, 1986).

Britain

The average field size over the whole of Britain was only 2 ha in 1947 (Pollard *et al.*, 1967), though much higher in the drier arable areas of the east where most partridges were found: 4 ha (now, 1985, 6 ha) in the North Riding of Yorkshire (*pers. obs.*) to a maximum of 10 ha in the later enclosed areas such as those in north-west Norfolk (Baird and Tarrant, 1973). Incidentally, this area was then, as now, the best area for partridge habitat in Britain. On the whole, fields are now undoubtedly larger, but sound data on this is difficult to find and not least is the problem that many small fields remain amongst the enlarged fields, distorting the average (Potts and Vickerman, 1974). Also, in the Sussex study area, even the large scale (1:10 000) Ordnance Survey maps did not give enough detail in order to judge the amount of nesting cover, so there are definite problems in calculating changes from maps. Old (1947) aerial photographs were also difficult to interpret.

However, samples in the arable farming districts which gave a field size of 6.5 ha in 1945, gave 11.0 ha in 1972 (Westmacott and Worthington, 1981) and the accumulated nesting cover removal over the period 1945 to 1985 must approach 50% (extrapolating from Potts, 1980a). The areas studied by Rands (Rands, 1982) had a similar size of field (15 ha) to those in the Sussex study area (16 ha), both above the average size of fields in the main partridge areas of eastern Britain. The central part of the Damerham study area now has fields of 20 ha; certainly well above the average even in the cereal growing areas of Britain. Areas covered recently by the British Trust for Ornithology Common Bird Census contained approximately 10 km of hedge km^{-2} (O'Connor, 1985), suggesting very small field size (about 5 ha).

Western Europe: Mainland

Western Europe is farmed on a smaller scale than Britain, indeed the average size of farms (of over 1 ha) in the EEC in 1984 was the same as the average size of *field* in the Sussex study area.

Most of central Europe was not involved in the enclosure movement; most farmers still lived in villages and much of the countryside in France, southern Germany and Austria still has much of the appearance of the open field system. The open fields were then divided into strips and small fields (until in many cases they were ridiculously small) according to the law enshrined in the *Code Napoléon*, which required farmers to share their land on death amongst all sons rather than to leave it solely to the eldest. In some areas fossilised landscapes occur with small fields, for example in south-east and central Poland (Dudzinski, 1986) and in parts of the upper Rhineland (Thieme, 1985). In most areas land consolidation schemes have enabled rationalisation of the field boundaries so that farmers could take advantage of modern technology and mechanisation.

In Germany, Frank (1970) reported fields averaging 1 to 1.5 ha and even in one of the major cereal growing areas (the Wetterau plain of Hessen) a sample of 390 fields averaged only 3.4 ha in 1978 (Döring, 1982; R. Schulz *in litt.*). The removal of many grass strips and baulks caused a great reduction of partridges in one part of Austria (Reicholf, 1973), but not in all (Petrjanos, *in press*). In Germany some similar schemes have not had notable effects on partridges, at least on breeding stock density (Dornberger, 1983; Mayer, 1983).

In France, partridge bags declined considerably in one of the major cereal growing areas, the South Gatinais, yet fields remained quite small (7 ha) (Gindre and Allion, 1971). In another cereal growing region where consolidation had proceeded for a number of years, fields averaged 16.0 ha in the early 1970s (Aubineau *et al.*, 1974) and in this case the provision of extra nesting cover increased breeding stocks compared to a 'control' area (Aubineau *et al.*, 1974). However, subsequently there was a big reduction in partridge density on both areas. More recently field sizes ranging from 7 to 12 ha were reported in Seine-et-Marne (Birkan, 1985), though still only a little over 3 ha at Witry-les-Reims (Pépin, 1981).

In a study area in Denmark fields increased from about 4 ha to 9 ha, the change taking place mostly in the mid-1970s (Møller, 1983). In Sweden a study area which contained 400 fields in 1947 contained 250 in 1967, and 130 in 1978 (Ishe, 1986). Land consolidation schemes began in the Netherlands in 1924 and peaked in 1976, at which time they were enacted at an annual rate seventeen times that which took place in 1924–1960 (Harms *et al.*, 1984).

Overall, a reasonable conclusion seems to be that despite the changes, fields are much smaller in Europe than in Britain but the nesting cover between them is poorer, due to the scarcity of hedges (Colour Plates IX and X). In the consolidated areas the amount of permanent nesting cover might approximate that in the Sussex study area; in the non-consolidated areas it is certainly better. There is no clear evidence of general adverse effects on partridge densities.

Eastern Europe

In eastern Europe the situation is radically different, though it too began with the same open field and strip system (Stys, 1957; Emmons, 1968). Indeed the medieval strip system with enforced rotation was in operation in most of the Soviet Union until well after the 1917 Revolution. As late as 1928, 74% of grain was still sown by hand, 44% cut with sickles and 41% threshed by flail and winnowing (Jasny, 1949), techniques phased out in Britain in the late nineteenth century.

The main drive towards collectivisation and mechanisation began in 1929, being virtually complete by 1938 (Jasny, 1949), and spreading to the adjoining countries in the early 1950s. Some strips remain as private plots but now most of the countryside consists mainly of large fields and as early as 1952 a mean field size of over 100 ha was reported from a study area in the Soviet Union (Poyarkov, 1955). Comparable studies in Hungary at that time reported fields of only 2 ha (Szederjei *et al.*, 1959).

In Hungary fields now range up to 300 ha though many are smaller, 50–100 ha (*Pers. obs.*), and with much smaller (still privately owned) plots around many villages. The area with the largest average field size is to be found in the more recently cultivated land east of the Volga and in Kazakhstan where analysis of satellite (Landsat) photographs shows typical wheat fields of 400 ha (1000 acres). However, in much of the country between the Volga and Moscow, the fields are smaller and broken by streams or sparsely wooded ravines, and so far as I could judge from the air, nesting cover will be better distributed than the size of the very large fields might otherwise imply. Nevertheless even from my own observations it is clear that in much of the Soviet Union, Czechoslovakia, Hungary, and north-east Yugoslavia, the amount of partridge nesting cover on farmland is much less than that found in the rest of Europe. Görner and Wegener (1978) reported increases in field size in East Germany, which show that this country too belongs to the above group, so far as nesting cover is concerned.

North America

The North American Prairies were mostly settled by planned square-mile sections, with most farms being a half-section or 130 ha with main fields of about 16 ha. Fields averaged 10 ha in the partridge range in Washington in 1940 (Yocum 1943); smaller in mixed farming areas such as Wisconsin. Fields were larger in the range states but were not comparable with modern eastern Europe; in the 1970s fields averaged 30 ha in a Montana study area (Weigand, 1977a). In the best partridge range in North Dakota, fields averaged 20 ha (Schulz, 1980); more marginal range in Iowa averaged about 24 ha in the late 1970s (McCrow, 1982). (In the least hedged parts of the Sussex study area, fields now average 24 ha.)

The rate of disappearance of partridge nesting cover in North America is difficult to judge, but it was perhaps first clearly evident (Colour Plate XIX) after the so-called 'great grain robbery' of 1972–73 and subsequent high prices (Trager, 1974). Perhaps the best data concern Colton's plot (10 km^2) in East Washington State. There, fence line lengths declined by 37% between 1940 and 1954 (Swanson and Yocum, 1958) but the total length of fence, hedge and banks with permanent cover declined by only 32% between 1947 and 1977 (Zeigler, 1978), and in 1980 there was still almost 5 km of nesting cover per km^2, higher than in one of the best hedged areas of North America (Conquest, Saskatchewan: Hunt, 1974). However, very many fencerows were removed in the early 1980s and Church et al. (1980) calculated a loss of nesting cover of 7.5% per annum during his study in Wisconsin. In Michigan there has been no decline in nesting cover in many of the old partridge areas, in fact the problem there, as in much of the eastern USA, seems to be that the partridge range has reverted to woodland, a situation similar to that which occurred in New York State (Murtha, 1967) and in parts of Scandinavia.

Field size

The relationship between field size and length of nesting cover per km² is given in Fig. 9.4. Approximate estimates derived from this relationship and from the text above for partridge range give mean field boundary lengths (only a proportion of which will be suitable nesting cover) as follows: in western Europe 7.5 km km^{-2}, regions with fully collectivised agricultures 2 km km^{-2}; and North America 6 km km^{-2}. The collectivised agricultures are clearly in a class of their own.

The main point to emphasise is that nesting partridges are so demanding of nesting cover because it is linear and because the pairs choose to space themselves out through it. In the Sussex study maximum nesting densities were reached at one nest per 200 m of nesting cover (Table 9.1), the same as the highest density of nests ever recorded, 70 km^{-2} at Great Witchingham in 1912. In some hedges nests are much closer than this (e.g. see Fig. 4.5) but on average one nest per 200 m of hedgerow seems to represent 'saturation'. Given one nest per 200 m of field border, the maximum settling of pairs would be reached

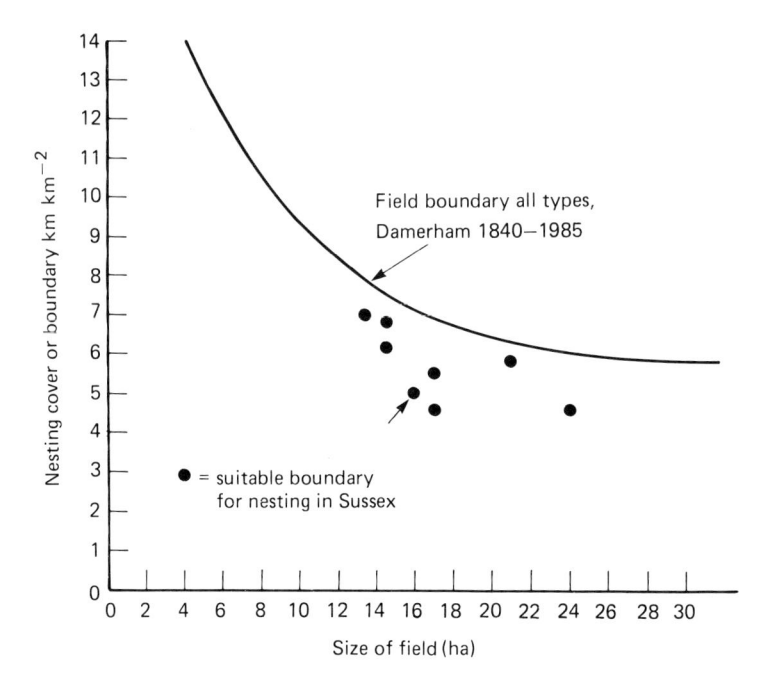

Fig. 9.4 Relationship between size of field and amount of nesting cover. Damerham, from Page (1985), Sussex, and, arrowed, Manydown.

with fields of 200 m × 200 m or 4 ha, equivalent to about 11 km of nesting cover km^{-2} (c.f. Fig. 9.4). However this would presume a very open landscape with few trees.

It would not need many trees around a 4 ha field to create a wooded landscape of the kind that partridges avoid. As we saw earlier partridges prefer less than ten trees per km of field boundary and the current average in Britain (even after the losses attributable to Dutch elm disease) is fifteen (Crowther, in press).

Dispersal to avoid inbreeding?

The previous section emphasised that density-dependent dispersal would space out nests, and thus prevent even more density-dependent predation than already occurs. But could it be that there are other advantages?

Most early authorities on partridges stress the need 'to change the blood' of partridges by swapping eggs from one nest to another, from one estate to another, or even by importing eggs or birds from central Europe. It is difficult to understand how these ideas originated, as Portal and Collinge (1932) state, 'It is hard to believe that inbreeding could occur to such an extent as to be detrimental'.

So far as I am aware, there is as yet no clear evidence that the density-dependent breeding dispersal of wild birds, as opposed to the differential movement of the sexes, is linked to the need to avoid inbreeding. Greenwood et al. (1978) suggested that this was the case in the great tit but it is a point which has been disputed (Shields, 1983). Recently the dispersal of young female red-legged partridges has been considered an adaptation to prevent inbreeding (Ricci, 1985) but if so this does not explain the *density-dependence* of the dispersal.

The most extreme example of inbreeding amongst gamebirds is perhaps the case of a group of brown-eared pheasants, a male and two females, which were collected in China in 1864 and which are the only ancestors of the entire population (about 600) of this species now in the West. Some of the birds have lost the ability to mate and fertility in these can now only be maintained by artificial insemination, but the majority are unaffected (Wise and Fuller, 1978, extended *in litt.*).

Inbreeding can be measured by the 'inbreeding coefficient', a term introduced in 1921, which is the probability that alleles (various forms of the gene) at the same locus (position on the chromosome) are identical in different individuals. With a maximum rate of inbreeding, i.e. brother/sister matings, the coefficient rises to about 0.75 after approximately five generations, and increases at each generation thereafter. The comparable figure for full cousins is 0.20 after five generations and it would not rise much above this level. Genetic traits with the lowest heritabilities are those most depressed by inbreeding: fertility and hatchability in the case of gamebirds (Abplanalp, 1974; Woodard *et al.*, 1982).

In wild partridges extreme forms of inbreeding have not been reported, in fact the separate dispersal of the sexes during covey break-up probably prevents it entirely. Not one of the 570 young birds back-tabbed in the Damerham study mated with a sibling. Full cousin matings occurred, but even if all matings were at this level for ten generations, the inbreeding depression would only amount to about a quarter drop in fertility, judging from the work of Abplanalp (loc. cit.) with chukars. In fact, as we have seen, fertility is very high in the partridge and usually around 90% of the eggs hatch in wild incubated nests. Shields (1983) has shown that a tendency towards some inbreeding is normal in birds; one large constraint to too much dispersal is that there must be a strong selective advantage in staying at or near the birthplace, because that place at least was once quite safe.

Inbreeding does not therefore seem a great threat to partridges; in any case it is prevented by the way in which the pairs are formed. The subsequent dispersal has nothing to do with avoidance of inbreeding since it occurs after pairing.

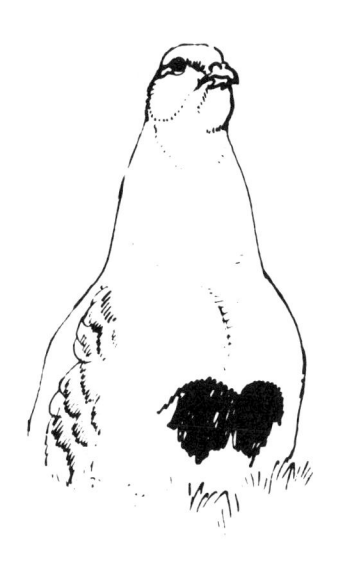

10 The Causes of the Decline in Partridge Populations

Up to this point in the study we have been dealing with the various stages of the breeding cycle separately. Now we shall consider all the factors such as nest predation, starvation amongst chicks, shortage of nesting cover and shooting rates together, and find out which matter to partridge conservation and which do not. The separate effects of these factors are difficult to assess and I know of only one way of using the mortality data presented so far to explore the reasons for fluctuations in partridge populations – simulation modelling on a computer. The methods are a little complex, but fortunately the outcome is rather clear.

The Sussex model

Structure and basis

This model essentially deals with the inter-relationship between chick mortality rates on the one hand, and population size and all the important variables dealt with in earlier chapters, on the other. The basic approach is to begin year 1 with a density of pairs km^{-2} (notional

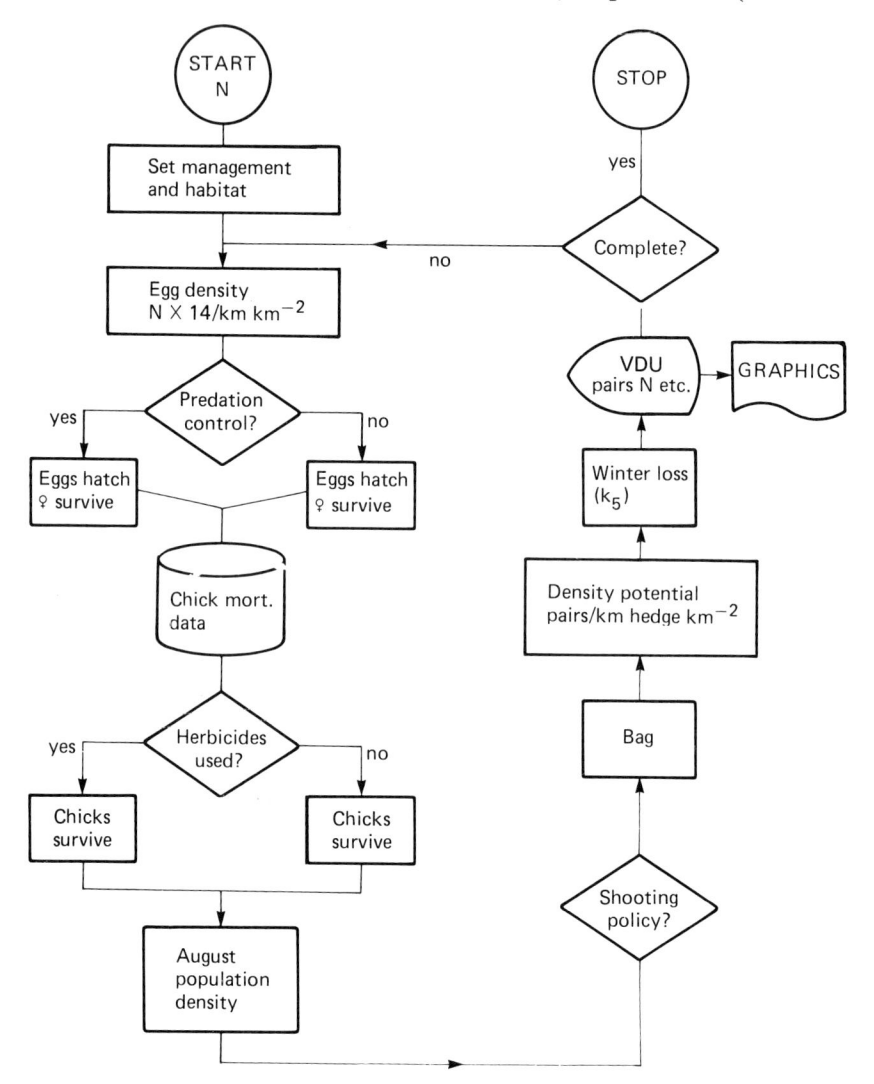

Fig. 10.1 Computer simulation model of the Sussex partridge population illustrating sequence of steps and options.

if necessary) and to estimate successively the number of eggs they lay and hatch, and the number of young surviving. The number of young are added to the old which survive nesting, and the shooting and winter losses then subtracted to give the pair density in year 2, whereupon the first computation cycle is complete. The flow diagram (Fig. 10.1) is given together with a full 'microsoft' BASIC listing (Box 10.1).

Box 10.1 COMPUTER PROGRAM FOR THE SUSSEX MODEL

```
10 REM ******************************************************************
20 REM *    COMPUTER SIMULATION OF THE SUSSEX PARTRIDGE POPULATION      *
30 REM *    Written in "MICROSOFT" BASIC.                               *
40 REM ******************************************************************
50 REM ********* SET UP THE RUN
60           INPUT "Number of partridge pairs /Km2 in spring.. ",PAIRS
70           INPUT "Kilometres of hedgerow /Km2................ ",HEDGE
80           INPUT "Were herbicides used on cereal crops.(Y/N) ",HERB$
90           INPUT "Were predators controlled............(Y/N) ",PRED$
100          INPUT "What shooting pressure..........(1,2,or 3) ",SHOOT
110 REM ******** CHICK MORTALITY DATA FROM 1957-1984
120 DATA .31,.59,.28,.28,.39,.55,.59,.47,.59,.46,.43,.66,.58,.42,.54,.77
130 DATA .54,.55,.61,.39,.89,.97,.67,.5,.91,.41,.5,.48,.59
140 REM ******** MODEL STARTS HERE
150      FOR YEAR = 1957 TO 1984
160          EGGS=(PAIRS*14)/HEDGE
170          LEGGS=LOG(EGGS)/2.303
180          IF PRED$ = "N" GOTO 220
190              K1 = 0.028 + (0.11*LEGGS)
200              K2 = 0.59*K1
210          GOTO 250
220              K1 = -0.217+0.578*LEGGS
230                  IF K1 < 0.2 THEN K1 = 0.2
240              K2 = 0.31*K1
250          READ CHIKMORT
260          IF HERB$ = "N" THEN CHIKMORT = CHIKMORT*0.53
270          K1SURVIV = 10^(-K1)
280          K2SURVIV = 10^(-K2)
290          CHSURVIV = 10^(-CHIKMORT)
300          YOUNG = PAIRS*14*K1SURVIV*CHSURVIV
310          FEMALES = PAIRS*K2SURVIV
320          AUGPOP = PAIRS+YOUNG+FEMALES
330          ON SHOOT GOTO 340,350,360
340              S2 = 0 : GOTO 370
350              S2 = 0.35/(1+2.178^(5.47-0.04*AUGPOP)) :GOTO 370
360              S2 = 0.35/(1+2.178^(5.47-0.023*(AUGPOP+150)))
370          S2SURVIV = 10^(-S2)
380          BAG1 = 1.43*(1-S2SURVIV)*PAIRS
390          BAG2 = 0.91*(1-S2SURVIV)*FEMALES
400          BAG3 = 0.87*(1-S2SURVIV)*YOUNG
410          BAG = BAG1+BAG2+BAG3
420                  LPRINT USING "£££££";YEAR;PAIRS*2;AUGPOP;BAG
430          OFEMALE = FEMALES-BAG2
440          YFEMALE = (YOUNG-BAG3)/2
450          FEMALES = OFEMALE+YFEMALE
460          LFEM = LOG((FEMALES/HEDGE)+1)/2.303
470          K5 = -0.07+(0.39*LFEM)
480          IF K5 < 0.11 THEN K5 = 0.11
490          K5SURVIV = 10^(-K5)
500          PAIRS = K5SURVIV*FEMALES
510      NEXT YEAR
520 END
```

(1) Chick mortality rate

The observed mortality rates for the Sussex study area from 1957 to 1985 inclusive were computer read in from a file – the data of Fig. 6.9. These observed data were designated the 'herbicides used' option. For the 'herbicides not used' option, the data of Table 6.7 were used to adjust the Sussex chick mortality rates (M) down with the equation:

$$M^1 = 0.53 \times M \qquad (r^2 = 0.85, P<0.05)$$

Over the period 1968–1985 this gives an adjusted chick mortality rate of 52% ($k_3 = 0.32$) with a standard deviation of ±10%. This seems very reasonable given that the longest pre-herbicide data set, Great Witchingham 1903–1932 inclusive, gave 58% ($k_3 = 0.38$) with a standard deviation of ±16%; moreover, that all pre-herbicide mortality rates combined (Table 6.11) gave a chick mortality rate of 53% ($k_3 = 0.33$) for Britain; and 47% ($k_3 = 0.27$) for other countries.

(2) Chicks hatching per brood

The number hatched per successful nest (c) varied very little between years and estates (i.e. in twenty-seven samples from 12.6 ± 0.5 to 14.6 ± 0.3, the mean was 13.84 (Table 3.3)), and 14 is used in the model.

(3) Effective density of pairs at nesting and of potential pairs before spring dispersal

Here partridge numbers km^{-2} were divided by the length of nesting cover such as a hedge, or equivalent, km^{-2} (as discussed in Chapter 9). Small patches of suitable cover (more than 100 m from other cover) were considered equivalent to 200 m of linear cover. Density was $\log_{10}(n + 1)$ transformed.

(4) Nesting mortality ($k_1 + k_2$)

A choice was introduced here, reflecting that made in the data analysed in Fig. 4.2. (note that k_1 and k_2 added are designated K1 in the BASIC listing of the computer program):

(i) Predation controlled

$$K1 = 0.03 + 0.11 \times \log[(C \times \text{pairs}) \div \text{length of cover}]$$

The slope of the regression coefficient was reduced from 0.15 (as

Fig. 4.2) to 0.11, with the incorporation of pre-1968 data (Table 4.5, row 1).

(ii) Predation not controlled

$$K1 = -0.22 + 0.58 \times \log[(C \times \text{pairs}) \div \text{length of cover}]$$

In this case estimates of K1 lower than 0.20 were made equal to 0.20 (see Fig. 4.2).

(5) Mortality of hens during incubation

With the predation choice as before:

(i) $k_2 = 0.59 \, (k_1 + k_2)$
(ii) $k_2 = 0.31 \, (k_1 + k_2)$

(6) Shooting

Where the partridge is the main quarry, the proportion of driven partridges which are shot increases in a logistic (S-shaped) curve with the density of birds available at the start of the open season. Also, at highest densities the bag very rarely exceeds 55% of the birds available (Potts, 1980a).

The small proportion shot at low densities is attributable to a reluctance to harvest wild stocks after a poor breeding season, combined with the practical difficulties and expense of finding and driving low numbers of partridges when the numbers shot will inevitably be low. At high densities the bag does not often exceed 55% of the initial density because of the need to conserve a good stock for the following year (when half of the available birds have already been shot), and because partridges become very wary after being driven; naturally they learn to avoid the line of guns.

The best data set on population size at the beginning of the open season and the associated shooting mortality, k_4, are those from the Damerham study:

$$k_4 = \frac{0.35}{1 + e^{(5.47 - 0.04 \times A)}} \quad (r^2 = 0.80, P<0.001)$$

Where A is the population density km^{-2} in August.

The North Farm data fit this equation very well ($P<0.05$) for the period 1957–1971, but from 1971 the shooting was aimed towards the exploitation of released, and much more numerous, red-legged partridge. Partridges (i.e. grey) were therefore shot even when densities were low; the equation is:

$$k_4 = \frac{0.35}{1 + e^{(5.47 - 0.02(A + 150))}}$$

(7) Shooting mortality according to sex and age

The data from the Sussex study are given in Table 10.1, which shows a higher percentage of males shot, $P<0.01$.

Table 10.1 Partridge mortality from shooting on farms in the Sussex study area with traditional partridge driving, 1968–1973, according to age and sex

	Number in area before shooting	Number shot	k_4	% shot
Males >1 year	1433	480	0.18	33
Females >1 year	1140	235	0.10	21
Young approximately 4 months	2888	568	0.10	20
Totals and means	5461	1283	0.12	23

Table 10.2 Partridge mortality from shooting according to age and sex; 'walking up' on Salisbury Plain 1984 and 1985

	Number in area before shooting	Number shot	k_4	% shot
Males >1 year	194	31	0.08	16
Females >1 year	149	17	0.05	11
Young approximately 4 months	542	74	0.07	14
Totals and means	885	122	0.07	14

Where partridges are shot by 'walking up', as they often are on Salisbury Plain, more old males (i.e. older than 1 year) were shot but the difference was not statistically significant (Table 10.2). A higher proportion of males shot is however kept for all models because lone birds offer easier targets and these are nearly always old males.

Simulation

Model calculations were started with a notional pair density for year 1, which was then taken through the steps outlined above to provide a new pair density for year 2. This cycle was then repeated each year with annual input of the relevant chick mortality rate and with other inputs changing as appropriate. One value of such a simulation modelling procedure is that it allows immediate testing of the effects of many combinations of habitats and management practices. More important, the modelling enables the evaluation of the net effect of applying factors which might in time offset or augment one another, and the formation of quantified hypotheses for testing by experiment.

We begin our first exploration of partridge population dynamics using a simple model of the Sussex population and by examining particularly the role of the density dependence in nest predation. Two simulations were run in parallel, with everything constant except for the density dependence in nest predation which was input as two cases, 'with' and 'without' nest predation control, as observed in the Sussex study (Fig. 4.2). A weighted mean of the two runs was calculated to reflect the proportion of the Sussex study area which was subject to predation control.

The resulting computer outputs of pair densities are compared to those we observed, in Fig. 10.2. The graph clearly shows that simulated breeding densities are very close to those we observed. One problem with simulations is that 'errors' once made tend to continue with observed and simulated trajectories trailing in parallel for many years. This occurred in our case (Fig. 10.2) but not to any notable extent and

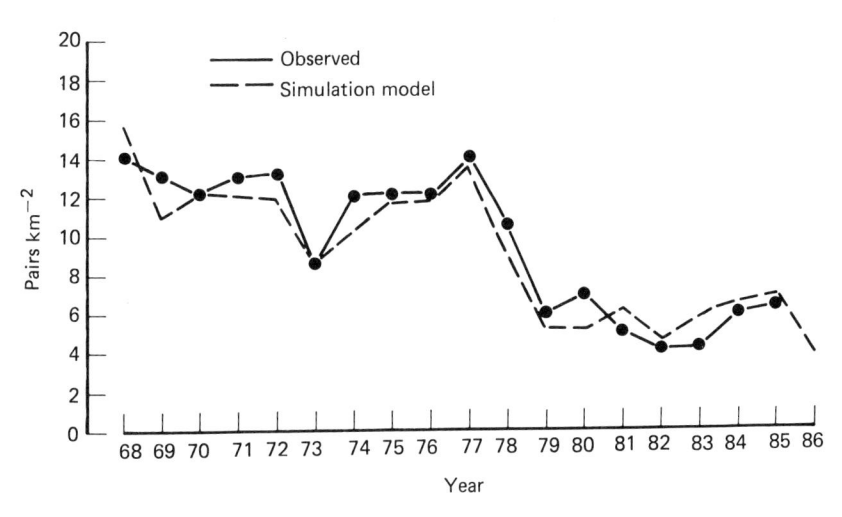

Fig. 10.2 Observed densities of partridge, pairs km^{-2}, 1968 to 1985, compared to computer simulation: the 'Sussex model'.

the simulated and observed mean breeding densities were as follows:

Simulation 11.15 ± 5.49 pairs per km^2
Observed   11.17 ± 3.85 pairs per km^2

There is, in addition, good agreement between the observed (x) and expected (y) pair densities each spring during the decline and the relationship between x and y is almost 1:1, i.e. $y = -0.139 + 1.06x$. Nearly three-quarters of the variation in breeding density from 1968 to 1985 was accounted for by our model; it is clearly valid.

Computer models can be valid and yet at the same time misleading because they may accurately describe fluctuations but only retrospectively, and not arrive at them in the way we imagine. In short, models need verifying – which in this case we can approach from two angles. First, a predictive model is particularly useful and the Sussex model has, when 'given' the observed chick mortality rates, predicted the population changes since 1977. The model described here is essentially the one completed in 1977 and published in Potts (1980a), though less complex and even more robust in its application to other studies. The essential logic and underlying rationale are the same. Second, as we saw in Chapters 4 and 9, considerable evidence exists which justifies the inter-relationship of density, nest predation and nesting cover and, Chapters 5 and 6, the relationship of chick survival to insects, which are the essential structures in the simulations. Relative to many other models there are few assumptions, and the model structure is strongly based on long-term field data and experiments rather than on theories or hypotheses.

Nest predation and competition for sufficient nesting space are by far the most important density-dependent factors regulating the equilibrium levels in the Sussex population model (Fig. 10.2), with the main effect of the decreased nesting cover being to increase predation, not to cause emigration to areas with better nesting cover. We can demonstrate the importance of density-dependent nest predation in two ways, both by using the Sussex population simulation model.

In order to illustrate how nest predation determines the population equilibrium level we compare two runs of the model by starting with a notional density of 100 pairs km^{-2} and by keeping everything constant except nest predation, with no shooting. One hundred pairs km^{-2} is far above the highest recorded density and it imposes unrealistic density-dependent nest predation, which quickly reduces the initial pair density as the simulation progresses. As this reduction of pairs takes place, so the density-dependent mortalities ease and this process continues until the density-dependent mortalities balance the density-independent mortalities: the equilibrium point. With predation controlled this is reached after ten years at 64 pairs km^{-2}, with predation not controlled after six years at 16 pairs km^{-2} (Fig. 10.3). Beginning with one pair the whole process is reversed but the same equilibrium levels are reached after the same time period. Equilibrium levels will be lower than achieved in these simulations if shooting is introduced, if nesting cover is removed and if pesticides are used.

A further simulation shows that in the absence of predator control, the amount of nesting cover regulates population equilibrium levels by adjusting nest predation rather than by creating an absolute shortage of nest sites and causing the emigration of pairs. In this simulation everything is kept constant except for nesting cover, which is input at two levels, 1 km km^{-2} (equivalent to the most extreme Eastern bloc collectivised agricultures) and 9 km per km^{-2}, giving maximum benefit so far as partridges are concerned. For these two extremes the results show

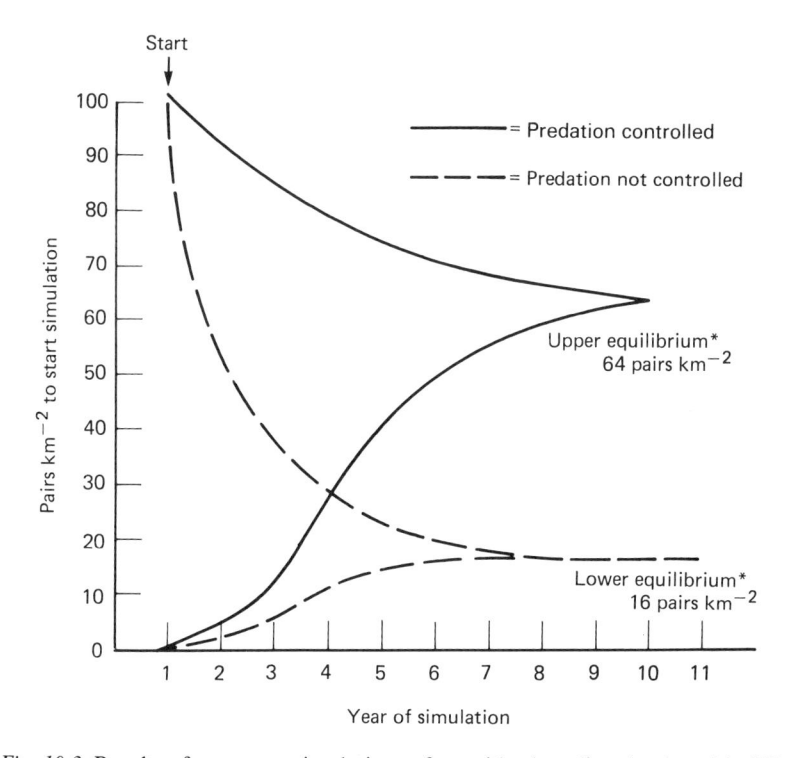

Fig. 10.3 Results of computer simulations of partridge breeding density with different starting densities, 1 and 100 pairs km^{-2}, and with and without 'predation control'.

*with 9 km of nesting cover km^{-2}, no herbicides, no shooting

Table 10.3 Computer-simulated partridge populations at two extremes of nesting cover availability

Nesting cover km km^{-2}	Young: old ratio August	Shooting mortality and winter losses $k_4 + k_5$	Pair density km^{-2}
9	2.17 ± 0.30	0.36 ± 0.02	20.1 ± 1.50
1	2.05 ± 0.30	0.35 ± 0.02	3.6 ± 0.58

(Table 10.3) that the breeding success and loss rates are approximately the same, though pair densities are more than five times as high with the greater amount of nesting cover. Actual densities will be lower than those given in the table if herbicides are used, higher if predation is controlled.

Incidentally, these data in Table 10.3 are a further illustration of the need to study breeding success and mortality rate in relation to density. It is not possible to determine from the table why the partridge population given poor nesting cover, is lower than that given good nesting cover. The rates of production and mortality are the same in both cases.

This emphasis on density dependence is very important to practical game conservation simply because it is counter-productive in any management programme to work against a density-dependent factor – the more work one does, aiming to increase numbers, the higher the mortality. Likewise shooting can only be compatible with partridge conservation where the survival rate or production rate of the survivors of the shooting, or both, are raised as a consequence of the reduction of the population by shooting (Chapter 11). Without natural density-dependent mortality, shooting would not be compatible with partridge conservation.

Causes of the population decline in the Sussex study

It is obvious from previous chapters that herbicides (affecting chick survival), increased nest predation, and reduced nesting cover would all have led to fewer partridges. But which factor was most important?

In the first simulation run (Fig. 10.4) the chick mortality rates were restored to their former levels (i.e. before the use of herbicides) and the extent of predation control was kept at the 1967 level. In this case the population decline is prevented altogether (Fig. 10.4, Run 1) and a

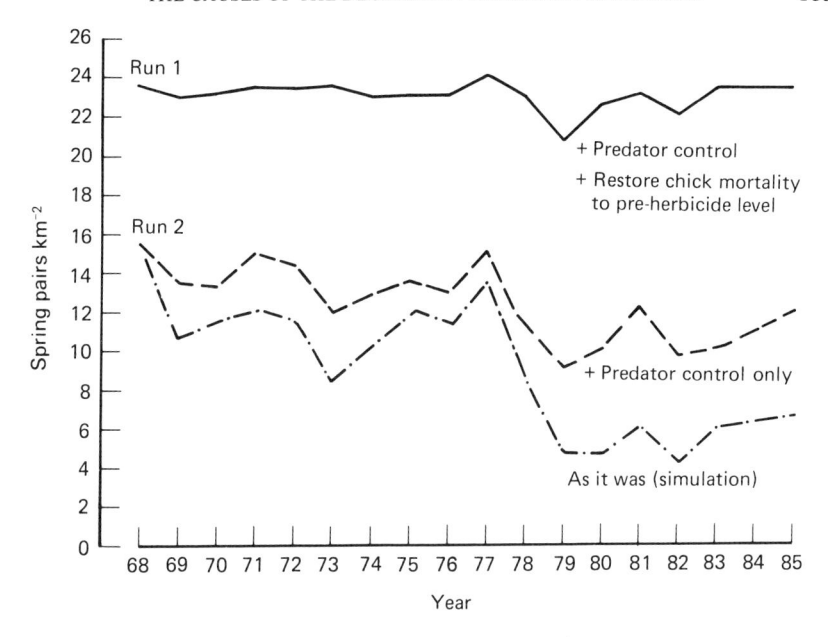

Fig. 10.4 Simulations of Sussex partridge population, restoring (Run 1) predator control to 1968 level and chick mortality to pre-herbicide level, or (Run 2) restoring predator control only.

shootable surplus, with driving, is produced yielding an average annual bag of 40 km^{-2} per annum without any downward trend.

Restoring predation control alone would have markedly increased breeding stocks in recent years – *but would not have prevented a steady decline* (Fig. 10.4, run 2). More important, it would not have enabled partridge driving to continue since bags would have averaged only 5 km^{-2} per annum. In these circumstances a gamekeeper would be far too expensive (£300 per partridge shot!), leaving two alternatives: either concentrate on released birds for shooting, or make the gamekeeper redundant. In the Sussex area both occurred – so the decline in predation control there in the late 1970s can ultimately be attributed to the 'herbicide effect' on chick mortality.

Only 5.1% of nesting cover was removed from the Sussex study area during the period 1968 to 1985 (see Table 9.1) – an amount so small that the effects are barely discernible by a simulation covering the whole area. Most nesting cover removal occurred at North Stoke (Chapter 3, Fig. 3.1c, d), but even there the breeding stock was always at a level below that which the nesting cover could sustain. Nevertheless, because of the removal of nesting cover, breeding stocks would only rise to 70%

of the pre-decline levels at North Stoke if chick mortality rates and predator control were restored. We return to these practical points in the next chapter. Meanwhile, it should be noted that the nesting cover in the Sussex study area in 1985 was sufficient for over 800 pairs of partridge – five times the current pair density.

It seems very clear that the main cause of the decline of the Sussex study area partridge population and of low numbers during the study was high chick mortality, accelerated by increased predation.

Damerham, Fordingbridge, Hants

Elsewhere in Britain the timing and sequence of events will have varied. For example, at Damerham the sudden drop in partridge numbers in the early 1960s (Fig. 2.7) was caused by increased chick mortality (Fig. 6.9), a reduction in the length of nesting cover (from 7 to 5.5 km km^{-2}), and the cessation of predation control when the ICI shooting rights lease expired, all within the space of a few years.

A detailed examination of the overall decline at Damerham shows that the contribution that each of these factors could separately have had can be obtained by modelling as set out below:

	Partridges 1 September
Observed:	
(1) 1950s	126 km^{-2}
(2) 1980s	18 km^{-2}
Simulations:	
(1) 1950s, no herbicides	151 km^{-2}
(2) 1980s, hedge change only	134 km^{-2}
(3) 1980s, herbicide change only	85 km^{-2}
(4) 1980s, predation change only	46 km^{-2}
(5) 1980s, all three changes	19 km^{-2}

Later (Chapter 11) we shall examine the relative value of restoring factors in various combinations.

The simulation above suggests that the withdrawal of predator control alone has brought about most of the large reduction of the population at Damerham. Similar changes have probably occurred on many estates in the past. In particular there was a large fall in the number of gamekeepers during both World Wars. However, the number of gamekeepers and therefore the potential for predator control (i.e. if it was effective for wild stocks as we discussed) has probably not changed since 1951, at least in Britain (Fig. 10.5).

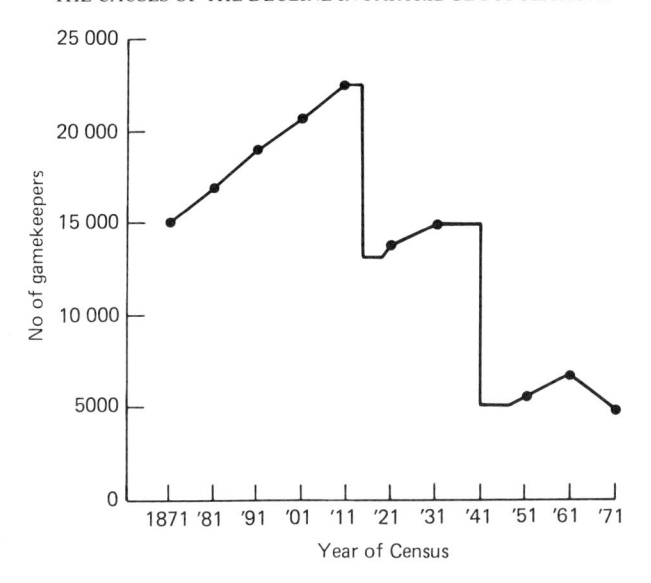

Fig. 10.5 Changes in the number of gamekeepers in the UK since 1871, National Census data.

World-wide decline

Data from population studies in addition to those in Sussex are summarised in Table 10.4 (a,b and c), with indications of whether or not the populations were stable or declining during the studies. Some postgraduate investigations have been too short to determine trends. In these cases, ancillary information such as bag records were utilised. However, this was difficult in the case of North America but it appeared that none of the listed studies there were definitely concerned with declining populations, or of populations at a significantly lower density than hitherto. The two studies in North Central Iowa were in localities where numbers had probably been higher but with no change after the mid-1960s (McCrow, 1982).

A population decline can result from one of two effects, or from both occurring together:

(1) A change in the density dependence of the mortality (increase in slope of regression of mortality on density). When this occurs the population will show a temporary increase in mortality until a new, lower equilibrium level is reached.
(2) An increase in density-independent mortality rate, which is sus-

Table 10.4a Reconstructed population data: Britain (all England)

No.	Start year	End year	Years studied	Area and county	Size area km^2	Mean pairs km^{-2}	k_1+k_2	k_3	k_4	k_5	K	Authorities
1	1903	1915	(13)	Witchingham, Norfolk	12	47	0.16	0.31	0.12	0.43	1.02	Middleton (1936a), and W. J. Barry diaries
2	1934	1938	(5)	Manydown, Hampshire	11	12	0.11	0.29	0.16	0.33	0.89	This study (archive data)
3	1935	1952	(7)	West Barsham, Norfolk	12	53	0.16	0.40	0.15	0.30	1.01	This study (archive data)
4	1946	1961	(15)	Damerham, Hampshire	14	24	0.16	0.40	0.11	0.22	0.89	Blank and Ash (1962) (archive data)
5	1952	1955	(4)	Micheldever, Hampshire	3	39	0.15	0.42	0.07	0.23	0.87	Jenkins (1956, 1961b)
6	1953	1978	(26)	West Barsham, Norfolk	12	40 ↓	0.17	0.46	0.08	0.31	1.02	T. H. Blank (+ archive data)
7	1957	1985	(29)	Manydown, Hampshire	11	8 ↓	0.19	0.42	0.10	0.29	1.00	This study (archive data)
8	1957	1967	(11)	North Farm, Sussex	13	23 ↓	0.19	0.54	0.17	0.17	1.07	This study (Chris Hunt and Fred Allen)
9	1962	1985	(24)	Damerham, Hampshire	8	7 ↓	0.20	0.51	0.00	0.33	1.04	This study
10	1961	1977	(16)	National Game Census	140	10 ↓	0.15	0.48	0.07	0.32	1.02	Potts (1980a)
11	1968	1985	(18)	Sussex study area (a)	}26	15 * ↓	0.20	0.60	0.10	0.19	1.09	This study
				(b)		6 * ↓	0.47	0.60	0.01	0.16	1.24	This study
				Applesham (c)	2.6	10 * ↓	0.31	0.43	0.01	0.27	1.02	This study
12	1977	1983	(7)	Boconnoc, Cornwall	22	<0.8 ↓	0.10	0.41	0.02	0.55	1.08	D. Clark (*in litt.*)

* *Note*: omitted from analysis in Table 10.5
↓ indicates decline

Table 10.4b Reconstructed population data: Mainland Europe and Soviet Union

No.	Start year	End year	Years studied	Country and area	Size area km²	Mean pairs km⁻²	$k_1 + k_2$	k_3	k_4	k_5	K	Authorities
1	1771	1868	(15)	Czechoslovakia, Trebon	82	7	0.33	0.30	0.14	0.30	1.07	Nováková and Hanzl (1966)
2	1886	1909	(23)	USSR, Gatchina, Leningrad	220	1	0.15	0.23	0.03	0.59	1.00	Dits (1917), Severtzoff (1934)
3	1922	1933	(12)	Hungary, Esterhazy	43	6	0.09	0.23	0.15	0.68	1.15	Prof. de Karkovany (*in litt.* 1935)
4	1939	1942	(3)	Czechoslovakia, Podebrady	82	21↓	0.63	0.30	0.11	0.40	1.44	Koteš and Knobloch (1947)
5	1946	1956	(n/a)	Hungary	4	25	0.18	0.39	0.15	0.28	1.00	Szederjei and Szederjei (1960) Szederjei *et al.* (1959)
6	1946	1973	(17)	USSR, N. Caucasian Plain	2200	<1↓	0.10	0.37	0.15	0.70	1.32	Loshkarev (1976)
7	1965	1985	(21)	Poland, Czempiń	140	7↓	0.23	0.36	0.02	0.48	1.09	Chlewski and Panek (1986)
8	1969	1982	(14)	France, Seine-et-Marne	7	20↓	0.30	0.51	0.07	0.40	1.28	Birkan (1977c, 1985 and *in litt.*)
9	1969	1980	(8)	France, SE Gatinais	10	7↓	0.13	0.46	0.14	0.40	1.13	Viart (1978)
10	1977	1980	(3)	FRG, Wetterau, Hessen	21	2↓	0.14	0.43	0.16	0.31	1.04	R. Schulz (*in litt.*), Döring (1982)
11	1979	1983	(5)	FRG, Winzenheim, Rhine	2	11	0.14	0.32	0.01	0.55	1.02	Döring and Helfrich (1966)
Bearded partridge												
12	1978	1983	(6)	USSR, Trans Baikalia	3543	1	0.07	0.19	0.08	0.69	1.03	Litun (1983)

↓ indicates decline

Table 10.4c Reconstructed population data: North America

No.	Start year	End year	Years studied	Area	Size area km^2	Mean pairs km^{-2}	$k_1 + k_2$	k_3	k_4	k_5	K	Authorities
1	1930	1933	(4)	USA, SE Michigan	7	8	0.34	0.24	0.00	0.24	0.82	Yeatter (1934)
2	1935	1943	(8)	USA, Faville Grove, Wisc.	10	5	0.35	0.48	0.05	0.23	1.11	McCabe and Hawkins (1946)
3	1940	1942	(3)	USA, Pullman, Washington	6	9	0.25	0.30	0.02	0.43	1.00	Yocum (1943), Knott et al. (1943)
4	1960	1966	(7)	USA, Waupun, Wisc.	108	6	0.37	0.38	0.05	0.23	1.03	Gates (1973)
5	1966	1971	(6)	USA, Hancock, Iowa	14	1	0.35	0.24	0.01	0.40	1.00	Bishop et al. (1977)
6	1968	1974	(7)	USA, Agawam, Montana	140	1	0.34	0.25	0.01	0.40	1.00	Weigand (1980)
7	1971	1972	(2)	Canada, Conquest, Sask.	16	4	0.16	0.11	<0.06	0.50	0.83	Hunt (1974)
8	1975	1977	(3)	USA, Hancock, Iowa	21	2	0.55	0.40	0.01	0.19	1.15	McCrow (1982)
9	1976	1978	(3)	USA, Latah, Idaho	13	14	0.35	0.22	0.05	0.49	1.11	Mendel and Peterson (1980)
10	1978	1979	(2)	USA, Calumet, Wisc.	72	2	0.41	0.28	0.05	0.32	1.06	Church (1980)
11	1980	1984	(4)	USA, NW New York State	20 20	1↓	— 0.14 }	0.49+	0.00 0.00	0.68 0.82* }	1.31	Enck (1986) Church (1986)

Note: omitted from Table 10.5
* indicates decline

tained, and not compensated for by other density-dependent mortalities.

In either of the above two cases population declines would be associated with increased mortality, though in the former the effect might be quite brief. The various mortality rates for stable and declining populations are compared in Table 10.5 which shows that the (density-independent) chick mortality is higher in declining populations. By contrast the other mortalities are practically the same with a tendency to be lower in the case of (density-dependent) nest predation.

Table 10.5 Comparison of mortality rates in partridge populations (excluding those for the Sussex study) and standard errors, according to their status.

		Populations		Significant
		Stable (21)	Declining (13)	
Nest loss	(k_1+k_2)	0.26 ± 0.02	0.21 ± 0.03	not sig.
Chick mortality	k_3	0.29 ± 0.02	0.44 ± 0.02	$P<0.01$
Shooting mortality	k_4	0.07 ± 0.01	0.08 ± 0.02	not sig.
Winter loss	k_5	0.38 ± 0.03	0.41 ± 0.05	not sig.
Total loss	K	1.00	1.14	

The world-wide data therefore clearly support the results of the Sussex study; moreover simulation modelling shows that the increase in chick mortality (Table 10.5) is sufficient to cause a major decline in typical partridge populations.

However, it must be pointed out that no study was made whilst the radical enlargement schemes were being carried out in the collectivised agricultures of the Eastern bloc countries. Modelling suggests such field enlargement will have, for a time, increased nest predation rates (by concentrating nests in less nesting cover). Nor were any of the thirty-four studies carried out near the northern limit of the species, where there has been a marked contraction of range. In this case modelling has shown that even quite small increases in chick mortality rate would extend the period of recovery after severe winters, from about three years with 50% chick mortality ($k_3 = 0.30$), to a decade or more with chick mortality of 75% ($k_3 = 0.60$). A small increase in chick mortality could therefore have a large and sustained impact especially where severe winters frequently occur (Potts, 1986).

Modelling further suggests that partridge populations would inevitably become extinct where annual chick mortalities exceed about 80% ($k_3 = 0.70$). The current figure for the Sussex study area (excluding

Applesham) is about 76% ($k_3 = 0.61$) and it is probably even higher in parts of the eastern counties where aphicides are used on a routine basis in cereals. At Czempiń, in Poland, chick mortality rates reached the Sussex levels in the late 1970s, causing a population crash (Figs 2.6, 6.9, and Chlewski and Panek, 1986). Almost exactly the same sequence of events occurred a year or two later in Seine-et-Marne, France (Figs 2.6, 6.9, and Birkan, 1985).

Taken overall, partridge populations appear as if they are on a down escalator, the position on the escalator depending on nesting cover, predator control, shooting rates, and so on. However, provision of nesting cover and attention to other management factors will only temporarily restore the population if chick mortality remains high. The only way to move back up the escalator or stop going down is to improve the supply of insects to the chicks – the main subject of our final chapter.

I have stressed many times in this book the importance of density dependence, but now in the light of the conclusions above it seems appropriate to conclude with the view of an entomologist with a long experience of the many controversies in ecology, and of the relative importance of density-independent and density-dependent factors. In our context it is indeed a pertinent warning:

'Clearly therefore, the ultimate control of decreases in numbers rests with the density-independent factors alone, for unless the density-independent factors stop causing a decrease then the remnants of the individuals that are left by the density-dependent factors must continue down towards zero.' (Milne, 1984).

The ground should be constantly patrolled, gun in hand.

11 Some Aspects of Traditional Partridge Conservation

Estimating the shootable surplus

'The good sportsman always lets the hen partridges fly, for on them depends the breed of the game.' (*The Beggar's Opera*, J. Gay (c. 1720))

At the Game Conservancy we often speak of shooting as the 'cropping' of game, and of the consequent reduction of the game population as the equivalent of the thinning out or pruning to produce new or better growth. This positive response of game populations to shooting mortality is said to be 'compensatory' and, like the compensation for natural predation, it takes several forms – for example, the replacement clutches which would never be laid if it were not for the removal of the first clutch.

If we are to look at this subject in more detail, the first objective must therefore be to identify the nature and extent of the compensatory response of partridge populations to shooting.

There is no doubt that compensation exists because the total annual mortality and losses in partridge populations do not increase in proportion to numbers shot. This is well illustrated by the data given for shooting mortality (k_4) and total mortality (K), which was summarised in Table 10.4. Even at the highest mean annual shoooting rate in the table, 32% ($k_4 = 0.17$), the total mortality (K) was increased by only 2%. This was not statistically significant, indeed regression analysis of the data show that K is similar throughout the range $k_4 = 0$ to $k_4 = 0.17$ ($P>0.95$).

The presence of compensation for shooting was tested by an experiment during the Damerham study. A 'control' area of 0.75 km² was selected (at Boulsbury), where shooting was prohibited for seven years (from 1952). Over the whole experiment 794 partridges were back-tabbed and ninety-three ringed out of a total of 1013 present on the 'control' area. Of the total marked (887), twenty-two (2%) were shot after they had moved off the 'control' area. As is usual in partridges, mortality did not vary with age, it averaged $51 \pm 2\%$ per annum (K – k_3 = 0.31). On the rest of the Damerham area (the 'experimental' area) the mean annual mortality rate could not be determined but overall losses including emigration and immigration were 55% (K – k_3 = 0.35, only 0.04 higher) despite a mean 24% ($k_4 = 0.12$) shot per annum. The breeding stock of partridges on the 'control' area did not build up because a higher proportion of the non-shot birds emigrated from the control area than from the 'experimental' area, thus offsetting some of the losses to shooting. Shooting would in this case be compensated for locally by reduced emigration, a point we shall return to shortly.

The comparative population data (Table 10.4) show a clear inverse relationship between nesting mortality and shooting mortality. At the highest rate of shooting, 32% ($k_4 = 0.17$), the nesting mortality was reduced by 28% ($k_1 + k_2 = 0.14$), the overall regression equation being:

$$k_1 + k_2 = 0.30 - 0.84 (k_4) \qquad (P<0.05)$$

This relationship, 84% compensation for shooting, has two component

XXV. Hemp nettle, its seeds are the favourite autumn food of partridge in Northern latitudes (*G.R. Potts*).

XXVI. Favourite foods of adult partridge, black bindweed and (front) chickweed (*G.R. Potts*).

XXVII. Adult knotgrass beetle (*Charles Coles*).

XXVIII. Favourite chick food – knotgrass beetle larvae (*Charles Coles*).

XXIX. Manydown, CDA sprayer with outer boom switched off over headland, note 'sterile strip' (*Michael Rands*).

XXX. Unsprayed headland with poppies, Eifel, F.R.G. (*Prof Wolfgang Schumacher*).

XXXI. Favourite food of chicks, larva of the sawfly *Dolerus gonager* (*David Hill*).

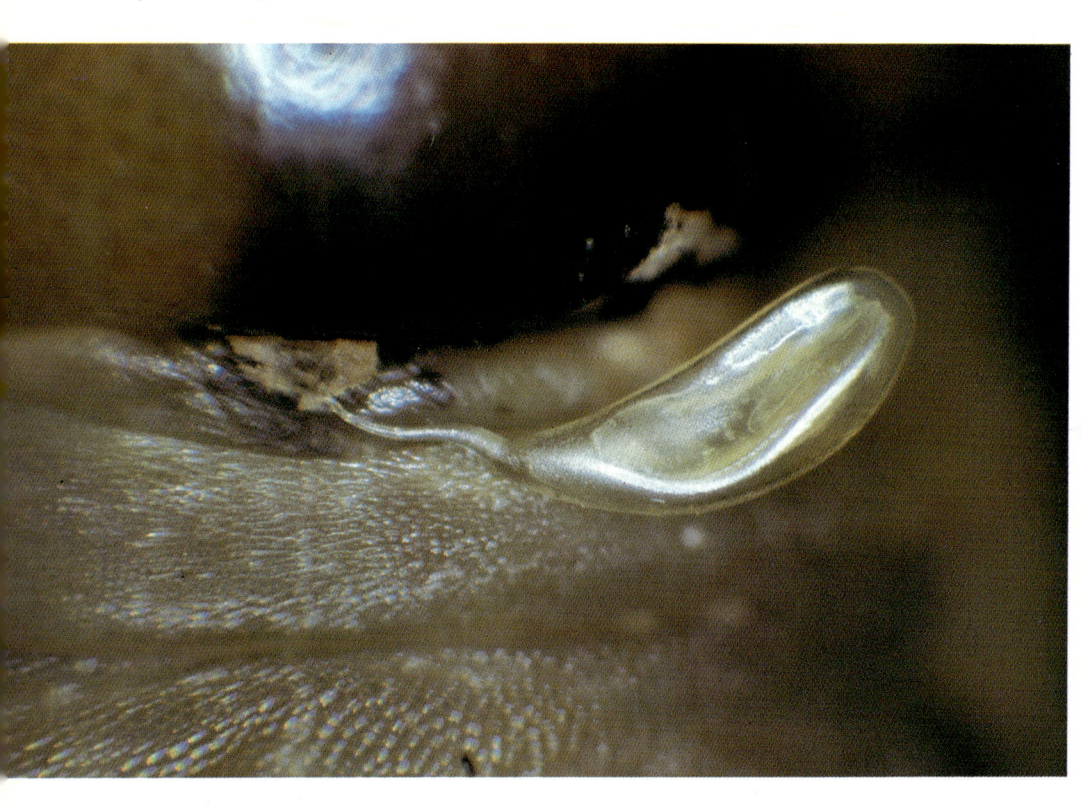

XXXII. Close up of egg of Ichneumon wasp parasite *Tryphon* sp. attached to neck of *Dolerus haematodes* (*Peter Copeman*).

parts:

(1) Predation control reduces nesting mortality, increases population size and creates a local shootable surplus of partridges which would have to emigrate in a *density-dependent* way to find nest sites.
(2) Where predation is not controlled, shooting reduces the nesting stock with the result that *density-dependent* nest predation is reduced, thus compensating for the shooting mortality.

No other source of compensation for shooting has been identified so there is a distinct limit to the available compensation. In general, nesting losses cannot be reduced below 20% ($k_1 + k_2 = 0.10$) with predation control or 37% ($k_1 + k_2 = 0.20$) without predation control. In case (1) above, the compensation will be exhausted at a shooting rate of 43% per annum ($k_4 = 0.24$); in case (2), at only 24% per annum ($k_4 = 0.12$). Beyond these rates of shooting, partridge populations will inevitably decline. The dynamics involved are best explained with the use of models.

Maximum sustainable yield

Computer models, which have been used for many years to assess the correct rates of exploitation of fish populations, are also, suitably modified, appropriate to assessing various rates of shooting. In both shooting and fishing the aim is to calculate the highest yield which can be sustained year after year, hence the 'maximum sustainable yield' or MSY. Unfortunately, the concept of MSY and to some extent the more sophisticated (because it allows for errors involved in estimating the population size) 'optimum sustainable yield' have fallen into some disrepute. Apart from political difficulties, such as are met in sea fisheries, this seems to be mainly because the exact nature of the density-dependent mortality, crucial to the calculation of MSY, is often not properly understood. For fisheries, Larkin (1977) was moved to write:

MSY
(1930s–1970s)

Here lies the concept, MSY.
It advocated yields too high,
And didn't spell out how to slice the pie.
We bury it with the best of wishes,
Especially on behalf of fishes.
We don't know yet what will take its place.

196   THE PARTRIDGE

But hope it's good for the human race.

RIP

In this study we explore the influence of different levels of shooting on partridge populations by using the Sussex model.

First we calculate the mean spring stocks and shooting yield for a ten-year period in relation to the percentage shot per annum. From this it is clear (Fig. 11.1) that there is a notable difference between the model outputs according to whether or not predation was controlled, and according to the chick mortality rates.

The effect of predation control on the MSY is clear – a fivefold increase in the bag in the low chick mortality era, reduced to a threefold increase in the high chick mortality era (Fig. 11.1).

The rate of shooting which gave the MSY was the same, whether or not there was predation control, though the size of the bag was affected greatly. In addition the rate of shooting at MSY declined from around 45% in the low chick mortality era, to around 30% in the high chick mortality era.

Increased rates of shooting reduced breeding stock densities in all

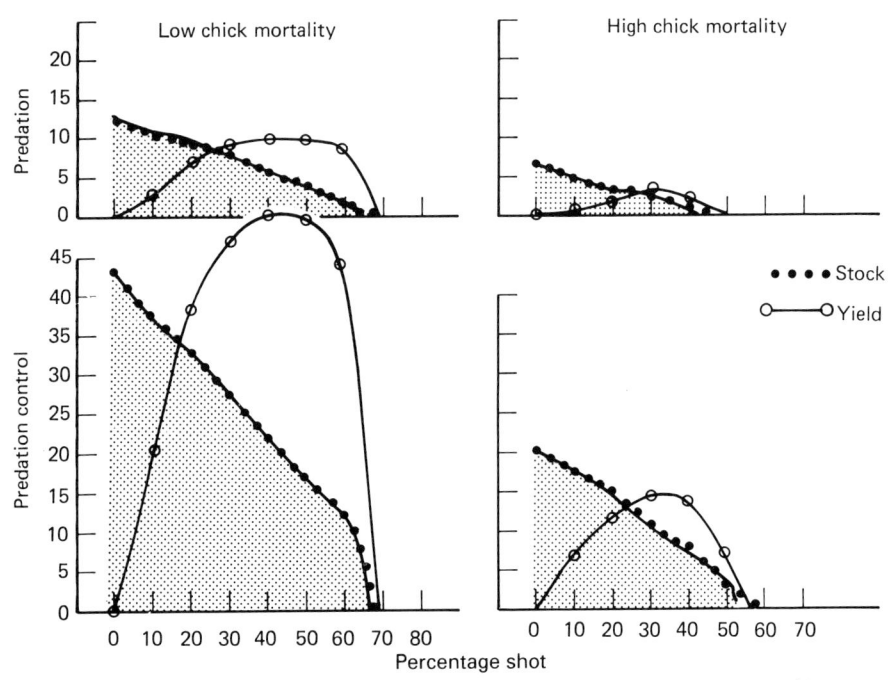

Fig. 11.1 Results of simulations relating equilibrium levels of stock and yield, partridges km^{-2}, to percentage annual shooting mortality.

Table 11.1 Results of computer simulation runs of partridge populations, showing that predation control results in increased losses (due to competition for nest sites), losses which can be replaced by shooting mortality

	% shot	(k_4)	Adult mortality and net losses % lost	(k_5)	Total	(k_4+k_5)
(1) No predation control	0	–	38	(0.21)	38	(0.21)
(2) Predation control, no shooting	0	–	64	(0.44)	64	(0.44)
(3) Predation control + shooting	41	(0.23)	42	(0.24)	66	(0.47)

Note: the equilibrium level in (3) is however much lower than in (2); (1) is lower still (see Fig. 11.1)

cases but, even after shooting the stocks were much higher where predation control was practised. Nevertheless, even with predation control, rates of shooting in excess of 60% in the low chick mortality era or 40% in the high chick mortality era led to extinction in the model. It is interesting to compare the estimate of 60% with one of the first attempts to warn against the dangers of overshooting. Kiessling (1923) warned that shooters should avoid, at all costs, risking the killing of more than two-thirds of the partridges present at the start of the shooting season.

The source of compensation for shooting mortality in populations without predation control is easy to see, i.e. a reduction in the density-dependent nest predation. Where there is no density-dependent nest predation, the compensation mechanism (involving dispersal, as we have seen) is best explained with the use of further simple models.

The reason why predation control increases the bag becomes apparent in a comparison of simulations with and without predation control (Table 11.1). Predation control, in the absence of shooting, doubled the adult losses, the cause being the competition for nest sites which results in emigration of pairs in spring (as described in Chapter 9). This explains why shooting 41% of the 1 September population increased losses at equilibrium by only 2% (Table 11.1, row 3). These results were not affected by changes in the amount of nesting cover in the range 1 to 9 km km^{-2}, but it is important to note that the point of maximum sustainable yield is now lower than 41% shot per annum (see Fig. 11.1) due to the higher chick mortality. The model used here employed chick mortality rates from the pre-herbicide era.

To estimate the proportion that should be shot and the bag (B), Birkan (1979) gave equations which have been widely applied in mainland Europe:

$$B = rs\frac{(1+j)-1}{(1+u)s}(1+a)x$$

where r = survival of adults between spring and the start of the shooting season (0.90); s = overall survival of partridges between the start of the shooting season and the following spring (0.55); j = young per adult at start of shooting (variable); u = non-retrieved shooting mortality and injuries as proportion of bag (0.15); a = the ratio of males to females in spring (1.2); and x is the density of pairs km^{-2} (a variable).

Substituting $j = 3.0$ and $x = 15$, we have:

$$B = \frac{0.90 \times 0.55 (1+3.0) - 1}{(1+0.15) \times 0.55}(1+1.2) \times 15$$

$$B = 51$$

However, Birkan did not allow for the extra shooting mortality of males and an alternative, simpler equation might be:

$$B = \frac{A - 2x}{s}$$

$$B = 53$$

where A = August population (108 in this case). Although simpler than Birkan's equation, the revised equation implies that A can be estimated as accurately as x.

The Game Conservancy calculated the shootable surplus for hundreds of estates in the 1950s and 1960s and arrived at a system of estimating A by combining the relatively simple spring count (x) and the August sample count and by analysis which is best shown by an extract from a typical report, that for Druid's Lodge, South Wiltshire:

'I thought you would like to know the details of our count and what we estimate you can shoot this season so I herewith give you the following figures:

Young partridges = 662   Old partridges = 546

(making a ratio of 1.2 to 1, which makes the average covey size 2.4 to a pair. This ratio brings your present stock (counted in spring) up, at the moment, to 3348).

Winter wastage 30%   1004

Next year's stock 750 (pairs)   1500
1961 total for your target this season   844 (or 422 brace)
                                                                3348

This, I would say, could make you two pleasant days' shooting.' (J. Brocklebank, 1961)

Apart from the understatement at the end we should note that the population was assumed to be at its ceiling (which, at 62 pairs km^{-2}, it probably was in this case).

Applying Birkan's equation to this example gives a bag of only twenty-four whereas the revised equation gives the more realistic 621. It seems that in general Birkan's model is too restrictive with low breeding success. On the other hand, with high breeding success it suggests rates of shooting well over 55%; certainly impracticable with driving. Therefore the revised equation seems reasonable and it should be good enough for all areas with predation control since it concentrates almost entirely on ensuring that breeding stocks are adequate. An adjustment should be made to s in areas with high winter mortality.

There is, however, one further adjustment that needs to be made to allow for the availability of nesting cover, the factor which determines much of the rate of emigration. For example, in the case where a farmer employs weedy headlands in order to increase chick survival rates, the population will be building; how then do we estimate the correct x? A good rule here is to allow 200 m of suitable hedgerow, or equivalent (particularly remembering the isolated patches of cover) per nest; or five pairs per km of nesting cover km^{-2}, as we discussed in Chapter 9.

On areas where compensation for shooting is brought about by reducing the breeding stock, it will be better to operate the percentage system; annual rates of 25–30%, *never* more.

Finally, we should try to ascertain whether the current level of shooting is depressing stocks to a serious extent. It should be evident from these studies that some reduction is inevitable with shooting. In fact the level of shooting currently recorded on National Game Census estates, about 17% per annum (Potts, 1980a), implies a reduction of about 20% in the stocks, but because of compensation, shooting is in equilibrium with density; *no progressive decline could be caused by this level of shooting.*

Overseas readers are probably well aware that Britain is rather unusual in the sense that the areas which are shot over are managed for shooting by the owner. Under no circumstances can anyone infringe the owner's shooting or shoot legally without permission of the owner of the shooting rights. Although some areas of farmland overseas are legally reserved for shooting by the owner (known as 'posting' in the USA), this is unusual. It might seem therefore, at first sight, that overshooting, like overfishing on the high seas, would be difficult to prevent. Fortunately in most countries local shooting associations are well organised and my impression is that shooting is in most cases remarkably restrained, despite some well known but local exceptions.

The possible exception is Italy – where hunters with access to partridges outnumber their quarry 7:1 or more (Renzoni, 1974; Lovari, 1975). New data are becoming available, a result of the studies of Laura Beani (from the University of Florence) at Castellina Fiorentini. On her study area there were eighty-six adults in spring 1984 but only eighty-two, many of them young of that year, in the following November. We can assume that breeding success was similar to that recorded by Meriggi and Prigioni (1985) in the same year, in similar country further north (Montalto de Pavese), because densities of insects in cereals were similar and there was ample nesting cover at both sites. On this assumption, 65% ($k_4 = 0.45$) of the partridges would have been shot by November 1984, a process the Italian conservationists refer to as 'hyper-hunting'.

By contrast, the reluctance to kill a large proportion of birds was very evident on many of the traditional partridge manors in Britain. It clearly shows the relationship between the shooter and his quarry which some find paradoxical. Concerning a shoot at Walsingham, North Norfolk, we have the view, in a letter to the author:

'Probably you are quite right in suggesting that we have undercropped our partridges since the good years of 1960 and 1961 but there are several factors which may have led me to err on the side of light shooting. Firstly the keepers and I have spent so much trouble trying to look after them, that one almost dislikes the idea of shooting them at all, certainly to any extent which might possibly prejudice next year's breeding stock; and secondly one always has to bear in mind the keeper's worried face, if, in a poor year, one happens to have several particularly successful drives and gets amongst the young partridges. They put in so much hard work and so many hours on the job, that, even if shooting pressure does not really materially affect next year's breeding stock, it is difficult to convince them of this, and one does not like to do anything which damps their enthusiasm or makes them believe that their efforts are being prejudiced by excessive greed in a poor year.' (G. Joyce, 1978)

Restocking

'Planting partridge stock is not yet successfully produced by artificial propagation.' (Leopold, 1931).

The history of the introduction, reintroduction, stocking and restocking of gamebirds is fascinating: countless failures and a few dramatic successes. The pheasant was introduced to Greece from the lowlands east of the Black Sea and then throughout Europe *via* Italy, to Britain possibly with the Romans (Vandervell & Coles, 1983) or more likely some time after the fourteenth century (Yapp, 1983), to Ireland by the sixteenth century (O'Rourke, 1970) and to America in the nineteenth century.

The successful introduction, after several failures, of the red-legged partridge from France to Britain in 1770, is also noteworthy. It is interesting that we now associate red-legged partridges, the genus *Alectoris*, with warm climates, for during the early-mid Pleistocene glaciation, the small western partridge *Alectoris sutcliffei* occurred in Devon (Harrison, 1980). The climate was then much colder, with Dartmoor resembling the tundra, and in caves in the area the remains of partridges were found alongside such species as the sea-eagle, eagle owl and wolverine.

The introduction of the partridge to North America at the beginning of this century was perhaps one of the most advantageous events for the species in its entire history. The origin of the hundreds of thousands of partridges that were taken across the Atlantic is not precisely known, but birds were sent from Hungary, Czechoslovakia, Poland, Bavaria and France.

As late as 1940, 50 000 live partridges were exported annually to the West from Hungary alone (Szederjei *et al.*, 1959), many to countries in the existing range of the species. In Britain, one of the eleven estates covered by a survey of partridge manors in the early years of this century had introduced partridges from Bavaria and four from Hungary (Maxwell, 1911). These practices continued until at least the 1960s. For example in our Sussex study area 200 eggs were imported from Denmark in 1962 and the resulting poults released in 1962/63, but to no apparent good effect. Glutz von Blotzheim *et al.* (1973) summarised the general situation very well when they said, 'These questionable experiments seem to be entirely without competent controls and sound documentation'.

The problems arising are of several kinds. First, the habitat may not be suitable, as for example in the southern parts of the United States (Leopold, 1933). Second, with hand-reared birds the mortality after release may be very high. In many cases such birds were released direct from carrying baskets, with no release pens, and this is still the practice in some countries. Some years ago in France, Birkan (1971) reported a 50% loss of partridges within three weeks of release. Third, the released birds may be bred from long lines of game farm stock with genetic weaknesses, as has been described in pheasants (Majewska *et al.*, 1979; Pielowski, 1981), although work we are now doing suggests that this may not be the most important factor.

Young released partridges are often 'adopted' by wild adults, in which case they soon develop some predator avoidance behaviour (Bouchner and Temmlova, 1974) – but how often does this occur and is their predator avoidance ever comparable to that developed by wild birds?

Estimates of the annual loss of released birds (k_6) can be made from ringing or tagging returns as follows:

$$k_6 = \log \left(\frac{\text{recoveries in year } t}{\text{recoveries in year } t + 1} \right)$$

Where this has been done for the birds released in the Sussex study area from 1962 to 1968 we have: $k_6 = 0.41$ for all ages and cohorts (see Fig. 11.2). Knowing the density, the amount of nesting cover, shooting rates and loss of hens, we would expect, on the basis of the main Sussex study, that k_6 would be approximately 0.35. From 1979 to 1982 inclusive, further releases were made though on a much smaller scale than in the 1960s. Taking all four years together, and after allowing for shooting, the population of females (potential recruits) was boosted from 9.8 km^{-2} (wild) to 15.9 km^{-2} (wild and released), giving an expected ten pairs km^{-2}. We observed an average 6.3 km^{-2}, giving overall winter losses of the wild and released partridges higher than ever encountered with wild birds in the Sussex study ($k_5 = 0.40$).

In Denmark, Paludan (1963) carried out a release experiment with trapped and released wild 'control' birds, concluding that the released birds did not survive so well as the wild ones. His data for released partridges are compared with those for Sussex and other comparable studies in Table 11.2.

Shooting rates are much higher in Italy but this alone could not explain the high rate of loss reported by Toschi (1962) and clearly cannot elsewhere. Allowing for the duration of snow, assuming 84% compensation for shooting and that $k_6 = k_5 + k_2 + k_4$, then k_6 should, overall, be approximately 0.52 for wild partridges in the areas given in Table

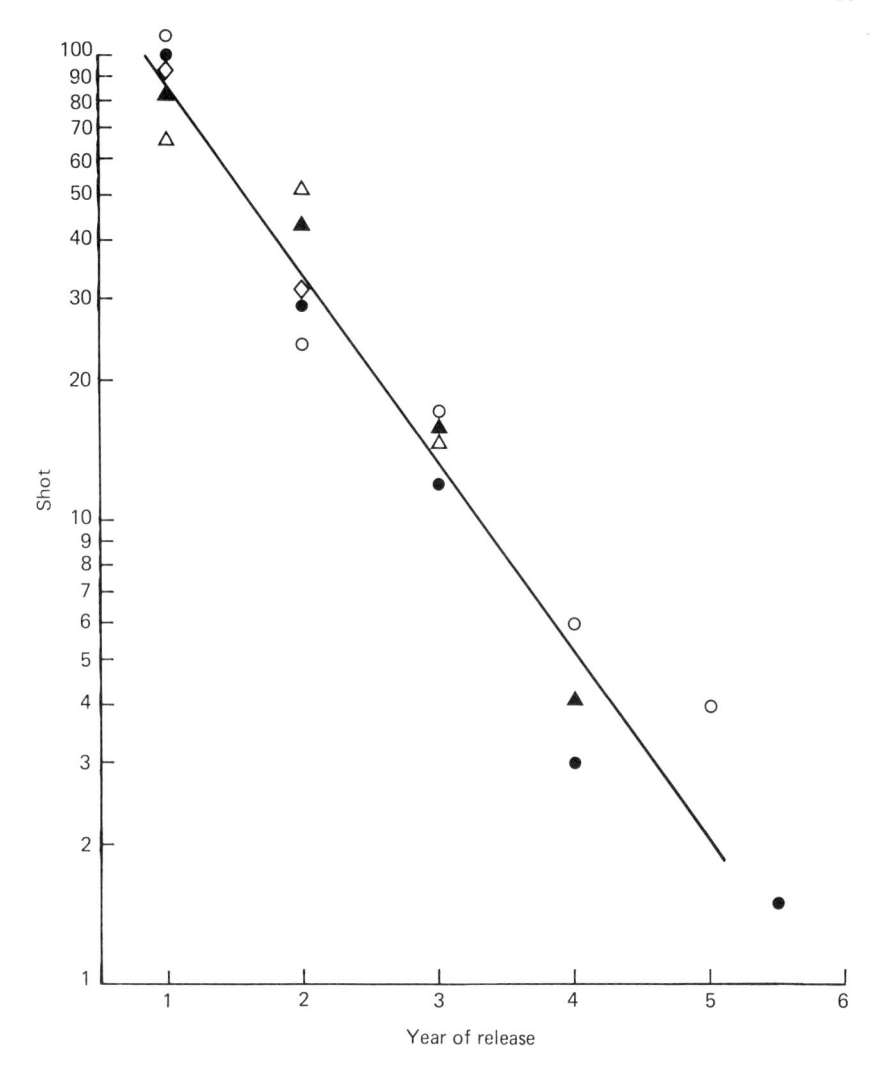

Fig. 11.2 Numbers of partridges shot at North Farm, Sussex, in successive years for cohorts released in 1963 (●), 1964 (○), 1965 (▲), 1966 (△) and 1967 (◇).

11.2, a third less than observed.

In France, Birkan (1977d) found a much higher dispersal of released birds (97% dying on or leaving an area of 12 km^2) compared to 70% for wild birds.

Released hen partridges with wild mates did hatch and rear young in the wild in Sussex, and released birds in Czechoslovakia contributed to

Table 11.2 Mean annual mortality rates for released partridges

	% mortality ± sd	k_6	Authority
Italy	82 ± 7	0.74	Toschi (1962)
Czechoslovakia	80 ± 4	0.70	Paleček and Toufar (1957)
Czechoslovakia	73 ± 6	0.57	Mottl (1973)
Czechoslovakia	91 –	1.05	Bouchner and Temmlova (1974)
Denmark	84 ± 3	0.80	Paludan (1963)
Sussex	61 ± 5	0.41	This study (1962–1968)

Note: losses between release and the start of the shooting season are excluded

sixty-three pairs in the wild as follows (Bouchner and Temmlová 1975):

Wild male and released hen	38 pairs
Wild female and released cock	17 pairs
Both released	8 pairs

In this way many of the surplus wild cocks are able to breed, as was described in France when pairs containing a wild cock and a surviving hand-reared female had only 11% fewer chicks than wild pairs (Birkan and Damange, 1977).

In studies (but not of individually marked birds) Rands (1982) found a much lower coefficient of recruitment among reared birds. He calculated the density of recruits for each year on his seventeen study estates but found only three areas (one of which was North Farm) where the released partridges made a substantial contribution to recruitment, compared to sixteen where wild yearling density significantly correlated with recruitment. A higher mortality rate of released partridges could explain their failure to recruit.

In radio-tracking studies of pheasants in England and Ireland, Hill and Robertson (1986) found much higher rates of predation on released pheasants throughout the first year compared to wild pheasants in the same areas. In the year starting at point of release each wild pheasant produced seven times as many young as each released pheasant.

There is a possible explanation for all this – a difference in predator avoidance behaviour. This is (and has to be) highly developed in wild partridges. For example there are special alarm calls according to whether the predators are on the ground or in the air and each can be altered to indicate the degree of urgency. The squatting alarm, given in response to aerial predators, is a low intensity call acoustically designed to conceal the whereabouts of the bird sounding the alarm, with a frequency of 0.5 to 1.5 kHz. The response to danger from ground predators is a sharp call delivered in the alert, upright position at 2 to 5 KHz and clearly signals the bird's intention to flee (Dessi *et al.*, in press).

The problem with released birds is that the reaction to alarm calls is not instinctive or inborn, but is conditioned by learning and experience – as shown in rock partridges (*Alectoris graeca*) by Menzdorf (1976, 1977), and brooder-reared chicks are deprived of the behaviour which wild chicks derive (non-genetically) from their parents.

Predation is normally the main cause of mortality among released partridges (Birkan 1973) though in Sussex only a third of released partridges found dead had been killed by predators: fox (24), stoat (22) and raptors (7). It therefore seems that the development of anti-predator behaviour would in most circumstances be crucial to survival. It remains to be seen whether game birds can be reared in such a way as to overcome their handicap in this respect.

This subject needs further research if only because rearing for release currently accounts for a large proportion of the expense in partridge conservation, especially in France, Italy and Denmark.

One additional danger with restocking is that it allows a rate of shooting which is sustained by the releases and not by the wild birds. An example of what can happen is shown in the simulation given in Fig. 11.3. Current shooting rates are too high for any yield from the wild birds and a large reduction in the percentage shot would still give a reasonable yield because the released ones not shot would be replaced by wild birds shot.

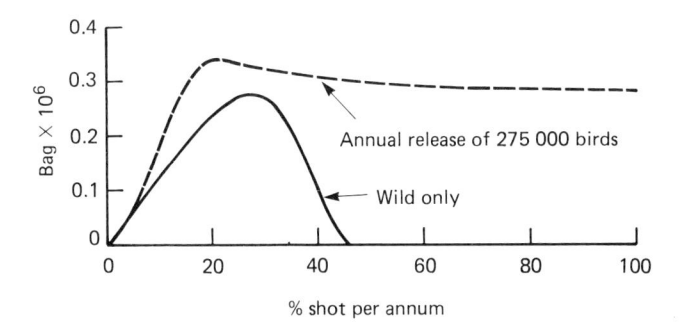

Fig. 11.3 Simulation of the partridge bag in a case where there is an annual release of 275 000 birds. In this case shooting rates above about 15% do not affect the bag much, though the maximum number of wild birds will be shot at about 30% shot per annum, and the maximum total bag is reached at approximately 20% per annum.

My view is that there are so many questionable features of the releasing of partridges for restocking, that it should not be regarded as beneficial to partridge conservation, at least using present methods.

Predator control

This subject is by far the most controversial aspect of partridge conservation, much of the problem being due to past reductions in the less common predators. The tolerance shown towards predators in general has steadily improved through this century, but even quite recently it has been estimated that a very large number, running into millions, of raptors and owls were trapped, shot or poisoned in Europe in the fifteen years prior to 1971 (Bijleveld, 1974), almost entirely in the supposed interests of game preservation. Even today most bird-watchers would readily agree that 'the obliteration of whole populations (of raptors) from large areas of Britain and Europe seems an extraordinarily selfish act by a small sectional interest' (Newton, 1979). The position with some rarer mammals, e.g. the polecat in Britain (Langley and Yalden, 1977), gave rise to similar views.

So far in this book it has been argued that predation on partridges is of crucial importance in population density regulation and that predator reduction is essential to create a reasonable shootable surplus. But in partridges the main egg predation is by carrion crows, and rats and foxes account for most of the predation on sitting hens. With the possible exception of the Eurasian badger (see Table 4.3), no birds or mammals currently protected in Britain were involved to a significant extent. Raptors were not controlled in Sussex, indeed in winter the main predator reduction area was noted by local bird-watchers as one of the best places in the county to see birds of prey such as hen harriers and, especially in 1974 and 1975, rough-legged buzzards; a gyr falcon once stayed for several months, and so on. Most important, the simulation models which accounted for the partridge population fluctuating did not include any inputs for predation outside the nesting season. In Sussex it was clearly not important.

At one time vultures were killed in Yugoslavia to protect partridges and throughout much of Europe nightjars and many insect-eating raptors such as the hobby, honey buzzard and red-footed falcon, as well as kestrels and many harmless owls, were killed by gamekeepers. Obviously we now realise this was barbaric and counter-productive but what of the sparrow hawk, goshawk and buzzard? Was all this killing

Table 11.3 Comparative bag of predators, three areas in Britain and one in Hungary

Estate	Decade beginning	Stoat and weasel	Corvidae	Sparrow hawks	Authority
Zsombloya (Hungary)	1889	19856	53000	4394	Maxwell (1911)
Elvedon	1904	9305	2649	670	Turner (1954)
Damerham	1947	2364	4940	613	Game Conservancy
Sussex (North Stoke and North Farm)	1962	2350	5675	0	This study

(see Table 11.3 for sparrow hawks) a tragic mistake too?

Evidence given in Chapter 8 showed that many partridges are killed by raptors, but especially where the habitat is marginal – poor food supply and hard winters, or in areas with many trees where the ambush species such as the goshawk have the advantage.

Despite a thorough search of the vast literature on partridges I can find no *evidence* that raptor predation reduces the numbers of partridges available for shooting, and much evidence that it does not. In mainland Europe the main problem is probably with the goshawk (Brüll, 1964) but even here the latest research shows that even where considerable predation occurs there may be no long-term effect on partridge numbers (Döring and Helfrich, 1986). So there is much to reassure the ornithologists and naturalists. The protected species deserve protection.

Nevertheless, it does seem that current attempts in parts of western Europe to give further protection to corvids are misguided. Some current research in eastern Europe has shown that magpie and hooded crow numbers can be controlled by an avicide which causes very little harm to other predators (Kalotás and Nikodémusz, 1982a, b; Nikodémusz and Imre, 1982). This practice would be illegal in Britain, but the control of crows can be remarkably effective by shooting and by cage trapping. The best and most up-to-date methods to use are described in the advisory booklet *Predator and Squirrel Control* (booklet no. 16), published by the Game Conservancy.

More studies are needed overseas where the predator and prey communities contain species very different from those in Sussex. For example the field vole *Microtus arvalis* is an important food of many potential partridge predators in the arable areas of mainland Europe but not present in Britain on farmland. It is possible that partridges can coexist with higher populations of raptors where this vole is common than would otherwise be the case. In North America, much of the partridge nest predation is by racoons and skunks, and the alternative prey of partridge predators is of course quite different from Europe.

Finally, some consideration needs to be given to the relative importance of fox control, especially since in Britain foxes are also valued as quarry species.

Computer simulations suggest that egg predators are more important than hen predators but that best results are achieved by controlling both kinds of predators – bags being higher than the sum obtained from each type of control in isolation (see Table 11.4).

Table 11.4 Computer simulation of partridge bags comparing control of egg and hen predators, the Sussex model

	Simulation	Bag at MSY, ± 1 sd
A	No predation control	3.4 ± 1
B	Hen predation controlled	5.1 ± 1
C	Egg predation controlled	8.0 ± 2
D	B + C	15.6 ± 4

Note: this is the current situation with herbicide use

There are no data available to check these results because gamekeepers are most unlikely to control foxes and not crows, but in many parts of mainland Europe fox densities have been reduced by up to 70% by the disease rabies (Macdonald, 1980). Spittler (1972) gave data showing partridge and fox bags before, during and after rabies outbreaks, indicating a clear increase in bags of partridges after a reduction in foxes. Sarcoptic mange is currently spreading amongst foxes in Sweden (Lindström and Mörner, 1985) and in its wake increases in partridges have been recorded (J.O. Peterson, *in litt.*). When foxes were reduced in numbers to prevent rabies entering Denmark, a similar response of partridges occurred (Jensen, 1970).

Legal aspects have been dealt with elsewhere (Anon, 1985) but ultimately the law will depend on the support which comes from those outside game conservation for rational, humane and sensitive predator control. Such support is likely to depend largely on improvements made to the environment as a whole in the interests of game conservation, the subject of the next chapter. Such improvements would count for very little, so far as partridges are concerned, without predator control.

12 Avoiding the Adverse Effects of Pesticides

'It may be advantageous to encourage minimal populations of pests and weeds to persist in and around crops, especially in winter, to sustain populations of beneficial insects at a level high enough to retard rapid multiplication of pests in spring.' (Graham-Bryce *et al.*, 1980).

There has been a steady increase over the past fifty years in the number of pesticides necessary to protect cereal crops. Taking, for example, the Sussex study area cereal crops as a whole, approximately five different treatments are now used between sowing and harvesting, involving twenty-five different chemicals plus a couple of seed dressings and herbicides to clear stubbles. Elsewhere in Britain MAFF survey data show that the situation in cereal crops is very similar (e.g. Stanley and Hardy 1984).

It is therefore appropriate that the first questions one should ask should relate to the reasons for the increase. Will it continue? Is the increase evidence of a gigantic pesticides treadmill? Will even more pesticides be used in future? The answers could profoundly influence the overall approach to the problem of adverse effects of pesticides.

Integrated pest control

Integrated pest control, now more often referred to as integrated pest management (IPM), is the harmonisation of existing natural pest control (e.g. by aphid predators or parasites) with the control exerted by the pesticide, so that the two controls work together rather than against one another. The opposite situation, a 'pesticides treadmill', occurs when the initial appplication of a pesticide reduces the natural control (for example the number of aphid predators), thus requiring the use of additional pesticides. The concepts describing these contrary conditions both originated from studies of the insect pests of cotton in California in the 1950s (Van den Bosch, 1980). The vast environmental implications were stressed by Moore (1967), but they have received little attention.

The first pesticides to be used in cereal crops were seed dressings and relatively narrow-spectrum herbicides used to control broad-leaved weeds such as charlock. Such chemicals were obviously not part of any 'treadmill' and they did allow farmers and consumers to benefit from higher yields, higher yielding varieties and from mechanised harvesting.

The succession of new, relatively specific herbicides which have been introduced for broad-leaved weeds such as *Polygonum* spp. was not usually caused by any upsurge of these weeds (Chapter 8), though in some circumstances this might be the case – Fryer and Chancellor (1971). Rather, the aim has been to eradicate weeds not previously controlled by herbicides (e.g. Fig. 6.4).

The reasons for the introduction of herbicides to control grass weeds (from the mid-1970s) are more complex but many grass weed infestations arose from a lack of control exerted by crop rotation and the desire for more autumn-sown cereals, rather than by the disturbance of any natural controls. Some cereal weeds are now resistant to herbicides (e.g. *Amaranthus* spp. to atrazine and simazine) but this does not explain the introduction of any new herbicide to cereals in Britain.

The introduction of many new fungicides in the 1970s might have been due to an increased incidence of pathogenic fungi but monitoring started too late to show that this actually occurred. The outbreaks of leaf blotch (*Rhynchosporium secalis*) and brown rust (*Puccinia hordei*) in the 1960s stimulated the search for new compounds but mildew (*Erysiphe graminis*) had been a problem in cereals for centuries. Even if an increase of fungus diseases occurred it cannot be blamed on the use of any pesticides though it may be attributable to certain other aspects of the extensive monoculture of cereals (Potts, 1977a). Later, high yielding but fungus-susceptible varieties were often grown because they could be protected with fungicides, but again this is not due to any counter-productive use of other pesticides.

Aphicide use has clearly increased rapidly (Fig. 6.8) and as we have seen (Table 6.8), all aphicides currently used are effective against insects preferred by chicks as well as against cereal aphids, which, although not preferred, are eaten in large quantities on occasion (Potts, 1970a).

Anticipating this increasing use of aphicides, we began to study the cause of outbreaks of cereal aphids in the Sussex study area. Our aim was to explore the possibilities of integrated control as a way to limit aphicide use. Like Adams and Drew (1965), we found fewer cereal aphids in crops not treated with herbicides and it soon became apparent that an important factor could be variations in the effects of the non-specialised aphid predators.

In 1970 we found that the rates of increase of cereal aphids were lower where their predators were most abundant (Potts, 1970c), a discovery later confirmed by a more detailed analysis (Potts and Vickerman, 1974). The most important variable appeared to be predation early in the season, but in order to establish this a lot more research was needed. In Czechoslovakia some work had already shown that nocturnal predators such as ground beetles and earwigs were eating aphids (Skuhravý, 1959, 1960), yet these predators seemed scarce in cereal crops, especially in the crop foliage. Could it be that the predation was not noticed because it took place at night?

By sampling on a twenty-four hour basis we showed that this was indeed the case (Vickerman and Sunderland, 1975). In particular the larvae of the rove beetle *Tachyporus* were adept at climbing up the tillers during the night to reach and feed on aphids in the ear, returning to the soil by dawn. Some recent work has confirmed these results, even concluding that *Tachyporus* predation, in conjunction with that of hoverfly larvae, prevented an outbreak of cereal aphids at Cranfield in 1982 (Holmes, 1984).

Our first experiments to check such effects used predator exclusion techniques, and we concentrated on the role of those predators which specialised in preying on aphids. For the three summers 1976–78, these predators were excluded from areas of winter wheat using cages of polyester netting, erected after aphids had established themselves but before aphid-specific predators such as hoverflies and ladybirds had arrived in the field. The experiments showed that the specialist predators could slow aphid multiplication rate prior to the population peak and that they significantly reduced the number of 'aphid-days' that the crop has to suffer (Chambers *et al.*, 1983). A recent review of this work has concluded that the specialist predators have a very important role in controlling cereal aphids – but they only prevent densities reaching the threshold at which insecticide application is recommended in years when they appear early in the season (Chambers *et al.*, 1986). The most important specialist predators appear to be hoverflies, such as *Syrphus corollae*, because they are so mobile and because they can lay their eggs after feeding on pollen. Unlike ladybirds they do not have to feed on aphids to lay eggs.

There are approximately 350 species of non-specialist aphid predators in cereal crops in Britain (Sunderland *et al.*, 1984), none of which depends on aphids because they can feed on Collembola or other prey and on fungi or even plant material. In our studies these predators occurred so early in the season that polythene barriers had to be used, and all predators removed.

The barrier work showed that the rate of growth of the aphid populations was increased where predators were removed (Edwards et al., 1979). It did not show which predators were important but the studies of aphids in the diet, in particular the diet in relation to aphid density (population functional-response curves) and tiller climbing behaviour, suggested that *Agonum dorsale*, *Demetrias atricapillus* and the earwig were particularly significant (Sunderland and Vickerman, 1980).

The same conclusion was reached using the annual monitoring data. Comparisons of the annual peaks in cereal aphid density (y) with the numbers of predators in the third week of June showed that, using log values:

$$y = 4.84 - 1.47x_i - 0.79x_{ii} \qquad (P<0.01)$$

where x_i was the combined density of *Agonum*, *Demetrias* and the earwig, and where x_{ii} consisted of the densities of *Tachyporus* spp., *Bembidion lampros*, and *Notiophilus biguttatus*. Only 40% of the variation in peak numbers was explained (Carter, 1984) but other important factors such as parasites (which are important in some years – Vickerman, 1982) and weather, altering seasonal development of the crop, were excluded.

The implications of the above equation are staggering, given that a level of about 3.3 (2000 aphids m^{-2}) represents the economic threshold for spraying. On a national scale, a doubling of predator numbers might replace the application of aphicides costing tens of millions of pounds per annum!

Table 12.1 The percentage of some species of predatory beetles on farmland which overwinter in hedges rather than in fields. Damerham; from Sotherton (1984)

	In hedges (%)
Percentage of total farm area	2
Ground beetles:	
Agonum dorsale	87
Demetrias atricapillus	89
Bembidion lampros	56
Rove beetles:	
Tachyporus hypnorum	43
Tachyporus chrysomelinus	43

Having due regard for the potential value of these generalist predators, a series of studies on them has been carried out at the University of Southampton (Griffiths, 1983; Carillo, 1985; Coombes, 1985a). It is especially interesting that *Demetrias* and *Agonum*, and also *Bembidion lampros*, overwinter in dry grassy hedges or fences of the type that partridges prefer for nesting (Sotherton, 1984, 1985a). For some of these aphid predators hedges are clearly vital in winter (see Table 12.1) and in summer numbers are higher in crops surrounded by this kind of cover (Coombes and Sotherton, 1986).

A final approach in our study of aphid outbreaks was the construction of a simulation model of cereal aphid peak numbers. Unfortunately, a year to year simulation model of cereal aphid populations has not yet been achieved because it is not yet possible to link the cereal aphid populations of one year with those in the next by equations. Problems also arise from the difficulty of relating D-vac density indices to absolute densities of predators in the crop. The diet of the many predators which extract only fluids from their prey also gave special problems, but these are now solved using enzyme-linked immuno-assay techniques (ELISA) (Crook and Sunderland, 1984).

Despite the fact that our knowledge of cereal aphid predation is obviously incomplete, a good deal of progress has been made using computer models. The basic approach was to calculate daily predictions of aphid population growth from known relationships of temperature and crop growth to cereal aphid development. Allowances made for predation improved the value of the predictions (Rabbinge *et al.*, 1979) and a model without predation predicted aphid numbers ten times higher than observed in 1978, a non-outbreak year (Carter *et al.*, 1982). Simulations of the seasonal growth of cereal aphid populations in the Sussex study area were more accurate when inputs were made to cover the role of predation (Carter, 1984). In summary, the evidence from simulation modelling is that predation is important. In future it is hoped that the models will become more accurate, for example, when the effects of parasitoids are included. However this will be difficult because each species of parasitoid has its own complement of hyper-parasitoids (Powell, 1982).

The role of web-spinning spiders, especially the money spiders (Linyphiidae), is also difficult to model but it could contribute significantly to cereal aphid predation (Nyffler and Benz, 1979; Nentwig, 1980; Fraser, 1982). Fraser found that cereal aphids were the second most frequent prey trapped in the webs of six species of money spider; 12% of prey were aphids, 72% Collembola. A total of 151 species of spider have been reported in cereal crops in Britain so far (Sunderland, *in press*).

The role of the many species of predatory flies, the Empididae (especially *Platypalpus* spp. and *Tachydromia arrogans*) and Dolichopodidae, is virtually unknown, though 11% of Empididae were positive for aphids in ELISA tests (Sunderland *et al.*, 1985, extended *in litt.*). In 1969 and the early 1970s these flies were very common in the Sussex study area cereals (together 30 m^{-2}), but with a marked decline in the mid-1970s to 4 m^{-2}, from which the recovery has been slow, 5 m^{-2} in 1984 but 16 m^{-2} in 1985. One species – the yellow dung fly, very common in cereals on stock farms – is difficult to catch in a D-vac but may be a significant aphid predator; 27% were positive with ELISA (K. Sunderland *in litt.*).

Attention is often focussed on aphid outbreaks but the most important feature of the aphid situation we have monitored in Sussex is that serious outbreaks turned out to be so infrequent (four times in seventeen years). Moreover, cereal aphids have tended to *decline* and the increased use of aphicides (at least on the study area) could not be the cause (Fig. 12.1). In fact the natural control mechanisms are still, at least in this study area, rather effective. A possible exception might be in autumn when increased incidence of barley-yellow-dwarf virus (spread by cereal aphids) has occurred, leading in recent years to much autumn use of insecticides. Effects on preferred insects the following summer are unknown but may not be important (Cole and Wilkinson, 1984).

In the early 1970s *Tachyporus* spp. (mainly *hypnorum* and *chrysomelinus*, but with some *obtusus* and *nitidulus*) were the most numerous non-specialised aphid predators in cereal crops, averaging in the third week of June ten adults and 220 larvae m^{-2} (corrected for D-vac efficiency but not for nocturnal 'increase' found by Vickerman and Sunderland (1975)).

Tachyporus spp. feed mainly on fungi, including the pathogenic fungi of cereals. Adverse effects (not necessarily including direct toxicity) on its numbers were noted with the first widely used foliar fungicide in cereals, tridemorph, in 1971 (Sotherton and Moreby, 1984a). *Tachyporus* began to decline at about the same time as fungicides were introduced, so could fungicides be the cause? At first glance (see Fig. 12.2) it appears as though this might be the case. However, a crude computer model was constructed which assumed that *Tachyporus* died in all fields as they were sprayed with fungicide: the worst possible case. Even this model gave a predicted decline from fungicides, but occurring two years *after* the one we observed. In recent years, with most fungicide use, there has been a recovery of *Tachyporus* densities.

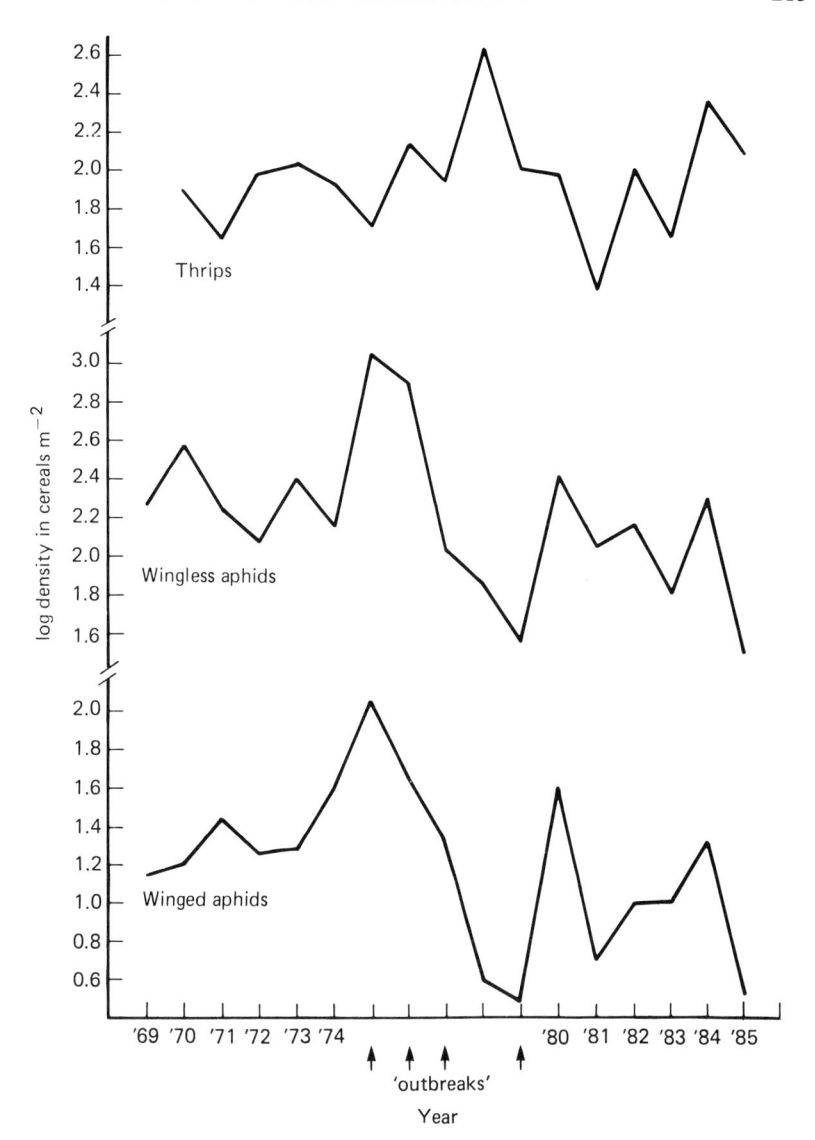

Fig. 12.1 Sussex study: trends in densities of cereal thrips and aphids in cereal crops in the third week of June over the period 1970–1985.

If fungicides did not cause the decline in *Tachyporus* spp., then what did? One possibility (no more than that) is parasitism. Even when *Tachyporus* spp. were at their lowest numbers in 1977–1981, 8% of emerging adults would not have been able to breed because of parasitism by the wasp *Centistes cuspidatus*. A further similar percen-

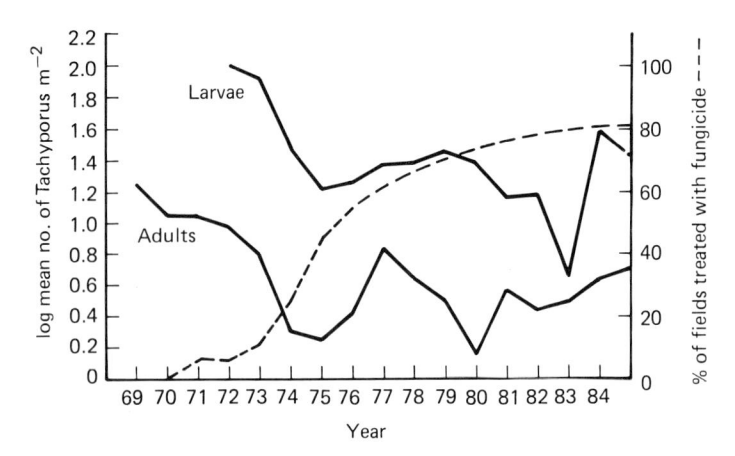

Fig. 12.2 Sussex study: densities of *Tachyporus* adults and larvae compared to use of foliar fungicides, 1969–1985.

tage were hosting various parasitic round-worms and 10% of larvae were parasitised by another minute wasp, *Blacus ruficornis* (Richardson, 1983).

Some effects of food-chain disruption on the fungus-dependent fauna are unavoidable. However in 1984, the organo-phosphate fungicide pyrazophos was cleared for use in barley by the Pesticides Safety Precautions Scheme and in 1985 supported by the Agricultural Chemical Approval Scheme, even though it was known to have insecticidal effects (Table 6.8). Fortunately the Cereals and Gamebirds Research Project was able to carry out trials and to warn conservation-minded farmers about its properties (Sotherton, 1985b). Used in wheat (as is allowed in Germany and was in Switzerland), pyrazophos can by its insecticidal effect on cereal aphid predators cause an upsurge of cereal aphids and necessitate the use of additional aphicides which would not be necessary in the absence of pyrazophos (Sotherton 1985b). An upsurge like this can usually be observed after using insecticides, due to the suppression of natural controls (Redfearn and Pimm, 1986).

There is pressure to introduce new fungicides such as pyrazophos because resistance to the early fungicides is developing. Widespread resistance of winter wheat eyespot (*Pseudocercosporella herpotrichoides*) and *Septoria tritici* to the benzimidazoles, or of mildew to ethirimol, and the reduced sensitivity of mildew to triazoles and other ergosterol inhibitors, each occurred within ten years of first use (MAFF, 1986). It is therefore fortunate that the Cereals and Gamebirds Project has developed a programme of monitoring the insecticidal properties of fungicides so that, where there is a choice, farmers can choose to protect insects in the interests of game management and other wildlife. Such vigilance is clearly necessary, and it is surprising that it should depend on shooting partridges.

Meanwhile the major problem appears to be with aphicides, particularly since they are not specific, indeed so far as insects are concerned becoming less so with the synthetic pyrethroids (e.g. cypermethrin, deltamethrin) though these are not cleared for summer use on cereals.

The smaller diurnal ground beetles are preferred both by chicks and by important aphid predators (e.g. *Demetrias*); it is therefore at least theoretically possible to solve both problems (chick food shortage and aphids needing control) in one stroke.

Apart from the Sussex studies there have been a number of indications that relatively unimportant, and therefore tolerable, cereal weeds can increase ground beetle densities, for example the grass weed *Poa annua* (Speight and Lawton, 1976), also legumes and grasses which have been undersown (Wichtrup *et al.*, 1985). In the latter case, in Germany, *Agonum dorsale* numbers were significantly increased and aphid peak numbers were halved, but at the time of writing there is no way of introducing integrated control of cereal aphids which would be reliable enough for most individual cereal growers. In addition yield penalties would be involved, in the short-term, with no compensation. However, many varieties of milling wheat grown by the leading 'organic' cereal growers, e.g. Mr C. B. Wookey of Upavon, Wiltshire, are less susceptible to aphids, and organic systems tolerate more weeds and employ the use of more clovers.

Cereal varieties have been bred which are semi-resistant to aphids (Lowe *et al.*, 1985) and this should enhance the role of aphid predators. The variety 'Huntsman', widely grown in our study area in the mid-1970s, was particularly susceptible. Some new wheats such as 'Rapier' are much more resistant (K. Sunderland *in litt.*).

There seems to be a general agreement among water suppliers in eastern Britain that too much nitrate is filtering through to the aquifers; indeed, some water boards are now considering reduced usage as an alternative to extracting directly from the water supplies. A nitrogen tax has been proposed, but from the environmental point of view incentives encouraging the use of more legumes would be a more advantageous approach. Such a system, in which legumes are established by the undersowing of cereals, is still continued at Applesham Farm. In fact it seems to have prevented any decline of partridges (Table 10.4), mainly by encouraging insects such as sawflies, as we saw in Chapter 6. It would be interesting to know what has happened in those parts of Poland and Canada where legumes and cereals are often grown together, as they were in Britain prior to the use of herbicides (the system known as 'dredge corn').

Many of the people who object to features of modern farming such as straw burning and slurry disposal prefer mixed arable and stock farms. Others wish to keep more labour on the land, or at least in rural areas, and would wish to help the smaller family farms in the less favoured regions, especially in the north. Traditional ley-farming with undersowing is a system which employs more labour and it is certainly kinder to the environment than any systems which replaced it; a grant to aid undersowing would help, especially where direct seeding is the alternative. The main problem with undersowing (though theoretically an advantage at present with huge cereal surpluses) is a yield penalty. This is caused by the need to encourage undersown legumes, brought about partly by using less nitrogen. In the recently designated environmentally sensitive areas, it will at least be possible to compensate farmers for using less nitrogen and fewer pesticides.

At the time of writing nobody seems to have come up with an acceptable solution of how to reduce cereal yields whether by quotas, land bank schemes or whatever. Grant aid to encourage undersowing (when appropriate) would in my opinion be one step in the right direction towards reducing the impact of modern cereal growing on the environment.

In future more consideration for the principles of integrated pest control could prevent many problems arising and even reduce the use of aphicides. But most trends are still in the opposite direction: only 2% of cereals are now undersown in the traditional way, and farmers with the organic approach account for an even smaller percentage.

It appears that there is no method by which a worthwhile overall increase in preferred insects can yet be achieved. In future it is hoped that the MAAF project 'Pest and Disease Control Systems: Their Ecological and Economic Effect in Intensive Cereal Production' at Boxworth, and the Lautenbach (near Stuttgart) project on integrated control in cereals (especially associated studies at the University of Tübingen), will help in rationalising pesticide use on cereals. It is encouraging that several similar projects have recently been established, particularly in Germany (FRG).

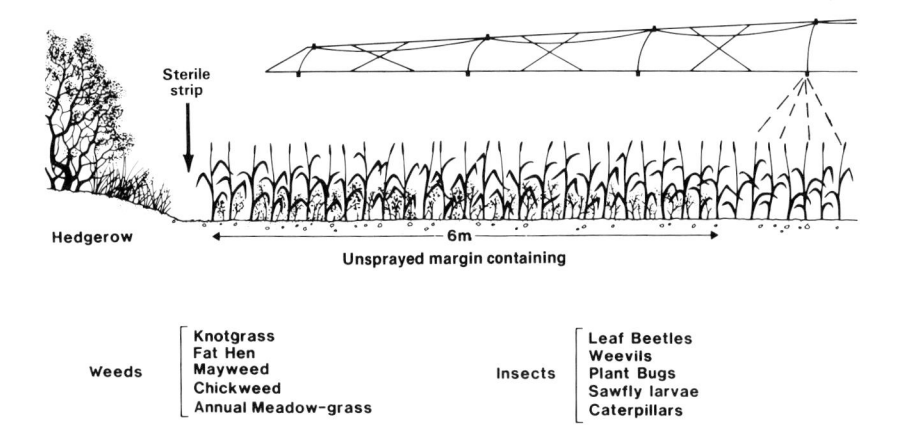

Fig. 12.3 Unsprayed cereal margin showing important features.

The cereal field: unsprayed margins

Our experiments, which were designed to assess the effects of herbicides, clearly showed that chick mortality rates could be reduced by not spraying the outer 6 m at the field margin (Colour Plate XXIX), equivalent in our case to 4% of the crop (Chapter 6; Fig. 12.3). Computer simulations suggested that the technique could restore partridge numbers, as is now becoming evident at Manydown (Rands, 1986c). These were controlled experiments – but could weedy margins be a practical proposition on a farm scale? The extent to which increased numbers of partridges and other wildlife might compensate for the hindrance to the cereal grower has to be considered, and how one might change the practices of a generation of cereal growers.

A principal concern of botanists has been for the endangered cereal weeds and of course the major benefit of not spraying headlands is that weeds are allowed to flourish. At the University of Bonn, Professor W. Schumacher has instigated a number of trials on cereal field margins (Schumacher 1980, 1981 and extended *in litt.*), and an arbitrary system of compensating cereal growers for weedy field margins is currently being developed as follows.

First the margins are selected by botanists, so far only in cereal fields and mainly in crops sown in spring. Margins with infestations of cleavers and any other weeds which will seriously reduce yields are excluded. Farmers are then invited (on a voluntary basis) to keep 3 m margins clear of herbicides (Colour Plate XXX). Although the prime purpose is to conserve rare weeds it is also recommended that insecticides are not used. By this technique a number of the endangered species of weed mentioned in Chapter 6 have been encouraged and in one headland strip fifty-four species of weeds were recorded. The weedy strips need not be in the same areas in succeeding years, though this is favoured by the botanists involved. If at any time the farmer sees a serious problem developing he can withdraw from the scheme. In 1985 twenty farmers in the Eifel district fulfilled the requirements of the scheme; one has now had a number of weedy headlands since 1978.

If the farmer keeps to the agreement he is reimbursed for the value of the lost yield, estimated to be 30% of five tons per hectare. Farmers in the FRG were thus granted £20000 for 500 km of weedy headland in 1985 and 2000 km are planned for 1986. In fact yield losses were found not to be the important factor; the main problems, as in this country were in harvesting crop margins when they were full of green and often damp weeds, and in reducing weed seed contamination of grain to meet the standards set by the Intervention (buying) Boards.

In all cases the main purpose of these schemes is to conserve flowering weeds which would otherwise become extinct. In Switzerland similar projects are organised by the charity Action Cornflower, and in several countries including England there are now arable weed reserves associated with rural open-air museums.

In our case (to conserve partridges), we would need to use the vast majority of available headlands (at least with fields >10 ha) and the unsprayed strips would need to be twice as wide as most of those employed in Germany, i.e. 6 m. In our experiments the unsprayed margins (which amounted to 6% of the area of the field) account for approximately 4% of total grain yield. So in a worst possible case where all the grain in the unsprayed margins was wasted (which in a normal season would be most unlikely), the returns would be reduced by only 4% and to offset this there would be savings on spray costs.

However, the main concern expressed by farmers interested in the technique and who have joined the Game Conservancy's Cereals and Gamebirds Research Project, is that there might, over a period of years, be a greater spread of weeds out into the rest of the field or to adjoining fields, than would otherwise be the case. Their particular concern was cleavers, by far the most competitive broad-leaved weed (Wilson, 1986), and the most difficult to separate from gain. Cleavers are a special problem too because they cannot be controlled by herbicides which would leave chickweed, mayweeds and the *Polygonums* unharmed. By contrast grass weeds, mainly a problem in autumn-drilled cereals, could be sprayed with some herbicides which would leave valued broad-leaved weeds unharmed, e.g. diclofop-methyl.

A sterile strip between the crop and the field boundary, about 1 m wide, can prevent grasses such as sterile brome (*Bromus sterilis*) or couch (*Agropyron repens*) encroaching into the crop. A practical herbicide for the purpose is a 1:5 mixture of glyphosate and atrazine. In practice, the margins on most farms can be treated in one day and an attachment can be fitted to prevent the herbicide drifting into hedge bottoms or into the weedy strip (Bond, 1986).

A great deal of research is still needed to perfect these techniques – in order to maximise benefits to partridges and minimise hindrance to farmers. This is in fact the main research activity of the Game Conservancy's Cereals and Gamebirds Research Project. Already it is clear that the major problem is that many margins in autumn-drilled cereals become very thick with weeds if no herbicides are used at all. Whether or not enough broad-leaved weeds will remain if damaging weeds are sprayed selectively is not yet established, though many trials are in progress. No detailed work has yet been carried out in maize but in this crop it would sometimes be practicable to undersow 6 m margins with peas. This would help where weedy margins are unlikely to be tolerated.

Finally we should consider the question of the overall costs involved in gamebird production and the financial implications of not spraying 6% of the crop.

To do this we can compare predicted bags on the Sussex study area with and without unsprayed cereal crop margins. For example on the 29 km^2 main study area we would need to employ 100 km of cereal margin, equivalent to 60 hectares. Assuming £100 per ton of grain, yields of 5 tonnes per hectare on margins, a notional 30% yield loss (to cover

Table 12.2 Expected cost per gamebird bagged and, in brackets, bag of partridge km^{-2}, according to whether cereal field margins were sprayed or not

	Spray normal	6 m margin not sprayed
Keeper	£47	£16
	(15)	(50)
No keeper	£ 0	£10
	(3)	(10)

harvesting difficulties), and that we would need six gamekeepers at a cost of £10000 per annum each to cover the 29 km² effectively, then the cost per gamebird bagged can be calculated. These and the bag of partridges km^{-2} are given in Table 12.2. Pheasants would benefit as much from not spraying as partridges (Rands, 1986c), and partridges would make up a third of the total gamebird bag.

The results suggest that the major consideration will be the cost of the gamekeeper, not that of the cost of the weedy margins. The Sussex study has, I believe, shown that full-time gamekeepering is essential to partridge conservation but also that it can be a highly seasonal occupation, February to July, if hand-rearing for release is abandoned.

Gamekeeper-associated costs would be much reduced if (for example) they helped at harvest time or with forestry and woodland management and if their value in controlling rabbits, rats, woodpigeons, moles, etc., and as 'unofficial farm policemen' was properly considered. Even so the cost of £16 per gamebird bagged compares favourably with the currently estimated cost of released partridges shot (£12), though of course with a lower bag. It therefore appears to me that the major effort needed to conserve partridges is simply to integrate farm, forest and game management.

Some gamekeepers might be alarmed by these views, but the plain facts are that traditional wild partridge keepers are needed to increase partridge numbers for shooting and that their very profession is endangered, as we saw in Chapter 10. An additional role for them in farming or forestry would create jobs, when otherwise the cost of a gamekeeper would be uneconomic.

In 1958 the Game Conservancy or, as it was then known, the ICI Game Research Station, stated 'We do not wish to do anything or make any suggestion which might hinder the progress and efficiency of modern food production'. Thankfully for the partridge, this does not seem necessary.

The potential that gamebird management has for reducing the impact of pesticides in the countryside generally is evident from the other benefits of not treating headlands with pesticides on a farm scale: the preservation of rare weeds (Schumacher 1980, 1981), avoidance of pesticide drift into hedgerows (Dobson 1986), increased numbers of butterflies, honey bees, grasshoppers and possibly song birds (Rands and Sotherton 1986 and series of Cereals and Gamebirds Research Project papers in preparation). However, these benefits are less easy to put into practice, if only because it is difficult to assess how many managed headlands would be needed. We need more butterflies, but how *many* more do we want?; and what proportion of headlands would suffice?

The future

At present it is of course difficult to place the economic arguments for game in full perspective, because many changes are difficult to predict. In western Europe there is a background of a high price support system for cereals – which can no longer be afforded. As prices decline in real terms, there is likely to be even further specialisation in farming with most cereals being grown in areas where high yields can be obtained. This might itself exacerbate pest problems and cause increased use of pesticides. Certainly there will continue to be increased efforts by the agrochemical companies, sometimes aggressive, to sell more pesticides.

On the other hand the financial support available to farmers for wildlife conservation is likely to grow in a number of ways, although these have so far been mostly concerned with hedges and spinneys. Financial incentives might be available to encourage wildlife in the crop and crop margins; there seems particular scope for this in the recently designated Environmentally Sensitive Areas or 'ESAs', although these are few and far between in the lowlands.

At time of writing, set-aside schemes are being considered as an alternative to cereal quotas. I hope that cereals in unsprayed margins can be exempt from quotas.

The extensive use of many insecticides on arable crops is a subject which attracts much criticism from wildlife conservationists and bee keepers as well as game conservationists. Measures to reduce pesticide inputs are therefore now identified as a priority by many environment protection agencies, as they are also by many of those concerned for cereal surpluses. Methods of encouraging natural enemies of insect pests at crop margins and in field boundaries could be significant in reducing the reliance on insecticides.

So far as partridges are concerned, my view is that the popularity of cereal margin management techniques will depend most of all on the value placed on conserving wild pheasants and partridges for shooting. I hope it is high. If it is low, the partridge seems destined, and soon, for a status similar to that of the corncrake.

13 Future Partridge Management: A Brief Summary of Recommendations

To restore partridge numbers to their pre-1952 level on farmland would require a five- or six-fold increase of the numbers currently present.

From the work reported in this book it appears that such a programme of restoration would be most likely to succeed if attention was paid to the following recommendations:

(1) Ensure at the start that the habitat is potentially suitable
Partridges prefer open countryside with relatively few trees, with cereal crops as the main habitat requirement in the absence of natural grassland.

(2) Ensure adequate good quality nesting cover
In suitable linear nesting cover (such as grassy bottomed hedges) the maximum density likely to be achieved is one nest per 200 m. The capacity nesting stock is thus five times the length of suitable field boundary km^{-2}.

The maximum utilisable field boundary length is probably 11 km km^{-2}, equivalent to a field size of 9 ha (22 acres). With more than ten trees per linear km of field boundary some of the field boundary length will be avoided by nesting partridges.

The best quality sites are on banks, 0.5 m or so above the field level so as to avoid water-logging in very wet weather. The preferred vegetation at the nest site in spring is long grass remaining from the previous season's growth, suitable for covering the eggs and concealing incubating partridges.

(3) Reduce chick mortality
The most effective method is to encourage the insect prey of partridge chicks by not using herbicides and other pesticides in the cereal field margins, in particular to provide broad-leaved weeds in a strip 6 m wide amounting to 6% of the crop. Some pesticides might be exempt from this rule: herbicides for the control of grass weeds (wild oats and various grasses) in autumn and non-insecticidal fungicides.

(4) Reduce nest predation

Predation on eggs is mostly by corvids and rats, and on incubating hens mostly by foxes, feral cats and stoats. These losses can be effectively controlled by gamekeepers reducing the densities of these predators during the nesting season. Such gamekeepers are effective at a rate of one full-time (though seasonal) keeper per 5 km² (one per 1250 acres).

(5) Shooting should not exceed the optimum sustainable yield

When the above methods (2–4) have been implemented a forecast of the bag (B) which can be shot is calculated:

$$B = A - \frac{2x}{S}$$

where x (the spring stock of pairs) is five times the length in km of linear nesting cover km^{-2}, S (the survival rate from autumn to spring) = 0.55, with a downward adjustment for areas with severe winters, and A is the number of partridges km^{-2} present at the beginning of the shooting season.

(6) Additional

Releasing for restocking is not advocated, though transfer of wild birds to an area with initially very low numbers (due to poor management) may be advisable.

Winter feeding of grain in areas out of range of trees, where raptors may be present, is advisable where snow cover is deep or where ice prevents normal feeding for more than about one week. Such conditions are rare in Britain.

Disease is no longer a serious problem but strongylosis may reappear as a significant cause of loss if numbers are restored. Methods of controlling the disease by using anthelmintics are now available, should they be needed.

Each recommendation would need to be adjusted to individual needs but always bearing in mind that they are a closely interrelated package, detailed recommendations and practical advice designed for gamekeepers and shoot managers are given in Advisory Booklet No 4: partridge management, published by the Game Conservancy.

References

Abplanalp, A.A. (1974) Inbreeding as a tool for poultry improvement. In: *First World Congress on Genetics Applied to Livestock Production*, pp. 867–908. Graficas Orbe, Spain.

Adams, J.B. & Drew, M.E. (1965) Grain aphids in New Brunswick. III. Aphid populations in herbicide-treated oatfields. *Canadian Journal of Zoology* **43**, 789–794.

Alington, C.E.A. (1904) *Partridge Driving*. Murray, London.

Almquist, A.J. (1952) Amino acid requirements of chickens and turkeys. *Poultry Science* **51**, 966–981.

Altieri, M.A. & Letourneau, D.K. (1982) Vegetation management and biological control in agroecosystems. *Crop Protection* **1**, 405–430.

Altum, B. (1894) Ueber Formen des Rebhuhns, *Starna cinerea* L. *Journal für Ornithologie* **42**, 254–269.

Anderson, M.R. & Shapiro, J. (1955) Control of the gapeworm in the ring-necked pheasant in Connecticut. *Bulletin of the Connecticut Agricultural Experimental Station* **315**, 12 pp.

Anon (1985) *Predatory Birds of Game and Fish* (Compiled by the Working Party on Avian Predators). British Field Sports Society, London.

Arrington, O.N. & Edwards, A.E. (1951) Predator control as a factor in antelope management. *Transactions of the 16th North American Wildlife Conference*, pp. 179–193.

Aschoff, J. & Pohl, H. (1970) Der Ruheumsatz von Vögeln als Funktion der Tageszeit und der Körpergrösse. *Journal für Ornithologie* **111**, 38–47.

Ash, J.S. (1960) Bird of prey numbers on a Hampshire game-preserve during 1952–1959. *British Birds* **53**, 285–300.

Ash, J.S. (1964) Observations in Hampshire and Dorset during the 1963 cold spell. *British Birds* **57**, 221–241.

Ash, J.S. & Taylor, A. (1964) Trials to measure the effects of a normal mercury/gamma BHC seed-dressing on breeding pheasants: interim report. *Annual Report Game Research Association* **3**, 36–41.

Ash, J.S. (1965) Toxic chemicals and wildlife in Britain. In: *Proceedings of the VIth International Congress of Game Biologists*, 1963, pp. 379–388. Bournemouth, Hampshire.

Ash, J.S. (1966) Some mutations of the partridge and red-legged partridge. *British Birds* **59**, 15–22.

Ash, J.S. (1970) Bag records as indicators of population trends in partridges. In: *Finnish Game Research* **30**, 357–360 (Proceedings of the VIIIth International Congress of Game Biologists, 1967. Helsinki, Finland).

Aubineau, J., Olivier, J. & Birkan, M.G. (1974) Effet d'aménagements de l'habitat sur la densité des couples et la réussite de la reproduction chez la perdrix grise (*Perdix perdix* L.) sur le territoire de chasse de Vauberon (Aisne). *Bulletin de l'Office National de la Chasse, Spécial* No. 2, pp. 121–152.

Bach, R.N. (1943) Strongylosis in Hungarian partridge. *North Dakota Outdoors* **6**, 13–14.

Bachthaler, G. (1967) Changes in arable weed infestation with modern crop husbandry techniques. *Abst. int. Congr. Pl. Prot. Vienna 6th*, pp. 167–168.

Badulin, A.V. (1983) Parasites and predators of the wheat leaf sawfly. In: *Noveishie dostizheniya sel'skokhozy-aĭstvennoi entomologii* (po materialam Ush s"ezda VEO, Vil'nyus, 9–13 oktyabrya 1979 g), (*ed.* V.P. Sem'yanov), pp. 13–16. Vilnius, USSR.

Bagliacca, M., Chiarcossi, M. & Mori, B. (1985) Effect of the amount of protein and amino acids in diets for grey partridges (*Perdix perdix* L.) during the first three weeks of life. *Avicoltura* **54**, 29–34.

Baird, W.W. & Tarrant, J.R. (1973) Hedgerow destruction in Norfolk in 1946–1970. Occasional reports, University of East Anglia, 47 pp.

Baker, T.H. (1911) *Record of Seasons, Prices of Agricultural Produce and Phenomena Observed in the British Isles.* Coates, Journal Office, Warminster.

Bărbulescu, A. (1973) Observations on the attack by hibernating adults of *Eurygaster* sp. on wheat. *Analele Institutului de Cercetări pentru Cereale și Plante Tehnice, Fundulea* **39**, 43–50.

Bayes, J.C., Dawson, M.J. & Potts, G.R. (1964) The food and feeding behaviour of the great skua (*Catharacta skua*) in the Faroes. *Bird Study* **11**, 272–279.

Beani, L. & Dessi Fulgheri, F. (1984) Leadership and social inter- actions in a group of grey partridges. In: *Monitore zool. ital.* **18**, 159–160 (The IXth Meeting of the Italian Society for the study of Animal Behaviour. Turin, Italy).

Beani, L. (1985) Comportamento sociale e bioritmi nella Starna, *Perdix perdix* durante il periodo gregario. In: Seminario tenuto all'Università della Calabria '*Biologia dei Galliformi, Problemi di gestione venatoria e conservazione*' (*eds* F. Dessi Fulgheri & T. Mingozzi), pp. 95–116. Dipartimento di Ecologia dell'Università della Calabria, Arcavacata, Italy.

Beani, L. & Dessi Fulgheri, F. (1984) Leadership and social interactions in a group of grey partridges. In: *Monitore zool. ital.* **18**, 159–160 (The IXth Meeting of the Italian

Beer, J.V. (1985) Prospects for the health of gamebirds. *Game Conservancy Annual Review* **16**, pp. 81–84.

Beljanski, B. (1960) Zimska ischrana i prezimljavanje jarebica. (Winter food and wintering of partridges). *Vojvodjanski Lovac* **6**, 171–173.

Benson, R.B. (1935) The alien element in the British sawfly fauna. *Annals of Applied Biology* **22**, 754–768.

Benson, R.B. (1950) An introduction to the natural history of British sawflies (*Hymenoptera: Symphyta*). *Transactions of the Society for British Entomology* **10**, 45–142.

Best, L.B. (1983) Bird use of fencerows: implications of contemporary fencerow management practices. *Wildlife Society Bulletin* **11**, 343–347.

Bey-Biyenko, G. Ya. (1939) Regional classification of crops by pest groups (based on the biocenosis of a wheat field). *Zap. Leningr. sel'skokhoz. inst., nov. izd.* **3**, 123–134.

Bey-Biyenko, G. Ya. (1961) Some features of changes in invertebrate fauna when virgin steppe is cultivated. *Review of Entomology URSS* **40**, 427–434.

Bezubik, B. (1959) Helminthofauna of partridge (*Perdix perdix* L.) in the Lublin

Palatinate. *Acta Parasitologica Polonica* **7**, 179-188.
Bijleveld, M.G. (1974) *Birds of Prey in Europe*. Macmillan, London.
Birkan, M.G. (1970) Le régime alimentaire de la perdrix grise d'après les contenus des jabots et des estomacs. *Annales de Zoologie – Écologie Animale* **2**, 121-153.
Birkan, M.G. (1971) Populations de perdrix grise (*Perdix perdix*) et agriculture sur un territoire de chasse près de Provins (Seine-et-Marne). *Bulletin Spécial du Conseil Supérieur de la Chasse* **15**, 1-8.
Birkan, M.G. (1973) Réussite des lâchers de perdrix grise (*Perdix perdix* L.) et de perdrix rouge (*Alectoris rufa* L.) d'élevage. In: *Proceedings of the Xth International Congress of Game Biologists*, 1971, pp. 345-358. Paris, France.
Birkan, M.G. (1977a) Reconnaissance du sexe et de l'âge chez la perdrix grise (*Perdix perdix*) et la perdrix rouge (*Alectoris rufa*). In: *Écologie du Petit Gibier et Aménagement des Chasses* (eds P. Pesson & M.G. Birkan), pp. 23-54. Gauthier Villars, Paris.
Birkan, M.G. (1977b) Analyse des tableaux de chasse de perdrix (*Perdix perdix* et *Alectoris rufa*): courbes d'éclosion, structure et dynamique des population, plan de chasse. In: *Écologie du Petit Gibier et Aménagement des Chasses* (eds P. Pesson & M.G. Birkan), pp. 55-77. Gauthier Villars, Paris.
Birkan, M.G. (1977c) Populations de perdrix grise et agriculture: évolution des tableaux de chasse et distribution des couples au printemps sur un territoire de chasse près de Provins (Seine-et-Marne). In: *Écologie du Petit Gibier et Aménagement des Chasses* (eds P. Pesson & M.G. Birkan), pp. 137-159, Gauthier Villars, Paris.
Birkan, M.G. (1977d) Lâchers de perdrix grises d'élevage, *Perdix perdix* L., valeur pour le repeuplement. *Bulletin de l'Office National de la Chasse, Numero Spécial Scientifiques et Techniques, Novembre* pp. 47-83.
Birkan, M.G. & Damange, J-P. (1977) Les lâchers de subadultes en novembre-décembre et d'adultes en mars. *Bulletin de l'Office National de la Chasse, Numero Spécial Scientifiques et Techniques, Novembre* pp. 84-118.
Birkan, M.G. & Angibault, J.M. (1978) Tracking léger sur perdrix grise (*Perdix perdix* L.) en plaine découverte. *Société Française pour l'Etude du Comportement Animal Bulletin Intérieur* **1**, 11-12.
Birkan, M.G. (1979) *Perdrix Grises et Rouges de Chasse et d'Elevage*. La Maison Rustique, Paris.
Birkan, M.G. (1980) Dynamique de population de perdrix grises (*Perdix perdix*): Analyse des facteurs-clé. *L'Oiseau et la Revue Française d'Ornithologie* **50**, 263-270.
Birkan, M.G. (1983) Influence de l'homme sur la répartition géographique de quelques espèces de gallinacés-gibier en France. *C.R. Soc. Biogéogr.* **59**, 382-396.
Birkan, M.G. (1985) Dynamique de population et relation avec l'occupation du milieu par la perdrix grise (*Perdix perdix*). In: *Proceedings of the XVIIth International Congress of Game Biologists*, 1985, 587 (abs, 8 pp, late paper). Brussels, Belgium.
Birkan, M.G. & Serre, D. (1986) Le problème du choix alimentaire chez le poussin de perdrix grise. In: *Proceedings of the Common Partridge (Perdix perdix L.) International Symposium Poland, 1985.* (ed. Z. Pielowski) Polish Hunting Association. Warsaw.
Bishop, R., Nomsen, R.C. & Andrews, R.D. (1977) A look at Iowa's Hungarian partridge. In: *Proceedings of the Perdix I. Hungarian Partridge Workshop* (ed. G.D. Kobriger), pp. 10-31. North Dakota Chapter of Wildlife Society.
Blank, T.H. & Ash, J.S. (1956a) Marker for gamebirds. *Journal of Wildlife Management* **20**, 328-330.
Blank, T.H. & Ash, J.S. (1956b) The concept of territory in the partridge *Perdix p.*

perdix. Ibis **98**, 379–389.

Blank, T.H. & Ash, J.S. (1960) Some aspects of clutch size in the partridge (*Perdix perdix*). In: *Proceedings of the XIIth International Ornithological Congress*, 1958, pp. 118–126. Helsinki, Finland.

Blank, T.H. & Ash, J.S. (1962) Fluctuations in a partridge population. In: *The Exploitation of Natural Animal Populations* (eds E.D. Le Cren & M.W. Holdgate), pp. 118–130. Blackwells, Oxford.

Blank, T.H., Southwood, T.R.E. & Cross, D.J. (1967) The ecology of the partridge I. Outline of population processes with particular reference to chick mortality and nest density. *Journal of Animal Ecology* **36**, 549–556.

Blank, T.H. (1969) The effect of Gramoxone on the hatchability of pheasant eggs. *Eley Game Advisory Station Annual Review*, 1968/69, pp. 82–83.

Boer, P.J. den, (1977) *Dispersal Power and Survival of Carabidae in a Cultured Environment.* H. Veenman & Zonen D.V., Wageningen, the Netherlands.

Bonacina, L.C.W. (1973) How extreme spells of weather could arise. *Weather* **28**, 382–385.

Bond, S. (1986) Management options for field margins – a farmer's view. *Proceedings of the British Crop Protection Conference on Field Margins*, 1986.

Borg, K., Wanntorp, H., Erne, K. & Hanko, E. (1969) Alkyl mercury poisoning in terrestrial Swedish wildlife. *Viltrevy* **6**, 301–379.

Borowiec, S., Kutyna, T., & Skrzyczyńska, J. (1975) Occurrence of crop field weed associations against environmental conditions in West Pomerania. *Ecologia Polska* **25**, 257–273.

Bouchner, M. & Fišer, Z. (1967) Contribution to the nesting bionomy of partridge. *Comm. Inst. For. Czechoslovakia* **5**, 19–28.

Bouchner, M. (1972) Prezivani umele odchovanych koroptvi po vypusteni do volne prirody. *Pol'ovnicky Zbornik (Folia venatoria)* **2**, 315–321.

Bouchner, M. & Temmlová, B. (1974) Factors influencing the survival degree of partridges from hand-rearing after release into free hunting grounds. *Práce Vúlhm* **45**, 73–92.

Bouchner, M. & Temmlová, B. (1975) Social behaviour of young partridges from hand-rearing after the release. *Práce Vúlhm* **47**, 43–53.

Bouchner, M. & Temmlová, B. (1977) Degree of the huntability of hand-reared partridges. *Práce Vúlhm* **51**, 7–18.

Brady, N.C. (1974) *U.S.S.R. Agriculture Atlas.* U.S. Central Intelligence Agency, U.S. Government Printing Office, Washington, D.C.

Branković, M. Davidović, M. & Popesković, D. (1967) Some thermogenic characteristics and the resistance of the partridge (*Perdix perdix*) against extremely low external temperatures. In: *Proceedings of the VIIth International Congress of Game Biologists*, 1965, pp. 251–253. Beograd-Ljubljana, Yugoslavia.

Brasse, D. (1975) Die Arthropodenfauna von Getreidefeldern auf verschiedenen Böden im Braunschweiger Raum. *Pedobiologia* **15**, 405–414.

Bresiński, W. (1976) Agrarian structure vs. the European hare population density. In: *Ecology and Management of European Hare Populations* (eds Z. Pielowski & Z. Pucek), pp. 195–197. Polish Hunting Association, Warsaw.

Brian, M.V. (1977) *Ants* (New Naturalist Series). William Collins Sons & Co Ltd, London.

Brisson, M. (1760) *Ornithologie* **1** (219), 26.

Broad, P.D. (1952) The occurrence of weed seeds in samples submitted for testing by the Official Seed Testing Station. *Journal of the National Institute of Agricultural Botany* **6**, 275–286.

Broadbent, L. (1980) Ecological aspects of agricultural pesticide application. *Biologist* **27**, 131–133.

Brown, A.W.A. (1978) *The Ecology of Pesticides*. John Wiley & Sons, New York.

Brugger, L. (1941) A survey of the endoparasites of the digestive and respiratory tracts of the Hungarian partridge (*Perdix perdix perdix* Linn.) in Whitman County, Washington. *Anatomical Record* **81**, 134.

Brüll, H. & Lindemann, W. (1954) Der derzeitige Stand unserer Kenntnis vom Leben des Rebhuhns. *Dtsch. J. Zeitung* **103**, 253–338.

Brüll, H. (1960) Der derzeitige Stand subtiler Äsungstudien des Flugwildes. In: *Proceedings of the IVth International Congress of Game Biologists, 1959*, pp. 18–31. Arnhem, Oosterbeek.

Brüll, H. (1964) A study of the importance of the goshawk (*Accipiter gentilis*) and sparrow hawk (*Accipiter nisus*) in their ecosystem. In: *Birds of Prey and Owls*. International Council for Bird Preservation, Caen, France.

Brüll, H. (1965) Grundsätzliches zur Niederwildhege. *Wild und Hund* **68**, 14–17.

Brüll, H. (1969) Der derzeitige Stand der Forschung zur Äsung des Rebhuhns. *Mitt. F. Schleswig-Holsteinsche Jäger* **16** No. 2.

Bull, A.L., Mead, C.J. & Williamson, K. (1976) Bird-life on a Norfolk farm in relation to agricultural changes. *Bird Study* **23**, 163–182.

Bureau, L. (1905) La perdrix grise de Pyrénées. In: *Proceedings of the IVth International Ornithological Congress*, pp. 494–512, London.

Bureau, L. (1911) L'âge des perdrix: I. La perdrix grise. *Bull. Soc. Sci. Nat. Ouest France (Nantes), Ser. 3* **1**, 124 pp.

Buturlin, S.A. (1906) On the birds collected in Transcaucasia (*ed* A.M. Kobylin). *Ibis* (Series No. 8) **6**, 407–427.

Byrkjedal, I. (1980) Nest predation in relation to snow cover – a possible factor influencing the start of breeding in shorebirds. *Ornis Scandinavica* **11**, 249–252.

Campbell, J.W. (1936) On the food of some British birds. *British Birds* **30**, 209–219.

Carillo, R. (1985) The ecology of, and aphid predation by the European earwig *Forficula auricularia* L. in grassland and barley. Unpublished Ph.D. Thesis, University of Southampton.

Carson, R. (1962) *Silent Spring*. Houghton Mifflin Co., Boston, U.S.A.

Carter, N., Dixon, A.F.G. & Rabbinge, R. (1982) *Cereal Aphid Populations: Biology, Simulation and Prediction*. Pudoc, Wageningen, the Netherlands.

Carter, N. (1983) Modelling the effects of predators on cereal aphid populations. *Game Conservancy Annual Review* **15**, pp. 68–71.

Carter, N. (1984) Modelling the effects of predators on annual variations in cereal aphid populations (1982–1984 inclusive). Final unpublished report (Ref. AG 63/161) to the Agriculture and Food Research Council.

Carter, N., Moreby, S.M. & Smith, G.L. (in press) Densities of insects in cereal crops in Sussex, at the margin and in the centre of the field.

Cartwright, B.W. (1944) The 'crash' decline in sharp-tailed grouse and Hungarian partridge in western Canada and the role of the predator. *Transactions of the 9th North American Wildlife Conference*, pp. 324–329.

Castroviejo, I. (1967) Zur Variation des Iberischen Rebhuhns *Perdix perdix hispaniensis*

(Reichenow, 1892). *Bonner Zool. Beitr.* **18**, 321–332.

Cergh, J.A. (1943) The European grey partridge in Persia. *Journal of Bombay Natural History Society* **44**, 297–298.

Chambers, R.J., Sunderland, K.D., Wyatt, I.J. & Vickerman, G.P. (1983) The effects of predator exclusion and caging on cereal aphids in winter wheat. *Journal of Applied Ecology* **20**, 209–224.

Chambers, R.J., Sunderland, K.D., Stacey D.L. & Wyatt, I.J. (1984). Aphid-specific predators and cereal aphids. *Glasshouse Crops Research Institute Annual Report for 1983*, pp. 86–91.

Chambers, R.J., Sunderland, K.D., Stacey, D.L. & Wyatt, I.J. (1986) Control of cereal aphids in winter wheat by natural enemies: aphid-specific predators, parasitoids and pathogenic fungi. *Annals of Applied Biology* **108**, 219–31.

Chambon, J-P. (1982) Biocenoses céréalières, rotations, insecticides. *Perspectives Agricoles* **64**, 44–56.

Chancellor, R.J. & Froud-Williams, R.J. (1984) A second survey of cereal weeds in central southern England. *Weed Research* **24**, 29–36.

Chapman, W.M.M. (1939) The bird population on an Oxfordshire farm. *Journal of Animal Ecology* **8**, 286–299.

Cheng, T-h., (1976) *Distributional List of Chinese Birds*. Institute of Zoology, Beijing, China (in Chinese).

Cheng, T-h., Dehao, Li., Zuxiang, W., Ziyu, W., Zhihua, J. & Taichun, Lu. (1983) *The Avifauna of Xizang*. Series of the scientific expedition to Qinghai-Xizang Plateau. Institute of Zoology, Beijing, China (in Chinese).

Chevin, H. & Chambon, J-P. (1984) Recherches sur les biocénoses céréalières: inventaire des Hyménoptères Symphytes. *La Défense des Végétaux* **227**, 156–162.

Chiriac, E., Manolache, L. & Constantinescu, Z. (1972) Contributions to the study of helminth fauna of the partridge (*Perdix perdix* L.). *Studii și Cercetări de Biologie, Seria Zoologie* **24**, 101–104.

Chiverton, P.A. (in press) Predator density manipulation and its effects on populations of *Rhopalosiphum padi* (Hom: Aphididae) in spring barley. *Annals of Applied Biology* **109**.

Chlewski, A. (1976) Estimation of the degree of danger to the European hare caused by pesticides. In: *Ecology and Management of European Hare Populations* (eds Z. Pielowski & Z. Pucek), pp. 231–236. Polish Hunting Association, Warsaw.

Chlewski, A. & Panek, M. (1986) Dynamics and some aspects of population structure of *Perdix perdix* in the Czempiń hunting grounds. In: *Proceedings of the Common Partridge (Perdix perdix L.) International Symposium Poland 1985* (ed, Z. Pielowski) Polish Hunting Association, Warsaw.

Church, K.E. (1979) Expanded radio-tracking potential in wildlife investigations with the use of solar transmitters. In: *A Handbook on Biotelemetry and Radio Tracking* (eds C.J. Amlaner Jr & D.W. Macdonald), pp. 247–250. Pergamon Press, New York.

Church, K.E. (1980) Grey partridge (*Perdix perdix* L.) nesting success and brood survival in east-central Wisconsin. Unpublished Master of Environmental Arts and Sciences Thesis, University of Wisconsin, Green Bay.

Church, K.E., Harris, H.J. & Stiehl, R.B. (1980) Habitat utilisation by grey partridge (*Perdix perdix* L.) pre-nesting pairs in east-central Wisconsin. In: *Proceedings of Perdix II Grey Partridge Workshop* (eds R. Peterson & L. Nelson), pp. 9–20. University of Idaho, Moscow.

Church, K.E. (1984) Nesting biology of grey partridge in east-central Wisconsin. In: *Proceedings of Perdix III Grey Partridge/Ring-necked Pheasant Workshop* (eds R.B. Stiehl, R.T. Dumke & R.B. Kahl), pp. 46–53. Campbellsport, Wisconsin.

Church, K.E. (1986) Comparative ecology of the grey partridge in occupied and potential range in New York. Unpublished Ph.D. Thesis, State University of New York, Syracuse.

Clapham, P.A. (1933) On the life-history of *Heterakis gallinae*. *Journal of Helminthology* **11**, 67–86.

Clapham, P.A. (1934) Experimental studies on the transmission of gapeworm (*Syngamus trachea*) by earthworms. *Proceedings of the Royal Society* (Series B), pp. 18–29.

Clapham, P.A. (1935) Some helminth parasites from partridges and other English birds. *Journal of Helminthology* **13**, 139–148.

Clapham, P.A. (1936) Further observations on the occurrence and incidence of helminths in British partridges. *Journal of Helminthology* **14**, 61.

Clapham, P.A. (1940) On wild birds as transmitters of helminth parasites to domestic stock. *Journal of Helminthology* **18**, 39–44.

Clapham, P.A. (1961) Recent observations on helminthiasis in some British gamebirds. *Journal of Helminthology*, R.T. Leiper Supplement, pp. 35–40.

Cole, J.F.H. & Wilkinson, W. (1984) Selectivity of pirimicarb in cereal crops. *Proceedings of the 1984 British Crop Protection Conference – Pests and Diseases* **1**, 311–316. Brighton, Sussex.

Connan, R.M. & Wise, D.R. (1977). Efficacy of tetramisole and dichloroxylenol against *Syngamus trachea* in pheasants and turkeys. *Veterinary Record* **101**, 34–35.

Coombes, D.S. (1985) The predatory potential of polyphagous predators in cereals in relation to timing of dispersal and aphid feeding. *Proceedings Ecology Aphidophaga II, Zvikov*, Czechoslovakia.

Coombes, D.S. (1986) Factors limiting the effectiveness of *Demetrias atricapillus* (L.) (Coleoptera: Carabidae) as a predator of cereal aphids. Unpublished Ph.D. Thesis, University of Southampton.

Coombes, D.S. & Sotherton, N.W. (1986) The dispersal and distribution of polyphagous predatory Coleoptera in cereals. *Annals of Applied Biology* **108**, 461–474.

Crook, N.E. & Sunderland, K.D. (1984) Detection of aphid remains in predatory insects and spiders by ELISA. *Annals of Applied Biology* **105**, 413–422.

Cross, D.A. (1966) Approaches toward an assessment of the role of insect food in the ecology of gamebirds, especially the partridge (*Perdix perdix*). Unpublished Ph.D. Thesis, University of London.

Crowther, R.E. (in press) Hedgerow trees. In: *Proceedings of the Royal Agricultural Society Conference on Hedges*, 1985. Stoneleigh.

Croze, H. (1970) Searching image of carrion crows. *Zeitschrift für Tierpsychologie* **5**, 85 pp.

Crudgington, I.M. & Baker, D.J. (1979) *The British Shotgun: Volume 1 1850–1870*. Barrie & Jenkins Ltd, London.

Csiki, E. (1912) Die Insektennahrung des Rebhuhns (*Perdix perdix* L.). *Aquila* **19**, 202–209.

Curio, E. (1976) The ethology of predation. In: *Zoophysiology and Ecology* (Volume 7). Springer-Verlag, Berlin.

Curtis, J. (1883) *Farm Insects, Being the Natural History and Economy of the Insects*

Injurious to the Field Crops of Great Britain and Ireland, and Also Those Which Infest Barns and Granaries, With Suggestions For Their Destruction. Von Voorst, London.

Dąbrowska-Prot, E., Karg, J. & Ryszkowski, L. (1974) An attempt to estimate the role of invertebrates in agrocenotic economics. In: *Ecological Effects of Intensive Agriculture (first attempt at a synthesis)* (ed, L. Ryszkowski), pp 41–62. Polish Scientific Publishers, Warsaw.

Dahlgren, J. (1986) Rapphönan. Fågelfaunan i Jordbrukslandskapet. *Swedish Wildlife Research* **13**. (In press.)

Dahlgren, J. (*in press*) Bird Fauna in the Agricultural Landscape.

Dawson, J.B. (1961) Hungarian partridge in Kemptville district. *Ontario Fish and Wildlife Review* **1**, 15–20.

Dean, A.M. (1978) Studies on the diet and weight of partridges *Perdix perdix, Alectoris rufa* and *Alectoris chukar*. Unpublished B.Sc. Hons Thesis, University of Southampton.

Delane, T.M., & Hayward, J.S. (1975) Acclimatisation to temperature in pheasants (*Phasianus colchicus*) and partridge (*Perdix perdix*). *Comparative Biochemistry and Physiology* **51A**, 531–536.

de Lavaur, E. (1967) Residus de Dinitro–4,6 orthocresol sur ble, après differents types de traitement. *Phytiatrie Phytopharmacie* **16**, 15–21.

de Lavaur, E. & Grolleau, G. (c.1983) Conséquences des Traitements Phytosanitaires sur le Gibier. Première partie: Effets Directs des Traitements Phytosanitaires, pp. 143–151. (Paper from Département de Phytopharmacie et d'Ecotoxicologie, INRA).

Dementiev, G.P. & Gladkov, N.A. (*eds*) (1952) *Ptitsy Sovetskogo Soyuza*. Moskva. [Translation by A. Birron & Z.S. Cole (1967), Programme for Scientific Translations, Jerusalem].

Denis, M. (1973) Influences des techniques agricoles sur les cultures et leurs adventices en relation avec l'étude de l'habitat de la perdrix grise, *Perdix perdix* L., dans les sud-est du Gatinais. Thèse présentée à la Faculté des Sciences D'Orléans, Université d'Orléans.

Dessi Fulgheri, F. & Mingozzi, T. (*eds*) (1985) Seminario tenuto all'Università della Calabria *Biologia dei Galliformi, Problemi di gestione venatoria e conservazione*. Dipartimento di Ecologia dell'Università della Calabria, Arcavacata, Italy.

Dessi Fulgheri, F., Beani, L. & Piazza, R. (in press) The vocalisation of the grey partridge (*Perdix perdix*): a spectrographic analysis. *Monitore Zoologico Italiano*.

Dewar, A.M. & Carter, N. (1984) Decision trees to assess the risk of cereal aphid (Hemiptera: Aphididae) outbreaks in summer in England. *Bulletin of Entomological Research* **74**, 387–398.

DeWeese, L.R., Henny, C.J., Floyd, R.L. Bobal, K.A. & Shultz, A.W. (1979) Response of breeding birds to aerial sprays of Trichlorfon (Dylox) and Carbaryl (Sevin–4–Oil) in Montana forests. In: *United States Department of the Interior, Fish and Wildlife Service*, Special Scientific Report – Wildlife No. 224.

Dietrick, E.J. (1961) An improved backpack motorised fan for suction sampling of insects. *Journal of Economic Entomology* **54**, 394–395.

Dits, V.R. (1917) Grey partridge in Imperial Hunting Preserves. *Orn. Vestnik* **8**, 57–58 (in Russian).

D'Mello, J.P.F. (1978) Factors affecting amino acid requirements of meat birds. In: *Recent Advances in Animal Nutrition* (eds W. Haresign & D. Lewis), pp. 1–17. Butterworths, London.

Dobson, C.M. (1986) Insecticide drift from sprayers and the effect on beneficial arthropods in winter wheat. Unpublished Ph.D. Thesis, University of London, Imperial College of Science and Technology.

Dobson, N. (1954) Chemical sprays and poultry. *Agriculture* **61**, 415–418.

Döring, V. (1982) Besatzshwankungen beim Rebhuhn und deren mögliche Ursachen. *Der Saarjäger* **34**, 7–10.

Döring, V. & Helfrich, R. (1986) Zur Ökologie einer Rebhuhnpopulation (*Perdix perdix*, L. 1758) im Unteren Naheland (Rheinland-Pfalz; BRD). Schriften des Arbeitskreises Wildbiologie und Jagdwissenschaften an der Justus-Liebig-Universität Giessen, Heft Nr. 15. Ferdinand Enke Verlag Stuttgart.

Dornberger, W. (1983) Winter observations on partridges (*Perdix perdix*) in middle Franconia, West Germany. *Anz. orn. Ges. Bayern* **22**, 169–176.

Doude van Troostwijk, W.J. (1968) Das Rebhuhn (*Perdix perdix*) in den Niederlanden. *Zeitschrift für Jagdwissenschaft* **14**, 1–12.

Douglas-Home, H. (1938) Partridge eccentricities. *The Field* (1938), 607.

Dritschilo, W. & Erwin, T.L. (1982) Responses in abundance and diversity of cornfield carabid communities to differences in farm practices. *Ecology* **63**, 900–904.

Dudziński, W. (1986) Importance of different elements of hunting ground structure for partridge populations. In: *Proceedings of the Common Partridge (Perdix perdix L.) International Symposium Poland, 1985.* (*ed.* Z. Pielowski) Polish Hunting Association, Warsaw.

Dumke, R.T., Stiehl, R.B. & Kahl, R.B. (eds) (1984) *Proceedings of the Perdix III Grey Partridge/Ring-necked Pheasant Workshop*, Campbellsport, Wisconsin. Wisconsin Department of Natural Resources, University of Wisconsin, Green Bay, U.S.A.

Dunachie, J.F. & Fletcher, W.W. (1966) Effect of some herbicides on the hatching rate of hens eggs. *Nature* **215**, 1406–1407.

Duncan, J.S., Reid, H.W., Moss, R., Phillips, J.D.P. & Watson, A. (1978) Ticks, louping-ill and red grouse on mooors in Speyside, Scotland. *Journal of Wildlife Management* **42**, 500–505.

Duncan, J.S. (1981) Louping-ill virus. *Game Conservancy Annual Review* **12**, pp. 63–66.

Dutt, T.E., Harvey, R.G. & Fawcett, R.S. (1982) Feed quality of hay containing perennial broadleaf weeds. *Agronomy Journal* **74**, 673–676.

Edwards, C.A., Sunderland, K.D. & George, K.S. (1979) Studies on polyphagous predators of cereal aphids. *Journal of Applied Ecology* **16**, 811–823.

Eggers, T. (1984) Some remarks on endangered weed species in Germany. *Proceedings of the 7th International Symposium on Weed Biology, Ecology and Systematics*, 1984, pp. 395–402. Paris, France.

Emmons, T. (1968) *The Russian Landed Gentry and the Peasant Emancipation of 1861.* Cambridge University Press, London.

Enck, J.W. (1986) The brood-rearing ecology of grey partridge in New York. Unpublished Master of Science Degree Thesis, State University of New York, College of Environmental Science and Forestry, Syracuse.

Ermolenko, V.M. (1983) Development of the fauna of sawflies (*Hymenoptera, Symphyta*) of man-made coenoses of cultivated lands in the south of the European part of the U.S.S.R. In: *Noveishie dostizheniya sel'skokhozyaistvennoi entomologii* (*ed.* by V.P. Sem'yanov) (po materialam Ush s″ezda VEO, Vil'nyus, 9–13 oktyabrya 1979 g.). Vilnius, U.S.S.R.

Errington, P.L. (1942) On the analysis of productivity in populations of higher vertebrates. *Journal of Wildlife Management* **6**, 165–181.

Fábián, G. (1979) Genetical consideration over the variation of the grey (Hungarian) partridge's breast colouration. *Aquila* **86**, 13–16.

Fagelfors, H. (1986) Weed flora in the agricultural landscape. *Swedish Wildlife Research* **13**.

Fant, R.J. (1953) A nest-recording device. *Journal of Animal Ecology* **22**, 323–327.

Farris, A.L. (1970) Distribution and abundance of the grey partridge in Illinois. *Transactions of the Illinois Academy of Science* **63**, 240–245.

Ferris, A.L. & Cole, S.J. (1981) Strategies and goals for wildlife habitat restoration on agricultural lands. *Proceedings of the 46th North American Wildlife & Natural Resources Conference*, pp. 130–136. Washington D.C.

Fimreite, N., Fyfe, R.W. & Keith, J.A. (1970) Mercury contamination of Canadian prairie seed-eaters and their avian predators. *Canadian Field Naturalist* **84**, 269–276.

Finch, S., Skinner, G. & Freeman, G.H. (1978) Distribution and analysis of cabbage root fly pupal populations. *Annals of Applied Biology* **88**, 351–356.

Folk, Č. & Bouchner, M. (1970) K Hnízdní Bionomii Koroptve Polní (*Perdix perdix*). *Lesnictví* **16**, 661–666.

Ford, J., Chitty, H. & Middleton, A.D. (1938) The food of partridge chicks (*Perdix perdix* L.) in Great Britain. *Journal of Animal Ecology* **7**, 251–265.

Formozov, A.N. (1946) Snow cover as an integral factor of the environment and its importance in the ecology of mammals and birds. In: '*Materials for Fauna and Flora of the U.S.S.R.*', New Series, Zoology, 5 (XX): 1–152. Moscow Society of Naturalists. (Translation published by Boreal Institute for Northern Studies, University of Alberta, Canada).

Frank, H. (1970) Die Auswirkung von Raubwild– und Raubzeugminderung auf die Strecken von Hase, Fasan und Rebhuhn in einem Revier mit intensivster landwirtschaftlicher Nutzung. In: *Proceedings of the IXth International Congress of Game Biologists*, 1969, pp. 472–479. Moscow, U.S.S.R.

Fraser, A.M. (1982) The role of spiders in determining cereal aphid numbers. Unpublished Ph.D. Thesis, University of East Anglia.

Freier, B. & Wetzel, Th. (1984) Abundanzdynamik von Schadinsekten im Winterweizen. *Zeitschrift für Angewandte Entomologie.* **98**, 483–494.

Fretwell, S.D. (1972) *Populations in a Seasonal Environment.* Princeton University Press, New Jersey.

Fröde, D. (1977) Changes in the numbers of grey partridge. *Zool. Anz.* **198**, 178–202.

Fryer, J. & Chancellor, R. (1971) Evidence of changing weed populations in arable land. *Proceedings of the 10th British Weed Control Conference*, pp. 958–964.

Furrer, R.K. (1979) Experiences with a new back-tag for open-nesting passerines. *Journal of Wildlife Management* **43**, 245–249.

Gair, R. (1975) Cereal pests. *Proceedings of the 8th British Insecticide Fungicide Conference* **3**, 871–874.

Gates, J.M. (1973) Grey partridge ecology in south-east-central Wisconsin. *Wisconsin Department of Natural Resources Technical Bulletin* **70**, 1–9.

Gätke, H. (1895) *Heligoland as an Ornithological Observatory.* Douglas, Edinburgh.

Gavrilov, V.M. (1980) Living energy of Galliformes: dependence on air temperature, season and body size. *Ornitologiya* **15**, 73–79.

Gavrin, V.F., Dolgushin, I.A., Korelov, M.N. & Kuz'mina, M.A. (1962) *Birds of Kazakhstan Volume II.* Publishing house of the Academy of Sciences, Kazakh S.S.R.

Alma-Ata (in Russian).

Georgiev, Ž. (1955) Materialien Über die Vermehrung des Feldhuhns (*Perdix perdix perdix* L.) in der Umgebung der Stadt Harmanli. *Isv. Zool. Inst. Mus. Bulg.* **7**, 385-392. (German summary).

Gerstell, R. (1942) The place of winter feeding in practical wildlife management. *Pennsylvania Game Commission, Harrisburg, Research Bulletin* **3**, 1-121.

Giban, J. (1953) Toxicité d'ingestion du chlorure mercurique et de deux produits fongicides à base de méthoxyéthylmercure. *Ann. Épiphyt.* **4**, 1.

Giban, J. (1965) Évaluation du risque théorique d'accident pouvant résulter pour les Gallinacés-gibier de la consommation de semences traitées. *Phytiatr. Phytopharm.* **14**, 59-65.

Giles, N. & Huntingford, F.A. (1984) Predation risk and inter-population variation in anti-predator behaviour in the three-spined stickleback. *Animal Behaviour* **32**, 264-275.

Gindre, R. & Allion, Y. (1971) Le Petit Gibier de Plaine dans un secteur du Gâtinais-est. *Bulletin Spécial du Conseil Supérieur de la Chasse Gallinacés Gibier,* Numero 15, pp. 9-22. Gauthier-Villars, Paris.

Gindre, R., Allion, Y., des Diguères, P., Denis, M., Ochando-Bleda, B. & Thonon, P. (1977) Études écologiques sur la Perdrix grise (*Perdix perdix* L.) réalisées dans le Loiret de 1969 à 1973. In: *Écologie du Petit Gibier et Aménagement des Chasses* (eds P. Pesson & M.G. Birkan), pp. 79-117. Gauthier Villars, Paris.

Gladstone, H.S. (1922) *Record Bags and Shooting Records.* Witherby, London.

Glutz von Blotzheim, U.N., Bauer, K.M. & Bezzel, E. (1973) *Handbuch der Vögel Mitteleuropas* (Volume 5). Akademische Verlagsgesellschaft, Frankfurt am Main, pp. 247-281.

Gooch, S.M. (1963) The occurrence of weed seeds in samples tested by the Official Seed Testing Station, 1960-61. *Journal of the National Institute of Agricultural Botany* **9**, 353-371.

Görner, M. & Wegener, U. (1978) Auswirkungen der Intensivierung in der Landwirtschaft auf die Vogelwelt. *Landschaftspflege u. Naturschutz Thüringen* **1**, 26-35.

Graham-Bryce, I.J., Hollomon, D.W. & Lewis, T. (1980) Pest and disease control in cereals: A research viewpoint. *Journal of the R.A.S.E.* **141**, 131-139.

Green, R.E. (1980a) Do red-legged partridge broods need insects? *Game Conservancy Annual Review* **11**, pp. 73-76.

Green, R.E. (1980b) Food selection by skylarks and grazing damage to sugar beet seedlings. *Journal of Applied Ecology* **17**, 613-630.

Green, R.E. (1983) Spring dispersal and agonistic behaviour of the red-legged partridge (*Alectoris rufa*). *Journal of Zoology* **201**, 541-555.

Green, R.E. (1984a) The feeding ecology and survival of partridge chicks (*Alectoris rufa* and *Perdix perdix*) on arable farmland in East Anglia. *Journal of Applied Ecology* **21**, 817-830.

Green, R.E.(1984b) Double nesting of the red-legged partridge *Alectoris rufa*. *Ibis* **126**, 332-346.

Green, R.E., Rands, M.R.W. & Moreby, S.J. (in press) Species differences in diet and the development of seed digestion in partridge chicks. *Ibis*.

Green, W.E. & Hendrickson, G.O. (1938) The European partridge in north-central Iowa. *Iowa Bird Life* **8**, 18-22.

Greenwood, P.J., Harvey, P.H. & Perrins, C.M. (1978) Inbreeding and dispersal in the great tit. *Nature* **271**, 52–54.

Greenwood, P.J. & Harvey, P.H. (1982) The natal and breeding dispersal of birds. *Annual Review of Ecological Systems* **13**, 1–21.

Griffiths, E. (1983) The feeding ecology of the Carabid beetle *Agonum dorsale* in cereal crops. Unpublished Ph.D. Thesis, University of Southampton.

Grigor'yeva, T.G. (1970) The development of self-regulation in an agrobiocoenosis following prolonged monoculture. *Entomological Review* **49**, 1–7.

Grolleau, G. & Biaddi, F. (1966) Note on the effects of Thiram on the laying and rearing of the red-legged partridge (*Alectoris rufa*). *Journal of Applied Ecology* **3**, 249–251.

Grolleau, G. & Giban, J. (1966) Toxicity of seed dressings to gamebirds and theoretical risks of poisoning. *Journal of Applied Ecology* **3** (Supplement), 199–212.

Grolleau, G., Lavaur, E. de & Siou, G. (1974) Effets du 2,4-D sur la reproduction des Cailles et des perdrix, après application du produit par pulvérisation sur les oeufs. *Annales de Zoologie-Écologie Animale* **6**, 313–331.

Gvozdev, E.V. (1957) The parasite fauna of the bearded partridge (*Perdix daurica* Pall.). *Trudy Inst. Zool. Akad. Nauk Kaz. S.S.R.* **7**, 166–169 (in Russian).

Gvozdev, E.V. (1958) Parasitic worms of galliform birds in Kazakhstan. Publishing house of the Academy of Sciences, Kazakh S.S.R. Alma-Alta, 265 pp (in Russian).

Gyrd-Hansen, N. & Dalgaard-Mikkelsen, Sv. (1974) The effect of phenoxy-herbicides on the hatchability of eggs and the viability of chicks. *Acta pharmacol. et toxicol.* **35**, 300–308.

Habermehl, K.H. & Hofmann, R. (1963) Geschlechts- und Alterskennzeichen am Kopf des Rebhuhnes. *Zeitschrift für Aus. Jagdwissensch.* **9**, 29–35.

Haftorn, S. (1971) *Norges Fugler*. Universitetsforlaget, Oslo-Bergen-Tromsø, 862 pp.

Hall, D.J., Cooper, W.E. & Werner, E.E. (1970) An experimental approach to the production dynamics and structure of freshwater animal communities. *Limnology and Oceanography* **15**, 839–928.

Hall, P.C. (1980) *Sussex Plant Atlas: An Atlas of the Distribution of Wild Plants in Sussex*. Borough of Brighton, Booth Museum of Natural History, Brighton.

Hamilton, W.D. & May, R.M. (1977) Dispersal in stable habitats. *Nature* **269**, 578–581.

Hammer, M., Koie, M. & Sparck, R. (1958) Investigations on the food of partridges, pheasants and black grouse in Denmark. *Danish Review of Game Biology* **3**, 183–208.

Hammond, M.C. (1941) Fall and winter mortality among Hungarian partridges in Bottineau and McHenry counties, North Dakota. *Journal of Wildlife Management* **5**, 375–382.

Hand, S.C. (1986) The capture efficiency of the Dietrick vacuum insect net for aphids in cereals and grasses. *Annals of Applied Biology* **108**, 223–41.

Hanf, M. (1983) *The Arable Weeds of Europe with Their Seedlings and Seeds*. B.A.S.F. U.K. Ltd.

Harms, W.B., Stortelder, A.H.F. & Vos, W. (1984) Effects of intensification of agriculture on nature and landscape in the Netherlands. *Ekologia (Č.S.S.R.)* **3**, 281–304.

Harrison, C.J.O. (1980) Pleistocene bird remains from Tornewton Cave and the Brixham Windmill Hill Cave in south Devon. *Bulletin of the British Museum of Natural History* (Geology) **33**, 91–100.

Harrison, J. (1952) On the history of the partridge in the German Friesian Islands, with the description of a new race from the island of Borkum. *Bulletin of the British Ornithologists Club* **72**, 18–21.

Harrison, J. (1968) On the 'Montana' variety of the common partridge. *Bulletin of the British Ornithologists Club* **88**, 48–53.

Hart, F.E. (1945) Mortality in summer and fall of ten coveys of partridges in Ohio. *Ohio Conservation Bulletin* **9**, 12–13.

Hartert, E. (1894) The migration of partridges. *Zoologist* **18**, 18–19.

Hartert, E. (1917) *Die Vögel der palearktischen Fauna* (Volume 3). Berlin.

Harting, J.E. (1884) *Hints on the Management of Hawks and Practical Falconry*. Horace Cox, London.

Haugen, A.O. (1941) Roosting and rising habits of the Hungarian partridge. *Wilson Bulletin* **53**, 235–236.

Hawker, P. (1844) *Instructions to Young Sportsmen in All That Relates to Guns and Shooting* (1922 edn. published by Herbert Jenkins Ltd, London).

Hawkins, A.S. (1937) Winter feeding at Faville Grove, 1935–1937. *Journal of Wildlife Management* **1**, 62–69.

Hay, R.J. (1968) The changing weed problem in the prairies. *Agricultural Institute Review* **23**, 17–19.

Hell, P. (1965) K niekotorým otázkam chovu jarabic y západoslovenskom kraji. *Zool. Listy* **14**, 37–46.

Hens, P. (1938) Einige Bemerkungen über die Kennzeichen und Verbreitung des Heidehuhnes *Perdix perdix sphagnetorum* (Altum). In: *Proceedings of the VIIIth International Ornithological Congress*, pp. 354–368. Oxford.

Herman, S.G. & Bulger, J.B. (1979) Effects of a forest application of DDT on non-target organisms. *Wildlife Monographs* **69**, 5–62.

Heydemann, B. (1956) Oberirdische biozönotische Horizonte in Kulturbiotopen. *Deutsche Pflanzenschutz-Tagung* **31**, 55–60.

Hick, L.E. (1950) Food habits of the Hungarian partridge in Ohio. *Department of Natural Resources, Ohio Division of Wildlife, Game Management Section Leaflet* No. 17, 4 pp.

Hill, D.A. (1984) Clutch predation in relation to nest density in mallard and tufted duck. *Wildfowl*, **35**, 151–156.

Hill, D.A. (1985) The feeding ecology and survival of pheasant chicks on arable farmland. *Journal of Applied Ecology* **22**, 645–654.

Hill, D.A. & Robertson, P.A. (1986) Hand-reared pheasants: how do they compare with wild birds? *Game Conservancy Annual Review* **17**, 76–84.

Hoffman, D.J. & Eastin, W.C. Jr (1982). Effects of Lindane, Paraquat, Toxaphene, and 2,4-5-Trichlorophenoxyacetic acid on mallard embryo development. *Archives of Environmental Contamination and Toxicology* **11**, 79–86.

Holmes, N.D. (1982) Population dynamics of the wheat stem sawfly, *Cephus cinctus* (Hymenoptera: Cephidae), in wheat. *The Canadian Entomologist* **114**, 775–788.

Holmes, P.R. (1984) A field study of the predators of the grain aphid *Sitobion avenae* (F.) *(Hemiptera: Aphididae)* in winter wheat in Britain. *Bulletin of Entomological Research* **74**, 623–631.

Holyoak, D. (1968) A comparative study of the food of some British Corvidae. *Bird Study* **15**, 147–153.

Homeyer, E.F. & Tancré, C.A. (1883) Beiträge zur Kenntniss der Ornithologie West Sibiriens, namentlich der Altai-Gegend. *Mittheilungen des Ornithologischen Vereines in Wein (Die Schwalbe)* **7**, 81–93+ attached colour plate by G. Mützel (1885).

Horstmann, H. & Zörner, H. (1986) Zur Situation des Rebhuhns in der DDR. In:

Proceedings of the Common Partridge (Perdix perdix L.) *International Symposium Poland, 1985.* (ed. Z. Pielowski) Polish Hunting Association, Warsaw.

Hudson, P.J., Dobson, A.P. & Newborn, D. (1985) Cyclic and non-cyclic populations of red grouse: a role for parasitism? In: *Ecology and Genetics of Host-parasite Interactions* (eds D. Rollinson & R.M. Anderson), pp. 77–89. Academic Press, London.

Hudson, P.J. (1986a) The effect of a parasitic nematode on the breeding production of red grouse.*Journal of Animal Ecology* **55**, 85–92.

Hudson, P.J. (1986b) *Red Grouse: The Biology and Management of a Wild Gamebird.* The Game Conservancy, Fordingbridge.

Hudson, R.H., Tucker, R.K. & Haegele, M.A. (1984) *Handbook of Toxicity of Pesticides to Wildlife* (Second edn.). U.S. Fish & Wildlife Service Resource Publication **153**. Washington, D.C.

Huffaker, C.B. (1970) The phenomenon of predation and its roles in nature. *Proc. Adv. Study Inst. Dynamics Numbers Popul.*, pp. 327–343. Oosterbeek.

Hume, L., Martinez, J. & Best, K. (1983) The biology of Canadian weeds. 60. *Polygonum convolvulus* L. *Canadian Journal of Plant Science* **63**, 959–971.

Hunt, H.M. (1974) Habitat relations and reproductive ecology of Hungarian partridge in a hedgerow complex in Saskatchewan. *Sas. Dept. Renew. Res. Wildl. Rep.* **3**, 1–51.

Hunter, M.L., Witham, J.W. & Dow, H. (1984) Effects of a carbaryl-induced depression in invertebrate abundance on the growth and behaviour of American black duck and mallard ducklings. *Canadian Journal of Zoology* **62**, 452–456.

Hupp, J.W., Smith, L.M. & Ratti, J.T. (1980) Grey partridge nesting biology in eastern south Dakota. In: *Proceedings of Perdix II Grey Partridge Workshop* (eds S.R. Peterson & L. Nelson), pp. 55–69. University of Idaho, Moscow.

Huss, H. (1983) Zur Ernährung des Rebhuhns (*Perdix p. perdix* L.) in einem Nordburgenlandischen Ackerbaugebiet. *Egretta* **26**, 1–14.

Inskipp, C. & Inskipp, T. (1985) *A Guide to the Birds of Nepal.* Croom Helm.

Isaković, I. (1970) Game management in Yugoslavia. *Journal of Wildlife Management* **34**, 800–812.

Ishe, M. (1986) Habitat changes in agricultural landscape. *Swedish Wildlife Research* **13**.

Jäckel, A.J. (1891) *Systematische Übersicht der Vögel Bayerns.* München & Leipzig.

Janda, J. (1956) Die Nahrung des erwachsenen Rebhuhns (*Perdix perdix* L.) in der Tschechoslowakei. *Acta Soc. Zool. Bohemosl.* **20**, 147–161.

Janda, J. (1957) Economic and agricultural importance of adult grey partridge (*Perdix perdix* L.) *Vědecké Práce Výzkumných Ústavu Lesnických und Myslivosti*, pp. 125–143 (in Czechoslovakian).

Janda, J. (1959) Užitečnost Juenilruch Koroptví (*Perdix perdix* L.). *Práce Výzkumných Ústavu Lesnických Č.S.S.R.* **17**, 27–66.

Janda, J. & Fišer, Z. (1960) Příspěvek ke studiu vlivu dlouhodobého komorování na tělesny stav koroptví. *Práce Výzkumných Ústavu Lesnických Č.S.S.R.* **20**, 45–66.

Janda, J. (1966) Seasonal development of ovaries of partridge in nature. *Práce Výzkumných Ústavu Lesnických Hospodářství Mysl.* **33**, 212–228.

Janda, J. (1974) Účinek Nových Pesticidních Přípravků (Birlane EC 24, Chlorophacinon, Nexion Saatgutpuder) Na Drobnou Zvěř. *Práce Vúlhm* **46**, 107–120.

Jasny, N.M. (1949) *The Socialised Agriculture of the U.S.S.R., Plans and Performance.* Palo Alto, Stanford University Press.

Javorszky, J. (1979) Feeding habits and behavioural activities of the partridge (*Perdix*

perdix L.) during winter under natural conditions. *Vadbiologiai Kutatas* **23**, 12–14.

Jenkins, D. (1955) Causes of death in partridges. *Bird Study* **2**, 142–143.

Jenkins, D. (1956) Factors governing population density in the partridge. Unpublished D.Phil. Thesis, University of Oxford.

Jenkins, D. (1957) The breeding of the red-legged partridge. *Bird Study* **4**, 97–100.

Jenkins, D. (1961a) Social behaviour in the partridge (*Perdix perdix*). *Ibis* **103a**, 155–188.

Jenkins, D. (1961b) Population control in protected partridges (*Perdix perdix*). *Journal of Animal Ecology* **30**, 235–258.

Jenkins, D. (1965) In: A discussion of ruffed grouse populations, Cloquet Forest Research Centre, Minnesota, by W.H. Marshall & G.W. Gullion. *Proceedings of the VIth International Congress of Game Biologists*, 1963, pp. 101. Bournemouth, Hampshire.

Jenkins, D., Watson, A. & Miller, G.R. (1967) Population fluctuations in the red grouse (*Lagopus lagopus*). *Journal of Animal Ecology* **36**, 97–122.

Jensen, B. (1970) Effect of a fox control programme on the bag of some other game species. In: *Proceedings of the IXth International Congress of Game Biologists*, 1969, 480. Moscow, U.S.S.R.

Johnson, C.G., Dobson, R.M., Southwood, T.R.E., Stephenson, J.W. & Taylor, L.R. (1955) Preliminary observations on the effect of weed killer DNOC on insect populations. *Rothamsted Experimental Station Report for 1954*, pp. 129–130. Lawes Agricultural Trust, Harpenden.

Johnston, E.L. (1972) Status of the Hungarian partridge population in eastern Ontario. Unpublished manuscript.

Jones, J.E. & Barnett, B.D. (1974) Effect of changing dietary energy and environmental temperature on feed consumption of large broad-breasted white turkey hens. *Poultry Science* **53**, 335–342.

Kalotás, Z. & Nikodémusz, E. (1982a) Selective reduction of the rook population (*Corvus frugilegus* L.) of Hungary by using 3-chloro-4-methyl-aniline HC1. *Zeitschrift für Angewandte Zoologie* **69**, 151–157.

Kalotás, Z. & Nikodémusz, E. (1982b) Controlling magpies (*Pica pica* L.) and hooded crows (*Corvus corone cornix* L.) with 3-chloro-4-methylaniline-HC1 using egg-baits. *Zeitschrift für Angewandte Zoologie* **69**, 275–281.

Kasimov, G.B. (1956) Helminth fauna of domestic fowls and gamebirds of the order Galliformes. *Trud Helmintologicheskoi Laboratorii: Izdatelstvo Akademii Nauk S.S.S.R.*, 554 pp. (in Russian).

Kasparyan, D.K. (1973) Ichneumon flies (Ichneumonidae) sub-family Tryphonini. *Fauna of the U.S.S.R.: Hymenoptera* 3 (No. 1), 320 pp. (in Russian).

Keith, L.B. (1962) Fall and winter weights of Hungarian partridges and sharp-tailed grouse from Alberta. *Journal of Wildlife Management* **26**, 336–337.

Kelm, H.S. (1979) Populationsuntersuchungen am Heidehuhn (*Perdix perdix sphagnetorum*) und Bemerkungen zur Taxonomie west- und mitteleuropäischer Rebhühner. *Bonn. zool. Beitr.* **30**, 117–157.

Kelso, L. (1932) A note on the food of the Hungarian partridge. *Auk* **49**, 204–207.

Kendeigh, S.C. (1970) Energy requirements for existence in relation to size of bird. *Condor* **72**, 60–65.

Khanmamedov, A.I. (1962) Ecology of partridge in north east parts of Azerbaydzhan. *Izv. Akad. Nauk Azerbaydzhan S.S.R. (Ser. Biol. medic.)* **1**, 39–51 (in Russian).

Khokhlov, A.N., Bicherov, A.P. & Mel'gunov, I.L. (1983) The Colorado beetle in the diet of birds. *Zashchita Rastenii* **11**, 38.

Kiessling, W. (1923) *Das Rebhuhn und seine Jagd* (ed. J. Neumann). Neudamm.

King, C. (1984) *Immigrant Killers: Introduced Predators and the Conservation of Birds in New Zealand*. Oxford University Press, Oxford.

Kirby, C. (1980) *The Hormone Weedkillers: A Short History of Their Discovery and Development*. British Crop Protection Council, Croydon.

Knapton, R.W. (1980) Winter mortality in a grey partridge population in Manitoba. *Canadian Field Naturalist* **94**, 190–191.

Knolle, F. & Heckenroth, H. (1985) Rebhuhn (*Perdix perdix* L.). In: *Die Vögel Niedersachsens und des Landes Bremen*, pp. 35–39. Niedersächsisches Landesverwaltungsamt, Hanover.

Knott, N.P., Ball, C.C. & Yocum, C.F. (1943) Nesting of the Hungarian partridge and ring-necked pheasant in Whitman County, Washington. *Journal of Wildlife Management* **7**, 283–291.

Kobriger, G.D. (1977) Foods of Hungarian partridge in North Dakota. In: *Proceedings of Perdix I. Hungarian Partridge Workshop* (ed. G.D. Kobriger), pp. 66–88. North Dakota Chapter of Wildlife Society.

Kobriger, G.D. (1980) *Food Habits of the Hungarian Partridge in North Dakota*. North Dakota Game and Fish Department, Bismarck, North Dakota.

Komarov, B. (1980) *The Destruction of Nature in the Soviet Union*. M.E. Sharpe Inc., New York. (Translated from Russian by M. Vale & J. Hollander).

Koskimies, J. (1962) Ontogeny of thermoregulation and energy metabolism in some gallinaceous birds. *Suppl. Ricerche di Zoologia Appl. alla Caccia* **4**, 148–160.

Koteš, O. & Knobloch, E. (1947) *Koroptev, Její Život, Chov a Lov*. Nakladatelstvi Studentske Knightiskǎrny v Praze, Prague.

Kozakiewicz, B., Maszewska, I. & Wiśniewski, B. (1983) Internal parasites of *Perdix perdix* in Wilkopolska (Poland). *Medycyna Weterynaryjna* **39**, 25–27.

Krüger, P. (1961) Lämpötilan vaikutuksesta pesäpaikan valintaan ja pesimistulokseen eteläsuomalaisella peltopyyllä suoritettujen tarhakokeiden valossa. *Suomen Riista* **14**, 112–120.

Krüger, P. (1965) Über die Einwirkung der Temperatur auf das Brutgeschäft und das Eierlegen des Rebhuhnes (*Perdix perdix* L.). *Acta Zoologica Fennica* **112**, 1–64.

Kubantsev, B.S. & Vasil'ev, I.E. (1983) Composition, distribution and numbers of birds in crop fields in northern regions along the Lower Volga River. *Ékologiya* **5**, 62–65.

Lack, D. (1947) The significance of clutch-size in the partridge (*Perdix perdix*). *Journal of Animal Ecology* **16**, 19–25.

Lack, P. (1986) *The Atlas of Wintering Birds in Britain and Ireland*. T. & A.D. Poyser.

Landry, P. (1985) Principaux résultats de l'enquête nationale sur les tableaux de chasse à tir en France pour la saison 1983–1984. In: *Proceedings of the XVIIth International Congress of Game Biologists*, 1985, pp. 359–366. Brussels, Belgium.

Langley, P.J.W. & Yalden, D.W. (1977) The decline of the rarer carnivores in Great Britain during the nineteenth century. *Mammal Review* **7**, 95–116.

Larkin, P.A. (1977) An epitaph for the concept of maximum sustained yield. *Transactions of the American Fish Society* **106**, 1–11.

Lascelles, G. (1892) *The Art of Falconry*. Neville Spearman, London.

Lasiewski, R.C. & Dawson, W.R. (1967) A re-examination of the relation between standard metabolic rate and body weight in birds. *Condor* **69**, 13–23.

Launay, M. (1975) Disponibilité en insects dans les cultures et dans les aménagements. Ses rapports avec le régime alimentaire du poussin de perdix grise (*Perdix perdix* L.). *Bulletin de l'Office National de la Chasse, Numero Spécial* **4**, 170–192.

Layher, W.G., Wood, R.D., Lambley, D., Bell, K.O., Irwin, J.C. & Hammerschmidt, R.F. (1985) Pesticide residues in Kansas pheasants. *Bulletin of Environmental Contamination and Toxicology* **34**, 317–323.

Lebeurier, E. (1958) Du régime de la perdrix grise (*Perdix perdix armoricana* Hartert) Ians le Finistere. *L'Oiseau et la Revue Française d'Ornithologie* **28**, 213–227, 300–308.

Lebreton, P. (*ed.*) (1977) *Atlas Ornithologique Rhône-Alpes.* Centre Régional de Documentation Pédagogique de Lyon.

Leopold, A. (1931) *Report on a Game Survey of the North Central States for the Sporting Arms and Ammunition Manufacturers Institute,* Madison, Wisconsin.

Leopold, A. (1933) *Game Management.* Scribner's, New York.

Leopold, A. (1945) The outlook for farm wildlife. *Transactions of the 10th North American Wildlife Conference,* pp. 165–168.

Lescar, L. (1984) Development of the protection of cereals against pests and diseases in France. *Proceedings of the 1984 British Crop Protection Conference* **1**, 159–168. Brighton, Sussex.

Lindström, E., & Morner, T. (1985) The spread of sarcoptic mange among Swedish red foxes. *Review Ecology (Terre Vie)* **40**, 211–216.

Linnaeus (1758) *Syst. Nat.* **X** (edn. 1), 160.

Lippens, L. & Willie, H. (1972) *Atlas des Oiseaux de Belgique et d'Europe Occidentale.* Tielt, Belgium.

Litun, V.I. (1980) Influence of agricultural activity on numbers of *Perdix perdix* in Kirov region. In: *Proceedings of a Scientific Conference 14–16 May 1980, The Influence of Man's Agricultural Activity on Populations and Habitat of Game Animals* (*ed.* V.G. Safonov). All-Union Science Research Institute for Game Conservancy and Fur Farming, Kirov (in Russian).

Litun, V.I. (1982) Partridge (*Perdix daurica*). In: *Migrations of Birds of Eastern Europe and Northern Asia,* pp. 180–196. Academy of Sciences of the U.S.S.R., Nauka, Moscow (in Russian).

Litun, V.I. (1983) Daurian partridge ecology in Southern Transbaikal. *Bulletin of Moscow Society of Naturalists, Biological Series* **88**, 25–31 (in Russian).

Logminas, V. & Petraitis, A. (1970) Population dynamics and population structure of the partridge (*Perdix perdix*) in Lithuania. In: *Proceedings of the IXth International Congress of Game Biologists,* 1969, pp. 435–439. Moscow, U.S.S.R. (in Russian).

Lokemoen, J.T. & Kruse, A.D. (1977) Populations and habitats of the Hungarian partridge in eastern North Dakota. In: *Proceedings of Perdix I. Hungarian Partridge Workshop* (*ed.* G.D. Kobriger), pp. 165–173. North Dakota Chapter of Wildlife Society.

Long, H.W. (1969) A Survey of the Agriculture of Yorkshire. County Agricultural Surveys No. 6. Royal Agricultural Society of England, London.

Long, J.L. (1981) *Introduced Birds of the World.* David & Charles, Newton Abbot.

Lorenz, H. & Kraus, M. (1957) *Insekten* **1**, 1–339. Die Larvalsystematik der Blattwespen. Akademie-Verlag, Berlin.

Loshkarev, G.A. (1976) Population dynamics of partridge in the foothills of the Northern Caucasus. *Ekologiya* **3**, 275–276. (Translation from Soviet Journal of Ecology).

Lovari, S. (1975) A partridge in danger. *Oryx* **13**, 203–204.
Lowe, H.J.B., Murphy, G.J.P. & Parker, M.L. (1985) Non-glaucousness, a probable aphid-resistance character of wheat. *Annals of Applied Biology* **106**, 555–560,
Lund, E.E. (1972a) Histomoniasis. In: *Diseases of Poultry* (eds M.S. Hofstad, B.W. Calnek, C.F. Helmboldt, W.M. Reid & H.W. Yoder Jr), pp. 990–1006. Iowa State University Press.
Lund, E.E. (1972b) Reciprocal responses of eight species of galliform birds and three parasites: *Heterakis gallinarum, Histomonas meleagridis* and *Parahistomonas wenrichi. Journal of Parasitology* **58**, 940–945.
Lutz, H. & Lutz-Ostertag, Y. (1971) Decrease in numbers of feathered game and the effect of pesticides; the effect of 2,4-D. *Bull. Soc. Zool. Fr.* **96**, 362.
Lutz-Ostertag, Y. & Henou, C.R. (1975) Teratologie – Paraquat: mortalite embryonnaire et effects sur l'appareil pulmonaire de l'embryon de poulet et de caille. *Comptes Rendues Academy Science* **281**, 439–442.
Lynn-Allen, E. & Robertson, A.W.P. (1956) *Partridge Year*. Geoffrey Bles, London.
Macdonald, D.G.F. (1883) *Grouse Disease*. W.H. Allen & Co., London.
Macdonald, D.W. (1980) *Rabies and Wildlife: A Biologist's Perspective*. Oxford University Press.
Macgillivray, W. (1837) *A History of British Birds* (Volume 1). London.
MacPherson, H.A., Stuart-Wortley, A.J. & Saintsbury, G. (1893) *The Partridge*. Longmans, Green & Co., London.
Madel, W. (1970) Herbicides and conservation in the Federal Republic of Germany. *Proceedings of the 10th British Weed Control Conference*, 1970, pp. 1079–1088.
Madsen, H. (1952) A study on the nematodes of Danish gallinaceous gamebirds. *Danish Review of Game Biology* **2**, 1–126.
Majewska, B., Pielowski, Z., Serwatka, S. & Szott, M. (1979) Genetische und adaptative Eigenschaften des Zuchtmaterials zum Aussetzen von Fasanen. *Zeitschrift für Jagdwissenschaft* **25**, 212–226.
Makatsch, W. (1950) *Die Vogelwelt Macedoniens*. Geest & Portig, Leipzig.
Manley, B.F.J. (1977) The determination of key factors from life table data. *Oecologica* **31**, 111–117.
Manolache, L. (1970) Răspindirea potirnichilor (*Perdix perdix* L.) in România şi extinderea lor in zona forestiera. In: *Comunicari de Zoologie* **14**, pp. 209–218. Societateă de Știinţe Biologice din Republica Socialistă Româniă.
Marcström, V. & Engren, E. (1986) About predation on tetraonids in northern Sweden. In: *Proceedings of the 3rd International Grouse Symposium* (eds T.W.I. Lovel & P.J. Hudson), pp. 94–98. World Pheasant Association and International Council for Game and Wildlife Conservation.
Marjakangas, A., Rintamäki, H. & Hissa, R. (1983) Thermal responses in the capercaillie (*Tetrao urogallus*) and the black grouse (*Tetrao tetrix*) roosting in snow burrows. *Suomen Riista* **30**, 64–70.
Markkula, M. (1969) The sales of pesticides in Finland in 1968. *Kemian Teoilisuus* **9**, 731–734.
Maskall (1581) *The Husbandlye Ordering and Governmente of Poultrie*.
Maskell, F.E. (1959) Wireworm distribution in East Anglia. *Plant Pathology* **8**, No. 1.
Matheson, C. (1956a) Fluctuations in partridge populations. *British Birds* **49**, 112–114.
Matheson, C. (1956b) Gamebook records of pheasants and partridges in Wales. *The National Library of Wales Journal* **9**, 287–294.

Matheson, C. (1957) Further partridge records from Wales. *British Birds* **50**, 534–536.

Matheson, C. (1960) Additional gamebook records of partridges in Wales. *British Birds* **53**, 81–84.

Mátrai, G. & Vallus, G. (1981) Tiz év vadgazdálkodása számokban. (Ten years of game management in figures 1970/1979). *Nimród Fórum Vadbiológiai Kutatás* **29**, 5–10 (in Hungarian).

Matteucci, C. & Toso, S. (1985) Note sulla distribuzione e lo *status* della Starna, *Perdix perdix* in Italia. In: Seminario tenuto all'Università della Calabria *Biologia dei Galliformi, Problemi di gestione venatoria e conservazione* (eds F. Dessi Fulgheri & T. Mingozzi), pp. 29–34. Dipartimento di Ecologia dell'Università della Calabria, Arcavacata, Italy.

Maxwell, A. (1911) *Partridges and Partridge Manors*. Black, London.

Mayer, K.A. (1983) Comparison of the bag for hare, pheasant and common partridge in consolidated and unconsolidated areas in Rheinhessen West Germany. *Zeitschrift für Jagdwissenschaft* **29**, 55–60.

McCabe, R.A. & Hawkins, A.S. (1946) The Hungarian partridge in Wisconsin. *American Midland Naturalist* **36**, 1–75.

McCauley, M. (1976) *Khrushchev and the Development of Soviet Agriculture*. Macmillan Press Ltd, London (in association with the School of Slavonic and East European Studies, University of London).

McCrow, V.P. (1982) Grey partridge habitat use and nesting biology in north-central Iowa. Unpublished Ph.D. Thesis, Iowa State University, Ames.

McCurdy, E.V. & Molberg, E.S. (1974) Effects of the continuous use of 2,4-D and MCPA on spring wheat production and weed populations. *Canadian Journal of Plant Science* **54**, 241–245.

McNeill, S. (1973) The dynamics of a population of *Leptopterna dolabrata* (Heteroptera: Miridae) in relation to its food resources. *Journal of Animal Ecology* **42**, 495–507.

Meinertzhagen, R. (1952) A note on *Perdix perdix* from Holland. *Bulletin of the British Ornithologists Club*, **72**, 55.

MEM STAGEK (1984) Az Üzemtervszerü vadgazdálkodás fontosabb mutatói 1981–1984 (Statistical Office of Ministry of Agriculture: Data of game management for 1981–1984). *Között*, 50 pp.

Mendel, G.W. & Peterson, S.R. (1980) Grey partridge population structure and densities on the Palouse prairie. In: *Proceedings of the Perdix II Grey Partridge Workshop* (eds S.R. Peterson & L. Nelson), pp. 118–136. University of Idaho, Moscow.

Mendel, G.W. & Peterson, S.R. (1983) Management implications of grey partridge habitat use on the Palouse prairie, Idaho. *Wildlife Society Bulletin* **11**, 348–356.

Menhinick, E.F. (1962) Comparison of invertebrate populations of soil and litter of mowed grasslands in areas treated and untreated with pesticides. *Ecology* **43**, 556–561.

Menzdorf, A. (1976) Ontogeny of some rock partridge calls. *Zool. Anz. Jena* **196**, 221–236.

Menzdorf, A. (1977) On the vocalisation of rock partridges. *Beitr. Vogelkd., Leipzig* **23**, 83–100.

Meriggi, A. & Prigioni, Cl. 1985) Productivité d'une population de perdrix grise (*Perdix perdix*) dans les Apenins de l'Italie du Nord et répartition du milieu avec la perdrix rouge (*Alectoris rufa*). In: *Proceedings of the XVIIth International Congress of*

Game Biologists, 1985, 351–358. Brussels, Belgium.

Merikallio, E. (1931) Kanalintujemme munamäärät. *Ornis Fennica* **8**, 1–10.

Merikallio, E. (1958) Finnish Birds. Their distribution and numbers. *Fauna Fennica* **5**, 1–181.

Messick, J.P., Bizeau, E.G., Benson, W.W. & Mullins, W.H. (1974) Aerial pesticide applications and ring-necked pheasants. *Journal of Wildlife Management* **38**, 679–685.

Mettler, B.J. (1977) Factors contributing to the increase of the grey partridge in Minnesota. *Loon* **49**, 205–210.

Michell, E.B. (1900) *The Art and Practice of Hawking*. Holland Press, London.

Middleton, A.D. (1934a) The population of partridges (*Perdix perdix*) in 1933 and 1934 in Great Britain. *Journal of Animal Ecology* **4**, 137–145.

Middleton, A.D. (1934b) Periodic fluctuations in British Game Populations. *Journal of Animal Ecology* **3**, 231–249.

Middleton, A.D. (1936a) Factors controlling the population of partridge (*Perdix perdix*) in Great Britain. *Proceedings of the Zoological Society of London* **106**, 795–815.

Middleton, A.D. (1936b) The population of partridges (*Perdix perdix*) in Great Britain during 1935. *Journal of Animal Ecology* **5**, 252–261.

Middleton, A.D. (1937) The population of partridges (*Perdix perdix*) in Great Britain during 1936. *Journal of Animal Ecology* **6**, 318–321.

Middleton, A.D. & Chitty, H. (1937) The food of adult partridges, (*Perdix perdix* and *Alectoris rufa*) in Great Britain. *Journal of Animal Ecology* **6**, 322–336.

Middleton, A.D. & Huband, P. (1966) Increase in red-legged partridges. *Annual Report Game Research Association* **5**, 14–25.

Middleton, A.D. (1967) Predatory mammals and the conservation of game in Great Britain. *Annual Report Game Research Association* **6**, 14–21.

Milne, A. (1949) The ecology of the sheep tick, *I. ricinus* L. host relationships of the tick Part 1. Review of previous work in Britain. *Parasitology* **39**, 72–85.

Milne, A. (1984) Fluctuation and natural control of animal populations, as exemplified in the garden chafer *Phyllopertha horticola* (L.). *Proceedings of the Royal Society of Edinburgh* **82B**, 145–199.

Ministry of Agriculture, Fisheries and Food (1986) *Use of Fungicides and Insecticides on Cereals*. M.A.F.F./A.D.A.S. Booklet No. 2257 (86).

Mitchell, B. (1963) Ecology of two carabid beetles, *Bembidion lampros* (Herbst) and *Trechus quadristriatus* (Shrank). I. Life cycles and feeding behaviour. *Journal of Animal Ecology* **32**, 289–299.

Mitchell, G.J. (1977) The effects of spring and summer weather on Hungarian partridge productivity in Southern Alberta. In: *Proceedings of Perdix I. Hungarian Partridge Workshop* (ed. G.D. Kobriger), pp. 201–209. North Dakota Chapter of Wildlife Society.

Mitchell, F. (1976) *The Irish Landscape*. Collins, London.

Moilanen, P. (1968) On the nest site selection of the partridge (*Perdix perdix*) in Southern Finland. *Suomen Riista* **20**, 105–111.

Møller, A.P. (1983) Changes in Danish farmland habitats and their populations of breeding birds. *Holarctic Ecology* **6**, 95–100.

Moltoni, E. (1964) L'ornitofauna della Sila (Calabria). *Rivista Italiana di Ornitologia*. Series II **34**, 1–183.

Montagu, G. (1813) *A Dictionary of British Birds.* Swan Sonnenschein & Co., London.

Moore, N.W. (1962) Toxic chemicals and birds: the ecological background to conservation problems. *British Birds* **55**, 428–435.

Moore, N.W. (1965) Pesticides and birds – a review of the situation in Great Britain in 1965. *Bird Study* **12**, 222–252.

Moore, N.W. (1967) A synopsis of the pesticide problem. *Recent Advances in Ecological Research* **4**, 75–129.

Moreby, S.J. & Potts, G.R. (1985) Insecticides and the survival of gamebird chicks in 1984. *Game Conservancy Annual Review* **16**, pp. 47–49.

Mottl, S. (1973) The age stratification in the partridge (*Perdix perdix* L.) and pheasant (*Phasianus colchicus* L.) population. *Actes du Xth Congrès de l'Union Internationale des Biologistes du Gibier*, 1971, pp. 317–325. Paris, France.

Mottl, S, & Krejčí, L. (1973) Vliv Stáří Koroptvích Slepiček A Bažantích Slepic Na Snůšku. *Lesnictví* **19**, 81–84.

Mühle, E. & Wetzel, T. (1965) Untersuchungen über die an Futtergräsern auftretenden Blattwespenarten (Hymenoptera, Tenthredinidae). *Zeitschrift für Angewandte Entomologie* **56**, 289–299.

Mukula, J., Raatikainen, M., Lallukka, R. & Raatikainen, T. (1969) Composition of weed flora in spring cereals in Finland. *Annals agric. Fennica* **8**, 59–110.

Muller, H.D. (1971) Responses of three generations of grey partridge to low level pesticide ingestion. *Poultry Science* **50**, 1610–1611.

Murdoch, W.W. & Oaten, A. (1975) Predation and population stability. *Advances in Ecological Research* **9**, 1–131.

Murray, R. (1983) A note on a summer index and summer 1981. *Weather* **38**, 88–89.

Murtha, P.A. (1967) Air photo surveillance of Hungarian partridge habitat change. *Journal of Wildlife Management* **31**, 366–369.

Murton, R.K., Isaacson, A.J. & Westwood, N.J. (1963a) The feeding ecology of the woodpigeon. *British Birds* **56**, 345–375.

Murton, R.K. & Vizoso, M. (1963b) Dressed cereal seed as a hazard to woodpigeons. *Annals of Applied Biology* **52**, 503–517.

Murton, R.K. (1965) *The Woodpigeon.* Collins, London.

Murton, R.K. (1971) *Man and Birds.* Collins, London.

Myasoedova, O.M., & Barabash, Ch.P. (1974) The grey partridge under conditions of the steppe in the Dnieper basin. *Proceedings of the VIth All-Union Ornithological Conference* **2**, pp. 282–283, Moscow.

Myrberget, S. (1972) Variations in a population of willow grouse in north Norway. In: *Proceedings of the XVth International Ornithological Congress*, pp. 107–120.

Nagy, E. (1975) Adatok a Hazai Fogolypopuláció Morfológiájához. *A Vadgazdálkodás Fejlesztése* **16**, 73–82 (in Hungarian).

Nagy, E. (1977) Apróvadtenyésztésünk müszaki fejlesztésének idöszerü kérdései. *Nimród Fórum* Vadbiólogiai Kutatás **20**, 1–5 (in Hungarian).

Naumann, J.A. (1833) *Naturgeschichte der Vögel Deutschlands* (Volume 6). Leipzig.

Neave, D.J. & Wright, B.S. (1969) The effects of weather and DDT spraying on a ruffed grouse population. *Journal of Wildlife Management* **33**, 1015–1020.

Nefedov, N.I. (1943) The agricultural importance of the partridge (*Perdix perdix*) on the lower Volga. *Zool. Zh.* **22**, 41–43.

Neill, D.D., Muller, H.D. & Shutze, J.V. (1971) Pesticide effects on the fecundity of the grey partridge. *Bulletin of Environmental Contamination and Toxicology* **6**, 546–551.

Nentwig, W. (1980) The selective prey of linyphiid-like spiders and of their space webs. *Oecologia* **45**, 236–243.

Neu, C.W., Byers, C.R. & Peek, J.M. (1974) A technique for analysis of utilisation-availability data. *Journal of Wildlife Management* **38**, 541–545.

Newton, A. (1861) On the possibility of taking an ornithological census. *Ibis* **3**, 190–196.

Newton, I. (1979) *Population Ecology of Raptors*. T. & A.D. Poyser, Berkhamsted.

Nice, M.M. (1937) Studies in the life history of the song sparrow, Volume I. *Transactions of the Linnaean Society of New York* **4**, 1–247.

Nicholson, A.J. & Bailey, V.P. (1935) The balance of animal populations. *Proceedings of the Royal Society of London* **3**, 551–598.

Nikodémusz, E. & Imre, R. (1982) Pathological features of 3-Chloro-4-Methyl Benzamine HC1 toxicity in rooks (*Corvus frugilegus* L.) and pheasants (*Phasianus colchicus* L.). *Gegenbaurs morph. Jahrb., Leipzig* **128**, 753–761.

Nøddegaard, E. (1984) Udvikling i brugen, godkendelse, anerkendelse og forurening af plantebeskyttelses-midler. *Statens Planteavlsmøde*, pp. 14–19.

Nolte, W. (1934) *Zur Biologie des Rebhuhns. Das Rebhuhn als Jagdwild 1932 und 1933* (ed. H. Neumann). Neudmamm.

Norris, C.A. (1945) The distribution of the corncrake (*Crex crex*). *British Birds* **38**, 142–148, 108–162.

Nováková, E. & Hanzl, R. (1966) Vliv anthropogenních změn prostředí na pocetní stavy koroptví v třeboňské pánvi a na Berounsku. In: *Symposium O Koroptvi*, pp. 45–71. Výzkumný Ústav Lesního Hospodářstvi A. Myslivosti Československý Myslivecký Svaz, Prague.

Nyenhuis, H. (1983) Die Einwirkung von Bodennutzungs- und Witterungsfaktoren auf die Siedlungsdichte des Rebhuhns (*Perdix perdix* L.). *Zeitschrift für Jagdwissenschaft* **29**, 176–183.

Nyenhuis, H. (1985) Die Veränderung der relativen Abundanz des Rebhuhns (*Perdix perdix* L.) im Bundesland Nordrhein-Westfalen von 1951–1983. In: *Proceedings of the XVIIth International Congress of Game Biologists*, 1985, pp. 579–586. Brussels, Belgium.

Nyffeler, M. & Benz, G. (1979) Zur ökologischen Bedeutung der Spinnen der Vegetationsschicht von Getreide-und Rapsfeldern bei Zürich (Schweiz). *Zeitschrift für Angewandte Entomologie* **87**, 348–376.

O'Cannon, M.W. (1893) Partridges migrating. *Zoologist* **17**, 433.

O'Connor, R.J. (1984) The importance of hedges to songbirds. In: *Proceedings of the N.E.R.C. I.T.E. Symposium No. 13 'Agriculture and the Environment'* (ed. D. Jenkins), pp. 117–123. Monks Wood Experimental Station, Huntingdon.

O'Connor, R.J. & Mead, C.J. (1984) The stock dove in Britain 1930–1980. *British Birds* **77**, 181–201.

O'Connor, R.J. & Shrubb, M. (1986) *Farming and Birds*. Cambridge University Press.

Office National de la Chasse (1976) Enquête statistique nationale sur les tableaux de chasse à tir pour la saison 1974–1975. *Bulletin de l'Office National de la Chasse, Spécial Scientifiques et Techniques*, No. 5, 83 pp.

Ogilvie, F.M. (1902) *Field Observations on British Birds*. Selwyn & Blount, London.

Ogilvie-Grant, W.R. (1891) Plumage of male and female partridge. The Field (November 31), London.

Ogilvie-Grant, W.R. (1912) Breeding and eclipse plumages of the common partridge. *British Birds* **5**, 234–236.

Oko, Z. (1963a) Pozywienie kuropatw dorosych (*Perdix perdix*) w cyklu rocznym na terenie wojewódatwa posnańskiego w latach 1960–1961. *Prace Komisji Nauk rolniczych Lésnych* **14**, 39–96.

Oko, Z. (1963b) Studies in analysis of food of young partridges. *Przeglad Zool.* **7**, 337–342.

Olech, B. (1969) Über Merkmale der Altersstruktur beim Rebhuhn (*Perdix perdix* L.). *Zeitschift für Jagdwissenschaft* **15**, 106–108.

Olech, B. (1971) Realised production, mortality and sex structure of a partridge (*Perdix perdix* L.) population and its utilisation for game purposes in Poland. *Ekol. Pol.* **19**, 617–650.

Olech, B. (1986) Polish population of *Perdix perdix* in 1964–1984/dynamics and age structure. In: *Proceedings of the Common Partridge (Perdix perdix L.) International Symposium*, Poland, 1985. (ed. Z. Pielowski) Polish Hunting Association, Warsaw.

O'Rourke, F.J. (1970) *The Fauna of Ireland*. Mercer Press, Cork.

Orts-Anspach, M. & Dalimer, P. (1954) *Perdix montana* Brisson, aberration, polymorphism, or mutation? *Gerfaut* **44**, 12–39, 304–306.

Orwin, C.S. & Orwin, C.S. (1967) *The Open Fields*. Oxford University Press, London.

Osmolovskaya, V.I. (1966) The population density and distribution of the partridge (*Perdix perdix* L.) in the European part of U.S.S.R. Biological-Pedological Faculty, the University of Moscow, pp. 90–98 (in Russian).

Page, J. (1985) An integrated approach to the management of semi-natural habitats on lowland farmland for conservation. Unpublished M.Sc./DIC Thesis, Imperial College of Science and Technology, London.

Paleček, J. & Toufar, J. (1957) Das Wandern der freigelassenen Rebhühner (*Perdix perdix* L.). *Zool. Listy* **20**, 133–138.

Pallas (1811) *Zoogr. Rosso-Asiat.* **2**, 62.

Paludan, K. (1954) Agerhønens Ynglesaeson 1953. *Danske Vildtunders* **3**, 1–20.

Paludan, K. (1963) Partridge markings in Denmark. *Danish Review of Game Biology* **4**, 25–60.

Paolo, M.P. & Piodi, M. (1986) Research into the consistency of the grey partridge in Piedmont, its presence and progressive rarity. In: *Proceedings of the Common Partridge (Perdix perdix L.) International Symposium*, Poland, 1985. (ed. Z. Pielowski) Polish Hunting Association, Warsaw.

Parker, E. (1927) *Partridges: Yesterday and To-Day*. The Field, London.

Parker, H. (1984) Effect of corvid removal on reproduction of willow ptarmigan and black grouse. *Journal of Wildlife Management* **48**, 1197–1205.

Páv, J., Zajícek, D. & Kotrlý, A. (1961) Parasitic worms of the European partridge (*Perdix perdix* L.) and their influence on partridge state of health. *Lesnictví* (Ročnik 7) **34**, 521–550.

Payne-Gallwey, R. (1892) *Letters to Young Shooters*. Longmans, Green & Co., London.

Pekić, B. (1968) The results of many years research on the partridge. *Glas. zav. zašt, prirode Titograd* **1**, 85–93 (in Serbian with English summary).

Penev, D. (1983) Study on the nutrition of the partridge *Perdix perdix* in Bulgaria. *Gorskostopanska Nauka* **20**, 71–75.

Pépin, D. (1981) *Sauvegarder et Développer les Populations de Lièvres*. La Maison Rustique, Paris.

Pesson, P. & Birkan, M.G. (*eds*) (1977) *Écologie du petit gibier et aménagement des chasses. Formation permanente en écologie et biologie*. Gauthier-villars, Paris.

Peterson, S.R. & Nelson L. Jr (*eds*) (1980) Proceedings of Perdix II Grey Partridge Workshop, Moscow, Idaho. Forest, Wildlife & Range Experiment Station, University of Idaho.

Petrjanos, S. (1983) Zur Ökologie des Rebhuhns in Kärnten. *Der Kärntner Jäger* **12**, 7–12.

Petrjanos, S. (in press) The influence of different types of agriculture on populations of the grey partridge in Austria. In: *Proceedings of the XVIth International Congress of Game Biologists*, 1983, Czechoslovakia.

Petròv P. (1963) Some aspects on partridge numbers restoration. *Gorskostopanska Nauka* **19**, 35–38.

Petròv, P. (1966) Die Dynamik der Rebhuhn-Ketten im Zusammenhang mit Koeffizientfeststellung des Nachwuchses. Beiträge zur Jagd- und Wildforschung 5, In: *Tagungsberichte* **90**, 99–108.

Peus, F. (1929) *Perdix perdix sphagnetorum* (Altum), eine aussterbende Rebhuhnrasse. *Orn. Monatsber* **37**, 129–135.

Phillips, J.C. (1928) Wild birds introduced or transplanted in North America. *United States Department of Agriculture, Technical Bulletin* No. 61.

Pielowski, Z. (1981) Weitere Untersuchungen über den Wert des Zuchtmaterials von Fasanen zum Aussetzen. *Zeitschrift für Jagdwissenschaft* **27**, 102–109.

Pielowski, Z. (1986) State and situation of the common partridge population in Poland. In: *Proceedings of the Common Partridge (Perdix perdix* L.) *International Symposium*, Poland, 1985. (ed. Z. Pielowski) Polish Hunting Association, Warsaw.

Pimentel, D. (1976) The ecological basis of insect pest, pathogen and weed problems. In: *Origins of Pest, Parasite, Disease and Weed Problems* (*eds* J.M. Cherrett & G.R. Sagar), pp. 3–31. Blackwells, Oxford.

Pleshkov, B.P. & Fowden, L. (1959) Amino-acid composition of the proteins of barley leaves in relation to the mineral nutrition and age of plants. *Nature* **183**, 1445–1446.

Podoler, H. & Rogers, D. (1975) A new method for the identification of key factors from life table data. *Journal of Animal Ecology* **44**, 85–115.

Pollard, E., Hooper, M.D. & Moore, N.W. (1974) *Hedges*. William Collins Sons & Co. Ltd, London.

Pontin, A.J. (1960) Field experiments in colony foundations by *Lasius niger* (L.) and *Lasius flavus* (F.) (Hymenoptera, Formicidae). *Insectes Sociaux* **7**, 227–230.

Popov, C., Mustetea, D., Vonica, I. & Tănase, V. (1981) Cereal bugs: forecasting and control measures in the year 1981. *Cereale şi Plante Tehnice, Produçtia Vegetala* **33**, 10–14.

Portal, M. & Collinge, W.E. (1932) *Partridge Disease and its Causes*. Country Life, London.

Porter, R.D. (1955) The Hungarian partridge in Utah. *Journal of Wildlife Management* **19**, 93–109.

Potts, A.S. (1982) A preliminary study of some recent heavy rainfalls in the Worthing area of Sussex. *Weather* **37**, 220–227.

Potts, G.R. (1969) The influence of eruptive movements, age, population size and other factors on the survival of the shag (*Phalacrocorax aristotelis*). *Journal of Animal Ecology* **38**, 53–102.

Potts, G.R. (1970a) Recent changes in the farmland fauna with special reference to the decline of the grey partridge (*Perdix perdix*). *Bird Study* **17**, 145–166.

Potts, G.R. (1970b) Studies on the changing role of weeds of the genus *Polygonum* in the diet of partridges. *Journal of Applied Ecology* **7**, 567–576.

Potts, G.R. (1970c) The effects of the use of herbicides in cereals on aphids and on the feeding ecology of partridges. *Proceedings of the 10th British Weed Control Conference*, 1970, pp. 299–302.

Potts, G.R. (1971) Agriculture and partridges. *Outlook on Agriculture* **6**, 267–271.

Potts, G.R. (1973a) Factors governing the chick survival rate of the grey partridge. In: *Proceedings of the Xth International Congress of Game Biologists*, 1971, pp. 85–86. Paris, France.

Potts, G.R. (1973b) Pesticides and the fertility of the grey partridge *Perdix perdix*. *Journal of Reproduction and Fertility Supplement* **19**, 391–402.

Potts, G.R. (1974) The grey partridge: problems of quantifying the ecologial effects of pesticides. In: *Proceedings of the XIth International Congress of Game Biologists*, 1973, pp. 405–413. Stockholm, Sweden.

Potts, G.R. & Vickerman, G.P. (1974) Studies on the cereal ecosystem. *Advances in Ecological Research* **8**, 107–197.

Potts, G.R. (1977a) Some effects of increasing the monoculture of cereals. In: *Origins of Pest, Parasite, Disease and Weed Problems* (eds J.M. Cherrett & G.R. Sagar), pp. 183–202. Blackwells, Oxford.

Potts, G.R. (1977b) Population dynamics of the grey partridge: overall effects of herbicides and insecticides on chick survival rates. In: *Proceedings of the XIIIth International Congress of Game Biologists*, 1977, pp. 203–211. Atlanta, Georgia.

Potts, G.R. (1980a) The effects of modern agriculture, nest predation and game management on the population ecology of partridges *Perdix perdix* and *Alectoris rufa*. *Advances in Ecological Research* **11**, 2–79.

Potts, G.R. (1980b) Sheep, sheep ticks, grouse and hill farming. *Game Conservancy Annual Review* **11**, 24–30.

Potts, G.R., Coulson, J.C. & Deans, I.R. (1980) Population dynamics and breeding success of the shag *Phalacrocorax aristotelis* on the Farne Islands, Northumberland. *Journal of Animal Ecology* **49**, 465–484.

Potts, G.R. (1981a) Insecticide sprays and the survival of partridge chicks. *Game Conservancy Annual Review* **12**, pp. 39–48.

Potts, G.R. (1984a) Monitoring changes in the cereal ecosystem. In: *Proceedings of the N.E.R.C. I.T.E. Symposium No. 13 Agriculture and the Environment* (ed. D. Jenkins), pp. 128–134. Monks Wood Experimental Station, Huntingdon.

Potts, G.R. (1984b) Grey partridge population dynamics: comparisons between Britain and North America. In: *Proceedings of Perdix III Grey Partridge/Ring-necked Pheasant Workshop* (eds R.B. Stiehl, R.T. Dumke & R.B. Kahl), pp. 7–12. Campbellsport, Wisconsin.

Potts, G.R., Tapper, S.C. & Hudson, P.J. (1984) Population fluctuations in red grouse: Analysis of bag records and a simulation model. *Journal of Animal Ecology* **53**, 21–36.

Potts, G.R. (1985) The partridge situation in Italy: a view from Britain. In: *Seminario tenuto all'Università della Calabria. Biologia dei Galliformi, Problemi di gestione venatoria e conservazione* (eds F. Dessi Fulgheri & T. Mingozzi), pp. 9–13. Dipartimento di Ecologia dell'Università della Calabria, Arcavacata, Italy.

Potts, G.R. (1986) A need for more research on the causes of the decline of the grey partridge in the nordic countries. *The Nordic Council for Wildlife Research Symposium*, 1983. Lund, Sweden.

Powell, W., Dean, G.J., Dewar, A. & Wilding, N. (1981) Towards integrated control of cereal aphids. *Proceedings of the 1981 British Crop Protection Conference – Pests & Diseases* **1**, 201–206.

Powell, W. (1982) The role of parasitoids in limiting cereal aphid populations. In: *Proceedings of a Meeting of the European Communities Experts' Group, Portici, Italy* (ed. R. Cavalloro), pp. 50–56. A.A. Balkema, Rotterdam.

Powell, W., Dean G.J. & Bardner, R. (1985) Effects of pirimicarb, dimethoate and benomyl on natural enemies of cereal aphids in winter wheat. *Annals of Applied Biology* **106**, 235–242.

Poyarkov, D.V. (1955) Ecology of partridge in steppes of European part of U.S.S.R. *Uchen zap. Mosk. gorod. ped. inst.* **38**, 157–213 (in Russian).

Priklonsky, S.G. & Sapetina, I.M. (1978) Results of the wildfowl bag count in the Russian Federation. *Proceedings of the Oka State Reserve, Scientific Foundations for Protection and Rational Wise Use of Bird Resources* **14**, 265–279.

Pulliainen, E. (1965) Studies on the weight, food and feeding behaviour of the partridge (*Perdix perdix* L.) in Finland. *Annals Acad. Sci. fenn. (A)* **4**, 1–76

Pulliainen, E. (1966) Food habits of the partridge (*Perdix perdix*) in autumn and winter. *Suomen Riista* **18**, 117–132.

Pulliainen, E. (1967) On the winter ecology of the partridge (*Perdix perdix* L.) in Finland. *Suomen Riista* **19**, 46–62.

Pulliainen, E. (1968a) Autumn weight of the partridge (*Perdix perdix* L.) in Finland. *Annals Zoologica Fennica* **5**, 241–244.

Pulliainen, E. (1968b) Sex and age ratios in a partridge (*Perdix perdix* L.) population in Ostrobothnia, West Finland. *Annals Zoological Fennica* **5**, 179–182.

Pulliainen, E. (1968c) Breeding success of a partridge (*Perdix perdix* L.) population in Ostrobothnia, West Finland, in 1967. *Annals Zoological Fennica* **5**, 183–187.

Pulliainen, E. (1968d) Peltopyyn kevaisesta ravinnosta. *Suomen Riista* **20**, 94–101.

Pulliainen, E. (1970) Productivity of a partridge (*Perdix perdix*) population in western Finland. In: *Proceedings of the IXth International Congress of Game Biologists*, 1969, pp. 432–444. Moscow, U.S.S.R. (in Russian).

Pulliainen, E. (1971) Clutch-size of the partridge (*Perdix perdix* L.) *Ornis Scandinavica* **2**, 69–73.

Pulliainen, E. (1983) Etela-Pohjanmaan peltopyiden syysravinnossa kahden vvosikymmenen aikana tapahtuneista muutoksista. *Suomen Riista* **30**, 15–21.

Pulliainen, E. (1984a) Changes in the composition of the autumn food of *Perdix perdix* in west Finland over 20 years. *Journal of Applied Ecology* **21**, 133–139.

Pulliainen, E. (1984b) On the gut size and chemical composition of the food of the partridge (*Perdix perdix*) in Finland. *Suomen Riista* **31**, 13–18.

Putnam, L.G. & Handford, R.H. (1964) Potential and actual populations of grasshopper nymphs in tilled and untilled cereal grain fields. *Canadian Journal of Plant Science* **44**, 365–375.

Pyrah, D.B. (1970) Poncho neck markers for gamebirds. *Journal of Wildlife Management* **34**, 466–467.

Rabbinge, R., Ankersmit, G.W. & Pak, G.A. (1979) Epidemiology and simulation of population development of *Sitobion avenae* in winter wheat. *Netherlands Journal of Plant Pathology* **85**, 25–29.

Rademacher, B., Koch, W. & Hurle, K. (1970) Changes in the weed flora as a result of continuous cropping of cereals and the annual use of the same weed control measures since 1956. *Proceedings of the 10th British Weed Control Conference* **1**, 1–6, Brighton, Sussex.

Randik, A. (1977) Polovné vtáctvo v polných krovinných formáciàch na slovensku. *Polovnićky Zbornik (Folia Venatoria)* **7**, 218–240.

Rands, M.R.W. (1982) The influence of habitat on the population ecology of partridges. Unpublished D.Phil Thesis, University of Oxford.

Rands, M.R.W. (1985) Pesticide use on cereals and the survival of partridge chicks: a field experiment. *Journal of Applied Ecology* **22**, 49–54.

Rands, M.R.W., Sotherton, N.W. & Moreby, S.J. (1985) Some effects of cereal pesticides on gamebirds and other farmland fauna. In: *Recent Developments in Cereal Production*, pp. 98–113. Proceedings of a Symposium on Cereal Production, University of Nottingham.

Rands, M.R.W. (1986a) The survival of gamebird chicks in relation to pesticide use on cereals, *Ibis* **128**, 57–64.

Rands, M.R.W. (1986b) The effect of hedgerow characteristics on partridge breeding densities. *Journal of Applied Ecology* **24**.

Rands, M.R.W. (1986c) Unsprayed headlands: The answer for gamebirds? *Game Conservancy Annual Review* **17**, 56–61.

Rands, M.R.W. & Sotherton, N.W. (1986) Pesticide use on cereal crops and changes in the abundance of butterflies on arable farmland in England. *Biological Conservation* **36**, 71–82.

Ratcliffe, D. (1980) *The Peregrine Falcon.* T. & A.D. Poyser, Calton.

Ratti, J.T., Smith, L.M., Hupp, J.W. & Laake, J.L. (1983) Line transect estimates of density and the winter mortality of grey partridge. *Journal of Wildlife Management* **47**, 1088–1096.

Redfearn, A. & Pimm, S.L. (in press) Insect outbreaks and community structure. *Insect Pests (ed. P. Barbosa)*. Academic Press.

Reichenow, A. (1892) Bericht über die März-Sitzung. Allgem Dt. Orn. Ges. zu Berlin. *Journal für Ornithologie* **40**, 222–226.

Reichholf, J. (1973) Der Einfluss der Flubereinigung auf den Bestand an Rebhühnern (*Perdix perdix*). *Anz. orn. Ges. Bayern* **12**, 100–105.

Reitz, F. (1983) Besoins énérgetiques du poussin de Perdrix grise (*Perdix perdix* L.) et ressourcc alimentaire disponible en plaine de grandes cultures. Possibilités d'exploitation trophique du milieu par les couvées. Thèse présentée à l'Institut National Agronomique, Grignon, Paris.

Renzoni, A. (1974) The decline of the grey partridge in Italy. *Biological Conservation* **6**, 213–215.

Rey, E. (1907) Rebhuhn, *Perdix perdix* (L.). *Mageninhalte einiger Vögel. Ornithol. Monatsschr.* **32**, 242–246.

Ricci, J-C. (1985) Influence de l'Organisation sociale et de la densité sur les relations spatiales chez la perdrix rouge. Conséquences démographiques et adaptives. *Revue Ecologique* (Terre Vie) **40**, 53–85.

Richardson, P.N. (1983) The role of parasitic Hymenoptera and entomophilic nematodes in the natural control of some insects in cereals. *Glasshouse Crops Research Institute Annual Report for 1981*, pp. 112–113.

Rivière, J.L. Bach, J. & Grolleau, G. (1985) Effects of prochloraz on drug metabolism in the Japanese quail, grey partridge, chicken and pheasant. *Archives of Environmental Contamination and Toxicology* **14**, 299–306.

Romić, S. (1975a) The fertility of the partridge (*Perdix perdix* L.) between 1933 and 1966. *Poljoprivrendna Znanstvena Smotra* **35**, 167–184.

Romić, S. (1975b) Changes of the biological potential of the common partridge (*Perdix perdix* L.) during the past 33 years. *Poljoprivrendna Znanstvena Smotra* **35**, 101–118.

Rörig, G. (1900) Arbeiten an der Biologischen Abteilung für Land-u. Forstwirtschaft am Kaiserlichen Gesundheitsamt. *Magenuntersuchungen Land – und Forstwirtschaftlich Wichtiger Vögel*, pp. 50–56.

Rothschild, M. & Clay, T. (1952) *Fleas, flukes and Cuckoos*. Collins, London.

Rowan, W. (1954). Reflections on biology of animal cycles. *Journal of Wildlife Management* **18**, 52–60.

Royama, T. (1981) Evaluation of mortality factors in insect life table analysis. *Ecological Monographs* **51**, 495–505.

Royama, T. (1984) Population dynamics of the spruce budworm *Choristoneura fumiferana*. *Ecological Monographs* **54**, 429–462.

Rudd, R.L. (1964) *Pesticides and the Living Landscape*. The University of Wisconsin Press, Madison.

Saint-André de la Roche, G. & Douville de Granssu, P. (1982) Influence of insecticide treatment of cereals on young partridges. *La Défence des Végétaux* **214**, 64–70.

Salvin, F.H. & Broderick, W. (1855) *'Falconry in the British Isles'*. Reprinted 1971, Thames Valley Press, Maidenhead.

Sargeant, A.B., Allen, S.H. & Eberhardt, R.T. (1984) Red fox predation on breeding ducks in midcontinent North America. *Wildlife Monographs* **89**, 1–41.

Saunders, H. (1899) *An Illustrated Manual of British Birds* (Second edn.). Gurney & Jackson, London.

Schifferli, A., Geroudet, P. & Winkler, R. (1982) *Atlas des Oiseaux Nicheurs de Suisse (1972–1976)*.

Schönnamsgrüber, H. (1970) Herbizide in der Landschaft. Ergebnisse der 8.dtsch. Arbeitsbesprechung über Fragen der Unkrautbiologie u. – bekämpfung am 26./27.2.70 in Stuttgart-Hohenheim. *Zeitschrift Pflanzenkrankheiten Pflanzenschutz*, Sonderheft 5, 153–161.

Schröder, W., Schröder, J. & Scherzinger, W. (1982) Über die Rolle der Witterung in der Populationsdynamik des Auerhuhns (*Tetrao urogallus*). *Journal für Ornithologie* **123**, 287–296.

Schulz, J.W. (1977) Population dynamics of Hungarian partridge in north central North Dakota: 1946–1975. In: *Proceedings of the Perdix I. Hungarian Partridge Workshop* (ed. G.D. Kobriger), pp. 133–145. North Dakota Chapter of Wildlife Society.

Schulz, J.W. (1980) Grey partridge winter movements and habitat use in North Dakota. *The Prairie Naturalist* **12**, 37–42.

Schumacher, W. (1980) Schutz und Erhaltung gefährdeter Ackerwildkräuter durch Integration von landwirtschaftlicher Nutzung and Naturschutz. *Natur und Landschaft* **55**, 447–453.

Schumacher, W. (1981) Artenschutz für Kalkackerunkräuter. *Zeitschrift Pflanzenkrankheiten Pflanzenschutz, Sonderheft* **9**, 95–100.

Sekera, I.J. (1959) Causes of the variation and diminution of the partridge populations in Tchekoslovakia. *Lesnictví* **5**, 493–500.

Sekera, I.J. (1966) Problém koroptví v Československu. In: *Symposium O Koroptví*, pp. 5-14. *Výzkumný Ustav Lesního Hospodářství A. Myslivosti Československý Myslivecký Svaz*, Prague (in Czechoslovakian).

Seoane, L.V. (1891) *Perdices de Europa (Perdix cinerea charrela)*. La Coruña.

Serre, D. & Birkan, M. (1985) Incidence de traitements insecticides sur les ressources alimentaires de poussins de perdrix grise. *Gibier Faune Sauvage* 4, 21-61.

Sevast'yanov, G.N. (1969) Information on the reproduction and diet of partridges in the sub-zone of the Taiga. *Trans. Kirov. sel'skokhoz. Inst.* 21, 39-53.

Severtzoff, S.A. (1934) On the dynamics of populations of vertebrates. *Quarterly Review of Biology* 9, 409-437.

Sharpe, G.I. (1964) Trials with thiabendazole as a cure for gapes in gamebirds. *Annual Report Game Research Association* 3, 26-35.

Sharrock, J.T.R. (1976) *The Atlas of Breeding Birds in Britain and Ireland*. British Trust for Ornithology and Poyser, Berkhamsted.

Sheail, J. (1985) *Pesticides and Nature Conservation: The British Experience 1950-1975*. Clarendon Press, Oxford.

Shields, W.M. (1983) Optimal inbreeding and the evolution of philopatry. In: *The Ecology of Animal Movement* (eds I.R. Swingland & P.J. Greenwood), pp. 132-159. Oxford University Press.

Sih, A., Crowley, P., McPeek, M., Petranka, J. & Strohmeier (1985) Predation, competition and prey communities: A review of field experiments. *Annual Review of Ecological Systems* 16, 269-311.

Siivonen, L. (1953) Kanalintujen Pesien Tuhoutumisesta Ja Sen Torjumisesta. *Suomen Riista* 8, 46-48.

Siivonen, L. (1956) The correlation between the fluctuations of partridge and European hare populations and the climatic conditions of winters in south west Finland during the last thirty years. *Finn. Game Found. Pap. Game Res. Hels.* 17, 1-30.

Simon, J.L. (1981) *The Ultimate Resource*. Martin Robertson & Co. Ltd.

Skuhravý, V. (1959) The food of field Carabidae. *Cas. csl. Spol. ent.* 56, 1-18.

Skuhravý, V. (1960) Die Nahrung des Ohrwurmes (*Forficula auricularia* L.) in den Feldkulturen. *Cas. csl. Spol. ent.* 57, 329-339.

Skultéty, J. (1965) The protection of nesting partridges in the cutting of agricultural cultures. *Comm. Inst. Forest. Cechosl.* 3, 49-60.

Sladek, I.J. (1966) Contribution to the problem of harmful influence of buzzard (*Buteo buteo*) on partridge. In: *Symposium O Koroptvis*, pp. 88-93. Výzkumný Ústav Lesního Hospodářstvi A. Myslivosti Československy Myslivecký Svaz, Prague.

Smith, H. (1913) *Partridges: Yesterday and Today*. The Field Press Ltd, London.

Smith, L.M., Hupp, J.W. & Ratti, J.T. (1980) Reducing abandonment of nest-trapped grey partridge with methoxyflurane. *Journal of Wildlife Management* 44, 690-691.

Smith, L.M., Hupp, J.W. & Ratti, J.T. (1981) Grey partridge trapping techniques. *Journal of Field Ornithology* 52, 63-65.

Smith, L.M., Hupp, J.W. & Ratti, J.T. (1982) Habitat use and home range of grey partridge in eastern South Dakota. *Journal of Wildlife Management* 46, 580-587.

Sokolov, N.S., Shipinov, N.A., Chesalin, G.A. & Yakovlev, B.V. (*eds*) (1964) *Herbicides in Agriculture*. Izdatel'stvo Sel'skokhozyaistvennoi Literatury Zhurnalov i Plakatov, Moskva 1962. (Translated by the Israel Programme for Scientific Translations, Jerusalem).

Somers, J., Moran, E.T., Reinhart, B.S. & Stephenson, G. (1974) Effect of external application of pesticides to the fertile egg and early chick performance. *Bulletin of Environmental Contamination and Toxicology* **11**, 33–38, 339–342.

Sotherton, N.W. (1980) The ecology of *Gastrophysa polygoni* (L.) (Coleoptera: Chrysomelidae) in cereals. Unpublished Ph.D. Thesis, University of Southampton.

Sotherton, N.W. (1982a) Observations on the biology and ecology of the chrysomelid beetle *Gastrophysa polygoni* in cereal fields. *Ecological Entomology* **7**, 197–206.

Sotherton, N.W. (1982b) Predation of a chrysomelid beetle (*Gastrophysa polygoni*) in cereals by polyphagous predators. *Annals of Applied Biology* **101**, 196–199.

Sotherton, N.W. (1982c) Effects of herbicides on the chrysomelid beetle *Gastrophysa polygoni* (L.) in laboratory and field. *Zeitschrift für Angewandte Entomologie* **94**, 446–451.

Sotherton, N.W. (1984) The distribution and abundance of predatory arthropods overwintering on farmland. *Annals of Applied Biology* **105**, 423–429.

Sotherton, N.W. & Moreby, S.J. (1984a) Contact toxicity of some foliar fungicide sprays to three species of polyphagous predators found in cereal fields. Tests of Agrochemicals and Cultivatars No. 5. *Annals of Applied Biology Supplement* **104**, 16–17.

Sotherton, N.W., Wratten, S.D. & Vickerman, G.P. (1984b) The role of egg predation in the population dynamics of *Gastrophysa polygoni* (Coleoptera) in cereal fields. *Oikos* **43**, 301–308.

Sotherton, N.W. (1985a) The distribution and abundance of predatory arthropods overwintering in field boundaries. *Annals of Applied Biology* **106**, 17–21.

Sotherton, N.W. (1985b) The effect of applications of pyrazophos on beneficial arthropods in cereal fields. The Game Conservancy, Fordingbridge, 26 pp.

Sotherton, N.W., Rands, M.R.W. & Moreby, S.J. (1985) Comparison of herbicide treated and untreated headlands on the survival of game and wildlife. *Proceedings of the 1985 British Crop Protection Conference – Weeds* **3**, 991–998. Brighton, Sussex.

Southwood, T.R.E. & Leston, D. (1959) *Land and Water Bugs of the British Isles.* Frederick Warne & Co. Ltd, London.

Southwood, T.R.E. (1965) In: A discussion of ruffed grouse populations, Cloquet Forest Research Centre, Minnesota, by W.H. Marshall & G.W. Gullion. In: *Proceedings of the VIth International Congress of Game Biologists,* 1963, p. 100. Bournemouth, Hampshire.

Southwood, T.R.E. (1967) The ecology of the partridge II. The role of pre-hatching influences. *Journal of Animal Ecology* **36**, 557–562.

Southwood, T.R.E. & Cross, D.J. (1969) The ecology of the partridge III. Breeding success and the abundance of insects in natural habitats. *Journal of Animal Ecology* **38**, 497–509.

Southwood, T.R.E. (1972) Farm management in Britain and its effect on animal populations. In: *Proceedings of the Tall Timbers Conference on Ecological Animal Control by Habitat Management* **3**, 29–51.

Soyez, J.L. (1978) Les facteurs de la mortalité du petit gibier sédentaire: pratiques agricoles, pathologie, produits chimiques. *Pesticides et gibier, maladies du Gibier* (ed P. Pesson), pp. 29–48. Gauthier-Villars, Paris.

Speight, M.R. & Lawton, J.H. (1976). The influence of weed-cover on the mortality imposed on artificial prey by predatory ground beetles in cereal fields. *Oecologia (Berl.)* **23**, 211–223.

Spittler, H. (1972) On the effect of the reduction of foxes due to rabies on the small game populations in North Rhine Westphalia. *Zeitschrift für Jagdwissenschaft* **18**, 76-95.

Sprake, L. (1934) *Perdix the Patridge.* H.F. & G. Witherby, London.

Stanley, P.I. & Bunyan, P.J. (1979) Hazards to wintering geese and other wildlife from the use of dieldrin, chlorfenvinphos and carbophenothion as wheat seed treatments. *Proceedings of the Royal Society of London*, Series B **205**, 31-45.

Stanley, P.I. & Hardy, A.R. (1984) The environmental implications of current pesticide usage on cereals. *Proceedings of the N.E.R.C. I.T.C. Symposium No. 13 'Agriculture and the Environment'* (ed. D. Jenkins), pp. 66-72. Monks Wood Experimental Station, Huntingdon.

Stantschinsky, W.W. (1929) Zur geographischen Variabilität des Rebhuhns. *Orn. Monatsberichte* **37**, 135-139.

Stewart, D.R.M. (1967) Analysis of plant epidermis in faeces. *Journal of Applied Ecology* **4**, 83-111.

Strandgaard, H. & Asferg, T. (1980) The Danish bag record II: Fluctuations and trends in the game bag record in the years 1941-1976 and the geographical distribution of the bag in 1976. *Danish Review of Game Biology* **11** No. 5. Game Biology Station, Kalø, Denmark.

Stresemann, E. (1924) Das Bergrebhuhn, *Perdix montana* (Gmelin). (Mutations-stadien XVIII). *Orn. Monatsberichte* **32**, 132-135.

Sturrock, F.G., Cathie, J. & Payne, T.A. (1977) Economies of scale in farm mechanisation; a study of costs on large and small farms. Agricultural Enterprise Studies in England and Wales, Economic Report No. 56. Agricultural Economics Unit, Cambridge.

Stys, W. (1957) The influence of economic conditions on the fertility of peasant women. *Population Studies* **11**, 136-148.

Sulkava, S. (1965) On the living conditions of the partridge (*Perdix perdix* L.) and the brown hare (*Lepus europaeus* Pallus) in Ostrobothnia. *Aquila Ser. Zool.* **2**, 17-24.

Sunderland, K.D. (1975) The diet of some predatory arthropods in cereal crops. *Journal of Applied Ecology* **12**, 507-515.

Sunderland, K.D. & Vickerman, G.P. (1980) Aphid feeding by some polyphagous predators in relation to aphid density in cereal fields. *Journal of Applied Ecology* **17**, 389-396.

Sunderland, K.D., Chambers, R.J. & Stacey, D.L. (1984) Polyphagous predators and cereal aphids. *Glasshouse Crops Research Institute Annual Report for 1982*, pp. 94-97.

Sunderland, K.D., Chambers, R.J., Stacey, D.L. & Crook, N.E. (1985) Invertebrate polyphagous predators and cereal aphids. *Bulletin of the International Union for Biological Control Working Group* **VII** (3), 105-114.

Sunderland, K.D. (in press) Spiders and cereal aphids in Europe. *Bulletin of the International Union for Biological Control Working Group 'Integrated Control of Cereal Pests'*, 1986.

Suomus, H. (1958) Wintering of Partridge. *Suomen Riista* **12**, 55-62.

Swanson, C.V. & Yocum, C.F. (1958) Upland gamebird populations in relation to cover and agriculture in south eastern Washington. *Transactions of the 23rd North American Wildlife Conference*, pp. 277-290.

Swingland, I.R. & Greenwood, P.J. (1983) *The Ecology of Animal Movement.* Oxford University Press, London.

Szederjei, A., Szederjei, M. & Studinka, L. (1959) Die systematische Stellung des Rebhuhns und seine Verbreitung. In: *Hasen, Rebhühner, Fasanen*, pp. 109-274. Terra-

Verlag, Budapest.

Szederjei, A. & Szederjei, M. (1960) Beobachtungen und Versuche über den Aktionsradius und die Vermehrung der Rebhühner. *Zeitschrift für Jagdwissenschaft* **6**, 1-15.

Tapper, S.C. (1976) The diet of weasels (*Mustela nivalis*) and stoats (*Mustela erminea*) during early summer in relation to predation on gamebirds. *Journal of Zoology* **179**, 219-224.

Tapper, S.C. (1979) The effect of fluctuating vole numbers (*Microtus agrestis*) on a population of weasels (*mustela nivalis*) on farmland. *Journal of Animal Ecology* **48**, 603-617.

Tapper, S.C., Green, R.E. & Rands, M.R.W. (1982) Effects of mammalian predators on partridge populations. *Mammal Review* **12**, 159-167.

Taylor, J. (1976) The advantage of spacing out. *Journal of Theoretical Biology* **59**, 485-490.

Taylor, J.C. & Blackmore, D.K. (1961) A short note on the heavy mortality in foxes during the winter 1959-1960. *Veterinary Record* **73**, 232-233.

Taylor, L.R. (1961) Aggregation, variance and the mean. *Nature* **189**, 732-735.

Taylor, R.J. (1984) *Predation.* Chapman & Hall Ltd, London.

Teixiera, R.M. (1979) *Atlas van de Nederlandse Broedvogels.* De Lange van Leer bv, Deventer, Netherlands.

Terrasson, F. & Tendron, G. (1975) *Evolution and Conservation of Hedgerow Landscapes in Europe.* Council of Europe, Nature and Environment Series, No. 8.

Thaisz, L. & Csiki, E. (1912) Über den wirtschaftlichen Nutzen des Rebhuhns (*Perdix perdix* L.). Erster Bericht. Vegetabilische Nahrung des Rebhuhns. *Aquila* **19**, 166-201.

Thieme, K. (1985) Biotoppräferenzen und Home-range des Rebhuhns (*Perdix perdix*). In: *Proceedings of the XVIIth International Congress of Game Biologists,* 1985, pp. 589-595. Brussels, Belgium.

Thom, V.M. (1986) *Birds in Scotland.* T. & A.D. Poyser, Berkhamsted.

Thomas, G.C. (1973) A study of the range of Hungarian Partridge (*Perdix perdix perdix*) in south western Ontario (Unpublished manuscript).

Thonon, P. (1974) Les populations entomologiques des *territoires* agricoles en tant que potentialités alimentaires pour les poussins de perdrix grise (*Perdix perdix* Linné, 1758) dans un secteur du Gâtinais du sud-est. Thèse Doctorale de Spécialité, Université d'Orléans, U.E.R. Sciences Fondamentales et appliquées.

Tinbergen, L. (1960) The natural control of insects in pinewoods. I. factors influencing the intensity of predation by songbirds. *Archives Neerlandaises de Zoologie* **13**, 266-336.

Tischler, W. (1965) *Agrarökologie.* 499 p, Jena.

Tomiałojć, L. (1976) *The Birds of Poland.* Translated by the United States Fish and Wildlife Service.

Tonkin, J.H. (1968) The occurrence of broad-leaved weed seeds in samples of cereals tested by the Official Seed Testing Station, Cambridge. *Proceedings of the 9th British Weed Control Conference*, pp. 1199-1204.

Toschi, A. (1962) Preliminary results of the release of partridges (*Perdix perdix*) in Italy. In: *Proceedings of the Vth International Congress of Game Biologists*, 1961, pp. 261-268. Bologna, Italy.

Trager, J. (1974) *Amber Waves of Grain.* Arthur Fields Books, New York.

Trautman, C.G., Fredrickson, L.F. & Carter, A.V. (1974). Relationship of red foxes and other predators to populations of ring-necked pheasants and other prey, South Dakota. *Transactions of the 39th North American Wildlife Conference,* pp. 241-252.

Trego, K.T. (1973) Radio telemetry monitoring of the spring and summer activities of the Hungarian partridge in north-central North Dakota. In: *North Dakota Game and Fish Department P-R Project Report* No. W-67-R-13, 56 pp.

Trego, K.T. & Upgren, T. (1975) *Hungarian Partridge Bibliography.* North Dakota State Game and Fish Department, U.S.A.

Turnbull, A.L. & Chant, D.A. (1961) The practice and theory of biological control of insects in Canada. *Canadian Journal of Zoology* **39**, 697-753.

Turner, T.W. (1954) *Memoirs of a Gamekeeper.* Geoffrey Bles, London.

Turtle, E.E., Taylor, A., Wright, E.N. Thearle, R.J.P., Egan, H., Evans, W.H. & Soutar, N.M. (1963) The effects on birds of certain chlorinated insecticides used as seed dressings. *J. Sci. Fd. Agric.* **14**, 567-577.

Twomey, A.C. (1936) Climographic studies of certain introduced and migratory birds. *Ecology* **17**, 122-132.

Ubrizy, G. (1968) Long-term experiments on the flora-changing effect of chemical weed killers in plant communities. *Acta Agronomica Academiae Scientiarum Hungaricae* **17**, 171-193.

Ulfstrand, S. & Högstedt, G. (1976) How many birds breed in Sweden? *Anser* **15**, 1-32.

Van den Bos, J. & Rabbinge, R. (1976) *Simulation of the Fluctuations of the Grey Larch Bud Moth.* Pudoc, Wageningen, the Netherlands.

Van den Bosch, R. (1976) Investigation of the effects of food standards on pesticide use. *Environmental Protection Agency Contract 68-01-2603,* Report No. 15, 147 pp.

Van den Bosch, R. (1980) *The Pesticide Conspiracy.* Anchor Press, New York.

Vandervell, C.A. and Coles, C.L. (1983) *Game and the English Landscape.* Debrett's Peerage Ltd, London.

Vaurie, C. (1965) *The Birds of the Palearctic Fauna (non-passeriformes).* Witherby, London.

Vertse, A., Zsák, Z. & Kaszab, Z. (1952) Food and agricultural importance of the partridge (*Perdix perdix* L.) in Hungary. *Aquila* **59**, 13-68.

Vetiska, T.K. (1979) Die botanische und zoologische Zusammensetzung des Kropfinhaltes bei Fasan (*Phasianus colchicus* L.) und Rebhuhn (*Perdix perdix* L.). (Dissertation for Doctorate in veterinary science, University of Vienna).

Viart, M. (1978) Nourrissage Hivernal d'une Population de Perdrix par Agrainage à Poste Fixe. C.T.G.R.E.F. Nogent sur Vernission Compte-rendu d'expérience 1977/83. *R.F.F.* **30**, 367-379.

Vickerman, G.P. (1974) Some effects of grass weed control on the arthropod fauna of cereals. *Proceedings of the 12th British Weed Control Conference,* 1974, pp, 929-939.

Vickerman, G.P. & Sunderland, K.D. (1975) Arthropods in cereal crops: nocturnal activity, vertical distribution and aphid predation. *Journal of Applied Ecology* **12**, 755-766.

Vickerman, G.P. (1977) The effects of foliar fungicides on some insect pests of cereals. *Proceedings of the 1977 British Crop Protection Conference - Pests & Diseases* **1**, 121-128. Brighton, Sussex.

Vickerman, G.P. & Sunderland, K.D. (1977) Some effects of dimethoate on arthropods in winter wheat. *Journal of Applied Ecology* **14**, 767-777.

Vickerman, G.P. (1978) The arthropod fauna of undersown grass and cereal fields.

Scientific Proceedings of the Royal Dublin Society **6**, 156–165.

Vickerman, G.P. & O'Bryan, M. (1979) Partridges and insects. *Annual Review of the Game Conservancy* **9**, pp. 35–43.

Vickerman, G.P. (1982) Distribution and abundance of adult *Opomyza florum* (Diptera: Opomyzidae) in cereal crops and grassland. *Annals of Applied Biology* **101**, 441–447.

Vickerman, G.P. & Sotherton, N.W. (1983) Effects of some foliar fungicides on the chrysomelid beetle *Gastrophysa polygoni* (L.). *Pesticide Science* **14**, 405–411.

Vrazic, O. (1957) Parasites of the common partridge (*Perdix perdix* L.) in Croatia. *Veterinary Archives* **27**, 25–32.

Vučković, M. (1967) The state and protection of game in Montenegro. In: *Proceedings of the VIIth International Congress of Game Biologists,* 1965, pp. 159–169. Beograd-Ljubljana, Yugoslavia.

Walsingham, Lord, & Payne Gallwey, Sir, R. (1895) *Shooting: Field and Covert.* Longmans, Green & Co., London.

Warner, R.E. (1984) Effects of changing agriculture on ring-necked pheasant brood movements in Illinois. *Journal of Wildlife Management* **48**, 1014–1018.

Warner, R.E., Joselyn, G.B. & Ellis, J.A. (1984) Declining survival of ring-necked pheasant chicks in Illinois agricultural ecosystems. *Journal of Wildlife Management* **48**, 82–88.

Watt, A.D., Wratten, S.D. & Vickerman, G.P. (1984) The effect of the grain aphid *Sitobion avenae* (F.) on winter wheat in England: an analysis of the economics of control practice on forecasting systems. *Crop Protection* **3**, 209–222.

Way, M.J. (1974) Integrated control in Britain. In: *Biology in Pest and Disease Control* (*eds* D. Price Jones & M.E. Solomon), pp. 196–208. Blackwell Scientific Publications, Oxford.

Wehr, E.E. & Olivier, L.G. (1946) Limitations of phenothiazine in the control of caecal worms and blackhead disease of turkeys. *Poultry Science* **25**, 199–203.

Weigand, J.P. (1971) Mercury in Hungarian partridge and in north central Montana environment. In: *Proceedings of the Oregon State University Workshop, Mercury in the Western Environment,* 19 pp. Portland, Oregon.

Weigand, J.P. (1977a) *Hungarian Partridge in North Central Montana.* Montana Dept. Fish and Game, Helena.

Weigand, J.P. (1977b) Mechanisms preventing inbreeding in a low density Hungarian partridge population. In: *Proceedings of the Perdix I. Hungarian Partridge Workshop* (*ed.* G.D. Kobriger), 99–107. North Dakota Chapter of Wildlife Society.

Weigand, J.P. (1980) Ecology of the Hungarian partridge in north central Montana. *Wildlife Monographs* **74**, 1–106.

Weiss, V. (1971) Keine winterverluste bei Rebhühnern (*Perdix perdix*) im Obererzgebirge. *Beitr. Vogelkd. Leipzig* **17**, 176–177.

Wellington, P.S. (1971) Assessment and control of the decimation of weeds by crop seeds. In: *The Biology of Weeds,* pp. 94–107. Blackwells, Oxford.

Wentworth Day, J. (1957) *Poison on the Land.* Eyre and Spottiswoode, London.

Westerskov, K. (1949) A comparative study of the ecology and management of the European partridge *Perdix perdix* in Ohio and Denmark. Unpublished M.Sc. Thesis, Ohio State University, Columbus.

Westerskov, K. (1951) On age composition and barrenness in the Danish population of partridges *Perdix perdix. Dansk Jagttidende* **68**, 26–28.

Westerskov, K. (1956) History and distribution of the Hungarian partridge in Ohio, 1909–1948. *The Ohio Journal of Science* **56**, 65–70.

Westerskov, K. (1957) The value of renesting in gamebirds. *New Zealand Outdoors* **22**, 25–26.

Westerskov, K. (1958a) Altersbestimmung und Schlüpfzeitdatierung mit Hilfe der Handschwingen europäischer Hühnervögel. *Zeitschrift für Jagdwissenschaft* **4**, 130–138.

Westerskov, K. (1958b) The partridge as a gamebird. *New Zealand Outdoors* **22**, 12–15.

Westerskov, K.(1960) Danish partridges in New Zealand.*New Zealand Outdoors* **25**, 9–12.

Westerskov, K. (1964a) The recent decline of the partridge in mid-western United States. *New Zealand Outdoors* **29**1, 16–19.

Westerskov, K. (1964b) Finland as an environment for the partridge (in Finnish with English summary.) *Suomen Riista* **17**, 14–21.

Westerskov, K. (1965) Winter ecology of the partridge (*Perdix perdix*) in the Canadian Prairie. *Proceedings of the New Zealand Ecological Society* **12**, 23–30.

Westerskov, K. (1966) Winter food and feeding habits of the partridge (*Perdix perdix*) in the Canadian Prairie. *Canadian Journal of Zoology* **44**, 303–322.

Westmacott & Worthington (1974) In: *Farming and Wildlife* by K. Mellanby (1981). William Collins Sons & Co. Ltd, London.

Whitlock, S.C. (1937) An apparent case of sexual difference in resistance to parasitic infection. *Journal of Parasitology* **23**, 426.

Wichtrup, L.G., Steiner, H. & Wipperfürth, T. (1985) The effect of clover as an undercrop on the population dynamics of aphids (Homoptera, Aphididae) and epigeic arthropods in winter wheat in the Lautenbach project. *Mitteilungen der Deutschen Gesellschaft für Allgemeine und Angewandte Entomologie* **4**, 430–432.

Wilson, B.J. (1986) Yield responses of winter cereals to the control of broad-leaved weeds. In: *Proceedings of the European Weed Research Society Symposium on Economic Weed Control*, 1986, pp. 75–82. Stuttgart.

Wilson, G.R. (1977) Another look at grouse disease. *Country Landowner* **28**, 30–31.

Wilson, G.R. & Wilson, L.P. (1978) Haematology, weight and condition of captive red grouse (*Lagopus lagopus scoticus*) infected with caecal threadworms (*Trichostrongylus tenuis*). *Research in Veterinary Science* **2**, 331–336.

Wilson, G.R. (1979) Effects of the caecal threadworm *Trichostrongylus tenuis* on red grouse. Unpublished Ph.D. Thesis, University of Aberdeen.

Wing, L.W. (1953) Cycles of European partridge abundance. *Journal of Cycle Research*, pp. 56–57.

Wise, D.R. & Fuller, M.K. (1978) Artificial insemination in the brown-eared pheasant *Crossoptilon mantchuricum*. *The World Pheasant Association Journal III, 1977–1978*, pp. 90–95.

Wise, D.R. (1982) Nutrition of wild red grouse (*Lagopus lagopus scoticus*). *The World Pheasant Association Journal VII, 1981–1982*, pp. 36–41.

Wishart, W. (1977) A review of the past and present status of the grey partridge (*Perdix perdix*) in Alberta. In: *Proceedings of the Perdix I. Hungarian Partridge Workshop* (ed. G.D. Kobriger), 48–65. North Dakota Chapter of Wildlife Society.

Woodard, A.E., Abplanalp, H. & Snyder, L. (1982) Inbreeding depression in the red-legged partridge. *Poultry Science* **61**, 1579–1584.

Woodford, E.K. (1964) Weed control in arable crops. *Proceedings of the 7th British*

Weed Control Conference **3**, 944–962.

Wood-Gush, D.G.M., Duncan, I.J.H. & Savory, C.J. (1978) Observations on the social behaviour of domestic fowl in the wild. *Biology of Behaviour* **3**, 193–205.

Wormald, J. (1912) *How to Increase a Stock of Partridges.* The Field, London.

Worthing, C.R. & Walker, S.B. (*eds*) (1983) *The Pesticide Manual: A World Compendium*, 7th edn. The British Crop Protection Council, Croydon.

Wright, B.S. (1960) Woodcock reproduction in DDT-sprayed areas of New Brunswick. *Journal of Wildlife Management* **24**, 419–420.

Wright, R. & Street, M. (1985) The influence of fish on survival of wildfowl broods. *Game Conservancy Annual Review* **16**, pp. 77–80.

Wright, V.L., Allen, L.F., Graham, D.L. & Fiedler, W.R. (1980) Effects of *Heterakis* and *Histomonas* on the survival of juvenile grey partridge. In: *Proceedings of the Perdix II Grey Partridge Workshop* (*eds* S.R. Peterson & L. Nelson), pp. 156–164. University of Idaho, Moscow.

Yapp, W.B. (1983) Gamebirds in Medieval England. *Ibis* **125**, 218–221.

Yeatman, L.J. (1976) *Atlas de Oiseaux Nicheurs de France.* Paris, France.

Yeatter, R.E. (1932) Housing problems of the Hun. *American Game* **21**, 11–12.

Yeatter, R.E. (1934) The Hungarian partridge in the Great Lakes region. *Bull. Sch. For. Mi.* **5**, 1–92.

Yocum, C.F. (1943) The Hungarian partridge (*Perdix perdix*) in the Palouse region, Washington. *Ecological Monographs* **13**, 167–201.

Young, B. (1983) *Prospects for Soviet Grain Production.* Westview Press Inc., U.S.A.

Zadoks, J.C. & Rijsdijk, F.H. (1984) *Atlas of Cereal Diseases and Pests in Europe*, Volume III. Pudoc, Wageningen, the Netherlands.

Zeigler, D. (1978) Upland gamebird populations in relation to cover and agriculture in eastern Washington. Report of the Washington Game Department, Upland Game Bird Investigation Study No. IV, 53 pp.

Index

2,3,6–TBA, 104
2,4–D, 96, 100, 102, 103, 104, 105, 109, 113
2,4–DB, 104
2,4–DP, 104
2,4,5,T, 96, 100

Action Cornflower, 200
Agawam, Montana, 96, 190
Age and clutch size, 45
  determination, 39
Ageing guide, 38
Agonum dorsale, 51, 112, 212, 213, 217
Agricultural Chemicals Approval Scheme, 216
Agropyron repens (Couch grass), 221
Alarm calls reaction to, 205
Albania partridge bag, 24
aldrin, 95, Plate IX
aldicarb, 98
Amara fulva, 79
Amaranthus spp. (Pigweed), 210
Amberley Mount, 117
Ametastegia glabrata, 107
Amino-acids, 82
Anaesthetic temporary, 43
Analysis time-series, 131
Animal protein, 83
Annual meadow-grass (*Poa annua*),219
Ant cocoons, *see* ant pupae
  eggs, *see* ant pupae
  pupae, 76, 83
Anti-predator behaviour, 205
Ants, 79, 155
Aphicide, 120, 121, 210, 216
  sprayed from air, Colour Plate XIV
Aphicides increased use in Britain
  1972 to 1985, 120
Aphid outbreaks, 120, 214, 215
  predators, 211
Applesham Farm, 31, 41, 62, 87, 116, 157, 217, Colour Plate VIII
Aquifers, 217
Arable land possible, 6
Arctic waders, 70
Ascot, 75, 78
atrazine, 210
Austria, 12, 19, 143, 153
  partridge bag, 23
Avicide for Corvidae, 207
Azerbaydjan, 22

BAA British Agrochemicals Association, 120
Badger, Eurasian, 60, 72, 206
Bags national partridge, 23
Banchory grouse research, 56, 80, 131
Bank height and partridge nesting, 164
Barley-yellow-dwarf virus, 214
Barrier work cereal aphid predation, 211
Bayern (Bavaria), 92, Colour Plate X
Beaters, 14
Beauce, 18, 79
Belgium, partridge bag, 23
Bembidion lampros, 212, 213
benazolin, 104
benomyl, 113
benzimidazoles, 216
bifenox, 104
Bilderdykia convolvulus, see Black bindweed
Biological control, 116
Black bindweed (*Polygonum*

convolvulus), 103, 107, 142, 143, 144, 145, 147, Colour Plate XXVI
duck, 122
Blackhead (*Histomonas*), 138
Body moult, 155
Borkum, 10
Boulsbury, 194
Boxworth, 218
British Trust for Ornithology, 12, 51, 65, 98, 169
bromophos, 120
bromoxynil, 104
Bromus sterilis (Sterile brome grass), 221
Brood Production Rate (BPR), 48
  size, 45
  size precision, 48
Broods hatching per pair (BPR), 48
Brown rust (*Puccinia hordei*), 210
Bulgaria, 10
  partridge bag, 23
Bunting reed, 114
Bureau of Animal Populations, 2
Burning stubbles, 112
Butterflies, 222
Buzzard
  common, 152, 206
  honey, 206
  rough-legged, 206

Caecal round-worm *Heterakis gallinarum*, 126, 138, 139
  threadworm *Trichostrongylus tenuis*, 126, Plate X
Calcicole flora, Colour Plate XI
Calcifuge flora cereals, 106, Colour Plate XIII
Calumet, Wisconsin, 190
Canada, 19, 96, 102, 146
  partridge bag, 23
Canadian prairies, 102, 110, 145, 146
captafol, 104
carbendazim, 104
carbophenothion, 96, 99
Carrion crow, 60, 61, 71, 72, 159, 206
Castellina Fiorentini, 92, 199
Cat, 60
Cataglyphus cursor (species of ant), 93
Caterpillars, 219
Caucasian foothills, 151

Cause of population decline at Damerham, 186
  of population decline at Sussex, 184
  of population decline world wide, 187
Cereal aphids, 52, 79, 88, 121, 210, 213, 217, Fig. 12.1
  grains on stubble, 142
  leaves protein, 153
Cereals and Gamebirds Research Project, 216, 220, 221, 222
  undersown, *see* undersowing
Charlock, *see* Yellow charlock
Charterhall Berwicks, 46
Chenopodium sp. usually *album*, *see* Fat hen
Chianti, 9, 19
Chick growth rate, 82
  mortality in relation to the density of preferred insects, 90
  mortality rate 1903 to 1985, 123, Fig. 6.9
  mortality rate according to herbicide use, 122
  mortality rate adjusted for effect of herbicides, 178
  survival and weather, 75, 90
  Survival Rate (CSR), 45
  survival rate as function of insect food, 87, 88, 89, 90, 91, Fig.5.3
Chicks hatching per brood, 46, 178
Chickweed (*Stellaria media*), 80, 104, 107, 144, 154, 219
chlorfenvinphos, 100
chlorpyrifos, 104
chlortoluron, 104
Cleavers corn (*Galium tricornutum*), 106
  (*Galium aparine*), 107, 220
Clover, 111, 113, 130, 142, 153, 154
Clutch largest of any bird, 1
  removal of the first, 194
  size, 8, 45, 153
Clutches collected (*see also* Euston System), 57
CMPP, 101, 104, 106, 109
Coccidiosis, 139
Code Napoleon, 169
Cold weather and adults, 146
  weather and chicks, 85
Collectivised agricultures, 170, 191
Collembola, 88, 213

Colorado beetle (*Leptinotarsa decemlineata*), 84
Compensating cereal growers, 219
Compensation mechanism (involving dispersal), 197
Compensatory responses of partridge populations to shooting, 194
Computer programme, 177
  simulation model, 176, 177, 182
  simulated partridge populations, 183
Confidence limits, xiv
Conquest Saskatchewan, 171, 190
Corn buttercup (*Ranunculus arvensis*), 106
  gromwell (*Lithospermum arvense*), 106, 144
  marigold (*Chrysanthemum segetum*), 106
  salad (*Valerianella dentata*), 106
  spurrey (*Spergula arvensis*), 106, 144
Corncockle (*Agrostemma githago*), 106, 108
Corncrake, 223
Cornflower (*Cyanus cyanus*), 102, 106, 144
Cornwall, 152, 188
Corvidae crows, 59, 60, 207, 208
Country Life, 2, 76, 126
Courtyard Farm, Norfolk, 36, 62, 63, 64, 91, 166, Plate XII
Coveys, daily movements of, 149
  defined, 2
Craggs Lane Farm, 102, 148, Colour Plate, XXIII
Craneflies Tipulidae, 76
Crop boundaries, 166
  contents of chicks, 76, 78
  filling, 142
  sprayers, 103
Cropping of game, 193
Crops in Sussex study area, 31
Cross of Lorraine effect, 37
Crossbill, 80
Cycle ten year, 130
cypermethrin, 104
Cystine, 82
Czechoslovakia, 9, 12, 14, 16, 18, 23, 24, 25, 26, 27, 67, 76, 79, 105, 111, 126, 131, 149, 171, 189
Czempiń, Poland, 26, 124, 189, 192,
Colour Plate XX

Damerham, Fordingbridge, Hampshire, 3, 27, 28, 36, 40, 42, 46, 47, 62, 63, 64, 67, 84, 91, 122, 136, 154, 160, 169, 179, 186, 188, 194, 207, 212
  partridge numbers 1914–1985, 27
Dandelion (*Taraxacum officinale* agg.), 142
Daphnia, 80
DDE, 94
DDT, 94, 96, 97, 99, 122
Decline in breeding stocks, 25
Delphacids, 113
demeton-s-methyl, 96, 99, 104, 121
Demetrias atricapillus, 117, 212, 213, 217
Denmark, 76, 105, 170, 201, 205,
  partridge bag, 23
Density estimates, 115, 188, 189, 190
  -dependent chick survival rates, 83
  -dependent dispersal, 173
  -dependent nest predation, 61, 62, 63, 64, 65, 67
  in August, 43
  in Spring, 43, 188, 189, 190
Desertion early, 56
dicamba, 104
dieldrin, 95, 96, 97, 98, 100
Diet, chick, 52
  of adult partridges in summer, 155
Dietrick vacuum insect sampler (D-vac), 50, 213, Colour Plate XII, Plate VIII
difenzoquat, 96, 104
Dikonert, 105
dimethoate, 96, 120, 121
Direct seeding, 218
Distribution of the partridge, bearded partridge and Tibetan partridge, 17, Fig.2.2
  of the partridge in Europe and North West Asia, 16, Fig. 2.1
  of the partridge in North America, 20, Fig. 2.3
DNBP, 95
DNOC, 96, 97, 98, 103, 106, 108, 109
Docking disorder, 99
Dog, nest predation by, 60

Dogs, pointing, 12
  retrieving, 14
Dolerus, 114, 116
  Dolerus gonager, 115, Colour Plate XXXI
  Dolerus haematodes, 115
  Dolerus puncticollis, 114
Dolichopodidae, 92, 214
Drainage improved, 108
Dredge corn, 218
Driving partridges, 14, Colour Plate II
Druid's Lodge South Wiltshire, 198
Dummy eggs, 58
Dutch elm disease, 173
D-vac samples, 115
  see Dietrick vacuum insect sampler

Earthworm, 135
Earwig, 211
Eastern Counties Partridge Study, 91
  Europe, 24, 170
Egg predators specialist, 72
  quality, 153
Eifel district FRG, 220, Colour Plate XXX
Eisenia foetida (earthworm), 135
Eley Cartridge Company, 2
  Game Advisory Service, 3, 15
ELISA, 214
Elvedon, 207
Empididae, 92, 214
Enclosures, 167
Energy assimilation efficiency, 145
  needs increase adult, 146
  needs increase chick, 85
Environmentally Sensitive Areas or ESAs, 223
Enzyme-linked immuno-assay techniques (ELISA), 213
Esterhazy, 189
ethyl-mercury acetate, 95
Eurygaster cereal bug, 84
Euston System, 55, Box 4.1
Exclusion cages and cereal aphid predation, 211
Experiments increasing or decreasing the number of predators, 73
Exploration by nesting pair, 160

Faecal analysis, 52
Faeces dissection of, 53
  location of, 43
Falcon gyr, 206
  red-footed, 206
  peregrine, 12, 13, 94
Falconry, 12, 13
Fasankert Field Research Station Hungary, 26
Fat hen *Chenopodium sp.*, 104, 105, 113, 144, 219
Faville Grove Wisconsin, 190
Feather-grass (*Stipa lessingiana*), 93
  -grass steppes, 110
  lice, 140
Feeding behaviour of broods, 86
Females, excess of, 37
fenbendazole (Wormex), 134
fenitrothion, 96
fenpropimorph, 104
fenthion, 122
Feral cat, predation by, 59
Fertilisers, 108
Field nigella (*Nigella arvensis*), 108
  pansy (*Viola arvensis*), 107
  size average, 168, 169, 170, 172
  size of and amount of nesting cover, 172
  sparrow, 70
  vole (*Microtus arvalis*), 207
Findon Meteorological Station, 88
Finland, 9, 10, 105, 143, 145, 147, 151
  largest clutch size of partridge, 8
  partridge bag, 23
Fisheries, 195
Flagellate protozoan *Histomonas meleagridis*, 126
Fleas, 140
Flooding of nest, 65, 160, 166
Fluellens (*Kickxia elatine* and *K. spuria*), 106
Flushing bar, 67
Fly Yellow dung (*Scopeuma stercoraria*), 214
Food and Agriculture Organisation, 105
Forget-me-not (*Myosotis arvensis*), 107
Fossilised landscapes, 169
Fox, 55, 56, 58, 60, 61, 70, 99, 206, 208
  bags, 208

control, 208
predation by, 58
France, 9, 11, 17, 18, 23, 24, 28, 76, 114, 124, 139, 169, 189, 202, 204, 205
FRG Hessen, 189
  Wetterau, 189
  Winzenheim, 189
Friesland island varieties of partridge, 10
Fungicides foliar, 99
  new, 210

Game Research Association, 3
  Research Station at Kalø, 21
Gamebird bagged cost, 222
  bagged expected cost, 221
Gamekeeper cost of, 185, 221
Gamekeepers increase bag, 186, 196, 197, Fig. 11.1
  number of in the UK, 187, Fig. 10.5
  reduces nest predation, 57, 63, 65, Figs 4.2, 4.3, 4.4
Gamma BHC, 96, 99, 104
Gapes, treatment of, 134, Box 7.2
Gapeworm (*Syngamus trachea*), 49, 126, 135, 137, 138, Fig. 7.3, Plate XI
Gapex, 134
Gastrophysa polygoni (Knotgrass beetle), 83, 88, 107, 111, 112, 113, Colour Plates XXVII, XXVIII
Gatchina, see Imperial Hunting Reserve
Geese, 99
Georgia, USSR, 10
Germany, 9, 23, 24
  DRG, 23, 114, 171
  FRG, 92, 101, 108, 165, 216, 217, 220
Goshawk, 13, 151, 164, 206, 207
Goslings, 80
Grain aphids, 108
  surpluses, 6, 223
  winter food of partridge, 146
Grass residual effect on site selection and predation, 163, 164
  residual on baulks, 165, Colour Plate XXII
  strips and baulks, 169
  weeds, 210
Grasshoppers, 76, 83, 92, 93, 139, 155, 222
Great grain robbery, 171
  horned owl, 150
  skua, 72
  tit, 173
Great Witchingham, 44, 75, 76, 91, 123, 127, 130, 172, 188
Greece, 19, 24
Grey squirrel, 2, 207
Ground beetles Carabidae, 76, 211
Grouse, 87
  chicks, 56
  red, 80, 131, 133, 140, 148, 153
  ruffed, 122
Growth rate of chick and diet, 80, 81
Gun breech-loading, 14
Guns, 14

Habitation behaviour of partridge pair when nesting, 160
Hancock, Iowa, 190
Hand-reared chicks, 205
  -rearing for release, 222
Hares, snowshoe, 130
Harrier, hen, 206
Hawking, 12
Hay seeds, 148
Headlands weedy, see weedy crop margin
Hedge removal, 167
  Britain, 168
  Eastern Europe, 170
  North America, 171
  Western Europe mainland, 169
Hedgehog, 60
Hedges, 161
Heligoland, 10
Hemp nettle (*Galeopsis tetrahit*), 106, 107, 142, 143, 144, 145, Colour Plate XXV
Hen loss on nest, 56
Henbit dead nettle (*Lamium amplexicaule*), 107
heptachlor, 96
Herbicide and other pesticides drifting into hedge, 221
  history of use, 101
  use, upward trends in, 103, Fig. 6.2
Herbicides, 99, 143, 210
  affecting chick survival, 184
  and herbicide-free cereal field

margins, 118
and insecticides effect on the mortality rates of partridge chicks, 118
effect of, 77
not used, 178
used, 104, 178
Heritabilities, 174
Hessen, FRG (Hesse), 92
Heterakis, see caecal worm
High protein diet of chick, 85
Histomonas, 139
Hobby, 206
Home range size, 119, Fig. 6.7
Honey bees, 222
Hooded crow, 207
Hoverflies especially *Syrphus corollae*, 211
Hungary, 18, 19, 23, 24, 25, 26, 67, 76, 102, 105, 106, 108, 161, 170, 189, 201
Hunstanton Estate, 36, 70
Huntsman, 217
Hursley Park, Hampshire, 46
Hyper-hunting, 199
-parasitoids, 213
Hypera postica (*Phytonomous variabilis*) lucerne weevil, 79, 83, 111
Hypothermia, 85
Hypothesis Siivonen's, 153

ICI, 2
  Game Research Station, 3, 36, 77, 222
  Plant Protection, 106
  shooting rights, 186
Ideal-free distribution Fretwell's, 158, 159
Image searching, 71
Imperial College Field Station, 77, 78, 80
  Hunting Reserve, Gatchina, 21, 151, 189
Inbreeding and dispersal, 173, 174
  coefficient, 173
Incubation, 154
Insect abundance in cereals, 87, 88, 89, 91
  monitoring in cereals Sussex study areas, 50, 51, 52, Figs 5.2, 6.4, 12.1, 12.2
Insecticides, autumn use of, 214

direct effects, 99
effect on partridge chick food supply and mortality, 120
Insects, as a percentage of items in the diet, 79
mean density of per m^2 from cereal fields, 111
other preferred, 117
preferred, 83
Integrated pest control/ management, 209, 210
International Foundation for the Conservation of Game, *see* acknowledgements
Ornithological Congress, 80
Union of Game Biologists, 77
Intervention buying, 220
ioxynil, 104
Iran partridge bag, 24
Ireland, 9, 19, 23
iso-proturon, 104
Italian Alps, 18
Italy, 9, 18, 23, 24, 100, 202, 205

Jassids (Cicadellidae), 113
Jealotts Hill (ICI Plant Protection), 3

k values defined, 49, 50
Kazakhstan, 10, 22, 24, 110, 114, 126, 155, 170
Kestrels, 60, 206
Kite, 13
Knebworth Estate, 3, 75
Knotgrass beetle, *see Gastrophysa polygoni*
  Polygonum aviculare (knotweed), 103, 107, 142, 144, 219, Colour Plate XXXVII

Ladybirds Coccinellidae, 211
Land consolidation schemes, 170
Larkspur forking (*Delphinium consolida*), 106
Lasius flavus (Yellow or mound ant), 76, 79, 83, 117
Latah, Idaho, 190
Lautenbach project, 218
Laxton, 167, 168
Laying median, onset of, 160, replacement, 57
Lead arsenate, 95
Leaf beetles, 88, 219

blotch (*Rhynchosporium secalis*), 210
weevil, 107
Lee Farm, 31, 32, 62, 122, 157
Lepidoptera, 79
  larvae, 88
Leptinotarsa decemlineata, see Colorado beetle
levamisole hydrochloride treatment of red grouse, 133, Box 7.1
Ley traditional, 30
Linnet, 80
Lithuania, 22
Lorraine, France, 11
Loss of clutches percentage per day, 71
Louping-ill, 140
Lucerne (alfalfa), 67, 111
  springtail (*Sminthurus viridis*), 79, 83
Lumbricus terrestris, 135
Luxemburg, 23

MAFF, 120, 209, 216, 218
  (ADAS), 111
  Tolworth Laboratory, 98
Magpie, 60, 72, 207
Maize, 100, 221
Manure, horse, 148
Manydown Estate, Hampshire, 36, 46, 47, 76, 84, 118, 119, 188, 219
Marking individual, 43
Maximum sustainable yield or MSY, 195
Mayweed *Matricaria perforata*, 107, 219
MCPA, 102, 103, 104, 105, 109
MCPB, 104, 109
mebendazole, 134
Mercury seed dressings, 95
Merlin, 72
methiocarb, 104
Methionine, 82, 154
methoxy-ethyl-mercury, 96
methyl-mercury dicyandiamide (MMD), 95, 96
metoxuron, 109
Micheldever, Hampshire, 76, 137, 188 (*see also* Sutton Scotney)
Migration of partridge, 149
Mildew (*Erysiphe graminis*), 210
  effect of ethirimol, 216
Missile, *see* pyrazophos

Model of the Sussex partridge population, 181
Moles, 222
monocrotophos (Azodrin), 96
Montalto de Pavese, 92, 199
Mortality annual rates for released partridges, 204
  attributed to hard weather, 150
  background: cause of chick, 84
  chick, 50, 81
  due to shooting, 50, 180
  egg, 50
  hen, 50
  increase in chick, 123
  nesting, 178
  of hens during incubation, 179
  rates in partridge populations in relation to status, 191
  rates partridge chick, 122
  rates using logarithms, 49
  related to snow cover, Fig. 8.4
  shooting and winter losses, 184
  variation in chick, 88
  winter, 50
Moult, 37, 155
Mountain partridge, *see Perdix perdix* ab. *montana*
Mowing, 65, 166
  machines, 67
Multiple regression model, 87, 122
Myxomatosis reached the Sussex study area, 117

Napoleonic wars, 167
Narrow fruited corn-salad, 106
National Game Census, 25, 36, 37, 39, 124, 161, 162, 199
Nest losses, 56, 57, 63, 64
  site quality, 160
  site selection, 161
Nesting cover, 157, 164, 183, 197
  abundance of, 162
  amount of dead residual grass in, 163
  availability of, 165
  permanent, 157
  quantified, 161
  removed, 157, 185
  period weather during, 65
  success effect of predator control, 62
Nests, 44
  flooded, 65

Netherlands, 9
  partridge bag, 9, 23
New York State, 21, 92, 150, 190
New Zealand shipment of partridges to, 21
NGC, *see* National Game Census
Nickersons, 106
Nitrogen tax, 217
Norfolk, 91, 92, 102
North America, 20, 29, 171
North Caucasian Plain, 84, 151, 189
North Dakota, 22, 25, 26, 43, 92, 93, 130, 146, 148, 155
North Farm tunnel traps, 61
North Farm, Washington, Sussex, 3, 29, 30, 31, 33, 56, 58, 59, 62, 78, 103, 118, 157, 160, 179, 188, 204, 207, Colour Plate VII
North of England Grouse Research Project, 80, 131
North Stoke shoot, 31, 34, 58, 157, 185, 207, Colour Plate XVI
Northumberland, 11
Norway, 18, 24
Notiophilus biguttatus, 212
Numerical response, 71
Nutrition maternal, 80

Official Seed Testing Station, Cambridge, 101, 143
Open field and strip system, 167, 170
Orache (*Atriplex patula*), 144
Ordnance Survey Maps, 168
Orenburg Steppes, 93
Organic cereal growers, 217
Overwinter loss (k_5) as a function of the log density of females, 158
Overwintering, 149
Owls, 60, 206

Pachynematus spp., 116
Palouse Prairie, 21, 147, 171, Colour Plate IXX
Panogen, 95
paraquat, 100
Parasitic dodder (*Cuscuta*), 106
  wasp *Blacus ruficornis*, 216
  wasp *Centistes cuspidatus*, 215
  wasp *Collyria calcitrator*, 116
  wasp *Tryphon* spp. (Ichneumonidae Tryphorinae), 116, Colour Plate XXXII
parathion-methyl, 96, 100, 122

Partridge bags, computer simulation of, 208
  brood size, 48
  chick gizzards, 81
  eggs hatchability of, 153
  Indian grey (*Francolinus pondicerianus*), 1
  introduction to North America, 201
  moor, 9
  mountain (*Perdix perdix* ab. *montana*), 11
  nest records, 70
  nesting cover in North America, 171
  nests distribution of on farmland, 165
  pecks per day, 147, 154
  populations computer-simulated, 183
  red-legged, 70, 81, 137, 139, 163, 173, 201
  Survival Project, 3, 55, 78, Plate VIII
  western (*Alectoris sutcliffei*), 201
Partridges migrated south, 149
  overwintering in barns, 149
  released, 202
  rock (*Alectoris graeca*), 205
Perdix daurica (Bearded partridge), 8, 10, 17, 18, 149, 150
Perdix hodgsoniae, 8, 17, 18
Perdix workshops, 19
Perdix perdix ab. *montana*, 11
  arenicola, 10
  armoricana, 9
  canescens, 10
  caucasica, 10
  charrela, 8
  furvescens, 10
  galliae, 9
  hilgerti, 10
  hispaniensis, 8
  italica, 9
  lucida, 10, 149
  perdix, 9, Colour Plate IV
  robusta, 10, 17, 149, Colour Plate IV
  rossica, 10
  sphagnetorum, 9
Peregrine falcon, 12, 13, 94
permethrin, 104
Pesticides Safety Precautions

Scheme, 216
treadmill, 209
Pheasant, 84, 137, 139, 166, 202, 204, 222
  brown-eared, 173
  eye (*Adonis annua*), 106
Philonthus cognatus, 112
phosalone, 120
Phytobius spp., 107
Phytonomous variabilis, see *Hypera postica*
pirimicarb, 120, 121, 122
Plant bug *Leptoterna dolobrata*, 114
  bug *Notostira elongata*, 108
Plant bugs (Heteroptera), 79, 83, 88, 93, 107, 113, 114, 120, 121, 219, Colour Plate XV
  bugs per 20 sweeps, 92
Platypalpus Empididae, 214
Plot Colton's, 171
Plumage, 37
Po Delta, 9, 92
Poa annua, 80, 81, 217
  spikelets, 154
  trivialis (Rough-stalked meadow grass), 109
Podebrady, 189
Poland, 10, 23, 24, 26, 28, 76, 84, 105, 106, 114, 124, 126, 166, 168, 169, 189
Polecat, 164, 206
Polygonum spp., 80, 81, 103, 104, 113, 143, 210, 222
  convolvulus, see Black bindweed
Population decline, 187
  decline, causes of in the Sussex study, 184
  equilibrium level, 182
  functional-response curves, 212
  studies, 53
Portugal, 8, 18, 24
Pre-herbicide data set, 178
Precision defined, xiv
  insect monitoring in cereals, 51
Predation by buzzards, 152
  by feral cat, 59, Plate V
  by fox, 58, Plate IV
  control, 195
  control, and shooting, 197
  control, effect on the MSY, 196
  control, no shooting, 197
  hypothesis, test of, 67
Predator avoidance behaviour, 204

control, 183, 206
protection, 68
reduction effect on nesting success, 65
reduction effect on partridge bags, 69
reduction effects of, 68
removal, 69
Predators, change in behaviour with higher partridge density, 69
  egg, 60
  hen, 60
  signs of, 59
  tolerance shown towards, 206
  which specialised on preying on aphids, 211
Predatory flies Empididae, 214
Preferred insects, 90
  insects adult, 155
  insects annual variation in densities, 90
  weeds, 143, 144
Probabilities defined, xiv
propiconazole, 104
Proportion that should be shot, 198
Protein adult diet, 153
  chick diet, 85
Provins Seine et Marne France, 26
Pullman Washington, 190
Pupae (cocoons) of ants, see *Lasius flavus*
pyrazophos, 121, 122, 216
Pyrenees, 18

Quail (*Coturnix novaezealandiae*), 21
  bobwhite, 130
Quasi-cycles, 115, 130, Fig. 6.6

Rabbits, 222
Rabies, 208
Racoons, 208
Radio-tracking of broods, 119
  -telemetry, 43
  -track coveys, 148
  -tracking, 43, 83, 204
  -transmitters solar-powered, 159
Rainfall, maximum daily, 66
Rapier, 217
Raptor predation on partridge in winter, 150
Raptors, 150, 206, 207
Rats, 60, 206, 222
Reapers and reaper-binders, 143

Reconstructed population data, 188, 189, 190, Table 10.4
Record partridge bag, 15
Recruitment among reared birds, 204
 efficiency, 162
Red Data Book, 9, 106
 poppy (*Papaver rhoeas*), 102, 107
 -spider mite, 97
 -tailed hawk, 150
Released partridges and predator control, 204, 205
Removal of nesting cover, 166
Residual grass, 163, 164
Respiratory metabolism, 145
Restocking, 201, 205
Rhineland-Pfalz, FRG, 92
Ringing, 149
Romania, 126
 partridge bag, 23
Rooks, 136
Roost in burrows in the snow, 146, 147
 sites in cereals, 43
Rothamsted Experimental Station, 108, 110
Rothwell, 15
RSPB, 98

Sainfoin (*Onobrychis viciifolia*), 11, 111
Salisbury Plain, 12, 67, 68, 111, 130, 165, 180, Colour Plate IX
Sandricourt, 18
Sandringham, 46
Sarcoptic mange in fox, 208
Sawflies, 76
 caterpillars of, 79
 cereal leaf-eating, 115
 fecundity of, 115
Sawfly adult (*Dolerus*), 94
 Ametastegia glabrata, 107
 Athalia rosae, 108, 109
 Cephus pygmaeus, 116
 consumption, 53
 larvae, 83, 88, 114, 121, 219
 larvae in Yorkshire, 78
 larvae per 20 sweeps, 92
 pre-pupal, 116
Scandinavia, 9, 171
Schleswig Holstein, 9, 105
Scotland, 79, 140
Scrapes for nest, 160

Scythes, effect on sitting hen, 67
Seed Testing station, *see* Official Seed Testing Station Cambridge
Seine-et-Marne, 189
Sentinel, 151
Septoria tritici, 216
Sex ratio, 37
Sexes, differentiation of, 37
Sheep tick (*Ixodes ricinus*), 140, Plate VI
Shepherd's cress (*Teesdalia nudicaulis*), 106
 needle (*Scandix pecten-veneris*), 108
Shooting, 49, 195, 202
 estimating the correct rate, 198, 200, 299
 mortality, 179
Shotguns, 13
Siberia, 10, 110, 149
simazine, 109, 210 (*see also* atrazine)
simulation model of cereal aphid peak numbers, 213
 model of Sussex partridge population, 185
Sinkiang, 10
Sites of Special Scientific Interest, 33
Sitting hens, 58
Six Mile Bottom, Cambridgeshire, 127, 128, 130
Skunks, 208
Slurry from cow kennels, 148
Smartweed, *see* Black bindweed
Sminthurus viridis, see Lucerne springtail, 83
Snares, 61
Snow and ice, 147
 depth greater than 50 cm, 149
 hole roosting, 146, 147
 ice-crusted (known as nast), 147
 in April, 151
 mean levels, 149
Snowy owl, 72
Soil, 30
Solar rechargeable batteries, 43
Song birds, 222
Source of compensation for shooting mortality, 197
South Dakota, 69
South Downs, 30
South-East Corner Sussex, 31, 62, 65, 157
South-East Gatinais, 189

South-East Michigan, 190
Soviet Union, 18, 22, 23, 25, 26, 76, 84, 93, 105, 148, 170
　partridge density, 22, 23
Spain, 8, 18, 24
Sparrow hawk, 72, 94, 99, 130, 150, 206, 207
Speedwells *Veronica* spp., 107
Spider, 213
Spiders, 93
　web-spinning, 213
Spring Census, 39
Spruce budworm, 122
Squatting alarm, 204
Stachys annua (Annual woundwort), 104
Stellaria media, see Chickweed
Stoat, 60, 61, 86, 87, 207
Stock dove, 99
Straw burning, 112, 113
Strip system, 168
Strongylosis, 129, 130, 131, 140, 148
Stubble count, 42
Stubbles, 142, 143
Sub-lethal effects, 100
Subspecies of partridge, 8
Sulphur amino-acids, 81
Sulphuric acid, 102
Summer plumage, 11, Colour Plate III
　weather and chick production, 75
Sunn pests, *see Eurygaster*
Surplus of cereals, 6, 223
Sussex model, 181, 196
　partridge population model, 182
　study, 4, 6, 14, 29, 31, 42, 96, 106, 107, 108, 109, 110, 113, 117, 137, 156, 157, 168
Sutton Scotney, 56, 91
Sweden, 18, 95, 154
　partridge bag, 23
Switching of predators to a diet of partridges, 71
Switzerland, 24, 216, 220
Syngamus, 135
　larvae, 138,
　trachea, 135, 136, 138
Synthetic pyrethroids (cypermethrin, deltamethrin), 217

Tachydromia arrogans, 214
Tachyporus, 211, 212, 216
　chrysomelinus, 212, 214
　hypnorum, 212, 214
　nitidulus, 214
　obtusus, 214
Temperature and chick mortality, 88
　and partridge in winter, 145
　daily 10 June–10 July, 89
　during laying, 21
tetramisole, 134
The Field, 126
thiabendazole, 134
thiophanate-methyl, 104, 113
thiram, 96, 100
Thistles, especially *Cirsium arvense*, 106, 113
Thorpe Malsor, 91, 152
Thrips, 88
tolyl mercury acetate, (TMA), 95
Tortoise-bugs, *see Eurygaster*
Traditional ley-farming with undersowing, 218
Traps, gin, 57
　spring, 61
Trebon, 189
Trechus quadristriatus, 79, 88, 92, 117
Trees, areas with many, 207
　as raptor perches, 165
　aversion to, 164
Trefoil, 111
Trends in densities of cereal thrips and aphids, 215
tri-allate, 104
triadimefon, 104
Triazoles, 216
Trichostrongylus tenuis (Mehlis), 126, 127, 130
　decline in 1910 to 1980, 129
Tryphon (Ichneumonidae), 116
Turkey, 24
Turnip flea beetle, 97
　sawfly (*Athalia rosae*), 108, 109
Tuscany, 19, 92

U46 combi, 105
Undersowing cereals with legumes and grasses, 116, 130, 217, 218
University of Bonn, 219
　of Dundee, 115
　of Durham, *see* preface
　of Florence, 199
　of Kiel, 110
　Oxford, *see* acknowledgements, 2
　of Southampton, 213

of Strathclyde, 100
of Tübingen, 218
Unsprayed margins, 119, 120, 219, 220
USA, 19, 103
  partridge bag, 23
USSR Trans Baikalia study of bearded partridge, 189

Vacuum samples, *see* Dietrick vacuum insect samples
Vegetation wetness of, 87
Virgin Lands, 21
Vultures, 206

Wales, 19
Walking up partridges, 14, Colour Plate I
Walsingham, North Norfolk, 200
Waupun, Wisconsin, 190
Weasel, 86, 87, 207
Weather and chicks, 87
  and nesting, 65
  in winter, 145
Weaver birds in Africa, 100
Weeds in cereal crops, trends, Figs 6.1, 6.3, 8.1
Weedy margins, 199, 222
  strip FRG, 220
Weevils (Curculionidae), 76, 88, 219
  and leaf beetles, 111
Weight loss during incubation, 155
  loss metabolism of proteins, 148
West Barsham, Norfolk, 37, 91, 148, 188
Wetterau Hessen, FRG, 114

Wheat bugs, *see Eurygaster*
  fields of 400 ha, 170
  grains, 147
  staple diet of hundreds of millions of people, 109
Wheat/rye leaves, 147
White campion (*Melandrium album*), 106
  chamomile (*Matricaria chamomilla*), 102
Widely-ranging broods, 87
Wild buckwheat, *see* Black bindweed
  radish (*Raphanus raphanistrum*), 106
Winter of 1947, 148
  wheat eyespot (*Pseudocercosporella herpotrichoides*), 216
Witchingham, Norfolk, 188
Woodcock, 122
Woodpigeon, 80, 99, 147, 154, 222
World partridge population, 1
  population, 24
Worthington Meteorological Station, 88

Yellow charlock (*Sinapis arvensis*), 102, 103, 106, 107, 209
Yorkshire Wolds, 12, 103
Young adopted by adults, 204
  hatched per successful nest, 45
  to old ratio August, 184
Yugoslavia, 9, 126, 153, 206
  partridge bag, 23